A Voyager Out

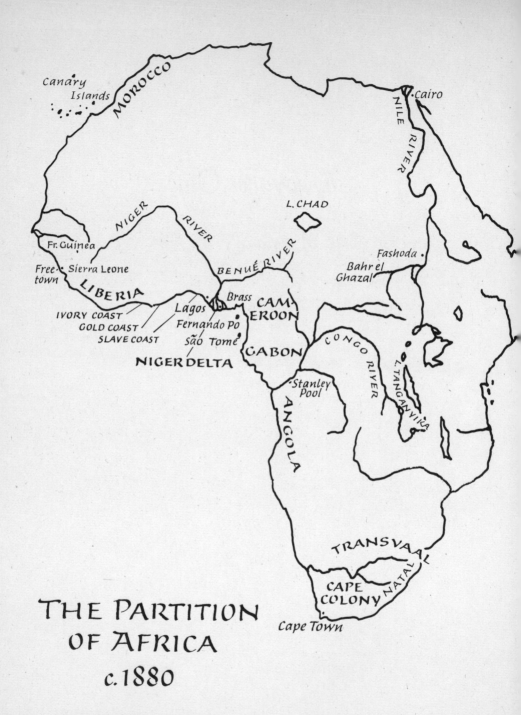

THE PARTITION
OF AFRICA
c.1880

KATHERINE FRANK

A Voyager Out
The Life of Mary Kingsley

Ballantine Books • New York

For
My Parents
and
Lee and Justin

Library of Congress Catalog Card Number: 87-91178

ISBN: 0-345-34830-3

This edition published by arrangement with
Houghton Mifflin Company.

Cover design by Richard Aquan
Photo courtesy of Mrs. Angela M.K. Covey-Crump

Frontispiece map by Jacqueline Sakwa

Manufactured in the United States of America

First Ballantine Books Edition: September 1987

10 9 8 7 6 5 4 3 2 1

Acknowledgments

My biography of Mary Kingsley was conceived and begun in the United States, researched in England, and lived and written in West Africa, and I have people and institutions in all these places to thank.

Professors Janet Sharistanian and William Kupersmith provided encouragement in the early stages of my work. My late and much missed friend Cheryl Miller helped me find the way to Africa. Laura Kalpakian followed in letters and lived this and volumes more with me.

At Houghton Mifflin Nan Talese's and Signe Warner's enthusiasm and inspired editing buoyed my spirits as well as improved the final form of the book.

In England I am indebted to the following institutions for assistance and permission to quote from their materials: the British Library; the British Museum (Natural History); the Bodleian Library, Oxford; Rhodes House Library, Oxford; the Pitt Rivers Museum, Oxford; the Royal Commonwealth Society; the Royal Geographical Society; the Highgate Literary and Scientific Institution; the Cambridge University Library; Christ's College, Cambridge; the Library of the House of Lords; the Library of the London School of Economics; and the University of Birmingham Library. I must express my special gratitude to Mr. Alan Bell at Rhodes House Library, Ms. Linda Cheetham at the Pitt Rivers Museum, Mr. Donald Simpson at the Royal Commonwealth Society, Mr. David Wileman and Mrs. Christine Kelly at the Royal Geographical Society, and Mrs. Gwynedd Gosling at the Highgate Literary and Scientific Institution.

I also wish to extend my thanks to the National Library of Ireland, Dublin, and the South African Library, Capetown.

Much of the material I have used I owe to the generosity of literary executors. I am especially grateful to Mrs. Angela Covey-Crump for allowing me to quote from all the Kingsley family materials, to Mrs. Joan Longdon for permission to use the Matthew Nathan papers, and to Mr. D. J. Holt for access to the Holt and Tylor papers, and also for producing a hitherto unknown photograph of Mary Kingsley. Mr. Holt, Mr. and Mrs. Matthew Nathan, and Mr. and Mrs. Peter Charles Kingsley Bailey were all kind enough to share their family histories, papers, photographs, and memorabilia with me. I am also indebted to Mrs. A. Pepper, the present occupant of 22 Southwood Lane, Highgate, and to Mrs. Margery Harris at 7 Mortimer Road, Cambridge, for allowing me to visit the houses in which Mary Kingsley lived for many years before going to Africa.

Mrs. Beth Urquhart's early work on Mary Kingsley's letters was extremely helpful. Roger Beck and Frank Dadswell also brought critical letters to light that I otherwise would have missed. Trish Krelingh and Merja Makineh led the way to the Highgate Literary and Scientific Institution and to Highgate Cemetery, and at the latter Jules Hardwick dispensed a good deal of interesting and macabre information. Mr. John Whale of the London *Sunday Times* and Mrs. Charity Hodge disclosed curious details of Mary Kingsley's funeral.

Also in England, I am indebted to Mrs. Dorothy Middleton, Mr. Richard Hall, and Lady Elizabeth Longford for their expertise and interest. Mandy Banton provided excellent research assistance, and Antonia Shooter a room of my own. Rosemary Grave also proffered shelter as well as enduring friendship over the years.

My debt to Deborah Birkett, friend, fellow traveler, oracle on Kingsley palaver and much else besides, is incalculable. In England and on "the Coast" we've sky-larked through so much together.

In West Africa countless people helped me "really to see" that world. My own travels were as dependent as Mary Kingsley's on the good will and hospitality of numerous friends, some fleeting and anonymous, and others whom I can acknowledge: Cady, Johannes, and Grace Mbong, Oumar Bah, Sylvaine Egneghe-Estughe, and Michel Mpira. At Bayero University, Kano, I am indebted to Dr. Munzali Jibril for allowing me to defer my teaching commitments in order to continue writing, and, just as importantly, for his interest and encouragement. A timely university research grant facilitated the final preparation of the manuscript, as did the typing skills of Mr. Michael Mhiuga Abo and Mallam Salisu Yahaya. *Na gode,* too, to my colleagues in the Department of English and European Languages and to Mr. Rodney Miles.

Most of all, on every continent, my deepest thanks to my husband Saeed-ul-Islam for seeing me through to the close of this particular chapter and for imagining with me the promise of the next.

Contents

x *Contents*

Illustrations

(following page 174)

Illustrations

Preface

Imagine this tableau: A tall, fair-haired, straight-backed woman in a proper high-necked English cotton blouse and a long black skirt — perhaps she has dispensed with her little sealskin hat in the jungle heat — stands on the shore of an African river awash with crocodiles. In a makeshift language, she speaks with a chief about lizards and snakes, about charms and prayer, about the goods she carries in her trader's case, of liquor and hairpins and colonialist designs on his village. She has come close to death, perhaps that morning or the day before, when her canoe was caught at the lip of a fast-moving falls, and she will go on (making light of it later for a massive audience of British readers in classically balanced, self-mocking prose) daring leopards, climbing mountains — she left her calling card at the peak of Mount Cameroon — approaching unfriendly guardians of forest villages, and maneuvering as best she can the ceaseless, murderous undertow of African disease.

She will also, without having invited any such notoriety, pursue a related danger of a different kind: back at home in England, she will raise her voice on behalf of the African peoples whose ability to legislate their own lives is, in the late 1890s, continuously and fatally under attack by British, French, Belgian, German — she is, of course, primarily concerned with British — colonial administrations. Imperialism, she will insist, misunderstands the intricacies of African self-rule, its own subtle interdependencies, its ability in spite of institutions like cannibalism and polygamy to deal justly, if not in the precise manner of Parliament, with its own laws and lawbreakers. Africans are not, she will explain with the help of dozens of examples confronted firsthand, pathetic undeveloped white men, deficient Europeans. Not alone in this view, she is nonetheless one of a small intrepid band and will become its most outspoken advocate, beloved by audiences, derided by government.

Six months later, another tableau vivant, the kind of stop-action scene the Victorians so enjoyed: The same woman in her London flat. Perhaps she is wearing an apron to protect a similar blouse from the spatter of grease. She is making beef-and-kidney pie for her brother, for whom she keeps house. She has been transformed, however far afield her memories and hopes might take her, into the spinster sister, guardian of the hearth. She does not approve of bicycles, this woman — she finds them unsafe — nor of omnibuses, which bring strangers into an unnatural and obnoxious closeness. She opposes the vote for women and remains permanently opposed to the movement afoot to admit women into Britain's learned societies. The women who apply to the Royal Geographical Society she calls "shrieking females and androgyns," and, angrily repudiating the idea that she is what one admiring journalist called "A New Woman," she iterates whenever the question arises that "every bit of solid, good work I have done has been through a man." "The presence of petticoats" would necessarily lower standards, she insists, perhaps with an angry flounce of her petticoat. Readers buy her books by the thousands, crowd into lecture halls to hear her, and she is much in demand as a celebrity at parties. Yet she goes home to that flat, which is crammed with West African artifacts, and keeps the heat turned uncomfortably high so that she can blot out the London chill and approximate the climate of her beloved continent. There she sits alone more often than not, caught between more contradictions than any single mind ought to ask itself to reconcile.

One of the marvels of personality is its resistance to prediction. One man's paralyzing trauma is another man's invitation to take control of his life; one woman's grounds for insanity is another woman's goad to a dramatic shaping of the self. Alcoholic parents breed alcoholic children — or teetotalers; violent circumstances produce violent offspring — or ones who are meek or saintly or desperate for security. All of us are hybrids of circumstance, habit, and genetics, mysterious compounds who bend toward the light or the darkness according to no plan or rule.

Mary Kingsley, who tended toward both in unique alternation, must be the most engaging heroine of surprise of the late-Victorian world. Given ample motive for self-abnegation (and very good at it, too), ill-educated but an autodidact of a sort almost unimaginable today, encouraged in duty first and then invisibility, for no necessary reason we can find except for the implacability of will that makes for genius — a sport — she stepped out of the shadows cast by the men who commanded her to female servitude to become a conqueror of danger, of convention, and of her own unpromising history.

She was the daughter of a dashing, infuriating man who had become a sort of society doctor, on retainer to dukes and earls, thus keeping the better part of his energy free for traveling around the world with them while giving the impression that he was gainfully employed. The wife he left behind, and apparently gave little thought to, was a cockney servant, whose child, born four days after their wedding in 1862, was Mary Kingsley. In futile retaliation, or merely despair, Mrs. Kingsley took to her bed and stayed there for the rest of her life. Saved by marriage from ignominy but not from neglect, she was able to indenture her daughter as her nurse; thus two lives were exchanged for the doctor's freedom. Mary Kingsley was encouraged to do as close to nothing as a lively young woman could do: she read the books in the family library, often surreptitiously; she raised fighting cocks, though of course not to fight; she tended her sick mother dutifully and directed the servant and the gardener, which took nearly as much out of our ancestors as tending a house unaided does nowadays. She was not socially at ease, she traveled nowhere (except for a holiday, once, in Paris, for which her mother punished her on her return by suffering a violent worsening of her condition); in general she planned little for herself. Later she was to say to the only man we know of who aroused romantic hopes in her constrained breast, "My life can be written in a very few lines. . . . It arises from my having no personal individuality of my own whatsoever. I have always lived in the lives of other people, whose work was heavy for them. . . . It never occurs to me that I have any right to do anything more than now and then sit and warm myself at the fire of real human beings. There is not one of them who has ever cared for me apart from my services. . . ." Then, when she was close to thirty years old, within two months of each other her parents died, and in the truest sense of the word, Mary Kingsley was born.

One can say that psychology often proceeds along lines analogous to physics: it is not far-fetched to say that Mary's life until this point was like a spring that coiled more and more tightly until, wholly without precedent or apparent conscious forethought, it could be said to have snapped in a single exorbitant burst of energy on whose trajectory she did the most implausible, impractical thing imaginable — she went to West Africa. She intended, she announced, to study fetish (what we might call religious customs and belief) and to bear with her a modest, because unsubsidized, set of preserving materials in which to pickle some unfamiliar fish to bring home to the British Museum. Like her father the doctor, she had a little ulterior motive to make her escape seem socially useful, hence justifiable.

The fact is, Mary seems to have seen this adventure as a kind of suicidal journey, spiritually speaking; or at least as a partly conscious invitation to death. She saw herself as a sacrifice to the loneliness of her early life and a mourner (anger unacknowledged) at the graves of her stupefyingly self-absorbed parents, who had so perfectly neglected her through all the years. And yet — the wonder of human inventiveness! — the roulette she chose to play was (perhaps one can thank her father for stimulating this) so much more interesting and engaging to a brilliant woman than any game she could have devised with a pistol and a single bullet. If her quest began in depression — anger at others, turned sharply against herself — it issued in gaiety, energy, compassion, and finally in a fiery rage aimed at a political situation in which she attempted with all her passionate articulateness to intervene.

That she never submitted to that fire of indignation her own position as nursemaid and subservient daughter and sister we can understand: was it not sufficient that she ventured into the world more daringly than even her father had done, he the "noble, perfect English gentleman . . . who never did a mean act or thought a mean thought, and never felt fear"? Must she betray her devotion to him, and to her endlessly, futilely nurtured mother, by becoming a champion of emancipated womanhood in word as well as deed? It is as if, given a limited amount of psychic energy, Mary could fight one battle or two or three: the inertia of her confined life, the extraordinary difficulties of her journeys, her attraction not to Christianity but to West African religious feeling, her political animosities. The battle on the home front, the sexual one, with all its implied repudiations of her past, seemed to have been one too many. (Though there are enormous differences, Mary Kingsley's resemblance to Isak Dinesen is profoundly telling: these were women whose fathers had managed to escape the dead hand of middle-class convention by leaving home and "productive enterprise" to become adventurers of the wild, dispatching occasional dazzling reports from distant seas and lands. For both women, the struggle for independence and excitement seemed more easily waged out of sight and in proximity to very alien social and spiritual mores, where few of their kind had gone before and few were likely to follow.)

So we cannot batter Mary Kingsley's spoken (as opposed to her acted) convictions about "women's place" into any semblance of a contemporary feminist's. Similarly, we need to be sensitive to the undercurrents of her apparent but highly complex brand of imperialism and the pressures she sometimes had to allay on the political as well as sexual front. She was, in short, a woman of her time, and, for better or worse, as if to encourage her in her own intimate confusions, that time was a confused and contradictory one. She lived on the cusp of a new century near the end of the elderly Victoria's rule, at a jagged moment when women were emerging in fits and starts from the clutter of artifacts and expectations that had made the Victorian parlor so stifling. So Mary Kingsley stands at a kind of crossroads for us in her preposterously incommodious lady's outfit ("because one would never want to go about in Africa in a way that would embarrass one to be seen in Piccadilly"), which she finally exchanged for the nurse's uniform that became — belatedly but perhaps to her relief — her burial dress.

Mary Kingsley is a heroine English children have grown up on. In the United States she has been largely unknown. Katherine Frank understands, and beautifully documents, the evolution of this woman uniquely unburdened by the kind of personal ambition that is fueled by ordinary expectations of success, and shows us how, therefore, she was free to cast off and go where chance propelled her. Mary Kingsley is an existentialist's dream child — and how she'd have laughed to hear herself so pompously described. We meet in her an unselfconscious heroine to add to our growing pantheon of women who, while they saved themselves and their sanity, became models too complex and original for us to follow, yet, in the history of vital accomplishment, too important to be forgotten.

Rosellen Brown

Part One

I thought for some reason even then of Africa, not a
particular place, but a shape, a strangeness, a wanting
to know. . . . . I have written "a shape," and the shape,
of course, is roughly that of the human heart.

Graham Greene

The Kingsley Family

It was well past midnight, and as usual Mary Kingsley was still up, writing in the small library of her house at 32 Saint Mary Abbott's Terrace, Kensington. The room was overheated and stuffy — she had never been able to readjust to the damp, chill English climate since returning from West Africa — and she worked in a pool of lamplight at her desk, which was cluttered with manuscript in various hands, indecipherable notes, maps, sepia-tinted photographs curling up at the edges. Books, shelves upon shelves of them, lined the walls, interspersed now and then by grimacing, carved ebony masks. The Benin bronzes were prominently displayed in the adjoining sitting room, and the three-foot-high, blood-encrusted, and nail-studded idol, Mu-vungu, held pride of place in the front entry hall. But in her untidy, cramped study Mary kept her handwoven baskets for catching human souls and her amulets to keep one on the right forest path.

The year 1899 was drawing to a close, and Mary — tall, slender, fair-haired, and still handsome at the age of thirty-seven — was attempting to create from the ocean of paper before her a memoir of her father, George Henry Kingsley, to preface a collection of George's writings that Macmillan, the Kingsley family publisher, wanted to bring out. It was a difficult task, far more taxing, indeed, than writing the two enormous and enormously successful books on Africa that Mary had herself already produced, *Travels in West Africa* and *West African Studies*. These had made her famous (some would even say infamous) as an intrepid African explorer and also, to the more discerning, as an authority on African culture and on African colonial policy. Scribbling far into the night, after days of wrangling with the Colonial Office over the Sierra Leone hut tax or lecturing in Liverpool or Manchester or nursing an aged Bailey or Kingsley relation, Mary now struggled to find some sort of meaning and order in the fragments of her father's inchoate life spread out on the desk before her.

Unlike his famous novelist brothers, Charles and Henry Kingsley, George had left behind a literary output so ephemeral as to be virtually nonexistent: lectures or addresses that evaporated into air upon delivery before one of the many learned societies he frequented; manuscript pages of his travel book *South Sea Bubbles,* which he coauthored with the earl of Pembroke; abortive beginnings of scores of articles that his wife or daughter fished out of his study wastebasket, uncrumpled, and preserved. Such were the fugitive jottings that Mary tried to weld into a volume for Macmillan. She labored at it foremost, perhaps, as an act of daughterly piety. But the work progressed slowly, in contrast to the speed and verve with which she produced her own books, because, whether she consciously realized it or not, to write her father's biography would also to some extent entail writing her own autobiography.

For all the years of her life, Mary considered George Kingsley to be the most important figure in her existence. Mary embraced, indeed inherited, her father's passion for travel, his hunger for an intense (and usually dangerous) life, his acute sensual receptivity to beauty in all its natural and human forms, and also his rather jaundiced and uncanny sense of humor. But at the same time Mary utterly repudiated her father's neglect of family and financial responsibilities — the way, for example, he left his wife and children for months or even years at a time with only the sketchiest financial support while he traveled about the world. Mary seemed to go even further, in fact, and tried to compensate for her father's neglect by assuming a sense of duty that was exaggerated, even for Victorian times. Her duty was first and always to her family, as nurse to her invalid mother, research assistant to her father, and, after her parents' deaths, housekeeper to her fastidious and demanding brother, as well as chief factotum and "doer of odd jobs" to the Kingsley clan in general. But in time Mary's vision of the horizons of her duty came to extend far beyond the demands of assorted Kingsleys to include the Colonial Office at Whitehall, the West African traders in Liverpool and Manchester, and finally that heart-shaped continent as a whole.

Given, then, this rather ambivalent relation to her father, Mary was not perhaps the best of candidates to write his biography. Originally

George Kingsley's fellow traveler and coauthor of *South Sea Bubbles,* the earl of Pembroke, was to do it, but Pembroke was first ill and then dying in the 1890s, and thus Macmillan suggested that Mary's younger brother, Charles, might take on the job. This seemed fitting, and so the thing was arranged, but in the years between the time the volume of essays and memoir was initially proposed by Macmillan in 1893, shortly after George Kingsley's death, and 1899, when George Kingsley's *Notes on Sport and Travel* finally appeared, Charley was unable to produce the introductory essay. He periodically reported that it was progressing handsomely in letters to George Macmillan and to his sister when she was out in West Africa in 1893 and in 1895. But Charley was more his father's child than was Mary, albeit with George Kingsley's passionate temperament considerably diluted and his ineffectualness increased several fold. "Master Charles," as Mary sometimes refers to Charley in her letters, traveled too — mostly in the Orient and Far East — but despite his desultory wanderings, his most striking gift was that of stasis. The fact that she dedicated both her books to him does not deny the fact that Charley was the bane of Mary's existence and for many reasons other than that he claimed to labor at the memoir for years until his sister reluctantly took it over and produced a two-hundred-page biography of her father in a matter of several months.

Mary's memoir of her father insists, quite rightly, that one cannot understand individual members of the Kingsley family without knowing about the "tribe" as a whole. There is a good deal Mary leaves out of her life of her father: her uncle Charles's manic-depressive episodes, for example, Henry Kingsley's probable bisexuality, her mother's obscure origins, and the unhappiness of her parents' marriage. But on the whole, Mary's portrait of the Kingsley "tribe" rings true. She commences thus:

> The old English family of the Kingsley has not been given to exhausting itself with rapidly successive outbreaks of intellectual brilliancy. It has gone on frequently for century after century hunting, fishing, fighting in an English gentlemanly kind of way; then it has turned out someone who was generally valuable, and settled down again. Money-making has, so far, never been its strong point; money-keeping still less so. . . . It is possible that if this family goes on down through the ages, in some far away time it may develop a generation excelling in the fine arts or music, or sound business capacity. Now and again a Kingsley shows symptoms of excellence in poetry and painting. . . .

Of music, as far as record goes, it has shown no such symptom. . . .
One member of the family only has been known to possess a taste for
figures, which, after 600 years', more or less, authentic record, and a
legendary past behind that of indefinite extent, is not an encouraging
percentage.

The Kingsley family did not, in fact, go on down the ages but
instead dwindled to an obscure halt in the generation following Mary's,
never having acquired any musical, mathematical, or — most unfortunately — any financial acumen. One can get along without fine arts
and multiplication tables, but not without money. The Kingsley family letters are full of discussions about money, or rather about the lack
of it. Throughout the correspondence of the various branches of the
family runs the leitmotif of financial woe, a nagging problem that even
best-selling novels, travel books, and royal patronage could never entirely alleviate.

Some six hundred years before Mary Kingsley was born in 1862, Sir
Ranulph de Kingsley of Cheshire won the favor of Ranulph, earl of
Chester, thereby acquiring for "his heir and assigns forever," the office
of "Baliwick and Keeper of the Forest of Delamere with divers other
liberties." Hence the Kingsley family device of a horn, the symbol of
the family's forestry rights.

Despite Mary's description of the family as anonymously hunting
and fishing and fighting its gentlemanly way through the centuries,
several figures emerge from this even historical tide and call attention
to themselves. A seventeenth-century Kingsley ancestor, the Puritan
Col. George Fleetwood, for example, was among those who signed the
death warrant for King Charles I. At the Restoration, he was convicted
of high treason, and his lands were seized by the Crown, though his
life was spared. William Kingsley (1584–1647) was archdeacon of
Canterbury. There was also Lt. Gen. William Kingsley (1698–1769),
the valiant soldier painted by Sir Joshua Reynolds who fought hero-
ically at Dettingen, at Fontenoy, and at Minden, where his horse was
shot from under him. Ten or so years after the gallant William Kingsley's
death, Mary Kingsley's paternal grandparents were born: Charles
Kingsley Sr. in 1781 at Battramsley House, New Forest, and Mary
Lucas in 1785 at Farley Hall, Barbados, in the West Indies. Mary
Lucas's father was a wealthy judge, and it is to her old, established,
plantation-owning West Indian family that Mary is referring when she
says she is descended from slave owners.

At this epoch in the family history one is struck by the limited choice of Christian names allowed themselves by the Kingsleys. Much to the consternation of their correspondents and postmen at the time, and of biographers and literary historians today, they used the same names over and over. By the time of Mary's grandfather, Charles Kingsley Sr., and for the next two generations, male Kingsleys were almost invariably named Charles, George, or Henry, often with one of the other two names serving as a middle name (as in George Henry Kingsley or Charles George Kingsley). Female Kingsleys were usually named Mary or Charlotte (the feminine form, of course, of Charles). Some of the Kingsley males carried consistency to the point of marrying women with the de rigueur names, as was the case with Charles Sr. and Mary's father George Kingsley, both of whose wives were also Marys. George went even further and gave our Mary Kingsley Henrietta as a middle name and thus neatly distinguished her from her first cousin, also Mary Kingsley, the daughter of Charles Kingsley Jr. (This second Mary Kingsley also grew up to become a famous writer, publishing her novels under the pseudonym of Lucas Malet.) Not surprisingly, Mary Henrietta Kingsley's brother and only sibling was christened Charles George.

Mary's grandparents, Charles Kingsley Sr. and Mary Lucas, married in 1804, though they did not produce a child until 1819 when Charles Kingsley Jr. was born. Fifteen childless years in those days when birth control was in a rather rudimentary state and when in any event people of the Kingsleys' class usually wanted large families is puzzling. Clearly the marriage was not altogether satisfactory, and its lack of intimacy should probably be attributed to Mary Lucas Kingsley rather than to her husband, for one of the most striking characteristics of the Kingsley men (which Mary understandably fails to mention in her memoir of her father) is their highly sensual nature and sexually active careers. Charles Kingsley Jr. wrote numerous explicitly erotic letters to his wife, which were sometimes accompanied by pornographic drawings, including one in which he and Fanny are copulating on a crucifix as they ascend heavenwards, for, as he explained, the life to come would consist of one perpetual orgasm. His younger brothers, Henry and George, were no less sexually avid, though neither felt compelled to make a religion of his sex life, and neither confined his sexual activities to his wife.

But sexual incompatibility or inactivity was not the only problem that plagued the early years of the marriage of Charles Kingsley Sr. and Mary Lucas Kingsley. In true Kingsley fashion, Charles managed to ride, hunt, and shoot his way through all his money by the time he was twenty-six, and even without children to support, he began to see that he would have to embrace some sort of profession in order to make ends meet.

At that time, the first quarter of the nineteenth century, really only two vocations were open to a gentleman: the military and the church. Given his robust country squire temperament, Charles Kingsley Sr. should have found the first option the most suitable, but he chose the latter, probably because Mary Lucas Kingsley preferred being a parson's wife to roaming about with a regiment.

Having cast his lot with the church, Charles Kingsley Sr. did not, however, hasten through his clerical training, yet another indication that like many other nineteenth-century clergymen, he felt no particular sense of religious calling. He entered Trinity Hall, Cambridge, in 1807 to study divinity, and it was not until a full nine years later that he came down, at the age of thirty-five, with a degree of LL.B. from Sidney Sussex College. Shortly afterward the long-deferred Kingsley babies began to arrive, no doubt because Mary Lucas Kingsley felt that her husband had finally attained a necessary standard of financial and social security. After the birth of Charles Kingsley Jr. in 1819, the rest of the children appeared with typical nineteenth-century frequency: Herbert was born in 1820, Gerald in 1821, Louisa May, who died in infancy, in 1823, Mary Kingsley's father, George, in 1826, Charlotte in 1828, and finally Henry in 1830.

It was, of course, Charles and Henry, both of whom were to become famous novelists, and most of all, George, who together initiated what Mary in her memoir of her father called the "intellectual outbreak," a kind of nineteenth-century "Elizabethan flowering" in the Kingsley family — all the more remarkable because of the rather dull, middle-aged parents who produced these three remarkable brothers. But the short careers of Herbert and Gerald are also of interest. A mere eighteen months younger than Charles, Herbert was sent with his older brother to a grammar school at Helston in Cornwall, whose headmaster was the Rev. Derwent Coleridge, son of the poet. Here at the age of fourteen Herbert stole a silver spoon, sold it, and ran away from school. But the next day he was arrested in Helston by a bailiff and marched back to the school in handcuffs. Here he was treated no better than was David Copperfield at Salem House: Herbert was locked in his room and fed only bread and water. Not surprisingly, he soon became ill with rheumatic fever, and within two months he was dead, officially from the heart condition that almost always accompanies rheumatic fever. But it was widely rumored at the time that young Herbert Kingsley took his own life by drowning himself in the nearby Looe Pool.

The fact that Mary Kingsley fails entirely to mention Herbert in her memoir lends credence to this more sinister account of his end. If Herbert was a suicide, he was not the only Kingsley to know serious psychiatric disturbance. There is, indeed, a clear Kingsley family history of severe depression and of other forms of mental instability. Charles Kingsley Jr. was a classic manic-depressive who during his thirties and forties experienced yearly bouts of prostrating depression, alternating with periods of frenetic activity during which he produced novels at breakneck speed while functioning as a full-time cleric and often as an academic as well. Less is known about Henry's and George's psychological make-up, though there is ample evidence of Henry's dark periods of excessive drinking, and George's "awful temper" is of nearly legendary proportions in all accounts of the family. Both Henry's and George's travels also include adventures that qualify as recklessly if not suicidally dangerous, as indeed do those of Mary Kingsley herself.

Gerald's fate, unlike Herbert's, Mary does recount in her memoir. It was, as she says, a "tragic one." Gerald was an officer in the Royal Navy who seemed to have a brilliant future spread out before him. But in 1844, when he was only just twenty-three, he met a gruesome end in the Gulf of Carpentaria off the coast of Australia on board a disease-stricken gunboat, the *Royalist*. For more than a year and a half the *Royalist* lay becalmed and stranded in the gulf of the Torres Strait with her wretched crew roasting, starving, and finally dying like the Ancient Mariner's parched sailors in Coleridge's poem. One by one they died, first the commander, then the officers and many of the crew. Gerald, the last surviving officer, died in September. The family, however, did not learn of his death until months later when Charles Kingsley Sr. was reading the newspapers at the Chelsea public library and overheard one gentleman observe to another, "Dreadful bad business this about the *Royalist* — every single officer on board her dead — those who did not die of fever were eaten by cannibals." Gerald, then, was enshrined in the family history as a romantic and tragic figure, unlike the unfortunate and shame-enshrouded Herbert.

Describing the three remaining Kingsley brothers who put the family on the nineteenth-century literary map, Mary said that "Charles was the greatest of the three . . . and shed honour on his name and credit on his nation for all time. Henry had possibly the greater literary gift; George was the most typical Kingsley, at the best, of all three." Mary actually held to two versions of her famous uncle, Charles Kingsley, a public and a private one. The memoir, of course, celebrates the first: the Victorian Great Man — chaplain to Queen Victoria, Canon of Westminster, Professor of History at Cambridge, Christian Socialist, champion of the working man, and author of best-selling novels. But privately Mary complained of the "cant and humbug" of Charles Kingsley and his family, of their utter conventionality and worship of propriety, both of which wrought ill treatment of George and Henry because of the two younger brothers' déclassé marriages.

Mary's dual vision of her uncle also stems, however, from the many contradictions in the man himself. Today Kingsley has become a fossilized footnote in nineteenth-century literary history: the author of books such as *Yeast, Alton Locke,* and *Westward Ho!* and the delightful children's story, *The Water Babies.* Charles Kingsley is also remembered and warmly appreciated for having been stupid enough to insult publicly John Henry Newman, thereby provoking Newman's rebuttal, *Apologia pro Vita Sua,* one of the great works of English autobiography. But to himself and to his family, Charles Kingsley was not footnote material, a shadowy figure hovering on the fringes of a nineteenth-century inner circle composed of Tennyson, Dickens, Browning, Mill, Swinburne, and Darwin, all of whom were his friends. Instead, as the underlying manic-depressive cycles of his behavior would suggest, Charles Kingsley was a deeply divided man: an exemplar and originator of the ideal of "muscular Christianity" (a sort of Victorian equivalent to today's Boy Scout code) and a periodically suicidal depressive; an eloquent, even mesmerizing preacher who out of the pulpit was a lifelong stutterer; the embodiment of Victorian propriety who drew pictures of naked women being tortured which Nathaniel Hawthorne said "no pure man would allow himself to look at"; a practitioner of fasting and self-flagellation who held that Paradise would consist of perpetual sexual intercourse.

What we find in Charles Kingsley, in fact, is the same passion and hunger for experience that we see in George and Henry and Mary. But in him these needs were all sadly thwarted for Charles Kingsley did not travel the world like his brothers and niece. He possessed and preached a religious faith to which neither of his younger brothers subscribed. And finally, Charles Kingsley was reined in by his profound love for his wife, Fanny, and it was Fanny whom we must hold responsible for the Victorian conventionality Mary so disliked in her illustrious uncle's family.

Frances Eliza Grenfell had married beneath herself when she accepted Charles Kingsley while he was still a young curate. Throughout their long, passionate union she never regretted this step down in the social world, but she did try to ameliorate the situation in two ways: by pushing her husband to rise and by alienating him from his brothers and their families. To a large extent both these strategies worked. While still a relatively young man Charles was appointed the Queen's chaplain and also personal tutor to the Prince of Wales at Cambridge. And by the time Mary was a young girl there was scarcely any contact between her family and the Charles Kingsleys. In fact, it was only after both her uncle and her father had died that she really had anything to do with Charles's two daughters, her cousins Mary and Rose Kingsley.

Fanny was less successful, however, in keeping her husband's youngest brother, Henry, at arm's length. Eleven years junior to Charles, Henry Kingsley was something of a foster son to him. Beginning at the age of twelve, Henry lived with Charles off and on until Henry himself married in 1864. Indeed, to Fanny's intense displeasure, Henry was on the scene when Charles brought her as his bride home to his curacy in Eversley in 1844, and Henry departed only when he commenced his entirely undistinguished and inconclusive academic career first at King's College, London, and then at Worcester College, Oxford. It was at Oxford that Henry first earned his reputation as a prodigious drinker and smoker. (He died at the age of forty-six of cancer of the trachea and tongue, which was undoubtedly caused by his excessive smoking.) After coming down without a degree in 1853, he decided to go off and make his fortune in the gold rush in Australia.

But Henry had even less luck than most Kingsleys in amassing wealth, and instead of striking it rich in the Australian gold fields, he wandered from one poorly paid job to the next, working at one time or another as a mounted policeman in Sydney, an agricultural laborer, and a stock driver. During his last year he had no regular job at all and drifted about as a "sundowner," a tramp who arrived at outstations at sunset seeking food and lodging. Grim and rugged as these Australian years were, they also possessed a definite romantic aura that animated Henry's first and perhaps best novel, *The Recollections of Geoffrey Hamlyn,* published in 1859 and immediately hailed as the Great Australian Novel. It was Henry's romantic Australian experience that also captured the imagination of his young niece. In later years Henry sought refuge in George Kingsley's home in Highgate from the noisy barrel organs and watercress women and also (though Mary fails to say it) from his demanding and unhappy wife and mother-in-law in his own house in nearby squalid Kentish town. In George's house Henry wrote his novels up in the slope-roofed attic, or, if the day was sunny, he could be found enveloped in a blue haze of tobacco smoke basking on the lawn, where he told Mary and Charley stories of his Australian adventures, "tales of corroborees, black snakes, and bushrangers as would have made sleep a curse to you for a week to come."

In 1864, five years after his return from Australia, Henry rather unaccountably married his second cousin, Sarah Kingsley Haselwood, a plain and penniless governess possessed of a dependent and domineering mother. It was a disastrous choice, for no matter how furiously Henry churned out his novels and journalistic hackwork, he could not keep pace with Sarah's and Mrs. Haselwood's extravagant spending. Moreover, when George was off traveling round the world Henry often had to provide for George's family as well, and so Henry found himself woefully "short of ready," as he confided to his publisher Alexander Macmillan. Henry's chronically dire financial straits play a prominent and enduring role in the Kingsley family correspondence. Anxiety, drink, and marital unhappiness all took their toll on him, and his novels deteriorated accordingly and ceased to sell well, thereby further jeopardizing Henry's affairs. In his later years he continually, often futilely, appealed for pecuniary aid to Charles, George, and Macmillan, and even to literary figures, such as Lord Houghton, who were personal strangers to him. With his debts and drinking and questionable sexual past, Henry indeed was the family black sheep. He was everything, in fact, that his famous older brother was not, and it is not surprising, then, that although Henry and George remained close until Henry's death, Charles Kingsley was scarcely on speaking terms with his unhappy youngest brother during the last years of his life.

There was one issue, however, on which Charles and Henry were in agreement, and that was the infamous Governor Eyre controversy. In October 1865 in Morant Bay, Saint Thomas, Jamaica, a rebellion of black Jamaicans against their white colonial rulers took place. The governor of Jamaica, Edward John Eyre, spared no time or brutality in ruthlessly putting down the revolt; almost five hundred Jamaicans were killed, hundreds more flogged and tortured, and thousands of homes burned down. News of the revolt and of Eyre's violent suppression of it reached England in November and caused an enormous furor. The public protest was sufficiently great that a royal commission was formed and sent to Jamaica to investigate the rising. Its conclusions were predictably conciliatory: Eyre was praised for "the skill, promptitude and vigour" of his actions, but he was also censured for excessive punishments and for overreliance upon martial law.

But the matter did not end with the publication of the commission's report in 1866. Instead of squelching the controversy, the report served to promote it further, and two opposing committees were soon formed to agitate against each other and to keep the issue squarely before the public. The Jamaica Committee wanted Eyre prosecuted for murder, and it numbered among its members John Stuart Mill, Thomas Huxley, Herbert Spencer, and Charles Darwin. The Eyre Defense Committee, on the other hand, was supported by the likes of John Ruskin, Alfred Tennyson, Charles Dickens, and Thomas Carlyle, who described their opponents as a "knot of nigger philanthropists." Also among the Eyre Defense Committee were Charles and Henry, but not George, Kingsley.

Henry's support of Eyre is perhaps more understandable than Charles's. His knowledge of Eyre actually came from Eyre's pre-Jamaican Australian years. In the 1830s Eyre had been one of the early explorers of the desolate region in southern Australia called the Australian Bight and had also, ironically enough, gained a reputation as a great protector of Australian aborigines during the time that he was resident magistrate for the Murray River Territory there. Henry most likely, then, felt that Eyre's actions in Jamaica were being misrepresented or at least exaggerated.

Charles Kingsley's support of Eyre, however, was straightforwardly racist. Despite his early Christian Socialism and support of the laboring masses, Charles had become very much a member of the establishment and a spokesman for the status quo by the 1860s. He was also very much his mother's son — the son, that is, of a woman whose family had owned slaves for generations in the West Indies — and he had never minced words about his attitude toward blacks. Privately he called them "ant eating apes." In the pulpit he was scarcely more restrained and marveled in one sermon that "out of sticks and stones, yea out of Hottentots, could the Lord raise up worshippers."

It is impossible to know whether Mary was aware of her uncles' support of Eyre. Certainly their views, especially Charles's, would have been abhorrent to her. And there is not a little irony — perhaps there is even some poetic justice — in the fact that the niece of these two men would gain fame as a writer who defended the people her uncles despised and explained the complexity, value, and beauty of black African life.

Both Charles and Henry Kingsley died when Mary was still a child, so her memories and understanding of them were necessarily fragmentary and incomplete. With her father, in contrast, she shared a rare if sometimes turbulent intimacy. "Infinite were the points of collision between him and me," Mary confessed in the memoir, "very largely from our similarity in taste." But it was much more than shared tastes that bound Mary Kingsley to her father. In addition to describing the chronological events of her father's life — his education, travels, family life, and death — Mary gradually unfolds in the memoir a parallel interior life, the inner man. The cast of mind, impulses, and desires that she explores here are the same as those that animated her own life: a conviction of irremediable isolation, a sense of fearlessness and an attraction to danger, a nonnegotiable need for personal freedom, a sense of profound alienation in England and a corollary quest for a "home" in remote and strange lands and cultures, and a passion for scholarship, the more abstruse the better. In short, this interior life of George Kingsley constituted what Mary repeatedly called his "many mindedness." If George was the most typical and the happiest of all the Kingsleys of his generation, as Mary claimed, it was because he protected and preserved this "many mindedness" from all incursions, from whatever quarter. Marriage, children, and financial worries entirely failed to thwart or curb George's need to lead a wandering life.

In fact, the only time George was in any way constrained was during his childhood, growing up in the gloomy, urban, Chelsea rectory of his father's parish. Like his daughter some forty years later, he escaped his dreary, cramped existence through books, the very same books, in fact, that were to be the chief nourishment of Mary's own youth. These books spoke of an unlimited, unnavigated world far beyond the dim rectory library and beyond the dirty lanes and courts and alleys outside its windows. In his father's library George first read the volumes that would eventually form the most valuable core — in his daughter's mind — of his own library: "Histories of the globe, and lordly folios, on whose maps full many a sturdy coast-line dwindled into dots — full many a line of dots went stumbling on to perish at the feet of pregnant nothingness. Volume on volume of famous voyagers —Dampier, Rogers, Shelrocke, Byron, Cook, and grand old Esquemeling — the Froissart of the Buccaneers — and respectable Captain Charles Johnson, deeply interested and very properly shocked at 'the Robberies and Murders of the Most Notorious Pyrates.' "

Mary emphasizes how George suffered because of the gulf between the fulfilling exciting world he found in such books and the actual life he had to submit to outside of the library. One can see his adulthood, in fact, as a restless quest to align these inner and outer worlds, as a search, as Mary makes clear, for a geographical home that would measure up to the needs of his imagination. Perhaps the most significant difference between the father's life and that of the daughter is that Mary eventually found a home in West Africa while George remained a rootless wanderer to the end of his days.

One cannot make a career out of wandering, however, and so George was forced to choose a profession. Rejecting his brothers' choices of the church and full-time authorship, he studied medicine, first at Saint George's Hospital, London, and then at the University of Edinburgh, where he earned his M.D. in 1847 when he was only twenty years old. George's reasons for becoming a doctor are unclear. He seems never to have contemplated either settling down as a practitioner or pursuing medical research. The only manner in which he practiced his profession was as the personal physician to a series of peripatetic noblemen whose mania for globetrotting was as unappeasable as his own. He may, then, have actually taken up medicine as a means of pursuing his travels. Whatever his reasons, however, in this as in so much else, Mary followed in his footsteps. She pored over his hefty medical textbooks as a child, studied medicine for a brief period in Germany as a young woman, and for the whole of her adult life she was constantly nursing friends and family in England, Africans, colonial officials, and traders in West Africa, and finally Boer prisoners of war in South Africa.

It was during his medical student days that George first began his ramblings, chiefly in Europe during his long holidays. In comparison with his later travels, these European jaunts through Germany, Switzerland, Austria, Bohemia, and Moravia seem rather tame, but they afforded him an exhilarating sense of liberation. *Free* and *alone,* Mary said, described the dominant needs of her father's life just as they did of her own. And the transformation these travels wrought in him she reveals in a favorite family anecdote: George's mother used to tell her grandchildren how once on a holiday in Dresden she was terrified when approached on the street by "a ragged, resolute, ruffian-looking young vagabond" who appeared to be demanding alms. But closer inspection showed that the beggar was "none other than her . . . son George, returning literally from Bohemia, with his clothes in tatters, the remnants of his boots tied together with pieces of string, and his face burnt as brown as a gipsy's, radiant with his freedom and his joy at seeing her again."

After completing his medical examinations in Edinburgh, George pursued further studies in anatomy in Paris. He did so just at the time when Louis Philippe was being driven from the throne, and George was swept up in the revolution — tending wounded rioters and getting wounded himself when he was shot in the arm while helping to build barricades out of paving stones.

When he returned to England in 1849, George lived briefly in Flintshire in northern Wales and there enacted perhaps the most heroic chapter of his life; a cholera epidemic swept through the district, and George cared for the multitude of sick and dying for days and nights on end. This episode was immortalized by his older brother Charles in the 1857 novel *Two Years Ago*. Tom Thurnell, the hero of *Two Years Ago,* is an almost exact likeness of George Kingsley: handsome (with his spare, athletic body and sensitive, mobile face, George was by far the best looking and consequently most romantically active of the three Kingsley brothers), fearless, indefatigably brave in attendance upon the cholera victims, and most significantly, once released from his medical duties, an incurable roamer. "Settle down in a country practice he would not," Charles Kingsley writes of his hero, "he vanished into infinite space and was heard of by occasional letters dated from the Rocky Mountains, . . . the Spanish West Indies, . . . Singapore, the Falkland Islands, and all manner of unexpected places." In time George Kingsley was to visit virtually all these unexpected and far-flung spots, but when *Two Years Ago* was published he had actually wandered no farther than Eastern Europe. Charles Kingsley may have possessed prophetic powers concerning his younger brother's life, or perhaps George found in *Two Years Ago* an appealing and challenging script for his life. In any event, though his serious travels did not begin until 1862, shortly after the Flintshire cholera epidemic George chose his vocation in 1850 as medical attendant to the noble, wealthy, and restless by becoming the private physician to the marquis of Aylesbury.

For the next twelve years George worked as a private doctor, employed initially by Aylesbury and afterward by the duke of Norfolk, the duke of Sutherland, and the first and second earls of Ellesmere.

The terms *worked* or *employed,* however, do not really accurately describe George's activities in these years. None of these noblemen was an invalid or was even particularly sickly. They all shared their young doctor's great pleasure in shooting, salmon fishing, and deer stalking, and just as important, the libraries of their great country houses provided George with the means to pursue his multifarious scholarly endeavors.

Mary venerated her father's learning and clearly was impressed by his membership in such scholarly fellowships as the Linnaean Society and the Royal Microscopic Society. But she concedes that despite all his erudition, he never fulfilled his early intellectual promise. During these years, George embarked on numerous projects, only a few of which were brought to completion. He published, for example, a translation of four novellas by the German writer Paul von Heyse, but never finished his more ambitious translation of Heinrich Heine. He also announced to Macmillan that he intended to write a novel set in the era of Charles II of England, but this too never saw the light of day. Access to the earl of Ellesmere's Bridgewater Library inspired him to undertake a study of early Elizabethan dramatists which also came to naught. In fact, apart from his contribution to *South Sea Bubbles* and the Heyse translation, the only writing George ever completed and published was an article on Christopher Marlowe and an edition of Francis Thynne's esoteric *Animadversions Upon the Annotations and Corrections of Imperfections and Impressions of Chaucer's Works* for the Early English Text Society.

Thus the years before George's marriage passed largely in vigorous sport and hunting, good society, and engrossing if desultory and inconclusive scholarship. But for George it was not an entirely satisfying life. He remained restless and could not settle down. By now, Charles was domestically immured in Eversley in Hampshire, and Henry was off in Australia. The lives of his two brothers may have represented for George the crossroads at which he stood — home, hearth, and conventionality, or travel, adventure, and danger. There was never really any doubt as to which road George would take. He still needed to find a geographical home that would correspond to the realm of his imagination created by his reading in childhood. And for George, as for Henry, and even more importantly for Mary, this home could only be found in the tropics. As Mary says, "The sunlight, the colour, and the magnficent exuberance of the life of the Torrid Zone absolutely called across the latitudes to every member of the Kingsley family. . . . No one of them . . . ever laid himself open to a charge of having spoken disrespectfully of the Equator. In truth, their happiness to no inconsiderable extent, depended upon their proximity to it."

George's pursuit of warmer climes at first took him no farther than a solitary cruise in the Mediterranean. But soon he was traveling to Spain, Egypt, Syria, and North Africa, and finally to the South Pacific, all in the company of one or another hypochondriacal nobleman.

From 1862 until the early 1890s George remained on the road and on the seas, returning to Britain every year or so for merely a few months before setting off again, like Tennyson's Ulysses, for "that untravelled world whose margin fades for ever and for ever when I move." It is Mary herself who quotes Tennyson in the memoir and compares her father to Ulysses, principally because of George's insatiable hunger for travel and experience. But Tennyson's hero, it will be remembered, left a wife and son behind in Ithaca to struggle on as best they could on the desert isle while he pursued self-fulfillment "beyond the sunset and the baths of all the western stars."

George, too, left neglected hostages of fortune behind. He had clearly opted to devote his life to travel, adventure, and danger, but he also at least made a gesture toward, if not actual commitment to, hearth and home. Scarcely three weeks before setting off for the Mediterranean in November 1862, handsome, elusive George Kingsley married — not into one of the titled, wealthy families he had served as a private physician, but rather to a thirty-five-year-old woman named Mary Bailey, an innkeeper's daughter who had been employed by George in some domestic capacity, very likely as his cook.

On October 9 at the grim little Islington parish church, in the presence only of the curate, W. J. Chapman, and two witnesses, George Kingsley and Mary Bailey exchanged vows and were nominally, at least, joined for the rest of their days.

This astonishing marriage and George's almost immediate flight from it both submit to an easy if still partially baffling explanation: on October 13, four days after George and Mary Bailey wed, their eldest child and only daughter, Mary Henrietta Kingsley, was born.

Mary's Childhood: Inner and Outer Worlds

It was extremely fortunate that George Kingsley decided at the eleventh hour to marry his pregnant cook and fortunate not only for Mary Bailey. If he had been a "bounder," as the type was called in those days, there would have been no *Travels in West Africa*, no *West African Studies*. British colonial policy, African ethnography, and English literary history all would have been impoverished, for it is inconceivable that the bastard of a destitute domestic would have grown up — if she survived infancy — to do anything other than follow in her mother's footsteps and go "into service," becoming at best, perhaps, a parlor maid. Despite all his gifts and talents, George Kingsley produced so singularly little that we can say his greatest contribution was acquiescing to wedlock, thereby providing a future for his daughter.

Matrimony for Mary Bailey, however, offered not so much a future as an isolated and lonely sinecure. It brought legitimacy for her two children but not really for her. After months of vacillation as he watched Mary Bailey grow larger by the day with his child, George Kingsley in the end did the decent thing. He behaved, as his daughter said he always did, like a gentleman. But though he gave Mary Bailey his name, he could not assimilate her into his family or his social world. How could Fanny Kingsley possibly receive a woman incapable of pronouncing her *h*s? Even Sarah Kingsley and Mrs. Haselwood would have airs that prohibited commerce with George's wife. Of course, there was still her own family, the Baileys, but marrying up in the world also to a certain extent alienated Mary Bailey from her own people. Bailey relations, particularly her brother William and his daughter Annie, continued to hover on the fringes of Mrs. Kingsley's life, and years later her daughter was far closer to her Bailey uncle and cousin than to any of the Kingsleys. Still, Mary Bailey Kingsley was trapped in a kind of social limbo by her marriage, and it was an exceedingly solitary limbo at that because her husband was almost always away from home.

Her response to this isolation was, given the age, predictable. At first she threw herself into dutiful ministrations to others, functioning, that is, an an exemplary Victorian Angel in the House by serving and nursing those in need. Mary said of her mother that "the only thing that ever tempted her to go about her neighbours was to assist them when they were sick in mind, body, or estate. So strongly marked a characteristic was this of our early home life that to this day I always feel I have no right to associate with people unless there is something the matter with them." And when she wearied of tending others or there were no more to nurse, Mary Bailey Kingsley became ill herself, took to her bed upstairs, drew the curtains, and was faithfully nursed in turn by her daughter. These languors were of a definite, if unspecified, psychological origin. Mrs. Kingsley suffered from that common ailment of nineteenth-century upper-middle-class women, neurasthenia, and taking to her neurasthenic sickbed, in fact, was really the only fashionable or socially acceptable thing she ever did in her life. Thus Mary Bailey Kingsley must have come to embody for her daughter two equally forbidding fates for Victorian women: the Angel in the House and the Madwoman in the Attic. The young Mary probably would not have precisely recognized and labeled the two stereotypes. Nevertheless, during the years that Mary was growing up, her mother was a wraithlike, often frightening figure and was also Mary's only model for what it meant to be a woman.

But in November of 1862 all these grim ramifications of the marriage of George Kingsley and Mary Bailey still lay in the future. The newlyweds, however, were already separated, for George was cruising in the Mediterranean on the HMS *St. George.* On the sixteenth his ship anchored off Lisbon, and he went ashore for the day, enjoying a delightful picnic luncheon on "the hot baking sand, with the air filled with the rich aromatic scent of the forest and bright butterflies and gigantic grasshoppers fluttering and bouncing about." In his log he congratulated himself on his pleasurable exile from "London the foggy with its dirty sloshing melting snow and cold rheumatising winds." His bride, of course, was still recuperating from childbirth in George's bachelor quarters in Islington in the midst of the dirty, melting snow, the windows firmly shuttered against the rheumatizing winds.

While George was cruising from Lisbon to Gibralter and to other Mediterranean ports, back in Islington Mary Kingsley had her first two hair-raising escapes in life. "Before I can remember anything," she later wrote in an autobiographical sketch for a popular magazine, "family tradition credits me with having plunged perambulator and all into a deep, dangerous area in Islington, upside down, headlong and calm." This incident, Mary confessed, "I believe to be only one I have been involved in in which I am held blameless of contributing negligence or reckless fooling."

She was actually equally innocent of the second mishap, which also marked her first appearance in print in the form of a headline reading thus: A GALLANT RESCUE BY A MEMBER OF THE ALL-ENGLISH ELEVEN. "I was not a member of the All-English Eleven myself," Mary explained, "nor do I exactly know who was; but, at any rate, at considerable risk to himself, he fished my nurse and me out of a deep pool down Hastings way. I remain grateful to him; but remember an opinion was subsequently expressed that in rescuing both of us he had gone too far." Thus began a life of a long series of close calls.

In early 1864, while home for one of his sporadic visits, George moved his wife and daughter several miles east to Highgate, in those days still a palmy, almost rural area, on the outskirts of London. It was here that Mary's brother, Charles George (or Charley, as Mary always called him), was born two years later in 1866, the product of another of George's brief stopovers in England in between travels. In Highgate George bought a small square house at 22 Southwood Lane, set back from the road and enclosed by a black iron fence. To the left was a Baptist chapel, from which issued fervently sung hymns at regular intervals, much to George's agnostic annoyance. Living next door to the chapel, however, instilled in Mary a humorous if unbelieving affection for Nonconformists. But the real disadvantage to living next door to the chapel was that people were constantly pulling the lion-headed knocker on the Kingsleys' door in quest of the chapel's minister. George became so exasperated at having his little house mistaken for a parsonage that he seriously considered putting up a brass plate, not with his own name engraved on it, but with the unadorned information that "the minister of the chapel does *not* live here."

On the other side was a lonely lane separating the house from the less prosperous, attached terrace houses farther down the street. The lane was a sort of no man's land, harboring as Mary described it, "all sorts of dangerous wild-fowl in the shape of burglars by night and distraught cattle by day, if the gate were open." Thieves, however, were kept at bay by the general awareness in the neighborhood that though reclusive and often bedridden, Mrs. Kingsley was an excellent shot with a revolver. It also helped that the Kingsleys kept a lot of dogs. Behind the house was a long, narrow garden, which steeply fell away to open fields beyond. Here it was that Mary kept her pet gamecocks and where her uncle Henry Kingsley loved to lounge and smoke his pipe on hot sunny summer afternoons.

The house looked out only onto this private back lawn, for one of its strangest features was the blindness of its front facade. The four main front windows facing the street were all bricked in, leaving only a single central window above the door. When George Kingsley was off on his travels his wife ordered that the shutters on the back windows be closed as well, and then the house was sealed off almost entirely, darkened day and night, winter and summer, except for the single shaft of light that could pour through the central front window onto the staircase. And even when George was at home, the wisteria at the back of the house was so thick that the rooms were almost as dim and musty as when the shutters were fastened shut.

Inside the house, then, reigned a perpetual dusk, and particularly when George was away, an almost unnatural silence, considering the presence of two little children.

Built around 1820, 22 Southwood Lane was a conventional and, by nineteenth-century standards, small Georgian house, scarcely opulent enough to merit the envy of the terrace dwellers down the street. On the first floor were the parlor and George's study, separated by the entry hall and stairwell. Directly above were two similar rooms, the nursery and the Kingsleys' bedroom, and above these in turn was the two-room, slope-roofed attic where Henry Kingsley wrote several of his novels. The kitchen and laundry room were in the two rooms at the bottom of the house, and the toilet, of course, in those days before modern plumbing, was in a shed outdoors.

It is easy enough to imagine the little house's parlor, with its heavy, dark, damask draperies, polished wooden floors, Turkish carpets, and fireplace; and also the stuffy bedroom Mrs. Kingsley lived in upstairs, with a table covered with vials and tonics next to the bed. Less easy to imagine is the nursery full of toys, with a rocking chair and two small cots, that lay across the hall from the sickroom.

The most vital room in the house, however, was none of these but rather George Kingsley's library on the ground floor opposite the parlor. Here could be found curiosities and mementos from all over the globe battling for space with piles of transactions of half a dozen learned societies. Shelves of arcane books on every conceivable subject stretched from the floor to the ceiling: Darwin jostled *Tristram Shandy;* Omar Khayyám nestled against Pliny; *David Copperfield* perched on top of Burton's *Anatomy of Melancholy.* The bookshelves also housed an abundance of travel and exploration narratives that George had assiduously collected over the years: classics from his boyhood and accounts of the most recent contemporary expeditions, including those to the Arctic and Antarctic poles, Australia, the South Seas, Arabia, the Himalayas, and, of course, Africa. Books, journals, correspondence, and maps covered every surface and overflowed onto the carpeted floor. And artifacts like Stone Age axes, Indian iron ornaments, and a set of arrowheads added to the library's exotic chaos.

In the midst of the darkened, claustrophobic house, George's study was an oasis of life, adventure, and excitement for his daughter. Mary's whole world during these early years was circumscribed by the walls of the Southwood Lane house, or, at the farthest, by the wrought iron fence that enclosed the garden. "The whole of my childhood and youth was spent at home," she later wrote, "in the house and garden. The living outside world I saw little of, and cared less for, for I felt myself out of place at the few parties I ever had the chance of going to, and I deservedly was unpopular with my own generation, for I knew nothing of play and such things. But this was not superiority of mind in me, at all, the truth was I had a great amusing world of my own other people did not know or care about — that was the books in my father's library."

But the problem remains of how she learned to read them. No governess ever entered the little Southwood Lane house, nor was Mary ever sent to school. Years later she rather bitterly confessed her lack of formal education to George Macmillan when she wrote him that "I do not know if I ever revealed the fact to you that being allowed to learn German was *all* the paid for education I ever had — £2000 was spent on my brother — I still hope not in vain."

Under normal circumstances, as an upper-middle-class young girl, Mary would have been taught to read, do sums, and manage globes, and perhaps to play the piano and draw by her mother if not by a governess. But of course very little about the Kingsley household was normal. Much of the time Mrs. Kingsley was indisposed, not quite "compos mentis," as one of George's club friends put it. Even when not down with nervous prostration, Mary's mother may not have been sufficiently literate herself to teach her daughter to read, and it is virtually certain that Mrs. Kingsley never sat down at a piano or stood before an easel. The only thing Mrs. Kingsley is on record as having instilled in Mary, in fact, was her cockney accent, a trait that always astounded her admirers and audiences, as Mary jokingly complained when she saw a newspaper account of one of her lectures that criticized her for dropping her *g*s "when I am trying so hard to hold on to the 'h's.' " Perhaps Charley taught Mary the alphabet and simple words and sentences and then passed on his primers to her after he began at grammar school. Or perhaps Mary, as some gifted children do, taught herself to read. In any event, despite years of voracious and wide reading, like so many self-taught people, Mary always thought herself to be poorly educated and intellectually incompetent. And this conviction of intellectual inferiority remained with her even after she had managed to teach herself Latin, physics, and chemistry — a curriculum that no Victorian girl would have studied under even the most erudite governess or at the most enlightened school.

Almost as puzzling as the question of how Mary learned to read was where or from whom she learned to swear. Her very earliest memory in life was of "being seized by the middle and carried horizontally downstairs by my justly irritated father, into the presence of my mother, whom he asked, 'Where does this child get its language from?' " Most likely she learned it from George himself, whose "awful temper" often produced volleys of oaths and hurled missiles. In later years, her curses elicited as much surprise as her lack of *h*s. Both, of course, were considered highly unladylike. But then there was nothing in Mary's childhood that could be considered appropriate training for a lady. The child was simply there, unplanned for if not positively unwanted. She unfortunately was a girl, which meant that there was nothing really to train her *for*. The nanny and the cook saw to her physical well-being, she herself saw to her own education, and then, because there was really no one else to do it, Mary took over the running of the house at an unusually early age. She became her "mother's chief officer from the day I could first carry a duster, and I had to do the tidying up . . . and became responsible for everything lost in the establishment."

Early on there were, of course, games and quarrels with Charley, but he was sickly like his mother and no physical match for his older sister. And Charley was in time sent to school, and then for months at a stretch, while George was off globetrotting, there were only Mary and her mother and the old servant, Mrs. Barrett, in the Southwood Lane house, and an elderly gardener outdoors who spent his mornings nailing up creepers or rolling gravel and his afternoons sleeping under the Jerusalem artichokes.

In 1867, when Mary was five and just beginning to carry a duster and tidy up, George embarked on his longest and most remote "ramble" yet — to the South Sea islands with Robert Charles Herbert, the earl of Pembroke whose health he was supposed to oversee and maintain. For the next three years "the Earl and the Doctor" (as the authors of *South Sea Bubbles* were identified when their book came out in 1872) cruised the South Pacific in their schooner the *Albatross,* dropping in now and then at Tahiti, Fiji, Bora Bora, and Samoa, as well as at ports in Australia and New Zealand. At irregular intervals George sent long, detailed bulletins of his adventures back to his family in Southwood Lane, giving lush descriptions of the lotosland beauty of the South Sea islands and hair-raising accounts of storms and the sinking of neighboring ships. He also included a certain amount of zoological and botanical information for his daughter, the "learned one," as he called Mary. These letters came to vie in Mary's imagination with the volumes of Richard Hakluyt and Captain Cook in her father's library. Moreover, they constituted an ongoing adventure and proved to her that excitement and danger were available at first hand and not merely through the medium of books. She thrilled to her father's descriptions of hurricanes, earthquakes, cannibal-inhabited remote islands, an attack by a wild bull, and finally the shipwreck of the *Albatross* on a coral reef in a lonely stretch of ocean near the Ringgold Islands, "the most cannibalistic part of the Pacific," as George wrote his wife and children.

He and Pembroke managed to navigate their lifeboat to a small island where they spent ten anxious Robinson Crusoe–like days, for although the island was uninhabited they found "evident marks of past cannibal feasts" on it. Day after day they were prevented by storms from leaving and so spent their confinement reading Shelley aloud, cutting down trees, and writing letters that they did not know whether they would live to send home. Eventually the weather cleared, and after thirty hours in their open boat at sea, George and Pembroke were rescued by an English ship.

Mary and Charley were spellbound by George's adventures, but Mrs. Kingsley could hardly share her children's enthusiasm. Despite their affectionate tone, his letters were, with all their close calls and reports of shipwrecks and drownings, extremely thoughtless accounts to send to a lonely, dependent, and high-strung wife. Nor could Mrs. Kingsley relish George's graphic descriptions of the beautiful Tahitian, Samoan, and other women of the South Seas he encountered on his travels, many of whom, he boasted, wished to run off and marry him. Given his passionate nature, it is unlikely that George put up much resistance to the obvious appeal and advances of these South Sea beauties, and as one who had herself succumbed to his charms, Mrs. Kingsley knew just how attractive her husband was to women.

But it was the risks George ran and the uncertainty over his fate — when and if he would ever return — that took the most serious toll on his wife. In some ways the three-year South Sea voyage was the worst of George's many absences for her. He was literally on the other side of the world; when mail came it described events that had occurred months earlier. Often George left his financial affairs in Henry's inept hands, and there were insufficient funds to pay the butcher and the coal man. And most of all, there was the constant specter of widowhood and two little fatherless children before Mrs. Kingsley's anxious eyes, particularly when she had, in her daughter's words, recently received "a letter eloquently setting forth the dangers of coral reefs to navigators, with a good deal about sharks and cannibals; then silence; then a paragraph in some newspaper to the effect that a schooner, name unknown, had been wrecked on some South Sea reef or another (in the region where she knew he might be) and that the crew had been massacred and eaten by natives."

George invariably managed, however, to escape being murdered and eaten, and he returned in his own good time to his lonely little family in Highgate. Mary was always overjoyed at the heroic return of her father. Mrs. Kingsley opened the back shutters in celebration, and for two or three or four months, until George was irresistibly drawn off to some other corner of the globe, they were a proper family once again. Not that perfect peace and harmony reigned in the little Southwood

Lane house. Mary idolized her father, but idolatry failed to avert collisions with him. George found it difficult to submit to domesticity after months of wandering in the South Seas. He could put up with privations on a desert island more easily than he could the constraints of domestic routine and the noise and interruptions produced by two little children. Mary, his devoted worshiper, had a close and familiar knowledge of George's "volcanic temper," finding it necessary on more than one occasion to duck from a copy of Brand's *Dictionary of the Arts and Sciences* "temporarily diverted into use as a projectile in consequence of some conduct of mine." George, buried in his books, was particularly sensitive to unwarranted sounds. Mary's fighting cocks in the back garden showed an uncanny ability to escape from their pen and reserve their "clarion crow" until they were directly beneath George's study window — "a performance rewarded promptly with miscellaneous projectiles and observations."

There were other mishaps as well. Mary had a fondness for filling the fire grates with neat, clean, white, willow shavings, "with just a twinkle of gold shavings on the top." George, a great smoker, frequently threw his matches — "never blown out, mark you" — into the willow-decorated grates. Minor conflagrations, both literal and metaphorical, ensued. George demanded of his wife why she allowed the "child [to] put that silly stuff into the fireplace." Mrs. Kingsley countered that "it amuses her, and you ought to be more careful with your matches." George prophesied that Mary would burn down the house one day, "just for all the world as if I, plus willow shavings, spelt spontaneous combustion, and he had . . . nothing to do with it whatsoever."

Explosions as well as conflagrations enlivened George's sojourns at home. Somewhere George had acquired a tin of particularly powerful gunpowder, the strength of which he praised to both his wife and his close friend Dr. Oakshott, one of the few visitors to Southwood Lane. Mary overheard these glowing descriptions of the gunpowder and "took an early opportunity to possess myself of that cannister, and desirous of testing the strength of the powder and of also seeing how military mines worked — affairs which I had been hearing and reading about just then in connection with the Franco-Prussian War — I inadvertently succeeded in blowing a tub of liquid manure over our great spring blanket wash that was hanging on a clothesline hard by."

George and Mary were also at odds over books, largely because of their similar literary tastes and shared appetite for science. Frequently, then, they would both want to read the same book at the same time. There was an especially bad "hurricane," for example, over Lockyer's *Solar Physics* — not exactly typical reading for young girls in the 1870s, but nevertheless a book for which Mary developed a great passion so that she hid it beneath some straw in the garden shed rather than surrender it to her father before she had finished reading it.

Mary was always engrossed in one volume or another of George's, usually something quite scientific, even technical, on such subjects as chemistry, physics, zoology, or medicine. She had little taste for fiction other than Dickens and her uncles' novels, and many of the staples of the nineteenth-century literary diet — Austen, the Brontës, George Eliot, and the Brownings — were unknown at 22 Southwood Lane. Nor did Mary succumb to the contemporary craze for sensation novels like *Lady Audley's Secret* or to the sentimental productions of Mrs. Oliphant or Mrs. Yonge, best sellers all.

In their monotonous circumscription and isolation, Mary's early years were to an unusual degree divorced from her times. But in one important respect her life was profoundly shaped by contemporary events. The second half of the nineteenth century was the culmination of the great age of African exploration by Europeans — the years when all the major geographical mysteries of the continent were, after centuries of effort, finally being resolved. Into the sealed-up little house on Southwood Lane the newspapers brought word of Henry Morton Stanley's discovery of Dr. David Livingstone on the shores of Lake Tanganyika in 1871, of Livingstone's death two years later, still in the heart of Africa, and of Verney Lovett Cameron's east-to-west walk across the whole continent in 1875. And in time the multivolume, gilt-bound, profusely illustrated books of these explorers also found their way into George Kingsley's library, where they were immediately devoured by his daughter.

Mary's close familiarity with the history of African exploration cast way back beyond contemporary exploration triumphs, however, to the earliest classical accounts of Herodotus and Ptolemy. These nourished her imagination the way fairy tales and ghost stories feed the minds of more conventional children. For the Western imagination Africa has always been much more than a geographical place; it is also a continent of desire — the repository of extravagant dreams and an arena of daring acts. The history of the opening up of this geographical terra incognita, then, is a fundamentally mythic one, a history of a land of fabulous beasts, gold, and diamonds, the lost kingdom of Prester John, the land of the White Man's Grave and the White Man's Burden, the Garden of Eden and the Heart of Darkness.

The African explorers Mary read about in her father's library — some of whom were still alive and even like Livingstone at that very moment wandering somewhere in the impenetrable reaches of the Dark Continent — were all associated with one or another of the major serpentine African waterways. And one after the other the nineteenth-century European explorers sought to penetrate the continent via these rivers, following their courses to vast, womblike lakes in the interior or back to their mouths on the coast where they emptied into the salt sea. In 1806 Mungo Park perished on the edge of the Sahara trying to find the mouth of the Niger. Alexander Laing was murdered by a fanatical sheik near Timbuktu on the same quest. Finally, in 1830 the Lander brothers survived a harrowing journey down the Great Brown God, as the Niger was called, to its delta network of streams and creeks that empty into the Atlantic between the Bights of Benin and Bonny.

The quest for the source of the Nile in midcentury was even more spectacular. This great mystery had haunted dreamers and adventurers since the times of Herodotus and of Ptolemy, and though it was effectively solved several years before Mary was born, the explorers' accounts that narrated the Nile search were coming out just as she was learning how to read. In 1858 Richard Burton and John Speke had discovered Lake Tanganyika in East Africa, and then Speke on his own had stumbled on to Lake Victoria, which, in a moment of unverified inspiration, he pronounced the source of the Nile. This led to irremediable hostilities between Burton and Speke, and in the early 1860s Speke returned to East Africa with James Grant and discovered the point at the northern tip of Lake Victoria where the Nile flows from the lake. Then he and Grant marched north to Gondokoro, where they met Samuel Baker and his mistress, who were shortly to discover Lake Albert. Finally, Speke and Grant sailed all the way up the Nile past Khartoum to Cairo.

The Nile question would seem to have been settled, then, but in fact the chagrined Burton would not let the matter rest. In 1864 the British Association for the Advancement of Science organized a debate over the great river's source to take place during the association's annual meeting at Bath. The old antagonists, Burton and Speke, were to argue for Lake Tanganyika and Lake Victoria respectively. But scarcely twenty-four hours before the Nile debate was to begin, Speke shot and killed himself — officially in a hunting accident, though it was widely rumored at the time that he had committed suicide rather than face defeat at the hands of Burton.

Certainly Burton, one of Mary's great heroes, held this interpretation of Speke's death, though instead of returning to East Africa to pursue his claims for Lake Tanganyika, he began to travel extensively on the western side of the continent, especially in Congo Français where he encountered the Fang people and visited the islands of Fernando Po and Corsico. Mary read his *Two Trips to Gorilla Land* when it came out in 1876, and it was perhaps the most influential of all the explorers' books she read as a young girl, for when she herself went out to West Africa nearly twenty years later she chose as her particular territory the places Burton had visited and as her particular people to study, the Fang.

Meanwhile, the source of the Nile was not definitively established until Henry Morton Stanley circumnavigated Lake Victoria in the mid-1870s. Stanley, in fact, pulled off major exploration coups all over the continent: he not only determined the source of the Nile, but that of the Congo as well; and he circumnavigated Lake Tanganyika, discovered Lake Edward and also Ptolemy's fabled Mountains of the Moon, Mount Kilimanjaro, in East Africa. But his greatest find — the one that brought him instant fame — was his discovery of David Livingstone at Ujiji on the eastern bank of Lake Tanganyika in 1871. Livingstone, a missionary, doctor, and explorer, had been wandering about central and southern Africa for more than twenty years, unsuccessfully seeking the source of the Nile and Congo (which he wrongly guessed were one river) but in the process discovering Lake Shirwa and Lake Nyasa. Even more spectacularly, Livingstone became the first European to cross the entire continent from east to west and then back again between 1852 and 1856, tracing as he went the course of the Zambezi River.

By 1870, however, Livingstone was alarmingly lost from sight and had not been heard from in months, so Henry Morton Stanley, a raw young journalist who had been knocking about the United States since the end of the Civil War, was dispatched by the *New York Herald* to find Dr. Livingstone. In 1871 Mary and the rest of the world read with amazement about Stanley's famous meeting with Livingstone and then two years later were even more stunned by the accounts of Livingstone's death. Livingstone died in April of 1873, emaciated and wasted in a remote Central African village, still in quest of the source of the Congo. His two devoted African servants, Susi and Chuma, embalmed his body and carried it on foot to the coast, an eight-month journey, where it was shipped back to England. It is possible that twelve-year-old Mary Kingsley was among the throng of mourners outside Westminster Abbey gathered to pay homage and to say farewell to the famous Dr. Livingstone, who was finally accorded a hero's funeral on April 18, 1874, more than a year after his death in the heart of Africa.

Livingstone's fate must have provided an important object lesson for Mary. More than any of the other major African explorers she read about, he embodied the syndrome of the expatriate European — his was the plight of the white man who cannot go home again, who finds in black Africa a desperately needed psychological and spiritual resting place.

Livingstone and his travels were very important to Mary in another respect as well. Like Burton, Livingstone was unusual among the African explorers in being keenly interested in the African peoples among whom he traveled and lived. All Livingstone's books contain a rich store of ethnographical as well as geographical information. He was not, like Speke or Baker, intent merely on solving certain geographical problems. Nor was he, like Stanley, out to conquer a continent through sheer force of will and strength of body, and then to bleed it dry for imperialistic gain as Stanley helped King Leopold of Belgium do in the misnamed Congo Free State. Livingstone recognized the value and complexity of the African culture that as a missionary he was, nominally at least, supposed to destroy and replace with European, Christian morals and mores. Of course, what in effect happened was that Livingstone himself, rather than the "heathen" Africans, was "converted" in the end. This was not spelled out in his books, but what was vividly portrayed and appealed most to Mary was the fascination and beauty of the people and the world which claimed him as their own.

Burton and Livingstone played a major role in Mary's inner life in the hours she spent reading in her father's library. But she singled out as her particular heroes several less flamboyant, less well-known travelers who explored and wrote about the Ogooué River region that she was to appropriate for herself. Foremost among these were Paul Belloni Du Chaillu and Pierre Savorgnan de Brazza. Du Chaillu, who went out to the Gabon in the late 1850s and again in 1864 and 1865, just missed striking the main stream of the Ogooué, but he carefully mapped out the area surrounding it — dense rain forest, for the most part, inhabited by pygmies and by the enormous equatorial African gorillas, neither of which had been seen by white men before. Du Chaillu's graphic accounts of both in Mary's great favorites, *In the Country of the Dwarfs* and *Stories of the Gorilla Country,* caused a sensation among the reading public, but also much skepticism among more erudite readers who thought that Du Chaillu's gorillas and pygmies were no more plausible than Prester John's streets of gold.

In the course of three journeys in 1875, 1880, and 1883, Brazza also explored the Ogooué some ten years after Du Chaillu. He traveled inland on the river from the Atlantic, signing treaties as he went with local chiefs that gained important territories for the French government. And Brazza also beat Stanley to the large, strangely placid lake in the Congo River known as Stanley Pool.

What sparked Mary's hero worship of Du Chaillu and Brazza, however, was not their sensational adventures with gorillas or pygmies or their races with competing explorers, but rather their fearless passage through what she liked to call "choice spots" in West Africa — regions of particular danger that required special gifts of strength of mind and body, or, as she put it, "pluck, perseverence, and tact." Brazza's extensive travels in particular became something of an obsession with Mary. Brazza did not publish a book-length record of his explorations, and so she had to piece together the magnitude of his achievement from scattered articles in journals and from transactions of geographical and scientific societies.

Like Burton, Brazza also provided Mary with a hero who had made a valuable scientific contribution; he was not a controversial public personality or a popularizer like Du Chaillu. Brazza was a brave government agent and a scientific investigator, both of the geographical features of the area and of the Fang, and this is why Mary always held he "was the greatest of all West African explorers."

Did Mary ever stop and reflect, however, that all these various explorers she read — Park, Burton, Livingstone, Stanley, Du Chaillu, and Brazza, to name only the most prominent, for she read many more — were all men? And did she perhaps wonder about the lives of women such as Samuel Baker's mistress (later his second wife), Florence Baker, who accompanied him down the Nile to Lake Albert; or Katherine Petherick, who covered much the same territory with her husband and coauthored their *Travels in Central Africa and Exploration of the Nile Tributaries;* or the long-suffering Mary Moffat Livingstone, who found her final resting place under a baobab tree on the banks of the Shire River in southern Africa? Even more important, did Mary recognize the essential pattern of male exploration in Africa, a pattern of masculine penetration, conquest, and, ultimately, self-aggrandizement, if not outright plunder? This was the pattern that Stanley — whom Mary openly criticized in her books — enacted above all, but not even her heroes entirely escaped enacting it.

There were no female role models in African exploration for Mary to emulate other than occasional explorers', government officials', or missionaries' wives, whose passages through Africa were, of course, not entirely voluntary, as stoical helpmeets to their husbands. Mary may have heard, though, of the Dutch heiress Alexine Tinné who sailed up the Nile to Bahr el Ghazal in the early 1860s and then attempted to cross the Sahara in 1869, only to have her attempt sabotaged by her guides, who slashed off her hands and left her to bleed to death in the desert while they made off with all her provisions and money. But even if Mary did know about Alexine Tinné, she would have found her an anomaly rather than a heroine. Tinné had no serious scientific motives for going to Africa, nor was she a serious explorer; her wealth enabled her to travel in a grand style with an enormous entourage, and she never wrote a word herself about her African experiences. Rather than seeking out female predecessors in Africa, Mary undoubtedly identified with the men she admired most, like Du Chaillu and Brazza, just as she identified with her father's globetrotting and scholarship while repudiating her mother's feminine dependence and immobility.

Altogether, it was a strangely circumscribed childhood in fact, but of almost limitless dimensions in imagination. The monotonous ticking of the grandfather clock dominated the hallway between the empty, chilly parlor and the library, but in the library a fire blazed in the grate and Mary could escape all boundaries of time and space through her father's books. For it was in these early, solitary years — cramped and lonely as they were in that darkened, silent house — that Mary first felt the stirrings of her pilgrim soul.

·ᢒᢞ 3 ᣔᢁ·

Changes

As the monotonous, uneventful weeks and months passed by, marked by little other than the presence or absence of snow, birds, or flowers in the back garden or by the postmarks on George Kingsley's infrequent letters, Mary passed from childhood into adolescence. Nothing ever changed behind the blank facade of 22 Southwood Lane, but Mary herself underwent baffling, disturbing, physical and emotional changes that she could share with no one, for there was no one to offer explanations, comfort, reassurance. The small, agile girl shot up into a tall, awkward, painfully shy adolescent with straight, pale hair and blue eyes. During this awkward stage, before Mary grew into a strikingly handsome woman, her body must have seemed an alien thing to her, her moods and fantasies and fears scarcely under her control, and her isolation at times insupportable.

For Mary was denied all the standard social forms and props; the late Victorian initiation rites of teas and carriage rides and dances were all unknown to her. She didn't even possess calling cards until she went out to Africa for the first time, and the only card she is on record as having used is the one she left to the elements at the top of Mount Cameroon. Even more important, Mary lacked the intimacy of close, intense female friendship so common among nineteenth-century girls and women that would have enabled her to negotiate her way, however falteringly, into womanhood. Because of the coolness that existed between the Charles and the George Kingsleys, Mary saw next to nothing of her cousins Rose and Mary Kingsley. Her mother, of course, was supine and helpless upstairs. And Mrs. Barrett was of no help, singing hymns as she mopped the floors.

It is not surprising, then, that during the years of her adolescence Mary seemed to repudiate entirely all conventional forms of female experience. The mischievous tomboy evolved into a neophyte scientist; the little housekeeper traded in her duster for a wrench. Physical, chemical, biological, and social sciences, mathematics, and engineering all absorbed her. Science in all its branches was, of course, then considered the domain of men; it measured, quantified, explained experience. It must have seemed a refuge, a safe place, to a young woman awakening to strange tides of change and desire within herself. Thus Mary wrote in her autobiographical sketch how "at this time I developed a passionate devotion for the science of chemistry and I went in for it — experiments not being allowed — in the available books in the library. Most of them were books on alchemy and the rest entirely obsolete. After most carefully getting up all the information these could give me, I happened on a gentleman who knew modern chemistry and tried my information on him. He said he had not heard anything so ridiculous for years, and recommended I should be placed in a museum as a compendium for exploded chemical theories, which hurt my feelings very much and I cried bitterly at not being taught things."

Despite the joke at her own expense, the denial of formal education continued to pain her deeply. When Mary "cried bitterly" after the chemistry episode, her "home authorities" presented her with a copy of Craik's *Pursuit of Knowledge under Difficulties*. From this book she learned how men had invented the steam engine by watching tea kettles and had taught themselves dead languages after finding a page of a book, written in one of them, in a dustbin. Craik's lessons, she claimed (but, one suspects, with no small degree of irony), "went home. I saw it was silly to go whining about looking for someone to teach me; if I wanted scientific knowledge there were kettles, and in addition, an extremely complicated pump which was always out of order, while if I wanted scholarship, there was the library to go on with, with the addition of my brother's school books."

The instructive broken pump was merely one of the numerous nonfunctioning elements of the rambling, dilapidated house at 32 Crook Log in Bexley Heath in northwest Kent to which the Kingsleys moved in 1879. The area was then a sparsely populated one (though large enough to sustain, to George's annoyance, two Nonconformist churches), with winding paths threading their way beneath tall, shady trees. Bexley Heath itself was and still is merely a big patch of grass with a cemetery adjacent to it, but it was in those days "a secluded spot," as

Mary described it, and the family had moved to its rural precincts on account of Mrs. Kingsley's continuing ill health. The wandering cattle, the noise of the Baptist chapel, and the threat of thieves in Highgate all played sorely on her nerves. Not that the "country air" of Bexley Heath had any immediate salubrious effect. On the contrary, the house was so run-down that the drafts that swept through its ill-hung doors and rotting shutters and the vagaries of that pump and the questionable source of the water it was supposed to produce could only have exacerbated Mrs. Kingsley's nervous ailments. And in its further remoteness from London, Bexley Heath also inevitably increased her daughter's isolation.

It was during these Bexley Heath years that Mary's devotion to science began to take a more practical turn as she blossomed into the household "handyman" with the aid of a magazine called the *English Mechanic*. It soon became her bible: "What I should have done without its companionship between sixteen and twenty I do not care to think."

Not that all the wisdom and illumination of the *English Mechanic* were immediately absorbed. One of Mary's greatest trials with the Bexley Heath house was connected with its faulty plumbing, and she met a crisis before she felt equal to it. A leaking pipe threatened to bring down the ceiling in the coach house. Before repairing it, she needed to cut through and double it back on itself. There was a boy about, "connected with odd jobs," and Mary "summoned him to attend on . . . my operations. . . . Standing on the box I cut the lead pipe gallantly through; swish came out a jet of water that knocked me over, box and all, and played on me as if I were a rick fire and it the local fire brigade and a wild yell of joy came from that wretched boy. Of course, I ought to have turned the water off from the main, and so on first, but as I have said, my education was unfinished in plumbing at the time."

The Bexley Heath years were not solely ones of applied science, however. One of the Kingsleys' few neighbors was the well-known electrical engineer, C. F. Varley, who was delighted by Mary's curiosity and quick mind and spent many hours initiating her into the mysteries and wonders of his discipline. Varley indeed was the first person other than her father who provided Mary with intellectual stimulation and companionship, and, however informal, real instruction as well. Mary's German lessons also began at this period, but only because her father wanted her to become his research assistant for a definitive tome on sacrificial rites that he was writing sporadically. By her late teens, Mary was proficient enough to plow her way through all the German scholarship available on the subject of such rites among various peoples around the world.

But George Kingsley's projected opus on sacrificial rites never saw the light of day, despite his daughter's labors in the German authorities. In part this happened because during the 1870s he was still the slave of his incurable wanderlust. Having "done" the South Seas with the earl of Pembroke, with his next patron and "patient," Lord Dunraven, George took on a new continent, North America. Between 1870 and 1875 he and Dunraven crossed it from coast to coast, venturing as far north as Canada and as far south as Florida and New Mexico. There was some talk of George's writing or at least coauthoring a book about these American travels on the order of *South Sea Bubbles,* but like all his literary endeavors, it came to naught. Dunraven did, however, produce a record of their adventures in the Yellowstone region of northwest Wyoming, *The Great Divide,* but George himself left only a few disconnected sketches of his American travels, along with the letters he penned over campfires in the Rockies or in tents hastily pitched in dense redwood forests after long days of elk, moose, and buffalo hunting.

The headings of these letters reveal an itinerary of extremely varied and extensive travels. After arriving in the northeastern United States, George and Dunraven proceeded to make their rambling way across the country by railroad, by carriage, and finally on horseback via northern Michigan, Chicago, Denver, Colorado Springs, Laramie, the Black Hills of South Dakota, Salt Lake City, and Yellowstone, Wyoming. The ostensible object and major activity of their travels was hunting, but it must have been George's accounts of the dramatic Indian wars then raging among the Sioux, Apache, and Pawnee that captured the attention of his daughter. For while he and Dunraven were stalking deer and elk on the plains of Wyoming or in the Black Hills, agents of the U.S. government were no less assiduously stalking the human indigenous inhabitants of the northwest.

George was no Indian lover, but he did glimpse the fundamental injustice of what was being perpetrated against the Indians, however inevitable he thought their fate. He described at some length the "incredible wrongs" they suffered and even affirmed that "before God, the Indian was in the right and was only doing what any American citizen would do in his place." The trouble over the North Pacific Railroad in particular aroused George's sympathy. The railway was being laid heedlessly right through choice, long-established Indian hunting grounds. Naturally, the Indians protested with bow and arrow and tomahawk against the coming of that paramount symbol of the white man's civilization. George wrote home that "one cannot be surprised at the poor wretches fighting; they depend wholly on the buffalo for food, and the railway and its consequent settlers will soon drive them away for ever. Quite lately these grand rolling plains were black with buffalo and the Indians lived in abundance, now we are considered lucky to have killed two!"

George only narrowly missed being involved — terminally involved, in fact — in the most famous or infamous episode in this sad history of the Indian wars. The worst shock Mrs. Kingsley ever suffered in connection with her husband's travels came in one of his last letters from America informing her that he and Lord Dunraven planned to join General Custer on an expedition. Shortly after the family received this letter the news came of the complete massacre of Custer's party. "A fearful period of anxiety followed," as Mary described it, and "then came a letter saying that providentially they had been prevented by bad weather from joining General Custer at all."

So fortunately George was deflected from meeting the legendary Custer and from participating in Custer's legendary last stand, but he did meet and become close friends with some of the other colorful figures of the American West, especially the renowned Buffalo Bill Cody and his only slightly less illustrious sidekick, Texas Jack. Dressed up in fringed buckskin and a wide Texas sombrero like his friends, George roamed the plains and mountains of Colorado with them, hunting buffalo and deer. He stinted no praise of Bill in particular, a man who seemed to George a paragon of masculine beauty, intelligence, and bravery. "Oh! That I had the pen of a lady novelist to describe his manly charms!" he wrote home to his wife and children, and then followed pages describing Bill's "large lustrous eyes, . . . pointed beard of silky brown, . . . his magnificent hair sweeping in natural curves over his strong square shoulders," and pages more were devoted to Bill's courageous adventures and to his remarkable skill with a gun. Buffalo Bill soon emerged as the larger-than-life hero of George's letters from America, and in Mary's imagination he must have come to rival even some of her revered African explorers.

Another legendary personage George came across in Colorado was Rocky Mountain Jim, the Wild West desperado and Indian scout who would figure so prominently in one of the few books by a woman traveler that Mary read, Isabella Bird's *A Lady's Life in the Rocky Mountains*. When George met Jim, however, the desperado was at death's door, having been almost mortally wounded by a nameless outlaw who had inflicted no fewer than five bullet wounds about Jim's head and face, one of which had penetrated the cerebellum. George tended Jim's wounds, and Jim miraculously survived, partly because of George's expert ministrations, but also because, as George noted, at that high Rocky Mountain altitude of eight thousand feet none of his wounds could suppurate.

One even more unexpected patient George encountered during his Colorado sojourn was none other than his older brother Charles, who was in the United States on a lecture tour. George, to his amazement, found Charles bedridden in a Denver hotel, suffering from pleurisy. The estrangement between the two brothers was overcome as the younger tenderly cared for the older in strange surroundings. But when Charles recovered, he went on to San Francisco, completed his tour, and returned to England, where he died at the end of January 1875 before George returned from his American travels; so the brief rapprochement in Denver turned out to be the last meeting between the two brothers.

George did not exactly hasten back to England, however, once he and Dunraven had done North America to their satisfaction. As Mary notes in the memoir, "After his wanderings in the Americas . . . he crossed Newfoundland, was away in Frobisher's Straits, down in Cape Colony, went round the world again, visited Japan, revisited New Zealand and Australia and so on; but none of these things were considered by him to be more than a mere stroll and quite incomparable with the experiences he had when with Lord Pembroke and Lord Dunraven in the South Seas and America."

By the time George finally returned from his "stroll," his young children had nearly grown up. Mary was quite a young woman — tall, studious, and beautiful, although she pulled her gold hair back severely from her narrow, pale face and had already taken to wearing black. Charley too was nearly an adult, a clever but unfocused young man. He had by this time completed public school and was ready for university studies. George settled on Cambridge for his only son and, deciding to stay in England for this culminating period of Charley's education, moved the entire family from Bexley Heath to Cambridge in 1884. Two years later Charley matriculated at Christ's College as a "pensioner" or paying student.

George installed his family at 7 Mortimer Road in Cambridge, several blocks down Parker Street and Mill Road from Charley's rooms at Christ's College. Mortimer Road, a short cul-de-sac overlooking the wide green of Parker's Piece, is lined by a row of identical semiattached brown brick terrace houses, four of them in all. The Kingsleys lived on the left-hand side of the last house at the end of the street. The house at 7 Mortimer Road was new, snug, and well built, standing three stories high, with two large rooms with fireplaces on each floor: a parlor and study on the ground floor, two bedrooms directly above, each with a small partitioned-off dressing room, and the servants' quarters, with sloped ceilings and tiny dormer windows, at the top. All the cooking and washing was done in the steamy, smoky precincts of the basement. The house is set very close to the road in front, with a low brick wall running along the curb, but to the back there is a deep, narrow strip of garden, separated from its neighboring plots by another brick wall.

Now for the first time in Mary's life her existence was not hemmed in by the boundaries of house and garden. During her early years there, at least, Cambridge offered a new, expansive, even exhilarating world of experience. After Highgate and Bexley Heath, it must have seemed a remarkably cosmopolitan place. It must also have seemed an extraordinarily beautiful one, combining the natural beauty of the River Cam and the Backs, with their feathery, drooping willows, shady paths, and flower-sprinkled green lawns, with the magnificent architecture of the university and town, including the Library at Trinity designed by Christopher Wren, King's College Chapel, and the series of ancient stone bridges constructed by Grumbold, Essex, and Wren that span the Cam. Soon Cambridge and its winding, cobbled streets and strategically placed greens became familiar to Mary. Of course, she was not allowed to enter the gates of any of the colleges, but she could go punting on the Cam with Charley and his friends; she also shopped daily at the sprawling central market overshadowed by Great Saint Mary's Church on King's Parade. And in time she even began to pay calls on her own, usually walking to her destination, but sometimes in bad weather or after nightfall using the popular Cambridge horse-drawn tramcars.

The increased social activity was largely because of George's unwonted presence at home. Dashing George Kingsley was now a graying if still urbane sixty, and his abiding hunger for travel and new experience was considerably appeased. At the same time, unlike Highgate or Bexley Heath, Cambridge possessed attractions that for a time at least persuaded George to stay put. Despite his rheumatism, he stood out in all weathers, watching the rowing on the river or the spirited cricket matches on Fenner's or Parker's Piece. And then there were old scientific friends like Aldis Wright, Robert Bowes, and Dr. Henry Guillemard (later Mary's editor, with whom she had a devoted but sometimes troubled friendship), and new friends as well among the Cambridge dons and the eager, young undergraduates Charley brought home on the weekends. George's life soon took on a placid new routine: his mornings were devoted to his continued desultory studies and writings, his afternoons to long walks, often with Mary at his side as they strode across Parker's Piece to the Backs, and his evenings to leisurely discussions with his scholarly friends over cigars and brandy or port.

Mary also benefited from her father's associations, and since her mother was as indisposed as ever, Mary presided over the tea table at 7 Mortimer Road when George's scientific friends or Charley's from Christ's College called. Mrs. Kingsley, in fact, was even more reclusive than usual during this period, and naturally eyebrows were raised and rumors whispered about her, the general consensus among the Kingsleys' acquaintance being that she was not entirely "compos mentis." Years later Henry Guillemard described the only time he ever saw Mrs. Kingsley, a rather extraordinary encounter that only enhanced the poor woman's reputation as a mysterious figure. He and George came back to 7 Mortimer Road late one evening to smoke a pipe after dining out at their club. George let himself in with his key, and the two men walked past the parlor to the study at the back of the house, and there, in Guillemard's words, "she was: . . . [George] was disconcerted. He went up to her and said in a slow, incisive voice, 'Hadn't you better go to bed?' She took no notice," Guillemard continued, "and uttered no word. He waited a moment or two and then with rising inflexion said, 'I think you had BETTER GO TO BED.' She slowly departed."

Mary of course still closely tended to her mother. Mrs. Kingsley refused to eat food prepared by anyone other than her daughter, and it was Mary too who she insisted push her wheelchair when the weather was warm enough for an outing across Parker's Piece. But despite her mother's needs and demands, Mary had more time at her own disposal than ever before, and, by now in her early twenties, she also enjoyed more freedom of movement than she had as a girl. These indeed were in many respects the happiest years of her life, for her father was home, and her mother's condition had stabilized. Mary continued her studies in mathematics and read Charles Darwin, Thomas Huxley, and also the Oxford ethnographer, E. B. Tylor. And for the first time, she came to know people beyond her small family circle. Her lifelong friend, Lucy Toulmin Smith, later described this blossoming effect on Mary: "The society of cultivated men and women of literature and scholarship whom she met in company with her father drew her out, and the shy, original girl gained confidence and was soon prized for her own sake."

Mary had actually known Lucy Toulmin Smith since her Highgate days when the Toulmin Smiths lived down the road at 30 Southwood Lane. More than twenty years Mary's senior, Lucy was something of a mother figure to Mary, especially when Mary was belatedly coming into her own intellectually and socially during these Cambridge years. Like Mary, Lucy had been a research assistant and amanuensis to her father in his scholarly labors on such diverse topics as geology, constitutional law, public health, and parish rights and duties. In 1870, after her father's death, Lucy embarked on original research of her own, despite the fact that, like Mary, she had received no formal education. Her particular area of interest was medieval history and literature, and her various publications included an edition of the York plays and extensive scholarship on fourteenth-century travel narratives. Here, at last, was a woman whom Mary could look up to, even emulate. Lucy Toulmin Smith, of course, was something of an anomaly: a nineteenth-century woman who was unmarried, independent, and intellectually gifted. In 1894 she was appointed librarian of Manchester College, Oxford, the first woman ever to hold such a post.

Emotionally, Mary was far closer, however, to a small group of women who were her contemporaries in Cambridge: Hatty Johnson, Clara Skeat, and Agnes Smith Lewis. Now, finally, in her midtwenties, Mary began to know the sort of sustaining female friendship she had so sorely lacked in her adolescence.

But Mary's closest woman friend in Cambridge was Violet Paget Roy. Violet was the daughter of the famous physician and friend of George Kingsley, Sir George Paget, and she was married to a Professor of Pathology at Cambridge. The bond between the two women was only strengthened after Violet was widowed while still young and childless, and though Mary never idolized or adored Violet the way she did Lucy Toulmin Smith, she cared for her more deeply. Violet was one of the few people Mary depended upon, from whom she was willing and able to receive help, and even at times consolation.

Mary's social, intellectual, and emotional horizons, then, were all expanding at Cambridge. Colorful figures, witty conversation, and serious discussion became regular features of her life, rather than things one received at second hand through the medium of books or the experience of others. To have a "lived" life had always been her great dream, and during these early Cambridge years the first tenuous bridges between her inner and outer worlds began to take shape. Life ceased to be something that went on only when one opened a book or read a letter posted from Tahiti or Wyoming; it could also happen at Mortimer Road on a damp November evening or on a balmy spring morning in 1884 or 1886.

Yet in one critical respect Mary's experience remained incomplete. It lacked suitors, romance, the entire complicated pattern of the Victorian courtship dance: teas and dance cards and strolls along the Backs. Among all of George's learned friends there was no young Professor Roy for Mary. Or perhaps there was one who was startled and put off by her sharp mind and obvious learning. Yet while she remained aloof from romantic entanglements of her own, Mary was often embroiled in those of others. Friends and relations were apt to use her as a decoy or smokescreen, or as "a sort of pause in affairs," as she put it.

The worst such case involved a young man — later to be a "full-blown vicar" — who had broken his spectacles. The object of this young man's attentions, Mary's cousin and Charles Kingsley's daughter, was herself ill, so Mary was commissioned to take him to the proper optician in a village some four miles off to have the spectacles repaired. All went well until they left the optician, when, as Mary described it, "I heard boys yelling. Looking around I saw that dreadful man was emitting from his heels portions of froth or foam and leaving them on the pavement. I took him home and said to the Intended, 'Look here, I will do a good deal for you, but I bar walking about with men who foam at the heels.' " Words passed between Mary and her cousin. And finally elucidation arrived in the information that " 'Dear James,' knowing the walk was long and rocky had profusely soaped his socks to prevent blistering."

However full her Cambridge life must have seemed to her, Mary would also have been aware of events and developments beyond her personal sphere. She could not have guessed, though, the determining impact on her future of an international political conference convening in Berlin at just about the time the Kingsleys were settling in at 7 Mortimer

Road in the autumn of 1884. The Berlin conference of 1884–85 marked the final partition of Africa among the European powers, a partition that had become inevitable since the "scramble" for the continent had begun some five or so years earlier. In time Mary would be able to discourse on the scramble and partition by chapter and verse because the Africa she came to know was the unhappy result. But in the late months of 1884 and on into the new year she probably followed only the broad outlines of the issues at stake in the wrangling in Berlin.

The two major African trouble spots that Mary would have read about in the papers were the Niger River, where Sir George Goldie's National African Company (later the chartered Royal Niger Company) was anxious about French incursions from the north on the upper Niger, and the Congo delta, where the French, Portuguese, and King Leopold of Belgium were all jockeying for positions of power. Most likely, Mary was more absorbed by the situation in the Congo, for it involved two of the leading African explorers: Pierre Savorgnan de Brazza and Henry Morton Stanley. Brazza, of course, represented French interests, while Stanley was King Leopold's agent. Both sought to secure the interior basin of the Congo, and thus ensued a kind of personal scramble between the two explorers-cum-agents of Empire as they raced each other to Stanley Pool in the interior. Brazza won when he reached Stanley Pool first, and he immediately negotiated a treaty that would safeguard France's colony of Gabon.

But the issue neither of the Niger nor of the Congo was really settled until the diplomats unrolled their maps in Berlin and dickered over boundaries and rivers. They finally cut up the west side of the continent into irregular chunks as if they were slicing a pie rather than vast tracts of land with heterogeneous peoples whose lives would be irrevocably transformed by the arguments, compromises, and final agreements reached in Berlin by men who had never set foot on the continent they were partitioning.

In 1885, however, the Berlin conference as it appeared in the newspaper accounts was just one of many stories that caught Mary's attention. Meanwhile, the even tenor of her Cambridge life continued. On at least two occasions, though, she tried to broaden her horizons beyond the spires and cobblestone streets of the university town. At one point, Violet Roy proposed a short holiday with her family in Wales. Permission was granted by George Kingsley, and Mary packed her valise. She was twenty-five years old, and this was her first trip away from home. But scarcely two days after she had left, a telegram reached

Mary in northern Wales. Her daughter's departure seemed to have provoked a sudden relapse in Mrs. Kingsley's condition. Her wings thus abruptly clipped, Mary of course obediently rushed back to 7 Mortimer Road.

It wasn't until several years later that she made another attempt to venture away from home, this time successfully. In the spring of 1888 she and Lucy Toulmin Smith went to Paris for a week — the first real holiday Mary had ever taken. Mrs. Kingsley's response to this second, successful journey to France was predictable. Shortly after Mary's return, Mrs. Kingsley had an attack of her "brain disease" even more violent than that which had summoned Mary back from Wales, with the result that it now became impossible for Mary to leave the house again for more than an hour or two at a time. Necessarily, many of her habitual Cambridge pleasures and routines, such as long walks and punting and dinners and teas out, had to be given up altogether.

Then in 1890 Mrs. Kingsley had a stroke, which left her partially paralyzed, unable to speak coherently, and reduced to the helplessness of an infant. Mary now had to feed, bathe, and do everything else for her mother. And though to others' ears, Mrs. Kingsley's attempts to speak sounded like senseless babbling, Mary was somehow able to grasp the meaning and to respond to and soothe her.

This unremitting attendance on her mother and her incarceration in the stuffy sickroom upstairs took a tremendous toll on Mary. Lucy Toulmin Smith suggested that Mary take up strenuous, demanding study in order to relieve the strain of the long, lonely hours at her mother's bedside, especially the interminable nights when Mrs. Kingsley slept only very lightly and fitfully. Mary did so, and the more abstruse her studies, the more comfort they seemed to provide. Light reading, except for Dickens or Kipling, was given up. Instead, unhappy, anxious, often on the verge of breakdown herself, Mary found adequate distraction only in teaching herself Latin, Arabic, or Syrian, or in poring over Bigfusson or Powell's *Corpus Poeticum*.

Mary described these as "years of work and watching and anxiety, a narrower life in home interests than ever, a more hopelessly depressing one, for it was a losing fight with death all the time." And before long it was a double battle as well because George Kingsley contracted rheumatic fever in the early 1890s after spending a winter in Suffolk caring for a patient.

In time George recovered, but, as is often the case with rheumatic fever, his heart was permanently affected. Somewhat like his prototype, the aging Ulysses in Tennyson's poem — for George was now sixty-five — he embarked on his last journey round the world. But for the first time, travel failed to be the universal restorative and panacea that George Kingsley (and later Mary herself) held it to be. In fact, George returned from his voyage considerably aged and enfeebled, though not yet chronically bedridden as was his wife.

But on the night of February 4, 1892, he went to bed feeling better than he had in some days, so much so that he mentioned to Mary that he planned to call on his friend Lord Sandwich the next day. Mary of course spent the night sitting up reading by candlelight in her mother's room. Early the next morning, after the postman's delivery, she took George's letters up to his room. He failed to respond to her knock, and after she entered, she found she could not awaken him. George Kingsley's erratic, adventurous, fulfilling, but also fundamentally inconclusive life was over, for in the course of the night he had died in his sleep.

Two and a half months later, on April 25, 1892, Mary Bailey Kingsley's twilit half-life also came to an end. With her husband gone, there was no more cause to linger. This second loss, however painful, must also have seemed a blessed release to Mary for both her own and her mother's sakes after the years they had together endured the odd and exhausting symbiotic relationship born of chronic invalidism.

Mary Henrietta Kingsley was now nearly thirty years old. Though she could not have imagined that her third decade would bring renewal and even rebirth, coming away from the grief of her parents' deaths and from the long years of duty and worry and loneliness that preceded those deaths was like awakening from a trance or spell. At first the prospect of her freedom made her positively dizzy. Then she realized the intoxicating possibilities: after a life of avid, vicarious travel, she might voyage out in reality as well as in dream and seek the confluence of her inner and outer worlds.

Part Two

Escape — it is the basket
In which the Heart is caught
When down some awful Battlement
The rest of Life is dropt.

Emily Dickinson

The First Voyage Out

Mary's domestic responsibilities, though greatly diminished by her parents' deaths, did not cease altogether. The dead, especially the Victorian dead, never vanish without a trace. A good deal of painful and time-consuming business is always left behind, and during the spring and early summer of 1892 Mary was much preoccupied. At first there were the callers and all the arrangements of two funerals to be dealt with. Mary answered countless condolence notes on black-bordered stationery and ordered black mourning for herself. For the rest of her life, she dressed exclusively in black, relieved now and then by a long-sleeved white cotton blouse. Perhaps her choice of such somber attire arose out of an enduring sense of loss; perhaps, in time, wearing the long, black, woolen skirts, black shawl, and black sealskin hat became so habitual that she felt they suited her. As indeed these garments did, though it is unlikely that she realized how they accentuated her pale blond hair and gray-blue eyes or that the dark severity of her dress emphasized her striking features and tall, slender figure. Almost certainly, too, she did not grasp the irony of the fact that she was covered in mourning weeds during that part of her life when she was most free and active and truly alive.

After the funerals and callers, there were drawers and closets to clear out, papers to arrange or throw away, all the flotsam of two long lives to sort through, preserve, or discard. Disposing of old clothes and cuff links and fans, sifting through boxes of photographs, and reading old letters would have stirred up a mass of memories for Mary, bringing home even more powerfully than during their lives the narrow futility

of her mother's existence and the irresponsible adventure of her father's. Above and beyond the magnitude of her own loss, Mary must
have been struck anew by the extremes exemplified by her parents'
lives.

Despite all her father's close calls and brushes with death, it was her
mother's fate that would have been most frightening to Mary. She
always referred to her mother in the most admiring terms, but a fri-
gidity creeps into her praise of Mrs. Kingsley's long-suffering trials
and patient endurance of ill health. Mary was not the first or last woman
to feel that a major object in her life was *not* to repeat her mother's,
but in Mary's case there were particularly strong reasons for her utterly
to repudiate her mother's shadowy half-life. Mrs. Kingsley's very helplessness and dependence had also, properly speaking, deprived her
daughter of any life of her own. Mary had been imprisoned by her
mother's need in the twilit world of the upstairs bedroom. But unlike
most captives, she was unable to turn the frustration and rage born of
such confinement against her jailer, nor could she dream of freedom,
for to do so would have meant wishing her mother dead. And this
painful psychological bind existed for years — from the time Mary
first took over running the house as a mere child, until Mrs. Kingsley
died nearly twenty years later.

Anger, pity, loss, relief: these were the governing emotions of Mary's
life in the days and weeks following her parents' deaths. But very likely
stunned disbelief — even horror — overshadowed them all. Among
her father's papers, tucked away behind his will and house deeds and
other documents, Mary almost certainly came upon her parents' marriage license and her own birth certificate. Their unadorned statistics
disclosed an appalling story. George Kingsley, "bachelor," "of full
age," and residing at 30 Tavistock Terrace, Islington, married Mary
Bailey, "spinster," also of full age and residing at the same location,
on October 9, 1862. Four days later, according to Mary's birth certificate, their daughter was born.

What did this revelation mean to Mary? Her initial thought must
have been that she had only very narrowly escaped being illegitimate,
a bastard, and that it was her birth, rather than her early scrapes with
her perambulator and nurse and the Hastings pool, that was her first
close call in life. And the discovery of her near illegitimacy must have
enhanced Mary's already ingrained sense that she was somehow different and isolated and alienated from others. In addition, her awareness
of the unhappiness of her parents' marriage must have been deepened

by this discovery of its origin. Above all, she now discovered that her very existence was not the product of an act of love and communion, but rather of an illicit, probably exploitative liaison.

The revelation of the circumstances of her birth, on top of everything else, must have reinforced Mary's decision to bolt: to flee the imprisoning house in Cambridge and the fresh memories of the past several years, to escape the society whose norms and values her parents had violated in the act of her conception. As soon as she had dispatched the last chores of the funerals and had settled her parents' affairs, she turned to her father's old friend, Henry Guillemard, telling him that she wanted to get away at once to restore her health. Guillemard, who was a physician as well as a geographer, suggested Madeira, where he had recovered his health after a lengthy sojourn in Africa. But Mary, whose previous travels consisted only of those several days in Wales and a week in Paris, rejected Madeira as "too civilised." Regaining her health after the strain of nursing her mother was, in fact, the justification rather than the real motive for getting away at once. And this is why she never even considered the obvious spas of southern France or Italy. Nothing less distant than the Canary Islands off the coast of northern Africa would do, she told Guillemard. Even this early on, Mary glimpsed her destination; a recuperative visit to the Canaries would be a kind of scouting expedition or preview of Africa. But she would have to work up to Africa slowly and carefully, for the idea of a twenty-nine-year-old woman setting off alone for the White Man's Grave was not merely implausible in Victorian England, it was utterly unthinkable.

As it turned out, the Canaries themselves had to be worked up to gradually as well. Mary's domestic servitude was not, in fact, really over. Charley's undistinguished Cambridge career had ended with a mediocre second class degree (he finished fifteenth out of nineteen in the law tripos), and he was now back living with his sister at 7 Mortimer Road. Charley was not as dependent as his mother, but he was exacting and fastidious, and if his surviving letters accurately reflect his personality, he could be tiresomely pompous and pedantic as well. As long as "Master Charles," as Mary rather acidly refers to him in several letters, was at home, Mary had to stay put and keep house for him. Fortunately, he too had a taste for travel, but the vagaries of his travel plans meant that Mary was always unsure of her own dates of departure and return. Shortly after their mother's death in April, Charley unveiled his intention of traveling to the Far East, whereupon Mary immediately turned to Guillemard with her plan of going to the Canaries. But the weeks rolled by, and Charley's scheduled departure began to look increasingly unlikely. Finally, Charley managed to pull himself together and get off in June, just in time for Mary hastily to arrange her own passage to the Canaries.

Mary left no connected record of the trip, and only one letter, to Hatty Johnson in Cambridge, survives from this first momentous foray into the tropics that she had been dreaming of since childhood. But from her letter to Hatty, scattered references in her books, and the reports of friends, we can piece together the general outline of this first adventure of her life. She booked a ticket on a passenger Castle liner, having been advised as a neophyte traveler that merchant "Liverpool boats were to be avoided." The run between Liverpool and Tenerife took only about a week, so she probably reached the Canaries by the end of July. The magnificent beauty of Tenerife and Grand Canary some two hundred miles off the coast of Morocco and at the westernmost edge of the Sahara never palled for her. Yet her first glimpse of these islands on this initial voyage must have made an indelible impression. For seven days she had stood on the deck of the Castle liner and gazed on the boundless, brilliant sea, watched schools of graceful dolphins cavorting in the ship's wake, and perhaps also seen at a distance the angular fins of sharks pierce the glassy water's surface; this was a landscape that finally answered Mary's need for space, beauty, release.

And then on the seventh or eighth day out, they sighted the peak of Tenerife, and "it displayed itself, as usual," Mary wrote later, "as an entirely celestial phenomenon." In the blazing afternoon sunlight its "superb cone . . . stood out a deep purple against a serpent green sky, separated from the brilliant blue ocean by a girdle of pink and gold cumulus." And looking up from the masses of mist that enshrouded its ocean-washed base to its summit more than twelve thousand feet above sea level, Mary saw the glittering snow-clad peak shining in the sun like a beacon.

Shortly after sighting Tenerife, Mary saw the island of Lanzarote loom up on the horizon and then finally Grand Canary looking as though it had been "formed from fantastic-shaped sunset cloudbanks that by some spell had been solidified." As the afternoon waned and the orange globe of the sun began to dip to the western platterlike edge of the sea, the sky turned a vibrant amethyst pink, and the setting sun outlined the massed, feathery clouds with rims of gold.

Mary found the Canaries no less beautiful on land than from the sea. The very air of Grand Canary, she said, was "a lovely lustrous blue," and she longed to take some of it home in a bottle and release it as a blue-violet cloud into the gray atmosphere of Cambridge. In both her books Mary describes the intoxicating beauty she discovered in the Canaries and her own intensely sensual response to it, an acute, aesthetic receptivity that remained an integral part of her love for the tropics and for West Africa in particular.

Her stay on the Canaries extended itself into many weeks, she wrote later, weeks during which she systematically studied the local trade and industries and spent time roaming into the more desolate reaches of the islands on obscure forest paths and paddling from one island to another by canoe. Her chief adventure, she told Guillemard, was an expedition to the little-known isle of Gomera and its impressive volcanic crater. As would be the case so often in later excursions, she miscalculated the amount of time needed for this trip and ended up having to spend the night in the open on the island under a rock before returning to Grand Canary and Las Palmas the next morning.

To Hatty Johnson Mary confided, "I have been having a wild time. . . . If I see you looking as if tonic shocks would benefit your system on my return, I will tell you dreadful stories of my conduct and experiences." Besides exploring the Canaries, Mary told Hatty how she also had been traveling on the boats that regularly plied between the coast of Africa and the islands, "on their way out with iron bedsteads, sperm candles, and salt petre, on their way home with black people of all ages and sexes, monkeys, parrots, snakes, canary birds, sheep, palm oil, gold dust and ivory."

Although Mary set foot only briefly on African soil on this trip, she learned how grave the threat to human life could be on that continent. On one of her excursions to the mainland, Mary went down to her cabin after the boat had been loaded and begun steaming back to Grand Canary, only to find, as she wrote Hatty, that it was "occupied by four gentlemen. On going to the steward to investigate the case I found him engaged with delirium tremens, and on looking up the purser, he said it was all right, the four gentlemen were dead, having died within ten days." With what was to become a characteristic macabre note in the face of such grim situations, Mary confessed that she "was somewhat reconciled to their decease . . . by thinking they might have been no better than their surviving passengers and none of them would have been missed."

Thus the most important part of Mary's Canary holiday was that it brought her into contact with West Africa for the first time, and not merely by means of her brief shuttle visits. The Canaries were a regular port of call for all the boats traveling to and from the coast, and what's more, traders, missionaries, and government officials at death's door with malaria or backwater or yellow fever were sent there to recover — or die. Doubtless, Mary ran into many "old coasters," as those who had seen even a short term of service in one of Britain's West African colonies or protectorates were called. And not even their grimmest tales about the intolerable climate, deadly diseases, and hostile Africans could deflect Mary from her growing resolution to return as soon as possible to the continent itself.

Among these veterans of West Africa whom Mary met and pumped for information was a young man named James Henly Batty, a Gold Coast trader who, some years later after Mary introduced them, became the second husband of Mary's close friend Violet Paget Roy. Batty told numerous stories of the trials and dangers of life on the Coast, stories about the various eccentric men he had known there which usually ended "but he is dead now." But in spite of these cautionary tales, Batty claimed responsibility for Mary's final decision to travel to West Africa rather than to South America, which for a short time at least she also considered visiting. For Mary realized while talking to Batty and to other traders and officials that despite their horror stories, despite the fearsome mortality rate, despite the extreme privation of their lives, West Africa had a peculiar hold on their imaginations, and that to some degree they fit in with the expatriate European syndrome that had characterized several of the African explorers she had read. Mary later claimed that if you took these old coasters "who most energetically assert that they wish they were home in England, 'and see if they would ever come to the etc. etc. place again,' and if you were to bring them home, and let they stay there a little while, I am pretty sure that — in the absence of attractions other than those of merely being home in England, notwithstanding its glorious joys of omnibuses, underground railways, and evening newspapers — these same men, in terms varying with individual cases, will be found sneaking back apologetically to the coast."

And so by the time she sailed back to England from the Canaries in the early autumn of 1892, Mary had firmly made up her mind to return to the West Coast and follow it as far south as possible, perhaps even as far as the Cape of Good Hope, or if not, at least to the mouth of the Congo River, to Brazza's and Stanley's territory in the Congo Free State, and down to Portuguese Angola.

It was nearly a year, however, before Mary was able to break away again, largely because of Charley. He returned home in the closing months of 1892, and as long as he remained in England, Mary had to stay put too and keep house for him. It seems never to have occurred to either of them to question this arrangement. As she wrote a friend some years later, when "my brother came back . . . I came home to look after him domestically as long as he wants me to do so. I must do it — it is duty — the religion I was brought up in. When he does not want me I go to West Africa." Thus was established the pattern for the rest of her life: when it took Charley's fancy to be off to the Orient or elsewhere, after all his tortuous, protracted travel plans were settled, Mary was free to get the next Liverpool ship for West Africa, knowing, however, that she might be recalled at any time by a cable from Charley informing her that he was returning to England.

In the winter of 1893, before either of them embarked again on travels overseas, Mary and Charley moved from Cambridge back to London, where they had not lived since they were small children. They no longer needed the three-story Mortimer Road house, which must have held too many painful memories for Mary especially. But why they moved all the way to London — away from friends like Violet Roy and Hatty Johnson and Henry Guillemard — is unclear. There were relations in London, both Kingsleys and Baileys, but they can scarcely have been the reason for leaving Cambridge. Perhaps the move was yet another manifestation of Charley's unfocused restlessness. In any event, the move was a great chore, and there is little doubt that Mary bore the brunt of the labor, packing up her father's books and papers and curious mementos, her mother's crockery, her own and Charley's possessions, plus all the furniture and carpets.

They did not return to their childhood home of suburban Highgate, but moved rather to Kensington across town where they rented a five-room flat at the top of 100 Addison Road, close to Uxbridge Station. Charles Kingsley's daughter, Mary Kingsley, who had already published several novels under the pen name Lucas Malet, lived close by, but Henry's widow, the chronically destitute Sarah Kingsley and her aged mother, Mrs. Haselwood, fortunately were farther afield in South Wimbledon.

The house at 100 Addison Road was, and still remains, a four-story terrace house of dull gray brick and wholly undistinguished architec-

ture. It was an urban residence, fronting directly onto the pavement
with no lawn or garden before the street. Addison Road was a busy
street, so the noise of traffic would be heard at all hours. The rooms
were high ceilinged but small, and with no back garden and no room
with a view, life must have seemed cramped and confined in the flat,
especially when both Mary and Charley were in residence.

And yet it was in these crowded rented rooms at the top of the house
that Mary later wrote *Travels in West Africa* and most of *West African
Studies* and also the countless articles and lectures that made her a
public and sought-after personage. And many of the period's most
powerful and famous figures later toiled to the top of the house's dark,
narrow staircase to consult, take tea, or dine with Mary. A cook prepared the meals, and a charwoman did the heavy cleaning and laundry,
but all the mechanics and organization and headaches of running the
house were handled by Mary. In truth, 100 Addison Road could never
have been much of a home to her. It was a house to return to from far
more exciting places, a place in which to write and keep her books and
papers. And she and Charley were cohabitants, not a real family.

In addition to the move from Cambridge to London in early 1893,
other practical affairs needed looking after, foremost of which was Mary's
and Charley's financial situation. Like a true Kingsley, Charley showed
not the slightest inclination to earn money, though for several years
Mary continued to hope that he might settle on some profession. She
of course could do no such thing because of her lack of formal education. She confided to several friends that she would have liked to follow
in her father's footsteps and trained as a physician, and it is not difficult to imagine her becoming a female Albert Schweitzer if she had
had the opportunity to study medicine. As it turned out, she did take
a brief nursing course at the Kaiserworth Medical Institute in Germany
shortly before she first went to West Africa the following summer. But
this was not to prepare her to practice medicine lucratively, but rather
to enable her to care for herself and for others — Africans as well as
Europeans — when she finally got to the Coast. The Kaiserworth course,
in all likelihood, consisted of little other than training in first aid for
things such as snakebites and common injuries and also in treatment,
where such existed, for the standard tropical diseases such as malaria
and yellow fever.

The only way for Mary to earn money was by her pen, which in
several years' time she did with a great deal of success. But in the
winter of 1893, she did not dream that she would ever be a best-selling

writer, Charley was not lifting a finger to bring in any money, and unlike Mary, he was "not indifferent," as she said, "to creature comforts." Their financial position was by no means desperate, but it still called for some concern and required careful planning for the future. George Kingsley had left some eighty-six hundred pounds in all to be divided equally between his two children. This legacy seems to have been invested in order to bring them in yearly allotments, for Mary later wrote George Macmillan of having a fixed annual income, which, of course, suffered from economic inflation and from Charley's apparently congenital inability to make any financial contribution to their domestic arrangements.

Given their somewhat straitened finances, it probably would have made sense for Mary and Charley to remain frugally at home in Kensington for a time at least. But shortly after settling in at Addison Road, they both began to make plans to be off and away again. The real stumbling block for Mary now was not so much money, for she was prepared to travel on a shoestring, as it was her need for a convincing or at least a marginally plausible explanation for her decision to go to West Africa. Her heart had been set on it since her trip to the Canaries because of a whole complex of motives and needs, some of them clearly formulated in her own mind, others not, but no less powerful for being semi- or even unconscious impulses.

At the beginning of *Travels in West Africa* Mary breezily explains herself as if her travels were some kind of lark. "It was in 1893," she writes, "that for the first time in my life I found myself in possession of five or six months which were not heavily forestalled, and feeling like a boy with a new half crown, I lay about in my mind, as Mr. Bunyan would say, as to what to do with them. 'Go and learn your tropics,' said Science. Where on earth am I to go, I wondered, for tropics are tropics wherever found, so I got down an atlas and saw that either South America or West Africa must be my destination, for the Malayan region was too far off and too expensive. Then I got Wallace's *Geographical Distribution* and after reading that master's article on the Ethiopian region I hardened my heart and closed with West Africa."

It is a charming but wholly misleading account, for Mary had become obsessed with West Africa ten and fifteen years earlier while reading Burton, Du Chaillu, and Brazza. West Africa, indeed, had seemed an ineluctable destination to her for years. Nothing could have been more premeditated, less like the whim she jauntily writes of here.

In later years, Mary offered other, more serious, but still incomplete explanations for her determination to go to Africa. After she had become famous, she transformed her motivation into an act of filial piety; she went out to Africa, she said in lectures and articles, to carry on her father's anthropological work. "My motive for going to West Africa," she told one large audience, "was study; this study was that of native ideas and practices in religion and law. My reason for taking up this study was a desire to complete a great book my father George Kingsley left unfinished. . . . So I, knowing how much my father wished that book finished, went out after his death to West Africa. . . . It was no desire to get killed and eaten that made me go and associate with tribes with the worst reputation for cannibalism and human sacrifice; but just because such tribes were the best for me to study."

This explanation holds almost as little water as the breezy, skylarking one. The "great book" George Kingsley left unfinished at his death was in fact never begun, though it is true that he and Mary had been haphazardly amassing data and scholarship for years on the religion and law of so-called primitive societies. But all this material lay uncodified and undigested in a mass of notes and files, and Mary never finished George's nonexistent great book, but instead wrote two of her own. Still, one can see the appeal of this filial explanation, both to Mary herself and to her readers and admirers. Anything, even going to West Africa, was permissible in the name of feminine self-sacrifice. Duty, Mary claimed — the "religion" she was brought up in — beckoned, and in the best Victorian fashion, she obeyed its call. It is hard to tell how honest she was with herself on this head. Certainly, the thought of carrying on George's work would have helped allay any feelings of guilt she might have had over recklessly pursuing intense experience in a new world.

The breezy repudiation in the lecture of any self-destructive motive contrasts dramatically with an extraordinarily intimate and revealing letter Mary wrote some years later to a close friend. She confessed how "dead tired and feeling no one had need of me anymore when my Mother and Father died within six weeks of each other in '92 and my brother went off to the East, I went down to West Africa to die. West Africa amused me and was kind to me and scientifically interesting and did not want to kill me just then — I am in no hurry. I don't care one way or the other for a year of so."

This startling confession, essentially describing a failed suicide attempt, is far more complicated than the explanation of daughterly duty. There was an abiding current of melancholy in Mary's personal-

ity, perhaps an inherited one and part of her Kingsley heritage that
had only been nurtured by her lonely, bleak childhood. There is no
doubt that she recklessly courted danger and death in West Africa, as
one does only when the life one is risking has little value. But if Mary
courted death by going out to West Africa, she also courted life. Like
the person who plays Russian roulette, Mary found life in Africa exciting and valuable, in part, because of the nearness or imminence of
death there. The ironic upshot of this situation was that she was far
healthier when she was out in Africa than when she was back in England. Of course she suffered from the inevitable bouts of malaria, but
these never interfered with her plans, for she continued to travel, fever
or no fever, by canoe or on foot. Otherwise, she almost never had to
use her medical kit on herself, except perhaps for minor bruises and
sprains or scratches. Her health on her return to England was another
matter. As soon as she landed in Liverpool, all her West African ro-
bustness and hardy well-being deserted her. Once settled back on Addison Road she became liable to a variety of incapacitating ailments:
influenza, neuralgia, migraines, heart palpitations, even rheumatism.
In Africa she pursued her travels with the stamina and energy of her
father, while at home in England she recurrently lapsed into her mother's passive invalidism.

Mary's motives, then, for setting her heart and sights on West Africa were complex and mixed, but once the choice had been made and
announced, she was unswervable, and she singlemindedly and energetically embarked on the extensive preparations for her first voyage out.
First of all, she set about filling "the vast cavity in [her] mind," as she
called it, that represented her "ignorance regarding West Africa." Not
anthropological, geographical, or historical ignorance, for she had been
studying all these for years. What she sought now was practical information for her travels, and what she was able to acquire she said could
be neatly categorized under one of the following headings:

> The dangers of West Africa.
> The disagreeables of West Africa.
> The diseases of West Africa.
> The things you must take to West Africa.
> The things you find most handy in West Africa.
> The worst possible things you can do in West Africa.

She needed, in short, a survival manual for the continent, and she
had no easy time compiling one for herself from the advice of her

various informants. For one thing, almost all of them tried to dissuade her from going, and when she made it clear that she was not to be deterred, their counsel was too often intimidating or irrelevant rather than helpful. The doctors she consulted warned her that it was "the deadliest spot on earth" and unrolled maps showing the geographical distribution of tropical diseases in West Africa. Next she turned to the missionaries and their voluminous reports, "alas! only to find that these good people wrote reports not to tell you how the country . . . was but how it was getting on towards being what it ought to be, and how necessary it was that their readers should subscribe more freely." The missionaries also confirmed the doctors' grim assessment of the unhealthiness of the place and then went into "various details of the distribution of cotton shirts over which I did not linger." She next came upon an acquaintance who had actually lived on the Coast for seven years, and his advice was more helpful, though scarcely less cheering. He told her to "abstain from exposing yourself to the direct rays of the sun, take four grains of quinine every day . . . and get some introductions to the Wesleyans; they are the only people on the coast who have got a hearse with feathers."

Mary also consulted her friends about the things she would need to take with her, and here they were much more lavish with their advice, since they seemed "to labour under the delusion," as she put it, "that I intended to charter a steamer and was a person of wealth beyond the dreams of avarice." For protection against malaria, two scientific friends urged her to take out "two devices": "One was a lamp which you burnt some chemical in; it certainly made a smell that nothing could live with — but then I am not nothing, and there are enough smells on the Coast now. I gave it up after the first half hour. The other device was a muzzle, a respirator, I should say. Well! All I have got to say about that is that you need to be a better-looking person than I am to wear a thing like that without causing panic in a district."

Even without the lamp and the respirator or the preparations of quinine, mustard leaves, patent filters, and hot water bottles that were also urged on her, Mary was still burdened down with her gear. No Victorian ever traveled light, and besides all the luggage to meet her personal needs, Mary was also saddled with cumbersome photography equipment, including a tripod and heavy photographic plates, and with collector's kits and specimen bottles of formaldehyde for the fish and insects she wanted to gather, in addition to ethnographic data. Besides her black medical bag and portmanteau, she had also acquired a most valuable long, waterproof sack that closed neatly at the top with a bar, and into it she stashed blankets, boots, books, and also a bowie knife and a revolver. The last two items she took somewhat reluctantly, feeling that it was both "utter idiocy" and a cowardly act to brandish a gun and threaten to fire it. Nevertheless, she realized the precautionary value of both arms and herself advised in *Travels in West Africa,* "always have your revolver ready loaded in good order and have your hand on it when things are getting warm and in addition have an exceedingly good bowie knife, not a hinge knife because with a hinge knife you have got to get it open — hard work in a country where all things go rusty in the joints." A knife was essential, she explained, "because after wading neck deep in a swamp your revolver is neither use nor ornament until you have time to clean it." She also confided to a close woman friend that she carried the gun and knife to use on herself in extremity should the need arise. But though Mary had her fair share of dangerous adventures in the course of her travels, she never had to resort to either.

Personal effects she tried to keep to a minimum. She brought along two diaries: a "bush diary" in which to record ethnographical, geographical, and other scientific information, and a personal journal in which she confided her emotional, or psychological, and aesthetic, even spiritual, response to the new world she was exploring. Her reading material was meager: Albert Günther's *Study of Fishes* and an old battered copy of Horace, with which she used to read herself to sleep at night. Shortly before her departure, a friend sent her a *Daily Telegraph* review of a Dahomey phrase book that he urged her to take along. This guide contained such useful sentences for the West African tourist as "Help! I am drowning!" and "The boat is upset," as well as queries on the order of "Why has this man not been buried?" and the "cheerful answer": "It is fetish that has killed him, and he must lie here exposed . . . until only the bones remain." Because the book "sounded discouraging to a person whose occupation would necessitate going about considerably in boats, and whose fixed desire was to study fetish" or African beliefs, Mary declined to add it to her standbys, Günther and Horace.

As for clothes, Mary took precisely the same wardrobe she wore in Cambridge and London, feeling that "you have no right to go about in Africa in things you would be ashamed to be seen in at home." She made no allowance, then, for the radical difference in climate between Kensington and the villages she would be visiting that straddled the equator. She packed her portmanteau with several long black skirts and cummerbunds, a dozen or so white cotton blouses, black leather boots, and also stays, which she persisted in wearing in the terrific heat, even when her stay laces broke and she had to use a shoestring to lace herself up. A long digression could be devoted to the controversy over whether or not Mary ever wore trousers. Her friend Lady Mac-Donald, who sailed out with Mary on her second trip, claimed that she brought along an old pair of Charley's and wore them on occasions under her long skirt; then if she had to wade across a river or through a swamp, she removed and carried her skirt and tied the trousers tightly around her ankles to ward off leeches. Mary herself, on the other hand, categorically denied ever wearing trousers. "As for encasing the more earthward extremities of my anatomy in" trousers, she asserted with mock primness in *Travels in West Africa,* "I would rather [have] perished on a public scaffold."

She failed to bring an adequate supply of hairpins, the lack of which is a source of recurrent lament in her letters, and also of toothbrushes, which became a very hot trade item among the Africans with whom she bargained. For Mary's plan from the very beginning was to trade her way through Africa, subsisting on local food and taking shelter in mud and thatch village houses or sleeping under the stars if darkness overtook her between villages. This scheme of travel was a radical departure from that of other African travelers, who would assemble a long caravan of porters to carry tinned food, tents, camp beds, and even portable commodes. Not infrequently, the travelers themselves were also carried in swaying hammocks with an African bearer at each end.

Mary dispensed with all these encumbrances, in part because her limited means — she took only three hundred pounds with her on the 1893 trip — prevented her from buying all these expensive provisions and equipment and from hiring a small army of porters to carry them. But her decision to travel as a trader, exchanging such goods as glass beads, wire, fishhooks, cloth, and tobacco for rubber and ivory, also reflected her acute anthropological sense. It was no good, she explained, to rush out to West Africa and start asking people rude questions about their religious and private affairs. She had read a book by a German ethnographer named Habbe Schleiden who had adopted this trading method and collected any amount of valuable information, and so she decided to follow his example.

As she explained to one of her lecture audiences, she found she got along best "in the guise of a trader; there is something reasonable about trade to all men, and you see the advantage of it is that when you first appear among people who have never seen anything like you before, they naturally regard you as a devil; but when you want to buy or sell with them, they recognize there is something human and reasonable about you." She went on to illustrate her point by suggesting that the members of her British audience put themselves in the Africans' place and "imagine a gentleman of inky complexion, mainly dressed in red and white paint, human teeth, and leopard tails and not too many of them, suddenly arriving in a village hereabouts. After the first thrill of excitement his appearance gave passed away, and he was found anxious to sell something, anything, say bootlaces, he would be taken much more calmly than if he showed no desire to do business at all." The guise of trader, in fact, gave Mary a kind of carte blanche in West Africa. It facilitated palavers with chiefs and "the confraternity of witch doctors," and also brought her under the wing of "that ever-powerful factor in all human societies, the old ladies."

After she had assembled all her equipment, personal necessities, and trade goods, Mary still had one last important task to perform before her departure. On July 31, 1893, she made out her will in the presence of her solicitor, an Addison Road neighbor named Eliza Ince, and her cousin Annie Bailey. Though Charley was absent, he was, not surprisingly, named as Mary's sole executor and beneficiary, save for five hundred pounds Mary specified to be left to Lucy Toulmin Smith "for her sole use and benefit." In the event that Charley died before Mary, the estate was to pass to Mary's uncle, William Bailey, a law stationer in Chancery Lane. Writing the will was Mary's final "odd job" before she set out for the Coast, and it mutely testified to her awareness that it was a highly risky journey she was embarking on and one from which she might very likely not return.

.⋅✵ 5 ✵⋅.

The Second Voyage Out

What with all these elaborate preparations, it was midsummer before Mary was able to book her passage to the Coast. She was not cheered to learn that she could only purchase a one-way ticket because the Elder Dempster Company, the West African steamer line, ominously enough, did not issue round-trip fares. In early August Mary took the train to Liverpool, in order to embark on the *Lagos,* a cargo boat, commanded by Capt. John Murray, who quickly became her great West African mentor. The *Lagos* was not a passenger ship like the Castle liner she had sailed on to the Canaries the year before. It was a decidedly unluxurious trade steamer crammed full of cargo and carrying a few traders and government officials, but, to Mary's relief, no missionaries. What first struck her most forcefully about the boat was its filth, and there was no way she could guess when walking across the gangplank in Liverpool that by the time the *Lagos* reached Luanda every square inch of its deck and cabins and holds would have been scrubbed down, scraped, and freshly repainted.

At the Canaries, the only other women on board — the stewardess with whom Mary rescued a careening piano in the saloon one stormy night, and a married woman traveling with her husband and child — both got off. Mary wrote Hatty that she initially felt a bit awkward about her solo female status on the *Lagos,* but "most unnecessarily," she added, for "everyone is most kind." Kind perhaps, but not exactly cheering. Almost all the other passengers, whether traders or government agents, had been to West Africa before, and their accounts of life there, especially as detailed in rather macabre dinner table conversations, were not reassuring. Whatever topic was introduced, the conversation eventually came back to disease and death. A trader would ask Captain Murray if he remembered a certain "J.," and the captain would recall the last time he took the said J. out to West Africa, "poor chap." Then Mary was held rapt by the particulars of the consequent "pegging out of J. and his funeral." Next a government official would inquire of the only other first-timer besides Mary, "'Brought any dress clothes with you?' [And] the unfortunate new-comer, scenting an allusion to the more cheerful phase of coast life, gladly answers in the affirmative. 'That's right,' says the interlocutor, 'you want them to wear to funerals. Do you know,' he remarks, turning to another old coaster, 'my dress trousers did not get mouldy once last season.' 'Get along,' says his friend, 'you can't hang a thing up twenty-four hours without its being fit to graze a cow on.'"

"This instruction of the young in the charms of coast life," as Mary explained, "is the faithfully discharged mission of the old coasters on steamboats, especially . . . at meal times." Besides the ubiquitous fever or malaria, Mary learned over the soup, she could expect to encounter, very likely experience, and perhaps, if she followed poor J.'s example, even "peg out" from numerous other tropical afflictions, such as kraw kraw, Portuguese itch, abscesses, ulcers, guinea worm, sleeping sickness, yellow fever, cholera, and smallpox. Whenever one of the diners gathered round the captain's table in the saloon tried to steer the conversation into less morbid waters by mentioning an amusing work that he had read recently, someone else would cut in and remark that "poor D. was found in bed at C. with that book alongside him."

Soon enough the *Lagos* itself had illness on board. No one succumbed like poor J. or D., but both of the stewards and the doctor came down with fever, and seasickness was rife. Mary wrote Hatty how she carried food to and nursed the worst off in their cabins and then went on to reassure her that "so far I have kept or rather got magnificently well, and I do not believe I have ever enjoyed myself so much in my life."

In this thriving, even exuberant state of health and mind, Mary delightedly mixed with her fellow passengers. The government functionaries were of a type not unfamiliar to her, for they came from the same middle- or upper-class background as her father and his family. But the traders were an entirely alien species. Many of these "palm oil ruffians," as they were called because palm oil was one of their principal commodities, had been engaged in the slave trade in the old days, and they were not, as a class, a very cultivated, sometimes not even a very literate, group of men. They tended to grunt and cough "for general social purposes" and to take frequent advantage of the spittoons in the corners of the saloon. Nevertheless, many of them became Mary's fast friends, both on shipboard and even more on her travels, when she depended far more on them than on colonial officials. Traders, in fact, were crucial to the success of her first trip because she had absolutely no government connections and was often wholly dependent upon the traders' good will and hospitality. They enabled her to visit places she could never have seen otherwise. When she turned up at their remote factories, "unheralded and in a delapidated state," they vacated their own beds and showered her with tinned food. Traders fished her out of the sea and out of fresh water with boat hooks, and she reciprocated when they got drunk — for they were almost always great drinkers — and ended up head downwards in a water butt or in some other awkward and inexplicable position. Whatever else one might say of the traders, they were absolutely free of sham and humbug, traits that all too often, Mary found, characterized missionaries and government officials. Even with its small sample of traders and government men, the *Lagos* initiated Mary into the ways of these two breeds, and before she reached the Canaries, she knew where her real sympathies lay.

What the traders and government officials made of *her*, on the other hand, is harder to say. At first they assumed she was a missionary, but her tepid performance at a Sunday service in the Bay of Biscay soon disabused them of this impression. When she failed to disembark at the Canaries — for a tourist holiday was the only other plausible explanation for Mary's presence on the *Lagos* — they finally inquired what she was up to going to West Africa. She began to explain her scientific motives and her plan to collect specimens of various species. The other passengers concluded that these must be botanical specimens and ominously mentioned that "they had known some men who had come out from Kew [Gardens] but they were all dead now."

The *Lagos* did not linger at the Canaries, but instead pursued its way south to the trade wind zone — "the hot breath of death," as those odorous winds were called — and the dangerous Almadia reef, where Mary saw the wreck of the *Port Douglas* (which had sunk the previous year). Both made her ask, "Can I live in this or no," but she concluded that "you have to leave it, like all other such questions, to Allah, and go on."

Mary of course did go on, farther south still to Cape Verde off the coast of Senegal at the westernmost bulge of Africa. Here the *Lagos* ran into the "mist universe" of the West African wet season. The familiar clear-cut realms of sky, air, and sea all dissolved damply into each other. Many days they could see only ten or fifteen yards from the ship. Occasionally another boat would suddenly loom up out of the dense, sodden atmosphere and be visible in the watery world of the *Lagos* for a few minutes, only to be swallowed up in the enveloping mist again. It was an eerie, sometimes beautiful world, but uncomfortable and inconvenient, too, for nothing, from table linen to bedsheets to underclothes, ever got completely dry.

August, in fact, was the very worst time of the year to sail out to West Africa, because the whole West Coast, from Guinea down to Cameroon, was saturated by "the rains." For the most part, the rains consisted of a steady, tedious downpour, the monotony of which was alleviated now and then by violent tropical storms. Mary experienced her first "tornado," as these spectacular storms were called, just south of Cape Verde. The *Lagos* was "surrounded by a wild, strange sky. . . . At one part of the horizon were great columns of black cloud, expanding and coalescing at their capitals. These were mounted on a background of most exquisite pale green. Away to leeward was a gigantic black cloud-mountain across whose vast face were bands and wreaths of delicate white and silver clouds, and from whose grim depths every few seconds flashed palpitating, fitful, livid lightnings. Striding towards us across the sea came the tornado, lashing it into spray mist with the tremendous artillery of its rain, and shaking the air with its own thundergrowls. Away to windward leisurely boomed and grumbled a third thunderstorm, apparently not addressing the tornado but the cloud-mountain, while in between these phenomena wandered strange wild winds, made out of lost souls frightened and wailing to be let back into Hell or taken care of somehow by someone."

It was several days later, in the evening, that the *Lagos* reached the coast of Sierra Leone. Here they dropped anchor, for the weather was too thick to see ten yards from the ship, and Captain Murray did not want to risk encountering Carpenter Rock instead of Cape Sierra, "a sandy promontory at the end of which was situated a lighthouse of irregular habits." All night long they remained enveloped in the murky mist off the coast of Freetown, mist that Mary's shipmates informed her was mixed with solid malaria coming off the land.

Mary could scarcely sleep with the prospect of finally setting foot on West Africa the next day. At dawn she was up on deck. The woolly gray mist of the night before had rolled back to swathe the densely forested mountains of Sierra Leone's exquisite coastline, and a huge orange sun was igniting the dim sky behind the mountains as it rose. Mary was overcome by a sense of déjà vu as well as excitement at seeing the beautiful scene. "It was with a thrill of joy that I looked on Freetown harbour for the first time in my life. I knew the place so well," she explained, principally from her childhood favorite, Charles Johnson's eighteenth-century account in *A General History of Robberies and Murders of the Most Notorious Pyrates.*

For the true Afrophile, the real Africa only begins when one has reached Sierra Leone. It was here that Mary finally came face to face with the world she had come so far to find. "On my first voyage out," she confessed, "I did not know the Coast and the Coast did not know me, and we mutually terrified each other." But after it was established that Mary was *not* a representative of the World Women's Temperance Association collecting shocking details for magic-lantern lectures on the liquor traffic and after Mary herself realized that sudden death at the hands of the "local nobility and gentry" was not on the immediate agenda, she at last "succumbed to the charm of the coast." Before her lay Freetown with all its noise, vibrant colors, heterogeneous structures and peoples, and terrific heat: she had finally arrived.

The place was a British colony that had been established as a home for freed slaves, who were brought there from England, Canada, and the West Indies, and also from slave ships bound for the United States that the British navy had intercepted. This population of freed slaves and their descendants, known as Creoles, was greatly outnumbered, however, by the indigenous peoples, Temnes, Mendes, Kono, and Fulani, for the most part, so the town was something of a West African melting pot. Not exactly cosmopolitan, but distinctly variegated.

Mary went ashore in the morning with Captain Murray, who spontaneously confided to her as they crossed the harbor to town that "he had looked forward with horror to having a single lady passenger to take down the coast but that he did not mind me somehow and was liable to forget my existence." Mary's first impression of Freetown was that it must be the world's capital of "ramshackledom"; most of the painted wooden houses and stores with corrugated iron roofs were in a state of "acute delapidation." But despite its enduring air of deterioration, Freetown possessed, and still possesses, an eccentric but compelling picturesque quality and charm. Nature peels the paint, rusts up the gates, and digs potholes in the laterite dirt roads, but it also covers the stone churches and markets with trailing yellow and mauve flowers and fills the air with the odors of frangipani, magnolias, and oleanders. And in marked contrast to the chronic decay of the town are the majestic, unchanging mountains, at whose base Freetown nestles, and the miles of white sand beaches, with their fringe of baobabs and graceful palms that line the coast.

It was market day when they arrived, and market day in Freetown, as Mary says, "has got more noise to the square inch than most things." "One wants the pen of a Rabelais," she said, to catalogue its riches. Freetown markets, whether open-air or inside the wall-less white stone market pavilions, are a kaleidoscope of color and noise. All manner of fruits, vegetables, fish, meat, live chickens, beads, vibrant print cloth, "and half a hundred other indescribabilia" are displayed, presided over by market women in flowing, colorful dress, yards of it usually, for, as Mary observed of the dimensions of most of the market women "but Allah! the circumference of them."

Leaving the market, she and Murray made their way under a blazing sun down the central thoroughfare, generously populated by stray goats and sheep, as well as by the most miserable looking dogs in West Africa. Almost as unattractive as these dogs were the huge, grotesque turkey vultures Mary saw perched on Freetown's largest church, Saint George's Cathedral. The human pedestrians, on the other hand, were most impressive: tall, graceful Fulani in long, pastel Muslim gowns, handsome young women, often bare-breasted, with long, vivid, cotton wrappers tied around their waists and carrying round trays of smoked fish or banana fritters or oranges on their heads. They also occasionally encountered what appeared to be a Creole dandy, clothed entirely in European dress, from his bowler hat to his finely pressed trousers, umbrella, and cigar, a black replica of the species who goes to "the city" every morning back in London.

Their destination was the store of a British trading agent in the center of town. Here, even within doors in the shade, the air was oppressive and hot, so the agent and Captain Murray refreshed themselves with a quarter of a pint of whiskey with a lump of ice in it. The poor captain, however, was then pecked by a large ostrich, unaccountably on the premises. Mary, in turn, was threatened by a dog-faced monkey, and in her haste to retreat she fell down the first of a number of holes she descended into in West Africa, into a cellar full of blacks arranging bundles of cotton goods, which fortunately made for a soft landing. She was soon hauled up safely by means of the cable and hook used to bring up the cloth bundles.

More excitement followed shortly when a swarm of locusts invaded Freetown for the first time within living memory. The insects approached from the wooded hills to the southwest, "a brown cloud of singular structure, denser in some parts than others, continually changing its points of greatest density, like one of Thompson's diagrams of the ultimate structure of gases, for you could see the component atoms as it swept by and the whole air rustled with the beat of the locusts' wings." This was Mary's first dramatic introduction to West African insects, a subject on which she soon became an authority. Initially what struck her most was the size of the locusts; she did not know this early on that almost all living things in West Africa (with the exception, perhaps, of the humans) are of almost surrealistically exaggerated proportions, particularly the insects. The next thing she learned was how uncomfortable they could make life. In one of her many discourses on insects Mary writes:

> I should say, looking back calmly upon the matter, that 75 per cent of West African insects sting, 5 per cent bite, and the rest are either permanently or temporarily parasitic on the human race. And undoubtedly one of the many worst things you can do in West Africa is to take any notice of an insect. If you see a thing that looks like a cross between a flying lobster and the figure of Abraxis on a Gnostic gem do not pay it the least attention, never mind where it is; just keep quiet and hope it will go away — for that's your best chance; you have none in a stand-up fight with a good thorough-going African insect.

After the uproar of the locust invasion had subsided a bit, Mary proceeded to the Custom House to get a bill of health for Fernando Po and Cameroon. Then they returned to the *Lagos,* it being by now late afternoon, for they only spent one day in Freetown on this first voyage out. More excitement awaited on board in the person of an enormous black woman "bearing a name honoured in English literature, and by profession a laundress, demanding that the body of the second mate in any condition should be rendered over to the hand of the law (represented by four Hausa policemen) on a warrant she held against him for not having discharged his washing-bill last time the steamer was in Sierra Leone." Apparently this was not an uncommon occurrence; according to Mary, there was "usually a summons or so awaiting a West Coast boat" at Freetown, "and many a proud vessel has dropped anchor in Freetown harbour with one of her officers in a ventilator and another

in a coal bunker." Unfortunately for this particular "accusatrix," the
Lagos's current second mate was not the same man who had held the
post the last time, and so she returned empty-handed to shore. The
Hausa policemen remained on board, however, until the *Lagos* departed in the evening, getting thoroughly drunk, so that when they
finally left in a small dinghy they draped their arms and legs over the
sides of their boat, unaware that these became tempting live bait for
the sharks in the harbor. Despite Mary's anxieties and the dire warn-
ings issued from the deck of the *Lagos,* they made it safely to shore.

By nightfall the *Lagos* left Freetown, and the following morning saw
them steaming past the Banana and Sherbro islands on their way to
the "Grain Coast" off Liberia. It was hazardous going because of all
the rocks lying in wait for them, many of which bore the names of
ships that had come to grief on them. And once again they entered the
saturated realm of "the wet," which made their way even more treacherous. "Why none of us started specialising branchiae," Mary wondered, "I do not know, but feel that would have been the proper sort
of breathing apparatus for such an atmosphere."

The next day the weather lifted some, and Mary saw for the first
time the elemental West Coast landscape that came to exercise an almost hypnotic effect on her imagination. It was a landscape devoid of
human imprint and possessed of an "eternal sameness [so] that you
automatically believe that nothing else but this sort of world, past,
present, or future can ever have existed: and that cities and mountains
are but the memories of dreams." It consisted of four, unchanging
parallel lines, lines that went away into eternity as far as the eye could
see: there was the band of unblemished white sand at the shore, backed
by a wall of dark, impenetrable forest, in turn backed by a sky that
varied from magenta-orange at dawn to a deep purple-blue in the evening before it became studded by glittering constellations, the moon
in all its phases, and the evening star of Venus. And finally there was
the fourth line of the surf before the shore; in the moonlight it gleamed
like an opaque diamond wall. For hours Mary would gaze at the un-
wavering four bands of surf, sand, forest, and sky and find in their
sublime monotony and imperviousness to human effort a profound sense
of peace, freedom, and permanence. They provided the first of a number of West African landscapes that complemented her own internal,
psychological geography. "Night and day and season changes pass over
these things," she wrote, "like reflections in a mirror, without altering
the mirror frame; but nothing comes that ever stills . . . the thunder

of the surf wall . . . or makes the forest wall brighter. . . . Mind you, it is intensely beautiful, intensely soothing, intensely interesting, if you can read it and you like it." But, she conceded, "life for a man who cannot and does not" in such a landscape "is a living death."

When they reached Liberia, the *Lagos* took on a number of Kru, the coastal people of what was then called the Grain Coast, who had long been in contact with the English and other Europeans and had proved themselves excellent workers, whether on board ship or trekking through the bush. Nevertheless, despite their familiarity with the white man and the white man's ways, they still came as something of a shock to Mary when they first joined the *Lagos*. The ship stopped at Tabou and fired its gun and sounded its whistle, whereupon a dozen or so canoes full of large and largely naked Krumen shot out from the inlets of the beach, "making a magnificently savage scene," as Mary wrote home to Violet Roy. They chanted a strange dirgelike song in time to their paddling as they approached the *Lagos* and, gaining the ship, swarmed up the sides in a fashion calculated to make Mary think of Addison Road with tenderness. She retreated to her cabin, only to find several Kru already in possession of it and apparently admiring and using her towels and hair and clothes brushes until she drove them off.

What with the added noise from these new passengers, sleep that night was impossible. Mary decided to pass the time fishing, as she would so often do in her travels when frustrated, thwarted, bored, waiting for a boat or a person to turn up, or when, as in the present case, sleep eluded her. There was something infinitely soothing about fishing in such situations. And so the night of the Kru invasion she got out her fishing gear in the moonlight "and getting behind a pile of parrafin tins in boxes proceeded to enjoy life once more." But the solace of her "piscatorial pursuits," as she called them, failed her this night. Instead of landing an interesting specimen to bottle up and take back to the British Museum, she managed to catch an octopus with a diameter of approximately eight feet that crawled over the paraffin cases in a repulsive way until Mary and one of the other passengers — a Scotchman whom she refers to as her "custodian" in her letters to Violet — drove it over the side of the ship with paddles.

The hubbub of the Kru, along with that of the Freetown markets, was Mary's introduction to the ubiquity of noise in this new West Coast world. "Woe to the man in Africa who cannot stand perpetual uproar!" she writes in *West African Studies*. "Few things surprised me more than the rarity of silence and the intensity of it when you get it."

The possibility of quiet in West Africa was threatened on all sides. Africans themselves, Mary found, tended to be more vocal than taciturn Englishmen for several reasons. First, they often, as she put it, "thought externally." Just as an Englishman will frequently write out something in order to get a grasp of it, she held that an African, not having writing, will talk it out to himself. In addition, while the devout Englishman will send up innumerable silent prayers to his Anglican God, the equally devout African tends to converse aloud to spirit guardians or to departed ancestors and relatives. On many occasions Mary was to see men at bush fires or in the village palaver house turn around and say, "You remember that, Mother?" to the ghost that to him was there.

Then there was the entire array of the West African orchestra to banish peace and quiet, especially at night. For the newcomer the nightly music of Africa — particularly the drumming — is deeply exciting, even before its significance is understood. The drums seem to answer one's pulse beat: they are both profoundly soothing and stirring. It is only later when one has grown accustomed to their inexorable rhythm or when one's head is throbbing from the parallel beat of a malaria headache that the drums can seem a no less inexorable torment. The ivory horn, wooden xylophone, and harp, however, are always pleasant to the ear, and Mary became adept at playing all three of them.

The other principal source of perpetual uproar was produced by the natural world, again especially at night, because in West Africa most living things — often including humans — sleep through the heat of the day and only make their existence known vocally once the sun has set. After the African orchestra had called it a night, the animal and insect world would take over. Many a night Mary would lie awake in stifling thatch houses listening to the grunting sighs of hippos, the whining bark of crocodiles, the thin cry of bats, the cough of leopards, and the unearthly yells issuing from little marmosets deep in the surrounding forest. Or if she was tide-trapped in a canoe in a mangrove swamp or visiting a trading hulk moored in a river, she heard the peculiar species of frog "who seems eternally engaged at night in winding up a Waterbury watch." Even more exasperating was the uneuphonious Ning Ning fish — named after its own "idiotic song" — which Mary described as a "deeply trying creature . . . who, when . . . you want to have a quiet night's rest, just as you have tucked in your mosquito bar carefully and successfully, comes alongside and ser-

enades you, until you have to get up and throw things at it with a
prophetic feeling, amply supported by subsequent experience, that hordes
of mosquitos are busily ensconcing themselves inside your mosquito
bar. What makes the Ning Ning . . . so maddening," she continues,
"is . . . it is a ventriloquist . . . and . . . it is not driven away or
destroyed by an artillery of missiles but merely lies low until its victim
has got under his mosquito curtain, and resettled his mosquito palaver — and then back it comes with its 'ning ning.'"

As they proceeded southward the *Lagos* called at both Cape Coast
Castle and Accra on the Gold Coast, and Mary took a day-long expedition up a coastal lagoon to a Kru village with her "custodian," the
Scotchman she identifies in her letters to Violet as "David." It was the
first of countless journeys up creeks and through mangrove swamps
and lagoons, and she was enchanted with the broad, glassy expanses of
silver water, the banks walled by intricately entangled mangrove roots,
wreathed about by deep green, creeping plants bearing large, white,
bell-shaped flowers. She also met her first crocodiles on this occasion:
great, long, sinister-looking creatures, lounging lazily on the red earth
banks of the lagoon. The excursion was less delightful toward the end,
however. When Mary and David were returning to the *Lagos,* they
were overtaken by the evening mists, and as they were passing underneath an invisible overhanging tree, David was smacked on the head
by a heavy branch and fell stunned and bleeding into Mary's lap. For
the several hours' return journey to the *Lagos,* he remained there, unconscious, his blood soaking through Mary's best skirt, as she told
Violet, and running down her stockings. She had neglected to bring
along her medical kit and could not easily ascertain whether he was
bleeding to death, permanently brain damaged, or just temporarily
knocked out. Hence it was a rather tense few hours, but by the time
they regained the *Lagos* David had begun to come around again.

Another Scotchman on board, the physician, Dr. McNab, had been
ill for three days, but the evening they returned from the lagoon expedition they found him up again, "crawling about . . . with an in-
describable tint of complexion . . . something like an ecru green."
McNab tended David's injuries and then proceeded to expend his remaining strength in a detailed and lurid conversation with Mary and
David on the topic of interracial marriage, citing, in particular, the
case of a Sierra Leonean lawyer, a barrister in fact, who had married a
white woman. Mary confided to Violet that such tales made her "mentally sick." In an earlier letter she had also cryptically referred to "a

revolting animalism" she had encountered on the West Coast that made her "inner soul sick and ashamed."

In coming out to West Africa, among the many geographical intellectual, and psychological voyages that Mary had embarked on was one that led to the reality of human sexuality — her own as well as that of others — a reality that in Britain she could have lived a whole sheltered lifetime without confronting. Miscegenation was just one of the forms in which this obtrusive sexuality was manifested, both between white women and usually very highly educated, Europeanized African men, or, much more commonly, between European men and African women. Mary's admired West Coast traders often took black mistresses and fathered their children, and government officials, who almost always had English wives back at home, sometimes did the same, though more discreetly. With her wide reading in the sciences and of frank travelers and ethnographers like Burton and Tylor Mary could scarcely have come out to West Africa in a state of innocence. Nevertheless, what she learned there came as a profound shock, and interracial sexuality and adultery were merely two manifestations of this new knowledge.

The real awakening for Mary derived from the high visibility of sexual experience in Africa. To begin with, there was the widespread institution of polygamy, which in time Mary was to spend a good deal of energy defending. Her ethnographical research into initiation rites made her familiar with both male and female circumcision and specifically how the various forms of female circumcision, such as infibulation and clitoridectomy, diminished, even destroyed, women's capacity for sexual pleasure. She learned also that nursing mothers refused to have sexual relations with their husbands, thus making polygamy essentially a necessity, since African women routinely suckled their children until they were well over two years old.

More generally, after Mary began her travels on land, she lived among Africans for weeks at a stretch. There is very little privacy in traditional African village life; circumcision, menstruation, sexual intercourse, and childbirth are all to some degree public events or activities, and all their pleasure and pain, joy and fearfulness, become almost communal experiences. Daily observing such things must have transformed Mary's awareness of her own body, its impulses, changes, even desires. Her monthly periods came and went; she bathed naked and washed her long hair in streams and rivers. And the Africans she lived among were constantly insisting upon her sexual identity in their per-

sistent questions regarding the whereabouts of her husband and children, it being inconceivable to them that a woman of her age could
possess neither.

   Most of these matters are of course only obliquely hinted at in Mary's
letters and scarcely appear at all in her books and lectures. What does
appear, however, with an extraordinary if unconscious clarity is Mary's
profound aesthetic and sensual response to the physical beauty of African men and women. She gives countless graphic descriptions of both
in her books. In the villages in the interior men and women were, of
course, scantily clad, sometimes completely nude. It is likely that Mary
had seen no naked body other than her own until she came to Africa.
Even so, she recognized that Africans, especially the men and the young
women, before ceaseless childbearing had begun to transform their
bodies, possessed distinctive physical attributes rarely found among
whites. Their bodies were smoother, with far less body and facial hair.
In addition, their diet and constant physical exercise — canoeing,
farming, hunting — meant that their bodies were well developed, firm,
and muscular. The mortality rate, of course, was fearfully high, so that
those who survived tended to be healthy and strong. Most of Mary's
admiring descriptions concentrate on the Africans' bodies, the muscular shoulders and chests of her bearers or canoe paddlers, or the round,
firm breasts of young girls on the brink of marriage. But she also
dwells on the varying hues of complexion among different peoples, the
large, doelike eyes of African children, the texture and plaiting styles
of women's hair, the whiteness of teeth even when filed, and the various patterns of facial scarring.

   Above all, there was the underlying physical and sexual sanity of
African experience, born of unconstrained openness and acceptance of
the body's needs, desires, and functions. Despite the existence of miscegenation, female circumcision, and the unfairness of polygamy, which
granted sexual freedom to men while denying it to women, Mary must
have found both harmony and honesty in the open sexuality of African
life. Even more important, it spoke to her, as did so much else in
Africa, of liberation. This liberation was not unqualified, because she
could never entirely repudiate her Victorian origins, however irregular
these may have been. She would often be torn; this early on, she must
have been confused as well. And Dr. McNab's tales of white women
with African husbands was an introduction to a realm she never completely fathomed. For, as she wrote a missionary years later who asked
her how she could champion traders when she knew they slept with

black women, her knowledge of human sexuality remained entirely theoretical. The sexual awakening West Africa brought her was never fulfilled because she never experienced physical love. Still, her views on and understanding of it were freer and more profound than were most married women's and mothers' back in England.

It was only several days' run from the Gold Coast to the Bight of Benin and on to the "oil rivers" of what is now Nigeria: the dense network of swampy rivers, streams, and creeks into which the great Niger river dissipates, creating a massive delta. The region of the oil rivers, so-called because they were used for transporting the major trade item of palm oil from the interior, is one of the most forbidding areas of the West Coast, particularly in the wet season when Mary reached it. The terrain consists largely of endless mangrove swamps rising out of rotting mud water, and the stench of the swamps is overpowering to the newcomer. The amount of stagnant water means the region is as dangerous as it is unattractive, because the swamps provide a fine breeding place for the malarial mosquito, though of course in Mary's day it was still believed that malaria was airborne — in the bad air of *mal'aria*.

The *Lagos* called in at the trading station of Bonny, a port in the midst of the oil river swamps. The first glimpse of Bonny filled Mary with a sense of horror, and she turned to Captain Murray and exclaimed, "'Good Heavens! What an awful accident. We've gone and picked up the Styx.'"

Mary went ashore in the evening and had tea with the resident agent at Bonny, a congenial man named Captain Boler who entertained her over tinned biscuits and tea with an account of the latest epidemic during which, in the space of ten days, nine of the eleven white men resident at Bonny died from yellow fever. At one funeral two junior clerks of the deceased, well fortified with drink, fell into the grave before the coffin, which was then lowered down on top of them so that all three had to be hauled out again. Another tea-taker explained that this was "barely necessary," however, since "those two had to have a grave of their own before next sundown." Poor Captain Boler himself had succumbed to the deadly climate by the time Mary passed through again in 1895.

Bonny, in short, was not a very scenic or cheerful spot; it was a relief to leave it the next day and be out at sea again, steaming south to Portuguese Angola. It was early September by the time the *Lagos* reached its southernmost destination of Saint Paul de Loanda. Here Mary's travels properly speaking really began: for the next four months she traveled, often by land, northward through Cabinda, the Congo Free State, Congo Français, and Cameroon, until she reached Calabar, just south of Bonny, whence she shipped home again in early January.

Saint Paul de Loanda, or just plain Luanda, as it is now called, is one of the most beautiful cities on the West African coast. It had been in the hands of the Portuguese for more than four hundred years, but it was only just shortly before Mary's arrival that anything had really been done to modernize the place, by introducing a regular water supply and streetlamps. Why in West Africa streetlamps should seem one of the most desirable manifestations of civilization is unclear, but they are to this day. Certainly the difficulties encountered by Loanda in its attempts to illuminate its streets might have proved a useful object lesson. As Mary tells it, Portugal ordered a set of streetlamps for the city from England, and in due course a set of old gas lamp standards arrived. But "there being no gas in Loanda there was a pause until oil lamps to put in them came out." These in turn also duly arrived, but without the necessary ladder for the lamplighter. "Hence that worthy had to swarm each individual lamppost, a time-taking performance which normally landed him in the arms of Aurora before Loanda was lit for the night."

Despite its beauty, Mary found Saint Paul de Loanda a rather benighted place and not just on account of the erratic streetlamps. She landed, as she later described it, "in an alarmed state and with no knowledge of the Portuguese language." She had been led to understand from a consular report that there were three hotels in the city, but she found none at all and so was driven to seek shelter with the English consul himself. This unfortunate man also had a drunken crew from a shipwrecked trading vessel on his hands, but eventually he found room for Mary in a merchant's store. Separated from her familiar *Lagos* companions, disoriented by the Portuguese language and by the rowdy trading vessel crew, Mary began to lose heart. Like so many new arrivals at the Coast, she was seized by the impulse to bolt. As soon as possible she got on a Portuguese boat bound for Cabinda where she hoped to be in time to catch an English ship heading north, for, as she said, "I began to feel that I had had enough of West Africa." But when she reached Cabinda, the small coastal Angolan enclave sandwiched in between the Congo Free State and Congo Français, Mary found that the English boat had sailed the day before, so she had no choice but to remain and stick it out.

Cabinda was, as it turned out, the most fortunate of places in which to be stranded, largely on account of the presence of a remarkable Englishman named R. E. Dennett, a kind of on-the-spot fetish tutor for Mary. Dennett had been in West Africa in the Congo Free State, Cabinda, and Congo Français for nearly eighteen years as a trader for Hatton and Cookson, the English firm Mary dealt with on both her journeys, bringing in her ivory and rubber to their stores, or "factories," as they were called, where she exchanged them for beads, cloth, fishhooks, and other trade goods. Unlike many traders, who lived only for the day when they could return to Britain on leave or for good, Dennett had become intensely interested in the Africans, especially the Fjort he lived among, and had carefully studied both their language and dialects and their folklore.

He had already published one book, *Seven Years Among the Fjort,* and several years after their first meeting, Mary contributed an introduction to his second book, *Folklore of the Fjort.* Dennett taught her a great deal during the short time she stayed with him, but it was his methodology, the way in which he collected and analyzed his information, that most impressed her, for she never studied or published anything on the Fjort herself, and her ethnographical interests focused on religion and law rather than on language or oral traditions.

Dennett installed Mary in a rather run-down but picturesque cottage that Henry Morton Stanley had stayed in while he was waiting for a boat to take him home after his first journey across Africa, and soon she was fully integrated into the Hatton and Cookson factory routine: tea at 6:00 A.M., breakfast at 12:15, and dinner at 7:00 P.M. This schedule gave Mary plenty of time to collect fish and insects and also to cultivate the friendship of two resident Portuguese women, Donna Anna de Chichorro, the wife of the resident Portuguese Secretary General, and her sister, Donna Maria de Coutinho. Conversation with Donna Anna and Donna Maria was not impeded by the language barrier. As Mary described it, "we either talked to each other placidly in our respective tongues or made ventures into each other's, and when we really wanted to indulge in some thrilling item of gossip we took refuge in Latin." Evenings were usually taken up with meandering conversations with Dennett on fetish and everything else under the sun. Dennett, as Mary put it, was "a dreamer." The two would sit up late in "a murky little room illuminated by a wick floating in oil, burning faintly, then flaming, then going into a sort of fizzle," and if they sat up late enough and Dennett got sufficiently dreamy, he would propose at some point, "let us have a little talk with God. It was not praying, it was conversation with the Deity, respectful but familiar, and now and then extremely critical."

One evening, however, when she was not with Dennett but rather was writing up notes by a kerosene lamp in Stanley's house, Mary was interrupted at about 11:00 P.M. by knocking at the shutters, and she opened them to find a local "fetish priest" or witch doctor. A person in a small village some miles distant was ill, he explained. Would Mary come along and help him treat the patient? She of course agreed and got her medical kit, and they set off. They walked several hours through the dark forest, "an alarming place to walk about at night, both for a witch doctor who believes in all his forest devils and a lady who believes in all the local, material ones." But eventually they made it safely to the village, where they found the patient extended on the ground outside one of the huts and surrounded by wailing women. Mary quickly recognized (but fails to identify in her account) a common West African disease treatable with European drugs. These she gave to her companion, who in turn administered them to the patient with the proper incantations. And then, after dispensing some further medical advice, they departed.

When they got back to Stanley's house Mary invited the healer in, even though it was now close to dawn, and asked him why he had performed the various rituals and charms that he had. The man gazed straight ahead and after a short silence began to talk, softly, wordily, and gently. The gist of what he said uncannily echoed in Mary's mind Goethe's "Prometheus." Not that she thought all fetish priests were Goethes or Spinozas, but it is clear that Mary realized even this early on the philosophical or spiritual basis of West African beliefs and felt a profound affinity with them. They corresponded to her own rather austere pantheism. And at bottom this correspondence — the sense that in pursuing fetish she was exploring and defining her own most fundamental ideas and values — was what made Mary recognize Africa as her home and declare at the beginning of *Travels in West Africa* that "you must make allowances for my love of this . . . country, with its great forests and rivers and its animistic-minded inhabitants, and for my ability to be more comfortable there than in England."

Over and over again in her books and lectures and letters Mary insists upon the primary importance of fetish, or African religious beliefs, in her work. Everything else, including fish, insects, and politics, she asserts, is secondary. And in pursuing fetish Mary was essentially pursuing the most basic and important questions one can ask: What is this universe and who created it? Why are we here, and to what purpose? What is our connection with other things, living and nonliving? What is the nature of the invisible, spiritual world beyond material reality? These are the same questions that plagued Spinoza and Goethe, the two most frequently invoked writers in Mary's books. In Africa Mary gradually discovered answers to such questions, answers that seemed both fascinatingly original and profoundly familiar. Thus her midnight excursion with the witch doctor in Cabinda was perhaps the most important of all her adventures during the 1893 trip.

Probably the most comical adventure — "a real knockabout farce," as Mary called it in *West African Studies* — also occurred in Cabinda. Like most places in West Africa, Cabinda possessed an abundance of mosquitos and dragonflies and also a species of enormous flying beetle that would sweep into a house, "go two or three times round the room and then flop into the soup plate, out of that, shake himself like a retriever and bang into someone's face, then flop on the floor." But it was the awful driver ant — an insect that both bites and stings and moves about in vast armies — that provided great excitement during her Cabinda stay. Drivers are also known as "visiting ants" because of their custom of swarming into or "visiting" houses, usually at night when the occupants are asleep, clearing the house of vermin and attacking any other meat, including human flesh. One evening Mary was passing through a Cabinda village, when out of one hut

came the owner and his family and all the household parasites pell mell, leaving the Drivers in possession; but the mother and father of the family, when they recovered from this unwonted burst of activity, showed such a lively concern, and such unmistakable signs of anguish at having left something behind them in the hut, that I thought it must be the baby. Although not a family man myself, the idea of that innocent infant perishing in such an appalling manner roused me to action, and I joined the frenzied group, crying, "Where him live?" "In him far corner for floor!" shrieked the distracted parents, and into that hut I charged. Too true! There in the corner lay the poor little thing, a mere inert black mass, with hundreds of cruel Drivers already swarming upon it. To seize and give it to the distracted mother was, as the reporter would say, "the work of an instant." She gave a cry of joy, and dropped it instantly into a water barrel, where her husband held it down with a hoe, chuckling contentedly. Shiver not, my friend, at [such] callousness . . . that there thing wasn't an infant — it was a ham!

From Cabinda Mary moved on to the neighboring Congo Free State. What she saw in King Leopold of Belgium's private empire — the forced labor and other atrocities that Joseph Conrad would bring to the world's attention in *Heart of Darkness* — were anathema to her, and she vowed never to pass through it again until it was in different hands. It was in Kacongo, as she called it, that Mary experienced at first hand the terrible lethality of the West Coast climate. Both small-pox and sleeping sickness were raging there in epidemic proportions during the autumn of 1893. Mary came across whole villages that had been almost completely depopulated by the "spotted death," as it was called by the Africans. Sleeping sickness was even more prevalent, and Mary saw numerous people in the last, listless stages of this tropical killer. And of course everywhere she went she encountered lepers, men and women whose limbs had become shapeless stumps or their faces blurred masks. Almost always they lived apart as outcasts, not because leprosy was understood to be contagious, but because it was associated with witchcraft.

All disease in Africa, as Mary learned, was held to be caused by witches or other evil spirits, including such psychological disturbances as "malignant melancholy" and suicide, which she found so common on the lower Congo. The notion that illness arbitrarily afflicts individuals or has some sort of "natural" source or explanation was alien to African thinking. Mary did not begin systematically to study witch-craft, or "fetish," as it was called, until her second West African trip in 1895, but she did gather a good deal of information on this first journey. In one Kacongo village she came across "five unpleasant look-ing objects stuck on sticks" in the middle of the village thoroughfare. Upon closer examination, these proved to be human livers and lungs, and Mary was informed by the villagers that these vital organs were the "witches" that had been found inside deceased witch doctors. Nor was this the only example of postmortem practice that she came across. In another village a woman had inexplicably dropped dead, even though, as Mary's informants related in pidgin English, the woman "no sick, she no complain, she no nothing, and then she go die one time." This portmortem, which Mary observed, showed a burst aneurism, as she immediately recognized from her medical training. But the African verdict was somewhat different. "She done witch herself," Mary was told; in other words, the woman was a witch who was eaten by her own familiar.

At the mighty Congo River Mary rejoined the *Lagos,* and the ship turned into the river's vast mouth, more than thirty miles wide, and steamed up to Matadi, which is about 140 miles from the sea. Matadi was the Congo Free State's major port, a colorful town built on terraces along rocky hillsides. The surrounding scenery was magnificent: mangrove swamps fringed the banks of the river, but behind them were palms and cotton and baobab trees. And beginning about 120 miles from the river's mouth, the mountains that seemed from the sea to loom in the distance moved to the river's banks, and the Congo itself shrank to a mere three or so miles across, walled in by the mountains' sheer cliffs rising six hundred feet toward the blue ribbon of sky reflected in the water's turbulent surface. The current was tremendous, and shortly before reaching Matadi, the *Lagos* passed through the stretch of treacherous whirlpools known as Hell's Cauldron.

The grandeur of the region more than lived up to the accounts Mary knew so well from Stanley's books. And it was enhanced by the bush fires set at that season to burn down the five- or six-foot-high grass covering the mountainsides. For miles the fires would rage, illuminating the darkened night sky, Mary wrote Violet, "with a wild, palpitating crimson glow." She conceded, though, that when the fires came right down to the river's edge, "with precipices and mountain slopes each side of it ablaze, Allah it was hot."

It was at Matadi that Mary had a harrowing experience on the Congo Free State Railway, which was built by King Leopold to carry ivory and rubber past the most unnavigable portions of the Congo to the coast, a venture that exacted an appalling toll in terms of African lives in the course of its protracted construction. Riding the Congo Free State Railway, Mary wrote Violet, was "one of the most risky things you can do in all Africa — it is casually laid out along a most terrific country and managed," she concluded, "by light-hearted lunatics." In the short history of its existence it had already known a good share of disaster, including a spectacular explosion the year before Mary rode on it when an engine plowed into a stash of dynamite left on the line. The train was filled with officials and Krumen, as well as "everyone in the state of the least importance," Mary wrote Violet, and she was "assured that . . . arms and legs still keep falling from the firmament to which they were hurled more than a year ago."

Mary, Captain Murray, and Dr. McNab, however, decided not to be scared by these macabre tales of past catastrophe and even cheerfully signed statements that they were embarking on the railway at "shipper's own risk," which McNab hazarded was tantamount to signing their own death warrants. They climbed into an open-air car, watched one official give the engine driver what looked like a last blessing, and then steamed rapidly out of the Matadi station.

"Never," Mary wrote Violet, "was there such a rickety and shaky concern driven in a more reckless way over such a perilous firmament. . . . We shook about like dice in a box and . . . we rushed into a sort of tunnel with one side out, heavy masses of insecure rock impeding over it, [and] 500 foot precipices at our elbows with . . . the rocky rapids of the Congo at [their] foot."

"We felt a trifle queer," Mary continued, "but still admired the scenery and enjoyed ourselves until the train took a hop, skip, and jump, and scuttled along and then stopped." They all hopped out of their open car and inched their way single file along the extremely narrow strip of ground between the train and the precipice and found that one of the rails had gotten loose. This problem was soon rectified with a crowbar, and in good time they proceeded to the end of the line, where they had lunch. The railway officials here, over cigars, confided to Murray and McNab that they were not sanguine about their engineer's ability to return them to Matadi without a "smash." And Mary reported that when they set off on their return journey, the three of them "all found [themselves] instinctively in the hindmost car, although it was a luggage one." Despite their anxieties, they survived all the hairpin turns and precipitous descents intact and returned to the little tin station at Matadi in good time in a quite jubilant frame of mind. The Matadi officials were also overjoyed to see them and "insisted on our having dinner and drinking health and prosperity to Leopold II, Congo Free State, the Commissaire de la Cataracts, The Magazine General, the Railway, and things in general." Mary reported to Violet that she "as usual confined myself to soda-water," and retired to the *Lagos* immediately after dessert was served. But as she lay in her cabin in the dark, she heard the sounds of revelry far into the night, and the next morning Captain Murray was ill and headachy.

After leaving the Congo Free State and parting again from her *Lagos* friends, Mary went by land into Congo Français, directly athwart the equator, the territory of Du Chaillu and Brazza, and also very soon the real heart or destination of her own travels in Africa. She spent at least two months here, most of that time in the interior and on her own. Unfortunately, her surviving letters to Violet fail to contain a detailed record of this central period of the 1893 trip, so that all we know of it derives from various episodes and allusions to it in Mary's books. She did relate to Violet that her "method of progression was . . . varied — hammocks, canoes, and walking." Soon she abandoned the first, unlike most white travelers in Africa, who favored being carried about by African porters.

She most likely hired a small band of African bearers, as she did later in 1895, including an interpreter who in theory spoke pidgin English and a cook, as well as three or four carriers. Communication was an enduring problem both with the French missionaries and officials, for Mary knew no French whatsoever, and with Africans, though she was amazingly adept at picking up the rudiments of most African languages.

As planned, Mary traded her way into the interior, bartering her beads and fishhooks and trade rum or gin for ivory and rubber. Her traveling in the capacity of trader meant that she was generally well received in villages despite her bizarre appearance, for most of the Africans she encountered, especially the Fang, had never seen a white person before. Thus, after the initial sensation caused by her arrival, Mary would be warmly welcomed, given the best thatch house to sleep in, and also plied with food and palm wine. For unlike nearly all other white travelers, Mary subsisted almost entirely on African "chop": palm oil stew, fried fish, snails, cassava or manioc in every conceivable form, plantain, yam, pumpkin, and pineapple. It was, as she conceded, a "dull, indigestible diet," and occasionally she supplemented it with a precious tin of smoked herring or biscuits from her capacious waterproof sack. She also brought along one necessity, the one thing she could not do without: tea. She lost weight, but except for the inevitable bouts of malaria, she remained essentially healthy under this regimen, and the daily trekking through the forest strengthened her body and greatly increased her physical stamina.

Even more than the coastal landscape of surf, sand, forest, and sky she had fallen in love with from the deck of the *Lagos,* the great equatorial forest of Congo Français held an irresistible power over Mary's imagination. But it took time and patience to penetrate the forest, and even more to learn how to read or really see it. "On first entering [its] . . . grim twilight regions," she writes in *Travels in West Africa,* "you hardly see anything but the vast column-like grey tree stems in their countless thousands around you, and the sparsely vegetated ground beneath. But day by day, as you get trained to your surroundings, you see more and more, and a whole world grows up gradually out of the gloom before your eyes. Snakes, beetles, bats, and beasts people the region that at first seemed lifeless. . . . It is the same," she goes on, "with the better lit regions, where vegetation is many formed and luxuriant. As you get used to it, what seemed at first to be an inextricable tangle ceases to be so." In time she learned to distinguish all the various networks of climbing grasses and blossoming creepers as well as the gigantic trees they enveloped. When Mary speaks of the charm and beauty of West Africa in her books and letters and lectures, it is this forest world she came to "see" and love that she is thinking of.

During these travels by land in Congo Français, Mary somewhat haphazardly began to pursue her dual purpose in coming out to West Africa: the study of "fish and fetish." The pursuit was somewhat haphazard because in many ways the 1893 trip was a trial run for the more extensive journey in 1895. This time out she was really just scouting the territory, but she acquired valuable techniques and information. The most efficient way of catching fish, she soon decided, was by stockade trap, but she also devoted many dreamy hours to drifting in a canoe with a pole and line in various creeks and lagoons, and during these hours, as she put it, "life slid away like a dreamless sleep."

Fishing expeditions were not, however, always so tranquil and idyllic. One lazy afternoon she was reading Günther's *Study of Fishes* in her canoe while waiting for a bite when one of her two African companions landed a huge catfish, "a three-foot long, grunting, flopping, yellowgrey, slimy thing," She describes the scene in *West African Studies:*

> The enormous fish came on board with an awful grunt, right in the middle of us; flop, swish, scurry and yell followed. I tucked the study of fishes in general under my arm and attended to this individual specimen shouting, "lef em, lef em; hev em for water one time." . . . "Bravi spatio interjecto," as Caesar says, in the middle of a bad battle, over went the canoe, while the cat-fish went off home with the line and hook. One black man went to the bank, whither, with a blind prescience of fate, I had flung, a second before, the most valuable occupant of the canoe, *The Study of Fishes.* I went personally to investigate fluvial deposits *in situ.* When I returned to the surface — accompanied by great swirls of mud and great bubbles of the gases of decomposition I had liberated on my visit to the bottom of the river — I observed the canoe floating bottom upwards.

Such "knockabout farces," as Mary liked to call them, also occurred in her pursuit of fetish. On one of her forest walks she came across a group of seven men in a clearing, each elaborately decked out in beads and shells and strips of animal skin and cloth. She immediately turned on her heel and beat a hasty retreat, her heart pounding furiously, because she thought she had intruded on a session of a male secret society, and to do so for a woman, or even for an uninitiated man, could mean death. Hastening down the forest path she was overtaken by one of the men, and since, as she put it, "there was no policeman round there [and] you cannot hail a cab and drive away from things in the Okanda country," she had no choice but to return to the clearing with her pursuer. After rejoining the others, they all set off down another bush trail while Mary's thoughts ran to the tune of " 'Oh to be in England now, it's spring time there,' " and her companions "made things all the more cheerful by now and again uttering strange cries, long clucks, melancholy whines and howls." When they reached a new clearing, however, Mary's companions revealed that they were not a secret society after all but merely a party of monkey hunters. Their method was to dress up in vivid attire and then seat themselves in the forest and pretend to be asleep, whereupon the monkeys in the trees overhead would be overcome with curiosity and would come down to investigate the hunters at close range. The hunters would then bag them. Mary, they explained through gestures, was an invaluable asset to their undertaking because she "was quite the queerest object they had personally ever seen . . . a heaven sent addition to a monkey hunt."

When Mary reached the Congo Français port of Libreville, the colonial and administrative center of Congo Français, she unexpectedly found an English ship, misleadingly named the SS *La Rochelle,* a two-thousand-ton vessel captained by one Captain Harrison, which could transport her back to Britain. But first the *Rochelle* had stops to make in both the German Cameroons and in Calabar. Mary wrote Violet in late October that the "S. S. Rochelle was . . . surprised at my arrival and I have been reveling in English language. Ever since leaving Loanda I have been wrestling with strange tongues: Portuguese, Dutch, French, [and pidgin], to the utter ruin of my conversational style which consists now of bald statements and questions and attempts at thanks."

After several days in Libreville the *Rochelle* proceeded to Cameroon where, of course, Mary was able to communicate because of her fluent German. Very shortly after arriving, she met two white Sisters of Mercy who asked her to come with them to Bimbi, near the Rio del Rey, to help them nurse a small, fever-stricken settlement of white traders and officials. As soon as they reached this "cheerful place," as Mary described it to Violet, they gathered all the sick men into the central agent's house, which was built on tall poles, open beneath, and surrounded on three sides by dense forest and bordered on the fourth by the river. They quickly dubbed the house "centipede villa," for the place was infested with the insects and, even worse, with scorpions.

Most of the men were delirious with fever and had to be watched carefully, day and night. Mary, long habituated to keeping vigils at sickbeds from the years spent nursing her mother, often volunteered to take night duty. But one evening, when she was not sitting up with the delirious men, she was awakened by the growling and barking of the trader's German boarhound. Going out on the verandah she was just in time to see a great black leopard spring at the dog. "I went to the rescue with a chair," she wrote Violet, "which I let into the leopard so lustily that the intruder let go its hold on the dog and turned on me, the look of its eyes which were green balls of fire."

"It crouched down to spring at me," she continued, "which was an error . . . for it gave me time to catch up a gourd full of lime water and sling it straight at its head where it burst like a shell. This discouraged the creature who turned and sprung off the verandah and vanished in the darkness." The next morning she measured the space between its front and back paws in the dirt and determined that the animal had been ten feet, two inches long.

The Rio del Rey in southwestern Cameroon was only a short distance from the British Niger Coast Protectorate, which was centered in the port of Calabar, the last African port of call for Mary on the 1893 trip. Here the *Rochelle* only called in to take on four hundred tons of oil. This took enough time, however, for Mary to make the acquaintance of Sir Claude MacDonald, the first governor of the newly established protectorate.

It was now mid-December and after several days in Calabar, the *Rochelle* departed once again and steamed northward, past Bonny and the Niger delta, the Bight of Benin, the Slave, Gold, Ivory, and Grain Coasts, round past Sierra Leone, and the western bulge of Senegal to Cape Verde and the Canaries. With each passing day they left the dazzling sun and terrific heat of West Africa farther and farther behind and with them all the grandeur of the equatorial rain forests and the four-banded beauty of the African coast.

In truth, it was no homecoming for Mary when she disembarked in the gray, chill drizzle of Liverpool one evening in early January. Returning to England, in fact, felt like a kind of exile. Most of her energies during the next twelve months would be devoted to returning once again to the Coast.

Exile in England

Jf you are susceptible to its spell, Mary later wrote in *Travels in West Africa*, West Africa "takes all the colour out of other kinds of living." This feeling was the most immediate and depressing legacy of her first voyage out in 1893. When she returned to London in the dead of winter in January 1894, her old life seemed almost unbearably dull and colorless. The sharp, cold winds, the dun-colored sky, the aloof, pinched, pale faces of passers-by on the street were all continual reminders of the contrasting African world she had left behind. Partly she was stunned by what we now call culture shock — by the omnibuses and hansom cabs and the din of their traffic, the daily newspapers, the multitude of shops, museums, galleries, and libraries, and all the other manifestations and appurtenances of "civilization." She swore never to ride one of the newfangled and enormously popular bicycles and warned others against them. She also avoided taxis and confided to one friend, "I am never quite happy on top of a bus." All these things gave her the "dazzles," as she complained in one letter.

But beyond the mental static wrought by feelings of culture shock was a more painful, abiding current of homesickness. In the cramped, dark rooms of the Addison Road flat, Mary was haunted by memories of her recent journey. "The charm of Africa," she explained in a lecture, "is a painful one. It gives you pleasure to fall under it when you are out there, but when you are back here, it gives you pain by calling you." This pain, she said, arose from visions "of a wall of dancing, white rainbow-gemmed surf playing on a shore of yellow sand before an audience of stately cocoa palms, or of a great mangrove-walled bronze

river, or of a vast forest cathedral, and you hear *nearer* to you than the
voices of the people round you, *nearer* than the roar of the city traffic,
the sound of that surf that is beating on the shore down there, and the
sound of the wind talking in the hard palm leaves, and the thump of
. . . tom-toms, or the cry of parrots passing over the mangrove swamps
in the evening time — and everything that is round you grows poor
and thin in the face of that vision, and you want to go back to the
Coast that is calling you, saying as the African says to the departing
soul of his dying friend, 'Come back, this is your home.'"

The flat at 100 Addison Road was not a home to her anymore, nor
could she consider Charley, recently returned from his own desultory
travels, her family. Mary stayed put in what had become for her an
alien environment, however, for the next eleven months until she departed once more for the Coast in December. And during this nearly
year-long interlude she tried to sustain the aura of her African life in a
number of small and large ways. She filled up the flat, for example,
with various African mementos: masks and woven country cloths, iron
and bronze armlets, amulets and charms of all sorts, and also a three-
foot-high carved "gentleman" named Muvungu who was covered in
dried blood and pierced with rusty nails. This striking figure, in fact,
was the first thing to greet callers who toiled up the stairs to the foyer
of the flat at the top of the house. She also kept the small flat heated
at most un-English, tropical temperatures, so that, as one friend described it, guests felt they were in a "vapour bath." As far as possible,
then, Mary tried to transform her cold, drab London rooms into a
West African bivouac.

It was not merely homesickness, however, that made Mary want to
keep alive her African experience in England. Africa had renewed, even
transformed her, and in the most radical possible ways. When she
departed for Africa she was a sheltered, reclusive, and awkward lady
"of a certain age," with little money and no prospects. What Mary
experienced and accomplished in Africa worked her metamorphosis.
Her modesty and chronic self-doubt persisted, but upon her return
from Africa she had to reckon with herself as an autonomous, self-
determining, and brave human being. It was impossible now to slip
back into the domestic servitude, the feminine self-immolation of her
pre-African life with Charley.

And so she defied this fate in part by creating a facsimile Africa in
the Addison Road flat, but also, and much more important, she sought
to protract or sustain her African life by writing about it. A writer

dwells in two worlds: on the one hand, the world of the clock and mealtimes and calls and the coal man and the post — the world one finds oneself physically inhabiting and growing old in; and on the other, the world of memory and dream and desire that one struggles to describe on paper. When Mary began writing about her African experience she was transported back to Africa, and so she energetically embarked on a lengthy account of her first voyage out, which she entitled "The Bights of Benin." The manuscript was woven together in part from the extensive diaries she kept on the 1893 trip and also from the letters she had written to and borrowed back from Violet Roy, though a good portion of the "Bights" was composed from scratch, as she reconstructed her journey in the small sitting room on Addison Road. In a remarkably short time, she had a large chunk of material to show to George Macmillan.

Mary began working on "The Bights of Benin" shortly after she returned to England in January, but she waited until August before broaching the subject of the book to her father's and uncles' publisher, George Macmillan. Somewhat hesitantly, she wrote Macmillan to inquire "if you would be likely to publish a book on the Bights of Biafra and Benin." It was Dr. Henry Guillemard, she hastened to add, who "tells me that I ought to make one out of journal or rather notes written for the benefit of my Cambridge friends — personally, I misdoubt that they are merely a mass of very curious information, as the old voyagers would say, never before published."

Though a wholly unsystematic writer, Mary was an extraordinarily fluent and prolific one. She never agonized over *mots justes* or wrestled with the most effective structural organization of her material. Instead, she tossed off pages with the reckless eloquence and élan of an Anthony Trollope or a Charles Dickens, almost never striking or revising passages. Despite all her protests that she was "no literary man" and that her books were mere "word swamps," Mary was an unselfconscious, effortless writer and one who was intoxicatingly readable. But like other kinds of inebriates, she had trouble discerning where and when to stop. George Kingsley's old Cambridge friend, Dr. Henry Guillemard, who helped edit *Travels in West Africa,* complained of the book's "undammable logorrhea of Kingsleyese," and, referring to one of its choicest anecdotes, insisted that when a "crocodile is coming over the stern of a canoe . . . he must not take six pages to do it, and . . . she must fetch him the necessary clip over the snout with a paddle in something under five minutes hard reading." Nor was it just in her published writing and lectures that Mary was excessively prolix; her personal correspondence was just as voluminous. A new acquaintance was stunned when Mary replied to a note with a ten-page letter, and when he protested that she had lavished on him material that a publisher would gladly pay for, she responded with six more pages and the explanation that "you pulled the string of a shower bath. . . . It is not everyone who can, but when he does who can, many pages of paper, half a gallon of ink, and writing no man can read without the support of swear words are his portion."

By December, shortly before she sailed for West Africa again, Mary had given Macmillan a narrative that covered her travels all the way down to the Bight of Biafra and southeastern Nigeria, including substantial sections on the Gold Coast and the Ivory Coast. She had, in addition, signed a contract with Macmillan that would give her half the profits on sales of the book, and the manuscript was near enough to completion for her to have a little skirmish with Macmillan over how its author should be identified. No doubt already imagining the "intrepid lady explorer" myth that would dog Mary's career, Macmillan made it clear that he wanted the gender of the author of "The Bights of Benin" clearly designated. Mary protested that "I really cannot draw the trail of the petticoat over the Coast of all places. Neither can I have a picture of myself in trousers or any other excitement of that sort." She preferred, she said, to publish the book anonymously, but if Macmillan insisted she use her name, she wanted to preface it with only her initials, identifying herself simply as M. H. Kingsley. "It does not matter to the general public what I am as long as I tell them the truth," she argued.

As it turned out, "The Bights of Benin" was never published at all, though large portions of it found their way in time into *Travels in West Africa* and *West African Studies* and into a number of Mary's lectures. What probably was the most important factor in her decision not to go ahead and publish it was what she had learned from the anthropological research she had been engaged in since her return from the 1893 journey. As originally conceived, "The Bights of Benin" was a fairly straightforward travelogue, with a good deal of miscellaneous ethnographic data and analysis thrown in along the way. As she pursued her reading in contemporary cultural anthropology, however, Mary must have been struck by the superficiality of her own observations and conclusions. Gradually, the conception of her book shifted from the "log of light-hearted lunatic," as she flippantly put it to Macmillan, to something far more ambitious and serious, and her reading convinced her that she had not seen and heard enough on the trip to fulfill this revised conception of the book. And so "The Bights of Benin" was scrapped, though as late as 1896 George Macmillan was still urging her to publish it and even went ahead and had the still uncompleted manuscript put into type: it came to about two hundred pages. But Mary was adamant in holding it back, dismissing it as "nothing but a series of notes," though she conceded it contained some of "the best stuff I have written."

Mary's anthropological studies had begun, of course, years earlier when she worked in her capacity as her father's research assistant. But during 1894 she set herself to master the new science of anthropology, which had come into existence, really, less than forty years earlier with the publication of Charles Darwin's *The Origin of Species* in 1859. (Mary herself was fully aware that Darwinism was the cornerstone of all contemporary anthropological thought, and more than once she referred to herself as a "Darwinian to the core.") In *Travels in West Africa* and *West African Studies* Mary gives an account of her course of study, prefacing it with the caveat to anyone else setting out to fathom West African culture to "burn all your notions about sun-myths and worship of the elemental forces. My own opinion," she adds, "is you had better also burn the notion, although it is fashionable, that human beings got their first notion of the soul from dreams." "Being a good Cambridge person," as she put it, she read Sir James Frazer's monumental and monumentally long *The Golden Bough* in its entirety but did not find it the "semi-universal key to the underlying idea of native custom" that she expected. Frazer's idea was "a true key to a certain quantity of facts, but in West Africa only to a limited quantity." And in her letters Mary goes even further in her criticism of what she calls "Frazerism." Instead of Frazer, Prof. (later Sir) Edward Burnett Tylor, the renowned Oxford anthropologist, became Mary's "great juju," as she described him, and his landmark book, *Primitive Culture*, became her bible; she instructs the reader in *Travels in West Africa* to "read [it] until you know it by heart." Other works Mary cites and praises in *Travels in West Africa* are today less well known than Frazer's and Tylor's: Edward Westermarck's *Human Marriage*, Theodor Waitz's *Anthropologie der Naturvölker*, which, of course, Mary was able to read in German, though she must have sought out translations of the French anthropologist Paul Topinard's *L'Anthropologie* and *Éléments d'anthropologie générale*. And finally, she read the specialized work done on West

Africa by A. B. Ellis, most notably his three-volume book, *The Tshi Speaking, Ewe Speaking, and Yoruba Speaking Peoples of the West Coast of Africa*. Ellis, indeed, became for Mary an intellectual ideal to emulate, for, as she said in *West African Studies,* "his books are . . . models of what books should be that are written by people studying native customs in their native land."

What Mary sought above all in these writers was a theoretical approach and methodology for her own study of West African religious belief (fetish) and law. She was, then, a cultural anthropologist but with comparatively little interest in such things as kinship and marriage and other kinds of social organization. And she was not in the least inclined toward physical anthropology, nor, as she said, "to go measuring peoples' skulls and chests . . . for no self-respecting person black or white," she added, "likes that sort of thing from the hands of an utter stranger, and if you attempt it you'll get yourself disliked in West Africa." No, what Mary wished to study in West Africa was not so much the social fabric of the culture or even how the people got on practically in day-to-day life, but rather what they lived *for,* what they believed *in* — their conception of and accommodation to the universe and the mystery of human existence. By focusing her attention on religion and law, she identified her interests as fundamentally spiritual and ethical ones, and these were at heart also highly personal interests. From the very beginning of the 1893 journey, Mary felt a profound sense of affinity with what she called "the black mind" and with animism, which struck a chord in her own austere pantheistic beliefs. For all her diligent study and the scientific meticulousness of her fieldwork (and she was one of the few early ethnographers actually to go out into the field rather than formulate theories in the cloistered libraries of Oxford or Cambridge), Mary was never really an objective or impartial scientist. Her need to find kindred spirits, as it were, and even to discover a spiritual home was too urgent and interfered with disinterested scientific inquiry. Hence when a fetish priest opened his mouth in Kacongo she heard familiar echoes of Spinoza or Goethe, the two major thinkers who had determined her own ontological vision. Thus it is more important to grasp how and why Mary found what she was seeking in West Africa than to assess historically her role and place in the development of cultural or social anthropology, as a forerunner, say, of Ruth Benedict or Margaret Mead. However much valuable scientific and ethnographic data Mary uncovered, she remained, above all and always, in quest of herself. And in time her major contribution as an ethnographer was her political role in colonial affairs: her overriding insistence that African culture be protected form the "smash" of British colonial policy.

At the same time she was vacillating over whether or not to publish "The Bights of Benin," Mary was still trying to put together the volume of her father's writings that Macmillan had proposed shortly after George Kingsley's death in 1892. She had gone carefully through her father's papers and retrieved and edited (and in some cases even completed) every article and lecture that might do for the volume, and she also combed through George's diaries and travel logs for more material. These essays and fragments ran the gamut from pieces on "Subglacial Angling," "Trout Tickling," and "Certain Delusions of the North Britons," to an article on Italian prisons that George had published in *Macmillan's* magazine and the log he kept of the solitary Mediterranean cruise he took in 1862 immediately after his marriage and Mary's birth. Lucy Toulmin Smith, who of course had known George Kingsley well, helped Mary with the editing and also read the proofs after Macmillan began putting the material into type. By the end of the year Mary and Lucy had selected, edited, and arranged the pieces that would eventually constitute *Notes on Sport and Travel*. But Charley, wrapped up as ever in his studies of Buddhism and other arcane matters, continued to make absolutely no progress on the introductory memoir of his father, and so the book remained maddeningly and indefinitely stalled.

In between work on "The Bights of Benin" and *Notes on Sport and Travel*, Mary also continued her ichthyological studies, under the tutelage of Albert Charles Günther, Keeper of the zoological department at the British Museum and author of Mary's other intellectual bible, *An Introduction to the Study of Fishes*. Mary's avowed purpose in going out to West Africa was to study "fish and fetish," and if E. B. Tylor was her "great juju," as she put it, for fetish, then Günther was her "great juju" or mentor for fish. He was one of those remarkably learned German scholars whose indefatigability proves crucial to other, more creative researchers. Darwin confessed to Günther, for example, that the sections of *The Descent of Man* devoted to fishes and reptiles "will be in fact yours, only written by me," and other scientists like Alfred Russel Wallace were equally indebted to Günther. Mary had probably originally found and read *The Study of Fishes* in her father's library, and it was her constant companion, as we have seen, on the 1893 trip. But though Günther was an old friend of her Uncle Charles, she had not yet met him personally. Upon her return from Africa she asked Charles's daughter, Rose Kingsley, to write her a letter of introduction to Günther. Shortly after, in February, Mary called on him at the new Natural History Museum in South Kensington. With considerable trepidation, she presented him with the specimens she had collected and carefully preserved in large, heavy bottles of spirit.

Günther was impressed with her collection, though somewhat dismayed perhaps by its haphazardness and by the amateurish preparation of the specimens. When she informed him of her intention to go out to West Africa the following year, he arranged for her to be equipped with a proper collector's outfit, and he also commissioned her to collect freshwater fish from the sparsely represented region between the Niger and Congo Rivers. For Günther kept the whole zoological globe in mind and was particularly eager to encourage travelers and collectors to bring home specimens from unknown or scantily studied regions. Thus Günther had a decisive influence on the area Mary was to claim as her own on her next journey: the Ogooué River in Congo Français, the largest river between the Niger and the Congo. The Ogooué is a mighty river running directly athwart the equator, and before it reaches the treacherous and spectacular rapids beyond Ndjolé, it is graced with a series of placidly beautiful freshwater lakes, brimming with fish unknown to the zoologists back at the British Museum.

Even more important than this encouragement from Günther was the new friendship Mary made this same year with Sir George Goldie, head of the Royal Niger Company. It is unclear exactly when and how they met, for Mary's social life was still essentially limited to her old Cambridge contacts, Violet Roy, Hatty Johnson, Henry Guillemard, and Lucy Toulmin Smith. She was not yet a habitué of the drawing rooms that Goldie, Cecil Rhodes, Frederick Lugard, and Lugard's future wife, the London *Times* writer on colonial matters, Flora Shaw, all frequented, drawing rooms that Mary would herself reluctantly and uneasily be visiting in a year or two's time. But somehow her path crossed Goldie's at some point in 1894, and it was a decisive meeting for many reasons.

Goldie was one of those singular and singularly gifted figures that the Victorian age threw up from time to time almost, it seems, to spite itself. Like George Kingsley, Goldie was a rebel, a wanderer, and an atheist, a handsome man with piercing blue eyes, a charismatic personality, particularly for women, and an atrocious temper. Born in 1846, he trained at the Royal Military Academy at Woolwich and obtained a commission with the Royal Engineers in 1865, which he resigned two years later. Then followed three years of travel in Egypt and the Sudan, much of the time in company with an Arab mistress. Shortly after his return to England in 1870, he ran off with his family's governess, Mathilda Elliot. The two fled to Paris, where unfortunately they were caught in the four-month seige of the city during the war between Prussia and Napoleon III. By the time Goldie and Mathilda were able to return to England they were, as one of Goldie's biographers put it, "unalterably compromised," so that Goldie, somewhat like George Kingsley before him, found himself virtually forced to wed a family employee.

Mathilda Elliot Goldie, however, was no Mary Bailey but was instead a handsome, gifted, high-spirited woman possessed of the same daring and ability to flout conventional society as her husband. She was indeed a match for Goldie, and though the marriage was not a faithful one on his side, it was a strong and enduring union. In addition, Mathilda Goldie became one of Mary Kingsley's dearest friends and one of the few women who was a match for Mary as well as for George Goldie. The two women understood each other, admired the misfit in each other, and, even more important, shared a common hunger for an intense life. Mathilda's life, after the dramatic commencement of her marriage, followed conventional lines, or lines as conventional as any life could with the mercurial Goldie. In time, they had two children, a son and a daughter. Mary's fate, in contrast, was solitary, husbandless and childless, and could not have been, of course, less conventional. But Mathilda was the only person Mary ever admitted had loved her; just as important, Mathilda was one of the few to sympathize and understand her.

It was perhaps fortunate that Mary was so close to Mathilda, for George Goldie was certainly her type, as indeed he was Flora Shaw's and numerous other women's. Goldie was a rebel, a stout Darwinian and follower of Huxley, an admirer of Ibsen and Wagner, and what's more, a man whose destiny for many years had been inextricably bound up with that of West Africa. Some seventeen years earlier, Goldie had first gone out to the Coast when his family bought a trading firm on the Niger River and put it into Goldie's hands. It is impossible to say now whether the Goldies were following that common Victorian method of dealing with family black sheep by sending them to the tropics or to some other insalubrious part of the world. In any event, Goldie survived the climate and saw that the new family enterprise would founder as long as cutthroat competition continued among a number of British firms on the Niger. The only solution was amalgamation and monopoly, followed by further penetration into the interior, which was being threatened in the north by the French.

By 1879 Goldie had succeeded in amalgamating the various commercial interests in the region into the United African Company, later to be turned into the National African Company, and finally, when a royal charter was granted to it in 1886 after the Berlin conference, the Royal Niger Company. This indirectly gave Britain control over the principal waterway in West Africa and in recognition of this fact Goldie was knighted in 1887 and became Sir George Goldie. The knighthood seems highly symbolic in retrospect, for the Royal Niger Company focused, even harnessed, Goldie's energies and gifts, and it also finally reconciled him with the society he had spent so much of his youth spurning. He became, indeed, a servant of Empire but of a rather peculiar and special sort, as Mary grasped. George Goldie was no Cecil Rhodes. When he turned over the Royal Niger Company territory to the British government in 1900 the governorship of the new crown colony was offered to him, and it was even suggested that the colony be named "Goldesia," in the mode of Rhodes's Rhodesia. Goldie rejected both offers out of hand. He had no taste for personal power or glory, as he made clear when he said late in life, "We (not I) bring our children up to think that fame, position, recognition by the public, are proper objects of human ambition. I loathe them all." Goldie was a capitalist and an imperialist — no longer pleasant sounding words — but he was also, as Mary understood, a humanitarian who wished to preserve and protect the peoples who inhabited the territory under his company's dominion.

This preserving, protective function of the Royal Niger Company was clearly stipulated in its charter. The only indigenous institution the company was authorized to interfere with was slavery, though even here its approach was moderate, for it was only enjoined "to discourage and gradually to abolish slavery." For the rest, the company was obligated "to tolerate the religion of the inhabitants and to uphold as far as possible their native laws and customs," especially those concerning marriage, inheritance, and land ownership, however much these might fly in the face of English mores. All of this provided a sharp contrast with France's policy in West Africa of military "pacification" and cultural assimilation.

The policy of the Royal Niger Company toward the peoples it governed was, in fact, a precursor of the doctrine of "indirect rule," which has become indissoluably associated with the name of Frederick Lugard. The essential idea here was that colonial powers should make use of existing social and political structures and institutions in order to govern their "dependencies" rather than impose alien British ones. In practice this meant that treaties were negotiated with African chiefs, and then the British governed the newly acquired territories through the existing chiefdoms and disrupted as little as possible the day-to-day life of the societies they ruled, all the while, of course, appropriating the region's rubber, palm oil, ivory, and other precious commodities to fill British coffers back home.

The system of indirect rule as it developed after Goldie was not, in fact, the product of altruistic humanitarianism but rather of good old English common sense. It was much easier and cheaper to use established African rulers and institutions than it would have been to bring in British personnel and resources to run African territories. It seemed better to work through the current chiefs than to bring out a contingent of district officers, most of whom would die of malaria or backwater fever in several months' time anyway. The beauty of the chartered company system, furthermore, was that it enabled England to gain vast territories without spending a penny, for the region was ruled by a private business corporation, not by the imperial government. The Royal Niger Company profits, along with the duties levied to defray the cost of administration, made the company virtually self-sufficient, for the time being at least.

No wonder Goldie was a hero at the Colonial Office. But for Mary his heroism lay in his refusal to tamper with the lives and culture of the peoples his company governed. And it was the example of the Royal Niger Company that sowed the seeds for Mary's later championship of trade rule in West Africa. Indeed, Goldie completes the great "juju" trinity that Mary established for herself during this interregnum year in England: Tylor for anthropology, Günther for fish, and Goldie for trade and politics. Goldie, on his side, was impressed with Mary and urged her to visit the Royal Niger Company territories and pursue "fish and fetish" there rather than in the Oil Rivers and Congo Français.

At the same time that Goldie was administering the Royal Niger Company in the hinterland, Mary's friend Sir Claude MacDonald, whom she had met in Calabar in 1893, was governing the Niger Coast Protectorate, a much smaller strip of land bordering the sea and to the east of the lands controlled by the Royal Niger Company. Relations between Goldie and MacDonald were not exactly cordial for several reasons, and Mary soon found that befriending both men put her in a rather delicate position. MacDonald was an army man who had fought in Egypt and served as consul general in Zanzibar. In 1889 he was appointed by the Foreign Office to go on a special mission to inspect the Niger territories, including those of the Royal Niger Company, and to prepare a report on the best method of administering them. In other words, he was sent out to West Africa to see how Goldie was getting on, which could scarcely have pleased the head of the Royal Niger Company.

Considering the era, MacDonald carried out this mission in a rather unusual way: he proceeded from the assumption that the wishes, ideas, and opinions of the Africans living in the Niger territories were of importance in making administrative decisions. And to determine these wishes, ideas, and opinions MacDonald made an extensive tour throughout the region and asked the people what form of government they preferred: a chartered company, crown colony, or Foreign Office protectorate. The option of self-government — of pulling out and letting the Africans take care of themselves as they had for centuries before the white man came — of course never occurred to him or to any other English person, including Mary. It was simply beyond British comprehension that they could trade with Africa just as they did with so-called civilized countries, by entering into equitable trade agreements, recognizing international boundaries, and so forth. Until well into the twentieth century, trade in Africa and in other countries inhabited by non-Caucasian peoples was always associated with conquest and Empire. But MacDonald's views, encompassing as they did African opinion, were for his day highly enlightened. On the basis of his tour MacDonald came to the conclusion that the crown colony system was the best form of government in West Africa, and it was largely as a result of his report that the Niger Coast Protectorate was formed in early 1891 and MacDonald himself appointed commissioner and consul general. Thus two very different systems of administration were in practice when Mary visited West Africa in 1893 and in 1895: that of the Royal Niger Company, monopoly, and indirect rule under Goldie in the hinterland, and that of the Niger Coast Protectorate, free trade, and direct rule on the coast. Mary's allegiance, even at this early date, was with the former. Trade rule, she was convinced, was the least damaging to African society and culture for the simple reason that traders' profits depended on the well-being of the African market; hence traders, Mary felt, would interfere least with the lives and culture of Africans. But at the same time Mary was highly impressed by Mac-Donald's responsiveness and concern for the wishes and needs of the people in his government protectorate.

MacDonald was still out in Calabar during 1894, but shortly after Mary arrived back in England she called on his wife, Ethel Mac-Donald, and the two soon became close friends, though not on the intimate terms Mary shared with Mathilda Goldie. Lady MacDonald was one of the early members of the species "Colonial Wife" that was soon to be scattered to the corners of the world as the British Empire burgeoned. Her career as a colonial wife had, in fact, begun before she married MacDonald in 1892, for she was the widow of an officer in the Indian Civil Service who had died of cholera along with their young children. Her photograph can still be found in the faded society pages of a popular turn-of-the-century tabloid, *Mainly About People:* a fair, tall, handsome woman with blue eyes and a round figure, who was, according to the accompanying profile of her, "an excellent hostess."

There would scarcely be much opportunity to entertain in Calabar, but Lady MacDonald was determined, as she soon informed Mary, to go out to West Africa and live with her husband. This was a highly unusual step for a West African colonial official's wife to take, both because of the deadliness of the climate on the Coast and because of the extreme privation and discomfort of day-to-day existence there for those who did somehow manage to survive. But the MacDonalds were virtually newlyweds and as yet childless, and Lady MacDonald must have found the protracted separation from her husband more unbearable than any hardship awaiting her in Africa. It was a bold move of hers to go out and join him, but Mary exaggerates Lady MacDonald's bravery when she claims in *Travels in West Africa* that Lady Mac-Donald's "courage in going to the coast was far greater than my own for she had more to lose had fever claimed her, and she was in those days by no means under the spell of Africa." Lady MacDonald's decision to join her husband may very well have been suggested by the example of Mary's own courage during the 1893 trip. At any rate, both she and her husband asked Mary to defer her departure until Lady MacDonald was due to sail in late December so that Mary could accompany her on the voyage. By this time Mary had, as she confessed, become Lady MacDonald's devoted admirer and "honorary aide-de-camp." And so of course she agreed, as she said, "to join her and make my time fit hers for starting on my second voyage."

Mary's stance in relation to Lady MacDonald was not atypical of her relations with other women. She revered her great jujus, Tylor, Günther, and Goldie, but her self-denigrating admiration of women such as Lady MacDonald, Mathilda Goldie, and later, Alice Stopford Green seems to have been caused by her own sense of feminine inadequacy. All of these women were or had been married; Lady MacDonald and Lady Goldie also had children. They were all handsome, charming women and gifted hostesses. They undoubtedly made Mary feel angular, awkward, and unwomanly. However certain she was of her own vocation as a traveler, ethnographer, and writer, and however much she longed for her "home" of West Africa, women like Lady Mac-Donald and Lady Goldie were a constant reminder of a feminine realm of love and sexuality and motherhood from which Mary was excluded. But at the same time, given the choice, she would surely have rejected the domestic conventionality of their lives. Unless she had found someone extraordinary on the order of George Goldie or had been fortunate enough to form a working partnership akin to that of her contemporaries Beatrice and Sidney Webb, it is impossible to imagine Mary as a wife. Her excessive praise of such women is of a mixed origin: she expresses genuine envy and regret on the one hand, but beneath this there is also a strain of mockery, perhaps even a sense of superiority. In her heart Mary must have known that Lady MacDonald was not more courageous than herself, and her apparent aside that Lady MacDonald was "by no means under the spell of Africa" is more damning than explanatory.

Mary delayed her departure, then, to suit Lady MacDonald. She also had to wait until Charley left for Singapore, and as usual, Charley's departure was a rather unsubstantial proposition. In the meantime, Mary continued to work late into the night on "The Bights of Benin" throughout the summer and autumn. And when there wasn't a sick relation or friend to nurse through some minor illness and the house was running smoothly and no morning callers were expected, she would often take the omnibus across town to Bloomsbury and spend the day reading ethnography in the domed sanctuary of the British Museum Reading Room. She continued to study E. B. Tylor, Ellis, and Sir Alfred Lyall, and also such German anthropologists and scholars as Kohler, Baumann, Buckholtz, Burkhardt, and Habbe Schleiden. It was bracing as well as taxing to read them all in the original, and when in difficulties she returned again and again to them, she said, "instinctively . . . because of the patience and soundness of their work."

Her reading further increased her doubts about "The Bights of Benin" and made her even more impatient to return to West Africa so that she could do the necessary fieldwork that would transform it into the ethnographically sound and valuable work she now wished to produce. She sought during this year to become a member of the "tribe" of anthropologists she most admired: Tylor, Ellis, Bastian, and Habbe Schleiden, and others "who study the African more than we study the geography of his country." These scholars had actually made commerce between Europe and Africa possible "because you cannot trade without a knowledge of the way of customers." Furthermore, as Mary saw it, the ethnographers' tribe was the only hope for sound and humane government in West Africa, for, as with trade, you cannot "govern without a knowledge of the nature of those for whom you legislate."

As the days became shorter and colder in October and November, Mary longed more and more to be back on the Coast with all its blazing heat and brilliant sunlight. For she would be returning this time not in "the wet" but in the middle of the West African dry season, when there is not a drop of rain for weeks on end and the sky is a brilliant azure blue, cloudless and unmarred except for the huge gold globe of the equatorial sun. In these closing months of the year, though Charley's and Lady MacDonald's moves were still disconcertingly vague, Mary began to make definite arrangements of her own to leave. Her own preparations this time were far simpler and less time consuming than they were in 1893. She knew now precisely what she needed and what she did not, and she was not distracted by a barrage of well-meaning but worthless advice. Günther had provided her with a proper collector's outfit, and she now knew which trade items were most popular and fetched the most rubber and ivory. She was returning home this time, not venturing into the unknown.

She was also returning without the financial constraints of the first journey. George Macmillan had made it abundantly clear that he was eager to publish and promote whatever she turned over to him. Hence she felt freer to spend what she had on hand, and she also saw that she could stay out in West Africa longer this time — up to a whole year in fact if she wanted. But financial security meant only prolongation of her second trip. Mary had no intention of using up her money in order to travel in a less rugged and hazardous way. She would carry on precisely as she had on her first trip, traveling "very hard . . . tentless, and living on native food," as she described it to Macmillan. No amount of money would ever persuade her to engage an entourage of African guides and bearers or to carry along cases of tinned food, a portable rubber bath, camp bed, or any of the other standard paraphernalia with which other white travelers in Africa equipped themselves. Mary did not even possess such standard colonial uniform items as a solar topi and mosquito boots.

But if Mary herself pared down her personal equipment to the absolute minimum, once others heard that she was returning to the Coast they showered her with things and messages to take back with her for their friends and relations. She wrote Hatty Johnson how "I am at present requested to see three men's mothers in three separate suburbs. I know what seeing men's mothers means by now having already done several. 'Does my son get on well with his local pastor?' 'Does he wear flannels next to his skin,' etc. . . . . A missionary's wife implores me to get 'three pairs of old fashioned braces, you know the sort' (as if I were at least neolithic) 'with no connecting straps and some cucumber seeds, the others wear Alfred's shirts out so.' Fortunately for the purchase of these articles, it is not needful for me to know whether it's the braces or the seeds that destroy the garments." A former trader asked Mary to buy £1.16 worth of toys for his half-caste daughter. By mid-December Mary was writing Günther that "I am getting rather nervous about my luggage which now includes a tombstone and several pairs of embroidered slippers and many other things entrusted to me to deliver to widely scattered individuals."

As the foggy London winter of 1894 set in, Mary's mood must have been one of impatient expectation. At last Charley bestirred himself and set off for Singapore. And then Lady MacDonald completed all her arrangements to go out and join her husband, and she and Mary were finally able to book their passage. The *Batanga,* captained by Mary's old friend from the *Lagos,* Captain John Murray, was scheduled to sail just three days before Christmas, on December 22. Mary and Lady MacDonald took the train to Liverpool on the twenty-first in good time for the departure, but a fierce storm came up on the twenty-second with such a strong gale that the dock gates could not be opened, so the *Batanga* was unable to leave. The bad weather also made it impossible for the ship's cannon powder to be taken on board, a loss, Mary says, that "nearly broke the carpenter's heart, as it robbed him of the pleasure of making that terrific bang with which a West Coaster salutes her ports of call."

On Sunday, December 23, however, the day broke fine and clear, and the *Batanga* set sail on the icy waters of the North Atlantic. Mary's heart must have lifted along with the ship's anchor. After a year of writing and study and yearning, she was finally, as she put it in one lecture, "homeward bound."

Part Three

I speak of Africa and golden joys.

Shakespeare

⋅ೕ 7 ೕ⋅

The Third Voyage Out

There is a painting by Toulouse-Lautrec dated 1895 entitled *La Passagère* of a woman with blond, upswept hair sitting on shipboard in a striped deck chair, intently gazing out to sea. The year, the golden hair, and the profile reflecting both absorption and expectation all conjure up a vivid image of Mary Kingsley en route to West Africa on the *Batanga* in the opening days and weeks of the new year. Mary, however, was seldom found passively lounging on deck. She could sometimes be persuaded to sit and relax, especially if she was writing a letter or mending a skirt hem. But for a good deal of the time Mary was standing against the deck rail, scanning the horizon for sight of the Canaries or Cape Verde or the coast itself. And especially during the early days of their voyage, Lady MacDonald was continually summoning Mary to observe "all sorts of marine objects overboard," which Mary would obediently admire, inwardly thinking "it would be the death of me if I had to work like this, explaining meanwhile aloud that 'they were very interesting but Haeckel had done them, and I was out after fresh-water fishes from a river north of the Congo this time,' fearing all the while that she felt me unenthusiastic for not flying over into the ocean to secure the specimens."

At the same time that she was trying to appreciate the fish Lady MacDonald pointed out to her, Mary was also carrying out preliminary investigations for what she termed a "natural history of mariners." In 1893 on the *Lagos*, the human organisms that had absorbed her attention had been the other passengers — the government officials and the traders. This time, on the *Batanga*, she took more notice of the crew, whom she found "valuable beings and their habits . . . exceedingly interesting." In *West African Studies* she delivered up her findings in a mock-ethnographical manner as she described with scientific precision the various members of the ship's company, their hierarchy, and peculiar signifying marks, just as she would later catalogue and explain all the salient traits of the Bubis on Fernando Po, the Igbo in Calabar, or the Galoa in Gabon.

"The sailor officer *(Nauta pelagius vel officialis)* is," she reported, a "metamorphic" creature. The particular stage of his metamorphosis, or the peculiar evolutionary niche an officer holds in the ship's scale, "is easily determined by the band of galoon round his coat cuff; in the English form the number of gold stripes increasing in direct ratio with rank. . . . The English third officer, you will find, has one stripe, the second two, the first three, and the . . . captain, four, the upper one having a triumphant twist at the top." The *Batanga,* of course, was a British ship, so the rank of all its officials from Captain Murray downwards was immediately discernible by the number of gold braided stripes they literally wore on their sleeves. In addition to the galloon stripes, some men were seen to sport red, white, or blue velvet bands on their cuffs, but inquiries soon yielded the information that these insignia identified the wearers as the doctor, purser, and chief engineer respectively, men who were not properly "marine organisms" at all, as Mary put it, "but more akin to the amphibia."

With this cuff-band key to rank worked out, Mary could easily assess the importance of the various individuals seated with her and Lady MacDonald round the captain's table at supper time. But in *West African Studies* she goes beyond description to analysis; she details the habits and activities as well as the appearance of her subjects. The third officer, she observed, "is a hard-working individual who has to do anything that the other officers do not feel inclined to, and therefore rarely has time to wash." The second officer is "the slave of the hatch," while the first is obsessed, above all, with the complexion of the deck. The captain has his mind on loftier spheres and takes no notice of the ship's "household affairs" at all.

The relations among these various functionaries could be both complex and troubled. The captain expected men and nations to sympathize with him if he had "a bad First." "It is almost unnecessary to remark," Mary said, "that the relationship between the first officer and the Chief Engineer" — men of equal power but different rank — "is rarely amicable." And the cook "although he always had a blood feud on with the engineer concerning coals for the galley fire, which should endear him to the first officer, is morally a greater trial to him than he is to his other victims."

One of the most remarkable characteristics of these *Batanga* officers was their superstitious reliance upon red velvet slippers when in difficulties, especially when literally in dire straits. Their belief in the talismanic power of this particular footgear was demonstrated shortly after the ship left Sierra Leone on January 8 when it reached the shoals of Saint Ann. First Captain Murray and then the chief and second officers all donned red slippers, which to Mary's initiated eyes seemed to blaze "like danger signals at the shore ends of all three" men's feet. She explained the significance of the footgear to the other baffled passengers, mentioning that "like all great discoveries," hers "was founded on observation made in a scientific spirit." She had noticed whenever a particularly difficult bit of navigation presented itself, it was negotiated in red velvet slippers — when they ran into heavy weather going into Puerto de la Luz rounding the Almadia reefs, and most recently, as they had seen, entering Freetown harbor in a dense fog. And subsequent events in the Bights of Biafra and Benin on this journey bore out Mary's deductions of the navigational efficacy of red velvet slippers: "We picked up rivers in them, always wore them when crossing bars, and did these things on the whole successfully." Only when they were rash enough to go up the Rio del Rey without their protection did they get into trouble. The *Batanga* got stranded on a sandbank and Mary swore would be there still, its "crew and passengers mere mosquito-eaten skeletons, had not the first officer rushed to his cabin, put on red velvet slippers and gone out in a boat, energetically sounding around with a hand lead."

After calling in briefly at the Canaries, the *Batanga* proceeded to Sierra Leone where a Wesleyan missionary named Dennis Kemp and his wife came on board. The Kemps were on a recuperative holiday away from their mission in the Gold Coast where Mrs. Kemp had very nearly died of fever. Just why they chose Sierra Leone, the White Man's Grave, as the site for her recovery is unclear. But her health did miraculously improve there, and the Kemps and Mary became well acquainted during the six-day run from Freetown to the Kemps' mission at Cape Coast. And who should Mary run into at the Cape Coast pier but James Henly Batty, the friendly Gold Coast trader and future

husband of Violet Roy who had persuaded Mary to go to West Africa
when she first met him at the Canaries after her parents' deaths in
1892.

It seemed perfectly natural that Mary and Lady MacDonald should
spend the night and the following day with the Kemps before proceed-
ing to Accra. The Kemps' Wesleyan mission was the largest and most
influential Protestant mission in West Africa. In 1895 Mary became
the guest of and fast friends with a number of British and French
missionaries, the first of these being the energetically hospitable Kemps.
But such friendships put her in a peculiar position: she came to rely on
these people almost as much as she had on the traders in 1893, and,
as we shall see in the cases of Mary Slessor in Calabar and Rober Nassau
in Gabon, she admired some of them enormously. And with Mary
Slessor she also established a rare intimacy that she never knew with
her trader-heroes or with government officials.

The awkwardness of Mary's situation with the missionaries — even
with the best and most enlightened of them — lay in the fact that she
felt that even more than the Colonial Office, they were out to "murder" African culture, and that far from being the Black Man's "savior,"
they were often agents of unalloyed destruction. In her letters Mary
also damned their cant and smug self-righteousness. She attacked the
kind of cant, for example, that spurred one Church Missionary Society
member to try to prevent Mary from going to nurse a solitary white
trader "ill unto death with fever [who] . . . had been neglected for
days with those other white Christians close by." The missionary protested that it was not "respectable" for her to go to the sick man's aid,
but, as Mary wrote a friend, "of course I went and I never forget or
forgive anything that vexes me and not a single Church Missionary
Society house door will I ever darken" again. Other Noncomformist
and Catholic doors she did continue to frequent but always somewhat
reluctantly and uneasily. A good deal of *Travels in West Africa* consists
of an attack on West African missions, and though Mary saved many
of her worst salvos for an appendix misleadingly entitled "Trade and
Labour in West Africa," even in her description of her Gold Coast
sojourn she does not entirely spare the Kemps' Wesleyan operations.

One thing the Wesleyans were doing on the Gold Coast that she
did approve of was introducing technical instruction to their educational programs. Indeed one of Mary's main axes to grind with missionaries was this: that the "civilization" they brought was inappro-
priate, consisting as it did primarily of Western academic education,

European dress, and so forth. And even when practical skills were taught in mission schools, they often were, as Mary put it, "arts of no immediate or great use in the present culture condition of West Africa," such as printing, bookbinding, and tailoring for men, while women learned such domestic accomplishments as embroidery and ironing, again not terribly useful activities in the standard West African family where clothing, pillowcases, handkerchiefs, and table linen were not common household articles. The Wesleyans, to their credit, Mary found, were introducing truly valuable technical instruction in smith's work, carpentering, bricklaying, and wagon building, but they were not offering, alas, the most needed technical instruction on improved agricultural methods and plantation work.

After inspecting the mission, the Kemps took Mary and Lady MacDonald on a tour of the town. Cape Coast was and remains a lovely city, surrounded by the three old Danish forts, later renamed by the British Victoria, William, and MacCarthy, each perched on top of a small hill overlooking the town. These forts, the castles of Cape Coast and of its satellite town of Elmina nine miles west of Cape Coast, and the new "Afro-Gothic" Wesleyan cathedral all bestowed on the place an "appearance of permanent substantialness so different from the usual ramshackledom of West Coast settlements." Perhaps one should qualify *ramshackledom* with the adjective *manmade.* There was nothing insubstantial or impermanent about the magnificent natural world of West Africa — its mountains, dense forests, and mighty rivers. Instead, it was the puny edifices humans had erected in the midst of the enduring works of nature which seemed doomed to perpetual dilapidation and decay.

Guarded by the Kemps, Mary and Lady MacDonald visited the vast stone Cape Coast Castle and Fort William, both of which, however, defied the usual West African fate of decay. It was a blazing hot day, but the party inspected both structures thoroughly. They climbed from the cool, tunnel-like slave barracoons, where captured Africans had been imprisoned until they were shipped off to the United States or to the West Indies, up to the top of Fort William, from which they were rewarded by a stunning view of the town and its patchwork of solid stone buildings jumbled up with mud and thatch houses and of Elmina and its own castle. And beyond the town lay the white surf wall and the brilliant blue sea, with the *Batanga* in the distance rolling to and fro on the long, regular sea swell. After their tour, Mary and Lady MacDonald returned to the mission, where they spent the night with

the Kemps before departing the next morning for the short run east to
the Gold Coast colony of Accra.

Accra too had its own substantial fort, and Christianborg Castle
overlooked it. Though larger than Cape Coast, Accra struck Mary as a
flimsy, unimpressive place: "a mass of rubbishy mud and palm-leaf
huts and corrugated iron dwellings for the Europeans." "Corrugated
iron," she laconically explained, "is my abomination." And no wonder: it turns houses into veritable ovens by day and into cold boxes by
night; it magnifies the sound of rain to the extent of making sleep
impossible by night and conversation virtually so by day; and it rusts
up and then peels rust almost as soon as it has been nailed into place.
And yet corrugated iron remains up to the present day the most ubiquitous building material in West Africa. In Mary's time it was largely
reserved for Europeans' dwellings; given all its drawbacks, it is not
entirely surprising that she was relieved when she found traders or
missionaries in the interior who were deprived of her "abomination"
and lived snugly, comfortably, and quietly in mud brick and thatch
houses.

In Accra, however, Mary and Lady MacDonald were the guests of
the governor, Sir Brandford Griffiths, whose residence was the massive
stone Christianborg Castle. After disembarking at Accra, Mary and
Lady MacDonald were transported to Christianborg by rickshaw, lo-
cally called a go-cart. These vehicles were pulled in front by one pair
of men and pushed by another pair from behind, something of a surplus of manpower, it would seem, given the slender dimensions of
Mary and Lady MacDonald. Not only were the go-carts overstaffed,
but the bearers were absurdly overdressed in the government uniform
of white jackets, knee breeches, and crimson cummerbunds. The last
caused no end of trouble on the sea-skirting road from Accra to Christianborg because the cummerbunds had no secure fastening and would
not stay put. Several times in the course of the two mile-journey "the
governmental cumberbunds" unraveled, "wound riskily round the legs
of their running wearers [and] we had to make halts while one end of
the cumberbund was affixed to a tree-trunk and the other end to the
man, who rapidly wound himself up in it again with a skill that spoke
of constant practice."

Christianborg Castle proved to be a large, solid, Danish-built edi-
fice. The go-carts entered by a sentry-guarded gate, and to the left of
the central courtyard Mary and Lady MacDonald espied evidence of Sir
Brandford's favorite hobby: a select little garden of Eucharis lilies and

other exotic plants in tubs. If she had failed to realize it before, Mary would have grasped now that as long as she was with Lady MacDonald she was destined to travel in the acme of West African comfort and style. But even Sir Brandford with his lilies could not entirely shut out the reality of West Africa from Christianborg Castle. The castle was perched on a hill overlooking the sea with the result that the surf spray penetrated every chink and cranny of the building. "Hence the place is mouldy — mouldy to an extent," Mary said, that "I with all my experience in that paradise for mould, West Africa, have never else-where seen." The floor carpets and mats wore a light glaze of it; the veneer hung off the furniture in strips, and "the looking glasses too were in a sorry plight." Because of the mold, "you only saw yourself in sections in them." This, of course, made shaving a rather hazardous operation. Mary noticed that one government official was liberally done up with sticking plaster about the jaw, "which I mentally put down to a shaky hand until I had trouble with my back hair with those governmental mirrors. One must never judge a fellow creature un-kindly, especially on the Gold Coast," she concluded.

The proximity of the sea also meant that inhabitants of the castle were continually subjected to the sound of its waves unendingly pounding on the shore. Social gatherings at tea and after dinner were held on a long verandah facing the ocean, the ladies seated in a hard and fast line of chairs along the wall while the men hung about or lounged and smoked cigars on the verandah rail. Conversation was difficult, what with the ceaseless roar of the surf. Mary describes a typical exchange with one young man who observed to her that

"You should have been here last week."
"Eh?"
"You should have been here last week when we had the races."
"Oh! You have a race-meeting?"
"Yes, we have a regular race-course, you know."
Then details regarding the races which you don't quite catch, but say "Indeed," "Really though!" "That must have been very nice," at random, and get regarded as being sympathetic, and are rewarded with more details. Another individual whose name you do not catch is intro-duced. He says something. You say,
"Eh?"
He says, "You should have been here last week when we had our races." Then come details as before and so on, *da capo,* throughout the evening.

What Mary fails to mention about the difficulties of conversing on the verandah of Christianborg Castle is the utter banality of the discussion "you don't quite catch." It is colonial conversation: the races last week and the new cathedral and who is due to go on or return from leave. We clearly sense, as Mary must have, that whatever she may not have caught, she had not really missed much.

Sir Brandford and Lady Griffiths and their governmental circle into which Mary was brought by Lady MacDonald lived an isolated existence on the Coast, as transplanted and out of place as their Eucharis lilies in the courtyard. This was not the case with another government official whom Mary met when she strolled out beyond the castle grounds to the nearby Christianborg cemetery the next day. This gloomy man guided her about the graves of all the Europeans who had succumbed to the climate and confessed that he walked there every afternoon "so as to get used to the place before staying permanently in it. . . .

"He took me across the well-kept grass to two newly dug graves, each covered with wooden hoods in a most business-like way. Evidently these hoods were regular parts of the cemetery's outfit. He said nothing, but waved his hand with a take-your-choice,-they-are-both-quite-ready style. 'Why?' I queried laconically. 'Oh! we always keep two graves ready dug for Europeans. We have to bury very quickly here, you know,' he answered. I turned at bay. I had had already a very heavy dose of details of this sort that afternoon." Mary remonstrated, " 'It's exceedingly wrong to . . . frighten people to death. You can't want new dug graves daily. There are not enough white men in the whole place to keep the institution up.' 'We do,' he replied, 'at any rate at this season. Why, the other day we had two white men to bury before twelve o'clock and at four, another dropped in on a steamer.' " And to confirm the official's veracity, Mary adds that just after she left Accra there was all along the Gold Coast "one of those dreadful epidemic outbursts sweeping away more than half the white population in a few weeks."

The two wooden-hooded graves seem a metaphor, in fact, for what Mary rather understatedly called the "grim realities" of life on the Coast. She wandered through a variety of West African worlds on her travels: the insipid one of colonial government life, such as that at Christianborg Castle; the missionaries' and traders' worlds; her favorite world of the unadulterated, "raw" African village in the bush; and the realm of physical beauty she found both on the magnificent coastline on the west side of the continent and in the immense equatorial forests in the interior. And finally there was the paramount reality of the world of Death, which underlay all these other realms. Death and Beauty, Beauty and Death, are the two inextricably intertwined motifs in everything Mary wrote about the Coast. Both yielded intensity; they were two sides of the same precious West African coin.

Death had many faces in West Africa, but lurking behind all of them was a kind of Conradian horror, the horror that made Mary — very uncharacteristically — "turn at bay" at the sight of the wooden-hooded graves. Years before Conrad, in fact, she wrote explicitly of how this "horror could get a grip" on one "out there," and cited as an example the case of a young English bookkeeper who had been forced by family reverses to take a situation at a tiny outpost, not even a real settlement, in the Bights, a young man, moreover, who had never before been outside the English country town where he was born. His ship merely dropped him on the factory beach and then departed. He was met by a contingent of nearly naked, friendly Kru, with whom, however, he found it impossible to communicate.

He approached the house of the agent he had come to serve under, looked into the dining room and onto the verandah, and when there was no response sat down and waited for someone to turn up. Sundry Africans did and said a good deal that the young bookkeeper could not understand, and finally he made a bolder tour of the verandah, "and noticed a most peculiar noise in one of the rooms and an infinity of flies going into the Venetian shuttered window. Plucking up courage, he went in and found what was left of the white Agent, a considerable quantity of rats, and most of the flies in West Africa." He did not die of shock from this but instead fell ill of fever and was taken off a fortnight later by a French ship the Kru signaled to come pick him up.

Mary had only heard of this agent and the bookkeeper. There was no way of knowing what exactly had killed the first or whether the poor young Englishman ever regained his balance once he returned to England. But on this same journey in 1895 Mary had a firsthand encounter with another "sad case." When she reached Gabon, she met a twenty-year-old French "boy-agent," as she described him, at Osoamokita on the Ogooué — a bright, intelligent, outgoing, but clearly lonely boy — whom she learned later committed suicide shortly after they visited him. This news left Mary depressed for days. She understood too well the peculiar nature of "the horror" that gripped and destroyed such sensitive men. It was the insupportable isolation of their position, in part, buried as they were deep in the forest, without seeing another white face for months on end other than the one in their looking glass, men who lived day in and day out with only "the one set of objects — the forest, the river, and the beach, which in a place like Osoamokita you cannot leave for months at a time, and of which you soon know every plank and stone." This staggering isolation seemed to swallow up the ego and all sense of self; monotony and tedium fed despair, and finally suicide must have appeared to such men as an affirmation of self rather than as an act of self-annihilation.

From Accra the *Batanga* sailed directly to Calabar where Lady Mac-Donald was at last joyfully reunited with her husband. She and Mary were "gorgeously" welcomed in Calabar by the entire white and black settlement and treated to a dazzling fireworks display in their honor. But Mary had scarcely set foot on land again when she sailed off once more for the neighboring island of Fernando Po with the MacDonalds. Sir Claude had some pressing business to transact there with its Spanish governor, Lady MacDonald did not want to be separated from him so soon after their reunion, and Mary was eager to accompany him and see again the island she had briefly visited in 1893. So they almost immediately re-embarked on the *Batanga,* which was to call at Fernando Po before turning around and beginning the northward journey home to England.

Fernando Po lies only nineteen miles off the mainland of West Africa. At thirty-three miles across and seventeen wide, it is the largest of all the islands on the West Coast, and is also, as Mary insisted, the most beautiful. Like its smaller sister islands, São Tomé and Principe, it is a slumbering volcanic mass with many craters, and it culminates in the magnificent cone of Clarence Peak. As they approached it on the *Batanga* from the north, the mountain presented itself, as the Canaries had, as an "entirely celestial phenomenon." Indeed, Mary wrote that it looked "like an immense single mountain that has floated out to sea, . . . a fairy island made of gold or of amethyst" in the brilliant sunlight. "Its moods of beauty" seemed to her "infinite; for the most part gentle and gorgeous, but I have seen it silhouetted hard against tornado clouds, and grandly grim. . . . And as for Fernando Po in full moonlight — well there! You had better go and see it yourself."

The dilapidated island port of Clarence where they landed con-

trasted sharply with the elemental grandeur of the island as a whole.*
Clarence, as Mary bluntly put it, was "the very dullest town . . . on
the Coast," and we should bear in mind with this judgment that it
took very little in the way of natural or acquired attributes to make
Mary enthusiastic about any West Coast settlement. But Clarence was
hopeless. In 1893 she had found it "in a flutter of expectation and
alarm not untinged with horror" over the imminent advent of a café.
This prospect boded ill, suggesting that "Clarence, nay the whole of
Fernando Po, was about to become so rackety and dissipated as to put
Paris and Monte Carlo to the blush." When they disembarked in late
January of 1895 Mary quickly grasped that the café alarm had been a
false one: "Clarence was just as sound asleep and its streets as weed-
grown as ever, although the cafe was open." She suspected that "the
sleepiness of the place infected the cafe and took all the go out of it."
In any event, she reported, "the cafe smoulders like a damp squib."

According to Mary, it took between ten minutes and a quarter of an
hour to exhaust the charms of Clarence — that is, to stroll down its
main street and visit the fly-blown café. She then applied to several of
the locals for other sights to see and was told by each and all "to go
and see the coals." Between 1827 and 1858 the island had been in
English hands, on loan from Spain as a naval station for the British
ships attempting to eliminate the slave trade in the region. The coals
Mary was urged to and obediently did visit were the remains of a stock
for English men-of-war that were left on the island when the naval
station was removed and Fernando Po returned to the Spanish. For the
past forty years these coals had moldered there, and Mary prophesied
that "the end of it will be that some few thousand years hence there
will be a serious quarrel among geologists on the strange pocket of coal
on Fernando Po, and they will run up continents and raise and lower
oceans to explain them and they will doubtless get more excitement
and pleasure out of them than you can nowadays."

They were not due to go to government headquarters at Basile until
the next day, and so, having utterly exhausted the tourism possibilities
of Clarence, Mary spent the rest of the afternoon visiting cocoa farms,
wandering the shoreline beyond the town, and wading through coves
and across dwarf rivers emptying into the sea. She also passed through
a number of highly "crocodiley-looking" spots but met no crocodiles

---

*Today Clarence is called Malabo. It is the capital of Equatorial Guinea, which consists of Fernando
Po, now called Bioko, and the mainland square of land in between Cameroon and Gabon known as
Mbini or Rio Muni.

and so concluded that Fernando Po was devoid of them because "it is the habit of these animals when they are handy to the sea, to lounge down and meet the in-coming tide." She did, however, encounter a number of wild pigs — the peculiar West African kind that seem to be about three-quarters head and the remaining quarter tail. These Fernando Po pigs were descendants of domesticated ones raised in Clarence that had become a municipal nuisance to such an extent that the government served notice that "all pigs without rings in their noses" — that is, pigs on the loose and free to wreak havoc in back gardens — "should be forthwith shot if found abroad." "This proclamation," as Mary recounts it, "was issued by the governmental bellman thus: 'I say — I say — I say — I say. Suppose pig walk — iron no live for him nose! Gun shoot. Kill him one time. Hear re! hear re!' " Nevertheless, despite this warning, "a good many pigs with no iron living in their noses got adrift and escaped into the interior, and . . . flourished like the green bay-tree."

The following day Mary accompanied Sir Claude and Lady MacDonald to the mountain town of Basile, where the government headquarters had been moved in the belief that it was healthier than Clarence. The Spanish governor, "a delightful person," in Mary's view, who was quite fluent in English, had had the seat of government removed literally to higher spheres when he was appointed governor of Fernando Po and arrived to find that his own immediate predecessor had died of fever.

The major problem of moving up to Basile was to get on with business at such a distance from the port, and so the governor had a telephone run up to him from Clarence through the forest, "and Spain at large felt proud of this dashing bit of enterprise in modern appliance." But telephones in West Africa to this day tend to be more decorative than functional, and this was certainly the case in Fernando Po in 1895. The leaves and branches of the forest tapped and brushed on the line to the extent "that a human being could not get a word in edgeways." So the governor ordered that a road be constructed along the telephone line to keep the trees off it, but the islanders themselves became interested in the line and began pilfering wire from it for their own use, the result being that "the Governor is thus liable to be cut off at any moment in the middle of a conversation with Clarence, and the amounts of 'Hellos,' 'Are you theres?' and 'Speak louder pleases' in Spanish that must at such times be poured out and wasted in the lonely forests before the break is realised and an unfortunate man sent off as a messenger, is terrible to think of."

Besides the governor, Mary and the MacDonalds found a surprisingly large number of white inhabitants on Fernando Po, though not of the colonial, racecourse set they had met on the Gold Coast. Up at Basile, the governor had helped to settle what Mary described as "the most unfortunate set of human beings I have ever laid eyes on" — the remnant of a group of Spanish colonists who had formerly been living in Morocco and who then moved to the no less deadly climate of Fernando Po when they began dying in great numbers in North Africa. In addition to these pathetic settlers, trying to eke out a living on small farms and plantations, there was a remarkably large contingent of Roman Catholic priests: fifty-four of them, in fact, which was two more than the fifty-two Spanish colonists. And in addition to the priests there were several Methodist missionaries left over from British days and also, Mary reported, "a white gentleman who had invented a new religion."

None of these could have made for very exciting society, but Mary was eager to escape official white circles in any case. The inhabitants of Fernando Po who interested her most were the indigenous ones, a people called the Bubi. Fernando Po and the Bubis were then, and remain today, what anthropologists call an "understudied" place and people. After serving as English consuls to the island, both T. J. Hutchinson and Richard Burton had produced some interesting but fragmentary observations on them, but Mary's only real predecessor in studying the Bubi was the German anthropologist Oscar Baumann, who wrote *Eine Africanische Tropen Insel Fernando Poo*, a work to which Mary liberally acknowledges her debt.

Before getting down to the Bubis themselves in *Travels in West Africa*, Mary gives a careful and detailed account of the physical, geographical, botanical, and climatic characteristics of the island and also a short history of the English and Spanish occupation of it. But her primary scientific interests are anthropological ones, and in the course of her short stay on Fernando Po Mary did fieldwork that produced remarkable results, for there is little in Bubi life and culture that she fails to cover. The nearly twenty pages she produces on them are, indeed, a kind of model ethnographical study of a little-known ethnic group.

The Bubis were particularly rewarding "anthropological material" because they continued to live in their "raw" state, as Mary liked to put it, uncontaminated by white culture despite the fifty-four Spanish priests lurking in Clarence and Basile. The Bubis lived in a number of small villages scattered over the island, and while Sir Claude and Lady MacDonald remained at the governor's residence in Basile, Mary spent her days in Fernando Po visiting these villages and gleaning as much information as she could about Bubi life. Much could be learned about the Bubis through simple if patient observation: their physical appearance; clothing; body decoration (wooden earrings and python bone, feather, and teeth jewelry, body painting, and facial scarring); the wooden, thatch-roofed housing in Bubi villages; the way the villages were surrounded by stake "hedges" for protection from other Bubis and from animals; the absence of ironworking and reliance upon stone implements; a local coinage or currency consisting of shells (coinage was a rarity in most West African societies); an economy based on hunting and fishing more than on agriculture; development of crafts such as pottery and basketwork; and also the construction and variety of Bubi musical instruments.

All these things Mary was able to report on from firsthand experience. In other areas, however, she had to fall back on Baumann, for one cannot work up an analysis of complex spiritual beliefs, government, and legal systems in the course of a few days' visit. And yet from Baumann and from Hutchinson's *Ten Years' Wandering among the Ethiopians* and from two other obscure Polish authorities on the island, Mary was able to round off her profile of the Bubis with information on secret societies, initiation rites, charms, and the connection between the chief god and the chief ruler of the Bubis. The Bubi people believed that they originated in the crater at the top of Clarence Peak, and this crater is also the home of their chief god or spirit, O Wassa. His chief priest is the king of all Bubis, a ruler named Moka, whom no white man nor even a non-Bubi African is allowed to gaze upon. Beneath Moka are the individual village chiefs, a number of whom Mary met and conversed with.

What did they make of her, this fair, slender woman who came to their villages off obscure paths deep in the Fernando Po forest? What did they think of Mary and her Porto interpreter* who asked them

---

*Porto is a Bubi word meaning a non-Bubi black man; Portos were the town-dwelling inhabitants of Fernando Po, immigrants from the mainland opposite and also from places as far away as Sierra Leone and Liberia. Because of their contact with Europeans they often served as interpreters for them with the indigenous Bubis.

questions and looked at their pots and tools and baskets and gave them gifts of beads and fishhooks rather than talking to them about an alien white God and his underworld? However much they may have been surprised by and may even have liked Mary, the Bubis must have regarded her as they did all white people: as a fish. For as Baumann was once told by a Bubi, "white men are fish, not men. They are able to stay a little while on land, but at last they mount their ships again and vanish over the horizon into the ocean." And so, after about a week in Fernando Po, did Mary and the MacDonalds. They mounted the *Batanga* again and vanished over the horizon back to Calabar.

By the time they returned to Calabar it was early February, and almost immediately upon arriving Sir Claude was forced to depart again because during their absence in Fernando Po a terrible uprising had occurred in the coastal town of Brass some 150 miles west of Calabar. It was an appalling episode and soon made front-page headline news in the *Daily Telegraph* and in the *Times* back in England, where it became known as the Brassmen's Revolt. Many killings took place, along with other atrocities, and the uprising also finally brought to a crisis the long-smoldering tensions between Sir George Goldie's Royal Niger Company and Sir Claude MacDonald's Niger Coast Protectorate.

The origin of the revolt was, as Mary would have put it, "trade palaver." After Goldie was granted his royal charter in 1886 a number of Liverpool traders cast about for ways to overcome Goldie's increasing monopoly on the Niger. These traders had stores or factories on the Coast and used African traders or middlemen to obtain their goods from the interior. In 1889 a number of these Liverpool concerns banded together to form the African Association in order to combat Goldie's growing power. But the friction between Goldie and his adversaries in Liverpool was finally diminished in 1893 when they reached a trade agreement whereby Liverpool agreed to keep out of the Niger in return for a share in the Royal Niger Company's profits and a seat on its board of directors. As a result, Goldie gained complete control of the Niger and its major tributary, the Benue River.

On the face of it, the 1893 agreement was a satisfactory compromise for everyone involved, except for the African middlemen traders, who depended upon Liverpool for their very survival. Neither Goldie nor the African Association seemed to take into account the desperate plight their agreement would leave the Africans in, especially the inhabitants of Brass, who were the major Niger middlemen on the Coast. For more than a year the people of Brass tried to carry on, largely by smuggling. But their canoes were fired upon by Royal Niger Company forces, their cargo confiscated, and the Brassmen who failed to escape the company officials were arrested and jailed. Finally, a smallpox epidemic broke out in Brass and its surrounding villages.

This was the last straw. Starving and dying, the people of Brass turned all their despair and rage against Goldie's company, which they held responsible for their terrible suffering. On January 29, 1895, more than one thousand Brassmen laid seige to the Royal Niger Company's headquarters at Akassa, twenty miles west of Brass. The resident British company employees just barely managed to escape on a mail steamer, but the Kru and other African company workers were brutally slaughtered in their huts. Then the Brassmen proceeded to sack and loot the company stores, to smash up all the equipment and machinery, and also to round up a few prisoners to take home with them. Most of these were later butchered and parts of their bodies eaten in order to appease the hostile spirits the Brass people believed were causing the smallpox epidemic.

The news of this terrible carnage greeted Mary and the MacDonalds immediately upon their return from Fernando Po. Brass was within the boundaries of MacDonald's protectorate, and however horrifying the attack was, MacDonald felt it was understandable. Goldie, of course, could scarcely agree, and so the already existing conflict and rancor between the two men was greatly intensified when they soon met in Brass and in Akassa. As the friend of both, Mary was put in a very difficult position. No doubt her initial impulse was to go to Brass with MacDonald and see for herself what the people there had first suffered and then perpetrated in revenge for their sufferings. Certainly the daily newspapers back in England would have welcomed on-the-spot dispatches from her on the situation. But it was more important to her to keep the good will and friendship of both these men, and this she could do only by remaining impartial and aloof from the explosive situation. In her two books, in fact, she makes no mention of the sensational Brass Revolt at all and explains that it was "for certain private reasons" that she decided not to collect fish from the Niger as she had originally intended, but rather decided to go farther south to the Ogooué in Gabon.

From various letters written during the 1895 trip we can get a good idea of Mary's and Lady MacDonald's early days in Calabar shortly after Sir Claude rushed off to Brass. Mary wrote her cousin Rose Kingsley that "the position of A.D.C. [aide-de-camp] to the Queen of the Oil Rivers [Lady MacDonald] is anything but a sinecure, let alone my own affairs." Mary found their reception by the local chiefs in war canoes "to my thinking perfect" but conceded that "Lady Mac did not share this view, and when it came to going up creeks for them she declined and sent me." "Lady Mac," it seems, was still very far from succumbing to the charm of Africa, while Mary herself was eager "to see some of those very little known towns with ju ju kings and temporal kings and human sacrifice galore and what not and a half." She had already visited a big walled town near Calabar, she wrote Rose, "where it was the local custom to put the bodies of all people who died in debt at the town gates until the relatives paid the amounts or decomposition cleared off the debtor. The stench at the three gates I saw was awful and I was in a hurry and three gates were one too many."

But initially, at least, Mary had little opportunity to explore Calabar and its surrounding villages, for she and Lady MacDonald were far too busy nursing patients of one sort or another. First an assistant of Sir Claude's fell seriously ill with symptoms that baffled Lady MacDonald but that Mary quickly recognized as those of delirium tremens, perhaps from her medical training but more likely from her 1893 sojourns with her hard-drinking trader friends. Shortly after the D. T. sufferer had been discharged, another man was brought in raving with fever to the MacDonalds' residence-cum-hospital, and this particular patient, as Mary wrote Rose, gave her

great sport devil hunting for him for 36 hours. Lady Mac wouldn't devil hunt and I had enough of it before I was done. You know what heat a tropic night can run to, and add to it the sweltering moisture and heavy rank earth smell of West Africa and bats and insects *ad infinitum,* and on top a lively young man who sees his "mosquito curtain swarming with devils." The mosquito curtain after a short time I bodily remove and cast out; then he sees them roosting on his towel horse; remove towel horse. By special request I then take a "quantity of squashy ones" out of the drawers — there are two chests in the room. That done I have to remove seven large devils from beneath the nursing table, "because they are making such a mess bringing up the blood they have been sucking" out of him that he can't take his food. The second night he reported a new devil on top of the wardrobe; he seemed puzzled about it, said it had a "quaint look, rather like his aunt, he fancied." I dog-tired and sweltering hot and no more intelligent than usual, thought it was one of the usual breed and made a swish at it with a towel while standing on a rickety chair, when hiss, scuffle, flop, down came a great grey brute of a poisonous snake, four foot and more long, which whif-fled itself off under the patient's bed: from this position I drove it with a broom on to the verandah, where it escaped down an iron column into the outer darkness. The patient took no interest in it, and on my return I found him engaged in a battle royal with "nine men and two women with drawn swords;" the only thing I could see being a rather strange shaving glass on a pedestal. I took him off this as best I could and whisked him back into bed and held him there until he thought of something else for a wee while. After thirty-six hours he confined his attention to supposing there was a general conspiracy to poison him, and he continued very ill and a considerable nuisance for ten days and nights, at the end of which time he was shipped on to the home-going steamer.

This exhausting patient, in fact, was only the trickle at the begin-ning of a subsequent flood of sick men, for they soon found themselves in the midst of a virulent typhoid epidemic, and it took all of Mary's physical and mental resources and stamina to nurse these men, to tie up their jaws when all her efforts failed and they died, and, most of all, to keep her sanity by continuing to laugh macabrely in the teeth of death as she had when devil hunting for her first fever victim. Some-times, in fact, her patients would come round and emerge from their delirium with unexpected suddenness and somewhat embarrassing re-sults. Years later Mary told her friend Rudyard Kipling about nursing a man whose mind was entirely clouded by fever, but her face, she explained,

> seemed to remind him of his school mistress and he'd gabble through his multiplication tables when he wanted . . . a drink. This was the only way to keep him quiet. I had several days of this. Then I felt I must get some sleep, so I covered him all over with tin biscuit box lids to wake me if he was restless. And he was. The lids made an awful noise. I jumped up half-asleep and began as usual, "Now steady! Say your tables, and I'll give you your drink. Twice one are two" . . . Well . . . the fever had left him and he was in his senses again and there was my face staring at him out of no where. *He* stared too and then he whispered, "Who the hell are *you?*"

For her first month or so in Calabar, then, Mary was once again immersed in the fundamental West African world of "grim realities" and death. She was also plunged once more into her old familiar role as nurse, especially night nurse, because it was Mary rather than "Lady Mac" who sat up until dawn with the fever-stricken men, reading

Horace and Günther just as she had sat up for years on end with her mother in the Mortimer Road house in Cambridge. But even in the midst of all her nursing duties, she wrote Hatty, how "I have made it a rule during my stay here to get, when patients permitted, a walk of eight or ten miles a day and so know a good deal of the surrounding country and drop in unexpectedly on unprotected native villages."

For more than a month the typhoid epidemic raged unabated. Mary wrote Hatty that she had not had an uninterrupted night's sleep for five weeks and, at the worst of it, doubted that "any of us would see the river bar again." But by the middle of March Calabar began to return "to its merely normal state of unhealthiness by reason of only too many of its inhabitants dying and the balance of the rest being carried on board homeward bound steamers."

By this time MacDonald was back from Brass, and yet Mary made no immediate plans to resume her voyage farther south to Gabon. She may have been hoping that the tensions of the aftermath of the Brass Revolt would subside quickly so that she could make at least a short visit to the Niger; thus she may have lingered in Calabar expressly to follow the outcome of the rising and to determine the state of affairs between MacDonald and Goldie. But the trouble between the two was not easily resolved, and in any event. Mary did not go to the Niger but instead remained in the Calabar region for the next two months until she departed for Congo Français toward the end of May.

During this extended Calabar visit, Mary writes in *Travels in West Africa,* "most of my time was spent puddling about the river and the forest round Duke Town and Creek Town," near Calabar, "collecting fish mainly through the kindness of Dr. Whitindale and insects through the kindness of Mr. Cooper then in charge of the botanical station." She was also collecting an enormous amount of information about the peoples of Calabar — the Igbo, Ibibio, and the Effik — who play almost as important a role in the fetish chapters of *Travels in West Africa* and *West African Studies* as the Fang. Mary in fact probably knew nearly as much about these Calabar or Cross River peoples as she did about the Fang and discussed them less openly perhaps because they had already been studied and written about, while the Fang were virtually unknown and unheard of. In addition, most ethnographers tend to choose one particular people as their "own," and this choice is usually to some extent an exclusive one. This choice would appear to be similar to choosing a subject or a person to write a book about or even to choosing a spouse in that it requires a major emotional investment that limits other allegiances and relationships. Then, too, there is the process of anthropological identification: to some degree, the anthropologist *becomes* one of the people she studies, however much she seeks to remain scientifically detached.

During these Calabar days and weeks Mary "puddled about" the Cross River and its mangrove-clogged creeks and swamps visiting the various villages for "fish and fetish." But these were not the only things she encountered. She wrote Günther of an excursion one day in a canoe full of men, women, and children and how they came across a smallpox victim floating down the river. As Mary described it, "my companions rowed or rather paddled hard towards" the corpse and "then carefully got it alongside the canoe. . . . They then drank calabash after calabash full of water from as close round it as they possibly could squeeze the vessel. . . . 'It's a good death charm,' they assured me. . . . 'Very,' said I, 'paddle away,' for I was fearful that they would drag the putrid thing bodily into the canoe to take home to their less fortunate relations."

In the course of these canoe outings, Mary also had encounters with crocodiles, for Calabar, unlike Fernando Po, was a most "crocodiley" place. On most of these ventures she was unaccompanied, and from her canoe she could see the crocodiles basking in the sun on rocks at the river's edge or flopping from the bank into the water and then gliding off — great, elongated, green-black creatures, with grotesquely dimpled hides and enormous, teeth-filled jaws. In *Travels in West Africa* Mary writes how

a crocodile drifting down in deep water, or lying asleep with its jaws open on a sand-bank in the sun, is a picturesque adornment to the landscape when you are on the deck of a steamer, and you can write home about it and frighten your relations on your behalf; but when you are away among the swamps in a small dug-out canoe, and that crocodile and his relations are awake . . . and when he has got his foot upon his native heath — that is to say, his tail within holding reach of his native mud — he is highly interesting, and you may not be able to write home about him — and you get frightened on your own behalf. For crocodiles can, and often do, in such places grab at people in small canoes.

In addition . . . you are liable — until you realise the danger from experience or have native advice on the point — to get tide-trapped away in the swamps, the water falling round you when you are away in some deep pool or lagoon, and you find you cannot get back to the main river. For you cannot get out and drag your canoe across the stretches of mud that separate you from it, because the mud is of too unstable a nature and too deep, and sinking into it means staying in it, at any rate until some geologist of the remote future may come across you, in a fossilised state, when that mangrove swamp shall have become dry land. Of course, if you really want a truly safe investment in Fame, and really care about Posterity, and Posterity's Science, you will jump over into the black batter-like, stinking slime, cheered by the thought of the terrific sensation you will produce 20,000 years hence, and the care you will be taken of then by your fellow-creatures, in a museum. But if you are a mere ordinary person of retiring nature, like me, you stop in your lagoon until the tide rises again; most of your attention is directed to dealing with an "at home" to crocodiles and mangrove flies, and with the fearful stench of the slime round you. What little time you have over you will employ in wondering why you came to West Africa, and why, after having reached this point of absurdity, you need have gone and painted the lily and adorned the rose by being such a colossal ass as to come fooling about in mangrove swamps. Twice this chatty little incident . . . has happened to me, but never again if I can help it. On one occasion, the last, a mighty Silurian, as *The Daily Telegraph* would call him, chose to get his front paws over the stern of my canoe, and endeavoured to improve our acquaintance. I had to retire to the bows, to keep the balance (it is no use saying because I was frightened, for this miserably understates the case), and fetch him a clip on the snout with a paddle, when he withdrew, and I paddled into the very middle of the lagoon, hoping the water there was too deep for him, or any of his friends to repeat the performance. Presumably it was, for no one did it again. I should think that crocodile was eight feet long; but don't go and say I measured him, or that this is my outside measurement for crocodiles. I have measured them when they have been killed by other people, fifteen, eighteen, and twenty-one feet odd. This was only a pushing young creature who had not learnt manners.

Mary also encountered numerous hippopotamuses during these Calabar excursions. In contrast to crocodiles, Mary found, hippos were generally shy rather than aggressive creatures but were also bovinely immobile. On more than one occasion, she had to prod one with her umbrella when it was blocking her way to get it to lumber off. On one of her overnight stays in a village, around 3:30 A.M., Mary was awakened by a terrific bellow and crash, and the whole line of huts, in one of which she was staying, was shaken and almost wrenched off the ground. Initially Mary had no idea what had happened, and indeed after the village clamor had subsided she prepared to return to bed again, only to be interrupted shortly by another bellow and crash, when "right through the south end of the village an immense hippopotamus tore full tilt, and went splash into the river." This beast was "about twelve feet long, and bulky as a small elephant and weighed a ton or two." The villagers told Mary that hippos frequently came out of the river and fed off their farms in the middle of the night, "and as each hippopotamus' stomach holds between five and six bushels, they cause an acute form of agricultural depression." Though gentle, hippos are also quite nervous "and prone to get flurried on land," especially when separated from their companions. This apparently had been the case with this particular hippo invader. "If you can picture to yourself a furniture van in hysterics," as Mary put it, "you will realise the sort of thing that went through that unfortunate village in the middle of the night."

But the most important encounter that Mary had during her Calabar stay was not with any tropical beasts, dangerous or benign, but rather with the remarkable Scottish Presbyterian missionary, Mary Slessor, who had been out on the Coast for nearly twenty years, most of that time spent alone in small Okoyong villages some miles north of Calabar in the Cross River creeks. Mary had heard of Mary Slessor — as everyone familiar with West Africa had — in 1893, but it was only during this second journey that she had the time and freedom to go seek her out in the village of Ekenge, situated in the forest in between the Cross and Calabar Rivers. Mary traveled from Calabar first by canoe and then on foot, arriving at Ekenge in the middle of some serious "twin palaver." For one of the great contributions Mary Slessor had made to the region was to discourage, if not absolutely stamp out, the custom of twin killing practiced by many of the Cross River peoples. The origin of this custom was unclear, but it was apparently believed that when twins were born, one was the child of the devil who had secretly mated with the mother, and since it was impossible to tell which was the diabolical offspring, both babies were killed and often the mother as well in punishment for producing such an abomination.

Mary turned up at Ekenge just when Mary Slessor was rescuing the mother of a set of twins. The mother was an Igbo slave woman from a nearby village, who, after giving birth to her babies, had fled to Mary Slessor for refuge. Mary Slessor, meanwhile, had received word of the poor woman and had set off to meet her: "By the time she had gone four miles she met . . . a procession, the woman coming to her and all the rest of the village yelling and howling behind her. On the top of her head was the gin-case, into which the children had been stuffed, on the top of them the woman's big brass skillet, and on the top of that her two market calabashes."

Mary Slessor did not take the woman and her babies back by the direct bush path to her house, because to have done so would have polluted the path and made it too dangerous for others to travel down, so they had to stand in the broiling midday sun while another path was cut through the forest to give them access to Mary's grounds and house. By the time they finally arrived home, one of the babies, a boy, had died, but his sister was still alive. The infants had been crammed so violently into the gin case the woman had carried on her head that the little boy's head had been smashed in the process. But the tiny girl cried lustily when they lifted her from the case, or rather when Mary Slessor did, for even the mother was very reluctant to touch her own child.

It was at this dramatic juncture that Mary Kingsley arrived on the scene. Besides the baby and its mother there were assorted other children of various ages in the house, for Mary Slessor took in orphans as well as twins and indeed any other creature, young or old, who needed a home. Mary Kingsley was immediately impressed by Mary Slessor, and instead of finding her the formidable, authoritarian missionary she had expected, was entranced by this unassuming, warm woman who, though forty-six in 1895, looked far younger and almost boyish with her short, cropped, auburn hair, plain cotton shifts, and canvas shoes. No stays or hairpins for Mary Slessor; she had entirely "gone for bush" in her years in Ekenge. She lived in a mud and thatch house, subsisted entirely on local "chop," except for the great necessity of tea, a need she shared with Mary Kingsley, and she went for months and even years without returning to Calabar or seeing another white person. When she was forced to go back to Scotland on leave, her holidays were fraught with trauma, for she found it impossible, for example, to cross a traffic-clogged street in Aberdeen or address a lecture hall full of admirers in Dundee.

That home and peace for Mary Slessor were Calabar and her house full of children was in part because of the misery and squalor of her childhood in Scotland. She was the second of seven children of an alcoholic shoemaker and his wife, who worked as a weaver. The entire family lived in a one-room flat in the Dundee slums with no water or light, and at the age of eleven Mary herself began working in the weaving mills. While still a child she heard the Calabar missionary, the Rev. William Anderson, speak in Dundee, and even more important, in 1866 Mary read reports of David Livingstone, another Scot from a working-class background, in the *Missionary Record*. These two experiences determined her eventual destiny, though it was not until she was twenty-eight that Mary finally sailed for Africa in 1876 as a female agent of the Scottish Missionary Society with a salary of sixty pounds a year.

Her influence on the world she embraced in Calabar, where she was known as Eka Kpukpro Owo — Mother of All the Peoples — was incalculable, but it was also, as Mary Kingsley realized, a reciprocal influence. Mary Slessor was perhaps "converted" to a greater degree than were her own Presbyterian followers, and this is what made her such a rare missionary and what won her Mary Kingsley's profound respect, just as her warmth and good humor won Mary Kingsley's affection. Like all good missionaries, Mary Slessor was as much ethnographer as proselytizer. As Mary Kingsley described her in *Travels in West Africa*, "her knowledge of the native, his language, his ways of thought, his diseases, his difficulties, and all that is his, is extraordinary, and the amount of good she has done, no man can fully estimate. . . . This instance of what one white can do would give many important lessons in West Coast administration and development. Only the sort of man Miss Slessor represents is rare. There are but few who have the same power of resisting the malarial climate and of acquiring the language, and an insight into the Negro mind, so perhaps after all it is no great wonder that Miss Slessor stands alone." Sir Claude MacDonald, to his credit, recognized what a rarity Mary Slessor was and appointed her vice consul of Okoyong, the first woman appointed to the post in the whole of the British Empire.

Mary Kingsley spent a number of days at Ekenge, no doubt prolonging her visit as time went on, for she would have felt much more at home with Mary Slessor than back at the consular residence in Calabar with "Lady Mac." There was no clock in Mary Slessor's thatch-roofed house, and so the two women often sat up talking until dawn, rocking the babies, discussing everything under the sun. Undoubtedly a great deal of what Mary Kingsley knew about the Cross River people came from Mary Slessor. But more intimate information was also exchanged during those long hot nights in the small house in the forest clearing: their reasons for coming to Africa, the hardships of their lives in the years before, their plans for the future. Mary Kingsley may have told the other Mary about her trials with Charley, and Mary Slessor, in turn, may have confided the details of her broken engagement four years earlier to a young man named Charles Morrison, another missionary in Calabar. The Mission Board had refused to allow Morrison to join and work with Mary at Ekenge, and shortly thereafter he was invalided home, and she never saw him again. Mary Slessor was left with only an opal engagement ring by which to remember her sensitive, delicate fiancé, who wrote poetry and at twenty-five was seventeen years younger than she. It had been a strange romantic interlude in an otherwise austere and laborious life, and for the next twenty-six years she lived and worked alone. If Mary Slessor did tell Mary about Charles Morrison, she would have found a receptive, sympathetic audience.

The tenor and texture of these days Mary Kingsley spent at Ekenge were beautifully described by Mary Slessor in a letter some years later, though she insists she cannot capture the reality of either the visit or Mary's personality:

> To give you an account of Miss Kingsley and her stay here — you may as well tell me to catch the clouds with their ever-varying forms, or catch the perfume of our forest jasmine, or the flashes of the sunlight on the river. Miss Kingsley cannot be portrayed. She had an individuality as pronounced as it was unique, with charm of manner and conversation, while the interplay of wit and mild satire, of pure spontaneous mirth and of profoundly deep seriousness, made her a series of surprises, each one tenderer and more elusive than the foregoing, No! There was only one Miss Kingsley and I can't define her character by speaking in this way, in the terms we speak of one another; or gather up the beauty and instruction and joy of those days of companionship and say, "There! She gave me this or that other impression or impulse or idea." It is like the languorous glamour of a summer day in which one bathed and lay still and let life go by in a sweet dream.

Mary Slessor also goes on in this letter to detail what she understood to be Mary Kingsley's religious ideas and convictions, for it is obvious that among all the things they discussed deep into the night were spiritual realities and Mary Slessor's role as a missionary in Africa. But we must treat with caution Mary Slessor's assertions about Mary Kingsley's fundamental adherence to Christian belief. Indeed, the whole subject of Mary Kingsley's faith or lack of it is an extremely vexed and confusing issue because Mary was reluctant to put herself on the line in the first place, and when she did, what she said varied greatly at different times and according to whom she was speaking.

Mary Slessor wrote as if Mary Kingsley had bared her innermost spiritual being to her, for she says, "I dare not betray the confidences sacred as the soul's secrets towards its maker only can be, else it were easy to prove that Christianity — for white and for the black alike — *alone* held hope and progress with Miss Kingsley." This assertion, in fact, is patently untrue as is Mary Slessor's insistence that "Miss Kingsley adored the Christ of God the Saviour of the world, and . . . all the trouble of her sensitive heart found rest at his feet." Mary Kingsley probably listened attentively and sympathetically to Mary Slessor's own avowals and perhaps vaguely stretched her own unorthodox beliefs sufficiently to suggest to Mary Slessor that she was within the Christian fold. But she was not, in truth, within it, and even Mary Slessor guessed at her waverings and knew of her grave doubts about almost all missionary activity in West Africa. Mary also felt secure enough with Mary Slessor to confide her fascination with Islam and her belief that it was far less disruptive of African society and culture than was Christianity. In fact, she told Mary Slessor that she longed to disguise herself and travel in North Africa and study and live among the Muslims.

To the American missionary Robert Nassau in Gabon Mary Kingsley also professed herself a believer — of sorts — for she plainly told him that she was *not* a Christian. Her confidences to Nassau were made in an extraordinary letter in response to one from him in which he berated her for taking the Lord's name in vain, and also the *wrong* Lord's name, for Mary was as much in the habit of saying "Allah!" as "Oh God," or "Good Lord." Essentially what Mary says to Nassau is that we see the God we are capable of seeing, according to the capacity and nature of our vision. "My mind," she says, "has a different feeling about God to that most people have . . . the God I know so well who I of late years have daily felt so close beside me is not the God you love. . . . If I could believe in that God of mercy you believe in I would . . . but I can see, hear, and feel that terrific God of infinite power, infinite knowledge, infinite justice, and I worship him in a cove of honour."

But in other contexts and to other nonmissionary friends Mary referred to herself as a "high and dry Darwinist," an agnostic who worshiped the "great God of Science." Although her grandfather and uncle were both Anglican clergymen, Mary herself seems to have been raised

without any sort of religious training whatsoever. George Kingsley
was an atheist, and Mrs. Kingsley appears to have entirely ignored her
children's spiritual welfare and instruction. There is no evidence that
either Mary or Charley was baptized or confirmed or indeed ever set
foot inside a church.

And yet if she was not a Christian, Mary was also not the purely
rational, scientific, secular person she sometimes affected to be, either.
Her love of Africa was at bottom a spiritual passion and her fascination
with fetish arose from the kinship she recognized between her own
heterodox beliefs and those of the Africans she lived among. Even Mary
Slessor recognized this last point, for she wrote in another letter that
Mary "respected [the Africans'] religious beliefs . . . and never either
ridiculed or laughed at them." And she recalled how "one day as we
stood before a huge tree which was worshipped by the natives, she
turned and said, 'I do not wonder they bow down to such a splendid
creation.' " "How different this was," Mary Slessor said, "from those
travellers and even officials who can put out their sticks and their hands
and touch contemptuously their sacred things and carry them off for
curios."

In a way, Mary was a tree worshiper too, which is to say, a nature
lover or pantheist. The spiritual power she felt in the universe she
found in the natural world — in the ocean, coast, and forest — not
in creeds or bibles or churches, and she found it most ubiquitously and
compellingly in West Africa. The most haunting and powerful passages in her books and letters are those describing this natural realm.
She once wrote that "it is the non-human world I belong to. . . . My
people are mangrove swamps, rivers, and the sea and so on." When
among "her people," she would experience an exhilarating sense of
release, of security, a sensation of some sort of benign power operating
beyond the fret and cares of human destiny. Not that Mary always
gives us this spiritual gloss on the beautiful landscapes she frequently
describes. But sometimes she does. In *Travels in West Africa,* for example, she tells of one particular night on the Ogooué at great length:
she describes the peaks of the Sierra del Cristal illuminated by the
rising moon, the wreaths and clouds of silver-gray mist "basking lazily
or rolling to and fro" in the valleys, the foaming, flying Ogooué in its
deep ravine, the thousands of fireflies flickering about her in the darkness, as she, sitting on the river's bank, brooded on the scene and
listened to the ceaseless thunder of the Ogooué rapids.

"The majesty and beauty of the scene fascinated me," she explains, "and I stood leaning with my back against a rock pinnacle watching it. Do not imagine it gave rise, in what I am pleased to call my mind, to those complicated poetical reflections natural beauty seems to bring out in other peoples' minds. It never works that way with me; I just lose all sense of human individuality, all memory of human life with its grief and worry and doubt, and become part of the atmosphere. If I have a heaven, that will be mine."

She is describing here the experience of transcendentalism, when "we are laid asleep in body and become a living soul," as Wordsworth put it. In such moments one bursts the boundaries of time, space, and ego. The ecstasy of the experience lies in the sense of powerful liberation from the constraints of the human, material world and in a feeling of union with a power or force that is immanent in nature. And this overriding sense of spiritual freedom is at the opposite extreme from the narrow, confining dogma that was preached by most missionaries on the Coast. But these are difficult experiences, sensations, and convictions to explain, especially to someone with more conventional, orthodox views. Mary Slessor grasped this fundamental spiritual impulse in Mary Kingsley's personality and then would seem to have draped it with her own Christian covering. But this distortion does not deny that the two women established a rare intimacy during Mary's visit to Ekenge, admired each other enormously, and at bottom understood the wellsprings — some shared and some not — from which their two lives sprang.

By the middle of May the rains had begun making "puddling" around the Cross River and its creeks too sodden and messy work even for Mary's tropical tastes. In any event, it was time she finally made her way farther south to her ultimate destination of Congo Français. But in order to reach her "beloved Southwest Coast," she first had to go back north to Lagos on her old friend the *Batanga*. Traveling from Calabar to Cameroon and Gabon, she said, was "a thing you ought to get a medal for," because the Liverpool ships bound for the southwest coast did not stop at the oil river ports such as Calabar but instead went directly from Lagos to Cameroon. This meant that Mary had to backtrack and take the *Batanga* to Lagos and then catch a "Southwester" outward bound — no simple operation, for as Mary says in *Travels in West Africa*, "I assure you changing at Lagos Bar throws changing at Clapham Junction into the shade."

This was because of the difficulty of negotiating the shark-infested

Lagos sandbar, which, like Lagos itself, was "a marvellous manifestation of the perversity of man coupled with the perversity of nature." Changing at Lagos bar involved being lowered over the side of the *Batanga* in a chair attached to a winch onto a small branch boat called the *Eko,* which was laden with passengers and mail that, like Mary, were to be picked up by the Southwester. The *Eko* was in an appalling condition; the deck was filthy, "rats ran freely about everywhere," and it was overflowing with soaking wet African passengers, most of whom seemed to be ill. Mary also encountered a white Lagos government official "in a saturated state. He said he had just come out to see how a branch boat could get across the bar at low water, a noble and enterprising thing," in Mary's opinion, "which places him in line with the Elder Pliny." The Southwester they were to meet was the *Benguella,* and the government official informed Mary that it was "hourly expected," as it had telegraphed from Accra. He was particularly eager that it should be on time because he was due to go upcountry on the small government steamer that he pointed out to Mary in the distance in Lagos harbor, and he wanted to return to Lagos as soon as possible.

But the *Benguella* did not appear as the afternoon wore away, and it was a most miserable afternoon at that, for "the little Eko rolled to and fro, to and fro, all the loose gear going slippety, slop, crash; slippety, slop, crash: coal-dust, smuts and a broiling sun poured down on us quietly, and the only thing or motion that gave us any variety was every three or four minutes the Eko making a vicious jerk at her anchor."

Finally Mary and the by now quite distracted government official were rescued, not by the *Benguella* but by another ship, a Danish one, that arrived around six in the evening. The *Janette Woermann* was commanded by one Captain Heldt, "a gigantic, lithe, powerful Dane," as Mary describes him, "clad in a uniform of great splendour and exceeding tightness, terminating in a pair of Blucher boots and every inch of his six feet four spick and span." He was a knight in shining armor or a fairy tale prince, in short. Captain Heldt insisted upon taking Mary and her government friend on board, vacating his own cabin for Mary, and offering them both delicious food (including a first course at dinner of what seemed a plateful of hot jam) and lively conversation. Mary was soon so comfortable and contented that she ceased worrying about the *Benguella.* Not the least of the charms on the *Janette Woermann* must have been the gallant and handsome Captain Heldt.

But the Lagos government official was becoming increasingly depressed and anxious over the government steamer waiting to take him upcountry and kept borrowing Captain Heldt's telescope to gaze at it yearningly. The captain did his best to cheer him up by offering him dry clothes, lager beer, cigars, and stories. Only one such story, recounting how the captain had severely injured his back and had had to navigate his ship among the shoals of Saint Ann while lying in agony for weeks, seemed to alleviate the government official's gloom, along with accounts of how the captain had broken various ribs on the high seas. "Still the Benguella came not," said Mary, "though we sat up very late looking for her, and at last we turned in" for the night.

"The next morning," Mary continues in *Travels in West Africa,* "we were up early. There was no Benguella." But though the captain provided them with an excellent breakfast, "my fellow countryman's anxiety had now passed into a dark despair. . . . Captain Heldt tried to cheer him with more stories, lager beer, and cigars, and at last produced an auto-harp." Finally the *Benguella* arrived at two in the afternoon, more than twenty-four hours after Mary commenced "changing" at Lagos Bar. While the government official reboarded the *Eko* to return to Lagos, Mary transferred to the *Benguella.* This time she climbed on board by means of a rope ladder rather than by being raised up in a chair, and as soon as she got her head over the top of the bulwark she saw directly in front of her on deck her first tutor in pidgin English — one of the *Lagos*'s crew from the 1893 journey.

Mary also made a valuable new friend on the *Benguella* as they sailed south to Gabon. The ship's purser was one Mr. Fothergill, who had formerly lived for some years in Congo Français as a merchant. Mr. Fothergill was extremely knowledgeable about all aspects of life in Gabon, for he was, as Mary put it, "one of that class of men, of which you most frequently find representatives among the merchants, who do not possess the power many men along here do possess (a power that always amazes me) of living for a considerable time in a district without taking any interest in it, keeping their whole attention concentrated on the point of how long it will be before their time comes to get out of it." Too often this was the attitude of government officials and missionaries, who, according to Mary, tended to live in West Africa like the guards who worked in the British Museum: they lived in the midst of cultural and historical wealth and treasure that they did not even notice, much less attempt to fathom or comprehend.

But Mr. Fothergill was a dramatic exception to this rule, and as the

Benguella proceeded south to the heart of the continent, he initiated Mary into some of the mysteries and wonders she would find there. Finally, on May 20, 1895, they landed at the port of Glass, a short distance from the capital of Congo Français, Libreville. It was nearly five months since she had set sail from Liverpool, and Mary must have felt that at last she had arrived home.

·୬୫ 8 ୫୬·

Traveling the Ogooué River

Gabon, part of Congo Français (the French Congo), as it was called
when Mary visited it in the 1890s, lies directly athwart the equator, below the great western bulge and the Gulf of Guinea of
West Africa. It lies, that is, almost exactly in the center of the western
side of the continent, in the geographical heart of Africa. Neatly sliced
in half horizontally by the invisible equator and by the Ogooué River,
which stretches like a shadow of this 0° latitude, Gabon was and remains a land of elemental presences and forces that simultaneously
attract and remain immune to all the incursions and efforts of man. In
a way, we can look at everything in Mary's life that had come before
her arrival in Gabon as preliminary, a prelude, and at everything that
came after, not perhaps as anticlimactic, but as a kind of postlude or
legacy. Some sort of consummation was worked within her here.

The African explorers Mary had admired most in her childhood reading — Du Chaillu, Reade, Burton, and most of all Brazza — had all
succumbed to the primal attraction of the place. But Gabon had been
discovered some four hundred years earlier in the late fifteenth century
by the Portuguese in their early voyages down the western side of the
Africa. They mistook its large, lake-like estuary for the mouth of a
river and called it Gabão, which means hooded cape, and the coastal
Mpongwe peoples they encountered there they called Gabonese. The
Portuguese, however, did not linger in Gabão or attempt to penetrate
its interior. Aside from minimal contact with the Mpongwe, the Orungu
at Cape Lopez, and the Vili along the Loango coast, they left the region
untouched, and so it remained until the French took an interest in it

much later, in the middle of the nineteenth century. The French established naval stations in Gabon and in 1837 and 1841 signed treaties
with Mpongwe chiefs that gave the French control of the entire estuary
region. For the next thirty years they continued to acquire more and
more territory through such treaties, with this process culminating in
the results of the three expeditions between 1875 and 1885 of Brazza,
Mary's hero.

In 1849 some fifty-two slaves who had been liberated from a slave
ship bound for the United States and then taken to Goree Island off
Senegal were shipped back south to resettle in Gabon. Here they were
consigned to a meagre existence as laborers on local plantations — a
fate that scarcely seemed the proper reward for their liberation from
servitude. Nevertheless, they formed a colony in the estuary modeled
after those in Sierra Leone and Liberia, and in fact the settlement was
named Libreville after Sierra Leone's Freetown. This colony, however,
did not prosper. No new "recaptives" (as slaves captured from slavers
were called) were sent to augment it, and eventually this small population of Gabonese "Creoles" was absorbed by the indigenous peoples.

At the same time, European missionary activity had begun to make
itself felt in Gabon. In the early 1840s American Presbyterians had
established themselves at Baraka in the estuary, and by the 1870s they
were on the Ogooué as far up as Lambaréné. The French Protestant
and Roman Catholic missions were not slow to follow, and by the
1880s and 1890s they had settlements at Lambaréné, Kangwe, and
even in more remote areas such as Ndjolé and Talagouga.

When Mary arrived in Congo Français in May of 1895 there was,
then, a threefold European influence operating in the region. The French
government ruled the colony, Congo Français, largely through its naval forces. In fact, Pierre Savorgnan de Brazza was the colony's gover-
nor-commissioner, though Mary unfortunately did not meet him because he was on leave in France between June and December of 1895
getting married. The French, then, held political rule over Congo
Français, but the colony's economic power was actually in the hands of
British traders, especially Hatton and Cookson and John Holt, both
old, established Liverpool firms that traded up and down the West
Coast. And finally, the Europeans who were most in touch with the
colony's inhabitants, their culture, beliefs, and way of life were the
American and French missionaries. These missionaries both outnumbered and were more influential than either the government officials or
the traders. They were also critical to the success of Mary's travels in

Gabon, for she repeatedly stayed with them in the interior settlements, and they helped organize and man her expeditions beyond their own and the government's and trader's spheres. But missionaries, officials, and traders were all as the shadows of clouds on the enduring Ogooué Mary had come to find — fleeting and insubstantial in contrast to the reality of Gabon she found when she left their stations, missions, or factories.

But this reality — the "raw" African world she sought — took some time to be reached. In the interim, from the morning of May 20 when Captain Eversfield safely landed the *Benguella* at Glass, Mary was necessarily in frequent contact with the world of European expatriates. Like all recently disembarked travelers, she had first of all to go through customs. Expecting to be reduced to a "financial wreck" by all her collector's cases and bottles of spirit, she was relieved when these were all passed through duty free in the name of science. But she was disconcerted when the customs officers "incarcerated" her revolver, "giving me a feeling of iniquity for having had the thing." Rather than pay a fifteen-shilling license fee and promise to shoot only French amunition, she left the gun in pawn.

Mr. Hudson, the agent general of Hatton and Cookson whom she had met in Cabinda in 1893, was away farther up the Ogooué on company business, and so Mary was taken in hand by his immediate subordinate, an energetic young man named Mr. Fildes. As she had done in 1893, Mary planned to trade her way through Gabon, and Hatton and Cookson, rather than its English competitor, John Holt, or the one German company in the region, Woermann, was the firm she had arranged to trade with. Hence her nominal status as an agent for Hatton and Cookson, their chronic anxiety in the coming weeks and months over her safety and whereabouts, and her own complementary anxiety that she should not let down her old friend Mr. Hudson and the company to which, as she put it, she was "invoiced."

It was the keen Mr. Fildes who saw Mary through customs and then took her to the Administration de l'Intérieur and the Palais de Justice in Libreville to register with the police and to acquire a permit to reside in the colony. And when these official chores were out of the way he evidently felt obliged to show her some of the local scenery. Or perhaps this young man in his straw boater and white shirt-sleeves was intrigued, even attracted, by Mary and was prompted to take her out in the company gig by feelings quite other than what Mary dismisses as mere "duty."

Bright and early on Sunday morning, May 26, they drove to a little river on the east side of the estuary and found "a perfect gem of a mangrove-swamp, and the stench . . . quite the right thing — real Odeur de Niger delta." Here they embarked in a small rowboat and oozed their way through "the stinking, stoneless slime . . . honey-combed with crab holes," under a broiling noonday equatorial sun. Mary "expected only to have to sit in the boat and say 'horrible' at intervals," but Mr. Fildes steered the boat to one particularly "awful-looking spot," cryptically observing "that will do," and then jumped "out with a squidge into the black slime." "For one awful moment," Mary says, she "thought it was suicide, and that before I could even get the address of his relations to break the news to them there would be nothing but a panama hat lying on the slime before me." But Mr. Fildes, in fact, only wanted to collect some crabs for Mary to put in some of the collector's bottles he had espied when he helped her through customs. And thus, as Mary describes him, this "powerfully built, lithe, six foot high young man" slogged through the swamp, brandishing his boat paddle in pursuit of crabs and managed to collect a good many. Mary "had never suspected we should catch anything but our deaths of fever, and so had brought no collecting-box, and before I could remonstrate, Mr. Fildes' handkerchief was full of crabs and of course mine too," and they consequently had nothing with which to wipe their profusely perspiring brows on the way back to Glass.

Over luncheon Mr. Fildes proposed an afternoon excursion to the German firm Woermann's farm, a proposal to which Mary gamely agreed, though by this time she had "lost all sense of reliance in Mr. Fildes' instinct of self-preservation." Again, one suspects Mr. Fildes may have been motivated by more than a sense of his obligation to the company in his devotion to keeping Mary occupied. Her doubts over the rationality of this expedition were not groundless. Woermann's farm turned out to be a six-mile hike from the company factory in Glass. But it was a splendid if exhausting one and a fine introduction to the region, for they got far beyond the European settlements of Glass and Libreville, traversed lovely flower-sprinkled meadows, climbed hills swathed in long saw grass with enormous butterflies and dragon-flies hovering in the air, descended into dense patches of forest, ma-neuvered across several streams, and, most important, passed through several Fang villages.

This was Mary's first encounter with "this tribe of evil repute," as she half-mockingly describes it in *Travels in West Africa*. She noted that their houses were constructed of sheets of bark tied to sticks, so different from the bamboo, mud, or thatch huts she had encountered in Calabar or even among the Mpongwe. The houses, in typical Fang fashion, were lined up on either side of the main thoroughfare in the middle of which stood a vast drum painted white with patterns in black and red and brown and with a piece of rawhide stretched across the top and one or two talking drums beside. By the time they finally reached Woermann's farm it was so late that they had to turn back almost immediately and hasten home before darkness overcame them. There was a slight altercation on this return journey in the gathering dusk over who should precede whom on the narrow Woermann Road. Mr. Fildes felt that he should now bring up the rear, but, Mary writes, "remembering the awful state that the back of my blouse got in at Fernando Po from a black boot-lace I was reduced to employ as a stay-lace, I refused to go in front, without explaining why."

Mary spent much of these first two weeks in Glass and Libreville wandering the roads and overgrown paths and visiting Fang villages, such as those she was introduced to on that first outing with Mr. Fildes. She quickly began to pick up the more rudimentary greetings and phrases of the Fang and would stop and converse with villagers or hunters she met on the wayside. One old man, understanding the purpose of the collecting gear Mary lugged about with her on her walks, caught her a choice lizard. She rewarded him with a gift of tobacco, and they launched into a discussion on the proper time to burn grass and on the differences for building purposes of the two kinds of bamboo. On another day Mary met a hunter in the forest carrying home a deer he had just shot and loaded down with an old musket and long, tufted, archaic-looking spears. He too was very garrulous, and Mary gave him tobacco and talked sport, and when they parted he gave her a charm that would enable her to see things in the forest.

In the course of these rambles, even before she reached the Ogooué, Mary wrote home to Günther that she was already collecting fish specimens from the swamps and creeks of the Libreville estuary. One morning's twelve-mile field trip led her into a stretch of "black stinking mud" that left her "unfortunate skirts" in a sorry state. She attempted to wash the worst of it off in a nearby stream, and "while so employed," she reported, "I noticed four human heads apparently floating on the mud but as they from time to time disappeared I thought there might be bodies belonging to them and opened up conversation genially with the usual coast greeting of 'You live?' 'Yes Ma,' said a head with a bland smile and I noticed that a mud encrusted hand every few minutes came up and threw something into a good sized basket which hung on to its left ear, so I continued the conversation until the entire human being came ashore and showed me his basket of our friends the African mud fish."

Mary had only been in Libreville a matter of days when she met Dr. Robert Hamill Nassau, the American medical missionary who had been out in West Africa since 1861, first on Corsico Island and then in Congo Français at various missions he had established on the Ogooué and in the region of the estuary. Nassau, like Mary Slessor, was one of the rare missionaries who ended up more Africanized than the numerous Africans he numbered among his flock were Christianized. He practiced what he called a policy of "assimilation," by which he meant that he lived and ate and slept and worked alongside the people he had come to Africa to serve. He refused to assume a posture of authority or power over the Benga, Galoa, and Fang he lived among. For a woman missionary, such as Mary Slessor, such activities were considered more acceptable than they would be for a man, especially a highly educated and cultivated man like Nassau, who held degrees in both medicine and theology and was an ordained Presbyterian minister.

Nassau was also an exceedingly astute and assiduous ethnographer, and like Mary Kingsley, his particular interest lay in what they called "native thought." For upwards of thirty years he had been studying and recording the customs, laws, and most of all the spiritual beliefs of the Africans he came to know so well, and among the many books he published were grammars of both Fang and Benga and his pioneering works, *Bantu Studies* and *Fetichism in West Africa.*

Mary was charmed by Nassau's "strangely gracious, refined, courteous manner." Many evenings when she returned from her long rambles she would sit up late with the sixty-year-old but still vigorous and energetic Nassau "talking ju ju" by the light of the flickering oil lamp. Nassau was giving her the sound theoretical and philosophical basis she needed to interpret and understand the observations she made during the day. And despite having been tragically twice widowed by the perils and deadly climate of West Africa, Nassau also gave Mary crucial encouragement to go beyond the "civilized" area of Libreville and Glass to study the Fang in their more remote interior villages. Nassau understood the depth of Mary's desire to penetrate what she called "the mind forest" of the Fang, and he also must have realized both how acute was her intelligence and how carefully and thoroughly she had prepared herself for her task. Later they would differ over the issues of liquor trade and polygamy, and, as we have seen, Nassau primly reprimanded Mary for her exasperated "Good Lords" and "Allah only knows." But as far as fetish went, they saw eye to eye, and Nassau recognized the strength of character in Mary that would enable her to travel into the hinterland alone.

That this prospect of a white woman traveling on her own through the interior of Congo Français was unheard of, indeed unthinkable, goes without saying. Hence the importance to Mary of Nassau's understanding and support. She gained neither from any other quarter. When Mr. Hudson arrived back shortly from his trip up the Ogooué he was not at all pleased when Mary disclosed her plans to him. Dismay over Mary's solitary state was to become a recurring theme in the course of her travels over the next several months. Wherever she went, whomever she encountered — black or white alike — she was met first with incredulity and then with stern disapproval.

If an unmarried female was regarded as an "odd woman" back in England, she was even more of an anomaly out in West Africa. One can count the number of single women who were there in the nineteenth century almost on the fingers of one hand; the few women who did risk their lives on the Coast were usually married to missionaries or to government officials. Unattached African women were even more of a rarity, for in polygamous societies there was no reason why any woman should remain without a husband, no matter how skewed the male-to-female ratio of the population was. And if an African woman was widowed, she was inherited by her dead husband's brother. Hence the consternation Mary would arouse among the Fang and among other African tribes when she materialized in their villages without any white male accompaniment.

In *Travels in West Africa* she relates a typical example of this reaction to her husbandless plight. She was being paddled between Lambaréné and Andande in Gabon by one of the products of American missionary activity there, an African named Samuel, "with an amazing knowledge of English which he spoke in a quaint, falsetto, far-away sort of voice." Samuel's "besetting sin was curiosity," and he was eager to ascertain Mary's spiritual as well as marital status.

" 'You be Christian, Ma?' " he asked her.

Mary evasively responded by asking him "if he had ever met a white man who was not?" Samuel replied that he had, to which Mary ob-

served, " 'You must have been associating with people whom you ought
not to know.'

Samuel fortunately not having a repartee for this, paddled on . . .
for a few seconds. 'Where be your husband, Ma?' was the next conversational bomb he hurled at me.

'I no got one,' I answer.

'No got?' says Samuel, paralysed with astonishment. . . . He recovered himself, however, and returned to his charge. 'No got one,
Ma?'

'No,' say I furiously. 'Do you get much rubber round here?'

'I no be trade man,' says Samuel refusing to fall into my trap for
changing the conversation. 'Why you no got one?' "

The lesson for Mary of this colloquy with Samuel was that it was
next to impossible for her to account for her single state. In a lecture
at Cheltenham Ladies' College she describes the new tack she began to
take when confronted with queries regarding her spouse: "I may confide to any spinster who is here present and who feels inclined to take
up the study of [the African] that she will be perpetually embarrassed
by inquiries of where is your husband? Not, have you got one or anything like that which you could deal with, but where is he? I must
warn her not to say she has not got one; I have tried it and it only leads
to more appalling questions still. I think that it is more advisable to
say you are searching for him, and then you locate him away in the
direction in which you wish to travel; this elicits help and sympathy."
Perhaps some at least of Mary's audience grasped the pathos as well as
the humor of this aside.

After about two weeks in Libreville and Glass, on the morning of June
5, Mary at last set off for the Ogooué River on the trim paddle steamer,
the *Mové*. As usual, she was the only woman on board, accompanied
this time by Mr. Hudson, who was going upriver again on Hatton and
Cookson business, several government officials, a Catholic priest, and
"black passengers galore." The *Mové* she found "a fine little vessel,"
her cabin snug and neat, "food . . . excellent, society charming, captain and engineer quite acquisitions." Altogether it was an auspicious
beginning for her long-awaited journey.

They steamed out of the estuary round Pongara Point and Point
Gombi with its erratic lighthouse. ("Most lighthouses on this coast
give up fancy tricks like flashing or revolving pretty soon after they are
established. Seventy-five per cent of them are not alight half the time

at all.") Then they turned due south and made for the north of the Ogooué at Nazareth Bay, keeping well within sight of land all the while. By afternoon they had crossed the equator, and shortly after they finally reached the Ogooué, the great brown river stretching more than seven hundred miles into the heart of the Gabon like "a broad road of burnished bronze," ignited by the late afternoon sunset. "The day closed with a magnificent dramatic beauty. Dead ahead of us, up through a bank of dun-coloured mist rose the moon, a great orb of crimson, spreading down the oil-like still river a streak of blood-red reflection. Right astern, the sun sank down into the mist, a vaster orb of crimson, and when he had gone out of view, sent up flushes of amethyst, gold, carmine, and serpent green, before he left the moon in undisputed possession of the black purple sky."

It was a two-day run from the mouth of the Ogooué to Lambaréné some 130 miles from the coast. This lower region of the Ogooué was a superb introduction for Mary to the world of the river because it was virtually untouched by human activity, its main population being "made up of malaria microbes and mosquitoes." They passed a trading hulk and also an Orogungou fishing village perched in the midst of the swampy delta on stilts and "very rickety stilts that look as if [each house] had taken to them some night hurriedly when an extra rise in the water round threatened to wash it away and gave it no proper ones." But mostly the *Mové* and its crew and passengers dwelt in the misty universe of river and forest, and a forest, as Mary says, "beyond all my expectations of tropical luxuriance and beauty." The Ogooué forest she found was "a Cleopatra to which Calabar is but a Quaker." While Mr. Hudson was immersed in his accounts, the engineer preoccupied with coal stoking, and the captain with navigating, Mary stood on deck lost in this magical forest world: a "great glorious strange world of gloom and grandeur" continually relieved from being a monotony of green by crimson, brown-pink and creamy yellow blossoming trees, splashes of pale pink lichen, and vermilion red fungus. All day they steamed on. For Mary the experience was more exhilarating than the most exquisite orchestral music to which she compared it. "Doubtless it is wrong to call it a symphony, yet I know no other word to describe the scenery of the Ogooué. It is as full of life and beauty and passion as any symphony Beethoven ever wrote: the parts changing, interweaving, and returning."

By late afternoon on June 7 they reached the island town of Lambaréné, which would be made famous twenty years later by the hospital Albert Schweitzer established there. Here Mary and Mr. Hudson disembarked and were welcomed by the Hatton and Cookson agent, Mr. Cockshut. While the two men strode up and down the beach, "doubtless talking cargo," Mary retired to the verandah of the Hatton and Cookson factory prepared to contemplate the wild beauty of the scene until dinner, but she was immediately stung all over by mosquitos and sand flies in "appalling quantities." Nor did the stinging of the tormenting insects abate when night fell and Mary was seated at supper between Mr. Cockshut and Mr. Hudson, yet she suffered the insect stings with stoical silence: "I behave exquisitely and am quite lost in admiration of my own conduct, and busily deciding in my mind whether I shall wear one of those plain ring haloes, or a solid plate one. . . . Mr. Hudson says in a voice full of reproach to Mr. Cockshut, 'You have got mosquitos here, Mr. Cockshut.' Poor Mr. Cockshut doesn't deny it; he has got four on his forehead and his hands are sprinkled with them, but he says: 'There are none at Ndjolé,' which we all feel is an absurdly lame excuse, for Ndjolé is some ninety miles above Lambaréné, where we now are. Mr, Hudson says this to him, tersely, and feeling he has utterly crushed Mr. Cockshut turns on me, and utterly failing to recognize me as a suffering saint, says point blank and savagely, 'You don't seem to feel these things, Miss Kingsley.' Not feel them indeed! Why, I could cry over them."

But of course she didn't, and indeed spent two very happy weeks in the Lambaréné district in the nearby missionary settlement of Kangwe with the Rev. Hermann Jacot, his wife, and their two children, "Edmond the Sententious aged five, and Roger the Great aged eighteen months and busy teething with phenomenal rapidity and vigour." For the most part, Mary devoted this first stay at Kangwe to collecting fish, though she also pursued fetish in the surrounding Fang villages, including one called Fula. "Through Fula," she writes in *Travels in West Africa,* one "ill-starred day, I passed with all the éclat of Wombell's menagerie." She was attempting to circumnavigate the village on the steep, pathless hillside overhanging it, when "I slipped, slid, and finally fell plump through the roof of an unprotected hut. What the unfortunate inhabitants were doing, I don't know, but I am pretty sure they were not expecting me to drop in and a scene of great confusion occurred. My knowledge of Fang . . . then consisted of korkor, so I said that in as fascinating a tone as I could, and explained the rest with three pocket handkerchiefs, a head of tobacco, and a knife which providentially I had stowed in . . . my pockets." Thus she propitiated the startled inhabitants. But aside from this adventure, the days at Kangwe passed serenely, so serenely, in fact, that Mary suspended her regular diary and subsequently notes in *Travels in West Africa* that she can't give precise dates or events for Kangwe because "it is one of my disastrous habits well known to my friends on the Coast that whenever I am happy, comfortable, and content, I lose all knowledge of the date, the time of the day, and my hairpins."

By June 22, however, she and Cockshut had left Lambaréné and Kangwe on a small stern wheel steamer, the *Éclaireur,* bound for Ndjolé, ninety miles farther up the Ogooué, which she hoped would be her point of departure for the treacherous Ogooué rapids. By nightfall on the twenty-third they reached Ndjolé and the nearby Mission Évangélique station at Talagouga. Their arrival provoked the "usual uproar, but, as Mr. Cockshut says, no mosquitoes." Just as they were getting off the *Éclaireur,* a very ill and feverish French official was carried on — grim realities again in the midst of the primeval forest beauty. Later Mary heard that he died before even reaching the mouth of the river. Talagouga, in fact, was a forbidding place. As Mary put it, it "is grand but its scenery is undoubtedly grim, and its name signifying the gateway of misery seems applicable." She photographed the mission station hitched on to a rocky, forest-covered hill: the mission house, the "prettiest church in Africa," a sawmill, and various outbuildings. Nearby stood the ruins of the house Dr. Nassau had built when he established the mission some twenty year earlier. And before the crumbling house was the grave of his wife, which somehow had withstood the forest's efforts to obliterate it with moss, creepers, and vines. It was almost impossible to move freely about the mission, which added to its gloomy, oppressive air. The hillside was so precipitous that only a very steep footpath led down to the river, and the enveloping forest was so thick as to be virtually impenetrable. Mary's explanation for its utter lack of bush paths was that "no Fang village wants to walk to another Fang village for social civilities, and all their trade goes up and down the river in canoes." Small wonder, then, that when the long dry season exposed the previously subaqueous sandbars in the river, as happened in the course of Mary's stay, everyone felt a sense of release at the sight — a dazzling white expanse in the midst of the dull bronze river and the deep, blackish green of the forest.

The Talagouga mission was staffed by two young French couples: the Forgets and their infant daughter Oranie, and the Gacons. Mary stayed with the Forgets, both of whom spoke excellent English and politely tolerated their strange guest's predilection for lengthy hikes under the equatorial sun when everyone else was sanely taking a siesta. For Mary spent most of her time in Talagouga wandering the pathless forest in search of specimens, often having to hack her way through with a machete and being rewarded for her efforts with "sensational meetings with blue-green snakes, dirty green snakes with triangular horned heads, black cobras, and boa constrictors. I never came back to the station without having been frightened out of my wits, and with one or two of my small terrifiers in cleft sticks to bottle." She soon became adept at catching snakes in cleft sticks, in fact, and in *Travels in West Africa* states that it is really "perfectly simple. Only mind you have the proper kind of stick, split far enough up, and keep your attention on the snake's head, that's his business end, and the tail which is whisking and winding round your wrist does not matter."

Mary also did a considerable amount of fish collecting at Talagouga. At first she bought specimens from fishermen in the nearby villages, but soon she was able to catch her own after she learned how to maneuver a dugout canoe. The current at Talagouga was swift and strong, and Mary's efforts to teach herself how to paddle and steer aroused both alarm and uncontrollable mirth in her hosts as they watched her from the bank whirl about in circles like a spinning top, crash into overhanging trees, and rush along with the current until mercifully halted by a raised sandbank. But the skill she eventually developed in handling a canoe was one of the few things Mary ever boasted about. She writes in *Travels in West Africa* that "there are only two things I am proud of — one is that Dr. Günther has approved of my fishes, and the other is that I can paddle an Ogooué canoe. Pace, style, steering and all . . . as if I were an Ogooué African." A strange, incongruous pair of things, she admits, "but I often wonder what are the things other people are really most proud of."

As her canoeing skills matured, Mary began to go farther and farther afield from her base and friends at Talagouga. At first these ventures were not solitary ones. She accompanied a small party of Azumba for example on an ivory-trading expedition. In order to pursue fetish while they pursued ivory, she asked them to drop her at a remote Fang village and then, after they reached their destination farther upriver, to pick her up on their way back. All went well as long as Mary's stock of trade goods held out, but as day after day passed and the Azumba failed to reappear and as her supplies of cloth and tobacco became depleted, she began to grow a bit desperate, for there were rumors that

the Fang sometimes killed empty-handed traders, recovered their ivory
and rubber, and then used them subsequently with other traders. Hence
Mary "kept [her] eye most anxiously on the lookout" for her Azumba
friends' canoe "for days in vain." When all her trade stock was exhausted, she was forced to sell her own belongings and for the first
time regretted her meager outfit. Nevertheless, she shrewdly made the
best of what she had. "My own clothes I certainly did insist on having
more for, pointing out that they were rare and curious. A dozen white
ladies' blouses sold well. I cannot say they looked well when worn . . .
in conjunction with *nothing* else but red paint and a bunch of leopard
tails, particularly when [the wearer] failed to tie the strings at the
back. But I did not hint at this and I *quite* realise that a pair of stockings can be made to go further than we make them by using one at a
time, and putting the top part over the head and letting the rest of the
garment float on the breeze." The last thing she parted with was her
toothbrush and then just as she was contemplating setting up business
as a witch doctor, the Azumba canoe came back and retrieved her.
Perhaps it was this experience of being stranded that made Mary even
more determined to perfect her canoeing so that future forays could be
solo ones.

Certainly there was something deeply rewarding about being able
to handle and propel a canoe. It gave Mary freedom, control, mobility.
She could leave the mission station and the gloom of its surrounding
forest, ride the swift inlets, and enter into the grim, twilit world of
the mangrove swamps. She loved to canoe in all seasons and weathers,
but most of all, she loved to be "dropping down" the river at night
when the moon was up and the constellations sprinkled across the deep
purple sky, and when the surrounding soft warm air was "be-gemmed
with fire-flies," as she described it in a lecture, "and . . . heavy with
the scent of flowers." Every so often she would drift past a village and
see shadowy figures "dancing by the light of the fires" and hear "the
thump, thump, thump of their drums, and the long drawn melancholy cadence of their songs."

Once she had mastered the art of canoeing Mary was determined to
attempt the rough Alemba rapids above Ndjolé and Talagouga. Her
scientific motive was to find new fish; since she had found new species
in Talagouga that did not exist at Lambaréné, she hypothesized that
the rapids too would hold new specimens. Most likely, however, she
set her heart on traveling the rapids for the sheer exhilaration the adventure was bound to yield. But there were many obstacles to her plans

to "do" them. Of course the Forgets and the Gacons tried to dissuade her from this particular "picnic." Once they realized her determination, however, they arranged for a large canoe and a crew of two Galoa and six Fang to accompany her. Mary was delighted; she packed her portmanteau, got some trade goods, wound up her watch, ascertained the date, and borrowed three hairpins from Madame Forget, and "then down came disappointment." The Talagouga Fang refused to go beyond Ndjolé for fear of their upriver Fang brothers. "Internally consigning the entire tribe to regions where they will get a raise in temperature even on this climate," Mary appealed to Monsieur Gacon, and he managed to provide her with additional Galoa.

And so Mary "screwed her courage to the sticking point," and departed with her Galoa crew, only to be stymied again by the authorities in Ndjolé. It was the old familiar story. They were loath to allow a single white woman to proceed to the rapids alone. Mary protested that another woman, a certain Madame Quinee, had been up them before, but officialdom countered that Madame Quinee had been with her husband and a large crew of Adjoumba, reputedly the best canoeists, whereas Mary was alone and had only eight Galoa with her. Mary conceded these facts, but went on to argue that she didn't want to go as far as Madame Quinee had but only a sufficient distance to collect fish. The Galoa, she insisted, were every bit as proficient at canoeing as the Adjoumba. As for a husband, Mary pointed out that "neither the Royal Geographical Society's list in their *Hints for Travellers* nor Messrs. Silver in their elaborate lists of articles necessary for a traveller in tropical climates make mention of husbands." Eventually permission was granted.

It was, in truth, a nearly suicidally risky journey. They kept close to the bank most of the time so that when the canoe threatened to capsize or the current threatened to smash it to bits on the rocks protruding from the foaming, rushing water, Mbo, the headman of the crew, who spoke a little pidgin English, would yell at Mary, "Jump for bank, Sahr!" and she would obediently jump. If there was a village in the vicinity the inhabitants would rush to the river to watch the porterage. And, as Mary describes one such incident in *Travels in West Africa,*

> seeing we were becoming amusing . . . they came legging it like lamplighters, after us, young and old, male and female, to say nothing of the dogs. Some good souls helped the men haul, while I did my best to amuse the others by diving headlong from a large rock on to which

I had elaborately climbed into a thick clump of willow-leaved shrubs. They applauded my performance vociferously . . . and during the rest of my scramble they kept close to me with keen competition for the front row, in hopes that I would do something like it again. But I refused the encore because bashful as I am, I could not but feel that my last performance was carried out with all the superb reckless abandon of a Sarah Bernhardt, and a display of art of this order should satisfy any African village for a year at least.

It was a three-day trip, this "knock-about farce before King Death in his amphitheatre in the Sierra del Cristal," as Mary sums it up in *Travels in West Africa.* These days were a series of close calls, drenchings, tedious porterage, and then breakneck movement down the river again. They stayed at island villages at night, where they were welcomed by astonished villagers who had never seen a white woman before. And finally, on the third day, they reached the mighty Alemba rapids. Even before they saw it they could hear its "elemental roar." Mary said to Mbo, " 'That's a thunderstorm away among the rapids.' 'No, sir,' says he, 'that's the Alemba.' " Regarding the great Alemba, Mary is for the only time in her travels rendered speechless. It was at Kondo Kondo Island, directly opposite the Alemba, that Mary wrote once again to Günther. Despite all their mishaps, she had managed to collect and bottle some precious new fish, and for once she glancingly refers to the danger of her present situation when she tells Günther that she has sent word to Hudson in Libreville that if she fails to turn up in a month's time, he is to forward all her specimens to Günther back in England.

In this same letter to Günther Mary enclosed a small white lily called by her companions "the lily of the spirit of the rapids." (If you go to the Natural History Museum in Kensington today you will find the white lily that Mary picked on the banks of the Ogooué ninety years ago folded up in the letter she wrote Günther; a tiny white butterfly will also flutter out of the envelope, now tinged ivory, like the lily, by the passage of time and of a papery fragility.)

The return journey back to Talagouga was every bit as harrowing as the trip to the great Alemba. At one point the canoe got brutally jammed on a clump of rocks and spilled its occupants out pell-mell into the rushing water. Mary and the French flag (which always accompanied her on what she called her "submergencies") took refuge on a nearby rock, unfortunately a rather inconvenient "smooth pillar affair." Because it was night and the atmosphere murky, there was considerable delay before the party could regroup and regain the canoe, and then they discovered that one of the men was missing. Just when they concluded that the Ogooué had claimed another victim, they heard the strains of "that fine hymn, 'Notre port est au ciel,' coming . . . above the rapids' clamour in an agonised howl. We went," Mary writes, "joyfully and picked the singer off his rock and then dashed downwards to further dilemmas and disasters." And so they succeeded in returning to Talagouga with a somewhat battered but intact crew and vessel.

For once Mary's timing was excellent; just several days after returning to Talagouga, the *Éclaireur* materialized again on its run down to Lambaréné. It was from Lambaréné, or rather from nearby Kangwe, that Mary hoped to launch her next and greatest adventure: an overland journey through the uncharted territory between the Ogooué and Remboué rivers, and thence down the Remboué to the estuary and back to Libreville.

But even more than the rapids excursion, Mary's projected overland trek required skillful and determined planning, and it encountered even greater resistance than had the rapids trip, which now indeed did seem a minor "picnic" compared with her desire to walk from the Ogooué through dense rain forest, swamps, and rocky hills to the Remboué. So she remained with the Jacots in Kangwe some days while her plans for the trip to the Remboué went forward by fits and starts. In the interim, she continued to practice her canoeing and to take long hikes in the surrounding forest in pursuit of wildlife and fetish. For the most part, these were solitary rambles, but one day she went out with a party of five Africans and several of their wives, and, as she wrote home to Günther, one of the men was suddenly attacked by a leopard that sprang out from the thick forest bordering the bush path. They all tried to separate man from beast, and in the process one of the men nearly cut off the victim's hand with a machete. It was one of those "fight or flight" situations in which one acts quickly and instinctively, and Mary swiftly found herself in the midst of the fray of snarling leopard and weapon-wielding men. But the leopard had bitten through the poor man's jugular — a fatal wound — so that in the end they could only avenge his death by killing the leopard, before bearing the dead man's body on their shoulders back to the mission station. This was the sort of experience that never found its way into any of Mary's books or lectures, for she was extremely loath to recount any tales of her own personal bravery. Indeed, she always insisted that she was quite devoid of both courage and fear. When in a tight spot, she said, she was aware only of a bitter salt taste in her mouth, and then she acted swiftly, without any conscious deliberation.

It was during this second stay at Kangwe that Mary also had her first encounters with gorillas. But along with her tight scrapes with leopards and snakes and crocodiles, she consistently understated her gorilla ancedotes, in contrast to her hero and predecessor Du Chaillu, whose fame derived largely from his sensational accounts of these enormous and disconcertingly humanlike beasts. Mary was repulsed rather than impressed by gorillas and objected to the way "they squattered across the open ground in a most inelegant style." Not that she lingered for long when she happened upon members of a gorilla family gorging themselves on the thick forest foliage or lazily lounging about in the trees, for she knew that they were liable to charge if they felt their young threatened. Just such a confrontation occurred later on in her travels so that one of her men had to shoot an enraged male gorilla in the chest at a distance of scarcely ten feet. In the midst of such crises Mary found it prudent to ignore the scientific advice of a British zoologist back home: "Always take measurements, Miss Kingsley, and always take them from the adult male." But at some point during this Kangwe interlude Mary came into possession of a baby gorilla — just how and why she does not say — which she told Günther she promptly sold because she was running short of money.

However great her affection for the Jacots and their two little boys, Mary's second sojourn at the Mission Évangélique only reinforced her misgivings about missionary activity in West Africa. Although she acknowledged the nobility of the missionaries' intentions, the bravery of their actions, and the strength and stoicism with which they endured (and sometimes succumbed to) the privations and deadly climate of West Africa, Mary could see little or no good produced by their efforts and even went so far as to say publicly that the missionaries "have produced results which all truly interested in West Africa must deplore."

To begin with, the missionaries' conversion rate, despite their tireless efforts, remained low, and backsliding among new converts was very common. Mary movingly describes the process in *West African Studies:* "I know no more distressing thing," she writes, "than to see an African convert brought face to face with that awful thing we are used to, the problem of an omnipotent God and a suffering world. This does not worry the African convert until it hits him personally in grief and misery. When it does, and he turns and calls upon the God he has been taught will listen, pity and answer . . . [it] is horribly heartrending to me, for I know how real, terribly real, the whole thing is to him and I therefore see the temptation to return to . . . [his] old gods." This psychological problem of the silence of the white man's god — a silence so alien to the prevalence of supernatural forces in all aspects of African life — was behind Mary's opinion that Islam was more appropriate to African culture than was Christianity. But ideally to her, this African culture would remain immune to the imposition of both Muslim and Christian proselytizing.

And the wish for this immunity was also behind Mary's continued hostility to education by the missionaries and to the missionaries' efforts to stamp out polygamy and the liquor trade. The schools run by most West Coast missions operated on the implicit and unquestioned principle of cultural hegemony: instruction was conducted in French rather than in any of the local African languages, and technical education, where it existed, consisted of teaching such skills as tailoring, bookbinding, and printing, "trades which," Mary observed, "Africa is not yet in urgent need to be taught." It was the Gold Coast all over again. "The teaching even of sewing, washing, and ironing" seemed to her "a little previous, . . . [and] . . . quite parlor accomplishments when your husband does not wear a shirt and household linen is nonexistent as is the case among the Fang and many other African tribes."

The issues of polygamy and the liquor trade were far more volatile, however, than mission schooling, and they got Mary into endless hot water once she returned home. She condoned, even defended, exporting trade gin and other alcohol to Africa on purely practical grounds. It was a convenient, economical and popular trade item — not bulky like cloth or perishable like tobacco. It procured a sure source of revenue, immune to fads and fashion. Furthermore, Mary condemned the colonial frame of mind that viewed the selling of liquor to Africans as equivalent to giving dynamite to children to play with. The fact was, she insisted, that the African could hold his liquor as well as any European, indeed even better in most instances: "I have no hesitation in saying that in the whole of West Africa there is not one-quarter the amount of drunkenness you can see any Saturday night you choose in the Vauxhall Road; and you will not find in a whole year's investigation on the Coast, one seventieth part of the evil, degradation, and premature decay you can see any afternoon you choose to take a walk in the more densely-populated parts of any of our own towns."

Mary even went so far as to have trade gin analyzed by the Chemical Society to demonstrate that it was less potent than such indigenous alcoholic drinks as palm wine or maize beer or even good old English whiskey or rum. But above all, she hated the hypocrisy of the anti-liquor-traffic school, most of whose members liked their port or sherry or whiskey as much as the next person. It was the condescension and accompanying assumption of moral superiority among the antiliquor-traffic party that Mary could not stomach.

Mary's stand on polygamy was far more complex and important than her defense of the liquor trade. For a late Victorian English spinster to take up, even champion, what her adversaries deemed institutionalized African promiscuity was, to say the least, rather unexpected. But Mary defended polygamy vehemently on both practical and ethical grounds because she realized that polygamy was an essential part of the fabric of African society and that to ban it heedlessly, as all missionaries did among their African flocks, was to wreak havoc with the structure and functioning of African culture.

"Now polygamy," Mary writes in *Travels in West Africa,* "is a very difficult thing to form an opinion on, if before forming that opinion, you go and make a study of the facts and bearings of the case. It is therefore advisable to follow the usual method employed by the majority of people. Just take a prejudice of your own, and fix it up with the so-called opinions of people who go in for that sort of prejudice too. This method," she continues, "is absolutely essential to the forming of an opinion on the subject of polygamy among African tribes that will be acceptable in enlightened circles." The view among "enlightened circles" of course was that polygamy was morally indefensible. The "facts and bearings of the case" that Mary marshaled to counter this "prejudice" were first of all pragmatic: it was quite simply impossible for one wife to perform all the duties and chores of African domestic life — the cooking, child care, water carrying, preparation of rubber, farming, marketing, and so on. In fact, African women themselves preferred to share their husbands with co-wives, for, as Mary summed it up, "the more wives the less work, says the African lady."

Mary was also fully aware that African women refused to have intercourse with their husbands while nursing and that African children were often not weaned until well over two years old. Recourse, then, to other wives was a virtual necessity for the husbands. One of the missionaries Mary discussed the matter with proposed another solution: " 'A blow must be struck at polygamy, and that blow must be dealt with a feeding bottle.' " And so a shipment of baby bottles was sent out to the Coast, but, as Mary reported, "they don't go off, and the missionary has returned to America."

Underlying her defense of polygamy was Mary's keen understanding of the nature of African marriage and more generally of the relations between the sexes in Africa. What the European missionary could not comprehend was the negligible importance of romantic love, with all its accompanying emotional baggage of sexual exclusiveness and fidelity, to African marriage. The rules and expectations of the marital game were different here, and the strongest emotional bonds were those of blood — between parent and child, sister and brother — rather than the bond between husband and wife.

There were also moral dilemmas arising from the missionaries' stand against polygamy. Suppose the convert had four or five wives or, on the other hand, if the convert was a woman, shared a husband with several other women. With hellfire and damnation looming ahead in the next world, the convert would be pressured into casting off all but one of his wives or into leaving her husband, with the result, in either case, of rendering the women vulnerable and without means of support. Mary tells of meeting with an old, recently converted chief with three wives who was ordered to desert all but one of them. But the women banded together, and each of them refused to marry him in his new church if it meant driving away the other two wives. "It was," as Mary described it, "a moral mess of the first water all round."

There was no place for the single "odd woman" in African society. Not merely a woman's status but her very survival depended upon her being some man's wife. To impose Christian monogamy on converted Africans would mean condemning certain women, especially those who were poor, older, or barren, to social and financial misery. Though her paramount interest as an ethnographer was in fetish, Mary was intrigued and profoundly moved by the lives of African women. In *West African Studies* she confesses, "I own that if I have a soft spot in my feelings it is towards African women, and the close contact I have lived in with them has given rise to this, and I venture to think, made me understand them." A large part of the affinity Mary felt with African women arose from their resistance and even hostility to European "civilization," "a reasonable dislike," as Mary put it, "to being dispossessed alike of power and property in what they regard as their own country." African women, then, came to represent for Mary a kind of indigenous purity and imperviousness to cultural contamination. They shied away from Western education, willingly shared husbands while retaining their own personal property, adhered to the African tradition of matriarchy in the face of colonial patriarchy, and so on.

But Mary was fascinated by the lives of African women on their own account as well. She devotes pages of *Travels in West Africa* and *West African Studies* to minute descriptions of their dress, hair-plaiting styles, cooking, farming, and so forth. She understood how they retained some measure of economic autonomy within marriage through petty trading, growing cash crops, and in some cases owning cattle. And Mary knew about the more intimate facts of their lives as well, data that she not infrequently had to convey to Professor Tylor back at Oxford via Mrs. Tylor. This delicate information would encompass such matters as African women's experience of menstruation and circumcision — and the ritual of initiation that often accompanied these events — marriage, childbirth, menopause, and often widowhood. What struck Mary again and again was the discrepancy between the political and social powerlessness of these women and the unstructured or un-institutionalized independence and strength they possessed within the rigid confines of their appointed spheres as daughters, wives, and mothers of men. Mary grasped that the seeming injustice of polygamy for African women was more apparent than real. Yes, it granted sexual freedom to men while denying it to women, but at the same time, through the division of labor shared by co-wives, it afforded them more time and freedom to pursue their own interests, often economic interests, which further liberated them from dependence upon their husbands.

In addition, and this must have counted heavily, albeit unconsciously, in Mary's endorsement of polygamy, no African woman need know the isolation of English spinsterhood, with all its pathetic braveries and hidden sorrows. To be sure, the African woman could know desolation, particularly if she was barren, but she would never be utterly alone. She would have a husband, a family, a home to which she belonged and contributed. She would be spared the plight of living in a dark, cramped flat at the top of a drafty house with only a frequently absent, undemonstrative and fastidious brother prone to a "dingy" frame of mind. In the stifling heat of the Kangwe night Mary probably lay awake under her mosquito net comparing her own lot with that of the Galoa and Fang women she was living among. Perhaps she even compared the fate of Madame Jacot and her two little boys with those of African widows when she learned of Hermann Jacot's sudden death from fever several months after she had returned to England. There was no brother-in-law to "inherit" Madame Jacot and her children. She took the next steamer back to France with "Edmond the Sententious and Roger the Great," to what meager future we can only guess.

Monsieur Jacot was hale and hearty, however, during this period while Mary was orchestrating her overland trip to the Remboué. After all her trade goods had been procured and packed; after Mary had gained grudging permission from the French authorities, although they refused her the protection of the French flag, which she had had on the rapids jaunt; after she had roughly plotted her own course through territory she could only guess the nature of, for no European had crossed it before; and after she had assembled all her own gear — her blouses and woolen skirts in her black waterproof bag, her papers, trade tobacco, and geological specimens in her portmanteau, and her brush, comb, and toothbrush in "a basket constructed for catching human souls . . . given . . . as a farewell gift by a valued friend, a witch doctor" — she turned her attention to the party of men she would need to accompany her. And here Monsieur Jacot proved indispensible. Even though Mary wished to limit her crew to the absolute minimum, as she had on the trip to the rapids, no one was very eager to volunteer because of the rumors of a "blood war" they felt certain awaited them en route to the Remboué. At last, however, Monsieur Jacot was able to recruit five men for her: a Galoa "interpreter" named Ngouta, whose repertoire of English Mary soon discovered consisted of "P'raps," "'Tis better so," and "Lordy, Lordy, helpee me," and four Adjoumba on whom Mary bestowed English sobriquets derived from their distinctive characteristics in apparel or character: Gray Shirt, Singlet, Silent, and Pagan. An unpaid Adjoumba hanger-on who attached himself to the party out of sheer adventurousness Mary named Passenger.

·✧ 9 ✧·

The Journey to the Remboué

Before dawn on the morning of Monday, July 22, Mary Kingsley awoke with a splitting headache, a sure indication that she was in for another bout of malaria. It was the long-planned-for date of her departure for the Remboué River, but none of the signs boded well. Rain poured from a leaden sky, and her crew of Adjoumba failed to turn up at daybreak as arranged. Eventually they arrived at a little past eight o'clock, and they decided to wait and see if the rain and/or Mary's headache would let up. Neither did, so they finally left Kangwe at two in the afternoon in order to arrive at their first stopping point, Gray Shirt's home, the Adjoumba village of Arevooma, by nightfall. Mary spent the long afternoon's paddle recumbent on the luggage and the copious stores of plantain and yam stowed in the bottom of the canoe. Because of her throbbing headache she was for once rather indifferent to her surroundings, not that they provided much that was new. The greater part of the journey to the Remboué would be overland, but in order to reach the best point from which to embark on their trek, they had to take the Ogooué affluents, the O'Rembo Vongo and the Karkola rivers some distance northwest of Kangwe.

The overnight stay at Arevooma was not uneventful. As soon as Mary was installed in Gray Shirt's house, she was summoned to a prayer service organized by Gray Shirt and Singlet, both enthusiastic Christian converts, and "of course [I] had to go headache or no headache," though "what with the hymns and the mosquitos the experience [was] slightly awful." Returning to Gray Shirt's abode at past midnight she settled into his luxurious bed — a real bed with a chintz mosquito bar and a calico coverlet — and read Horace by candlelight until a fat marmalade-colored cat demanded to join her. The two had a rather fitful night of it, because the cat kept dashing to and from the bed to kill marauding rats scurrying about in the one-room house.

In the morning Mary was greeted by the news that a man "done die" in the night. The only explanation she could elicit for the sudden decease was that "he just truck luck, and then he die." Not that Mary was likely to get anything in the way of medical explanations; she well knew that all illnesses and deaths were ascribed to witchcraft. But if inquests were unknown in West Africa, funeral rites were common and predictable. As soon as Mary emerged from Gray Shirt's house she saw the dead man's "widows . . . having their faces painted white by sympathetic lady friends and . . . attired in their oldest dirtiest clothes." The omens for the trip remained grim; on the other hand, at least Mary's headache and the dreaded bout of fever had subsided.

But her hosts were extremely pessimistic about her chances of getting safely through the territory of the "fearful Fang." And momentarily at least their vivid prophecies of misadventures ahead daunted Mary. Great predeparture palaver ensued while the white-faced widows wailed and moaned in the background. " 'How are we going to get through that way?' says I, with natural feminine alarm, . . . far from a French station, and without the French flag. Why did I not obey Mr. Hudson's orders not to go wandering about in a reckless way! Anyhow, I am in for it, and Fortune favours the brave. The only question is: Do I individually come under this class?" Of course she did, but the critical factor in Mary's decision to go ahead was that Pagan had made friends and done business with two Fang in the first Fang village they were to visit, and Pagan felt confident that his friends would receive them hospitably and would provide protection farther on down their route. This was the first and last time Mary wavered in the course of the journey; she decided in the early morning hours at Arevooma to forge ahead.

Having made up her mind, Mary marshaled her men and made an early start of it. The entire day was spent on the small rivers and streams leading to the freshwater lakes where they would leave their canoe and proceed on foot. Only rarely was the surrounding dense forest relieved by any signs of life. They came upon a solitary snow-white crane perched on a sandbank, which, when Gray Shirt took an unsuccessful shot at it, raised itself up, made a small graceful "curt-sey," and then sailed off, its broad wings outspread and its long legs trailing behind it, like a figure on a Japanese screen. In the afternoon they stopped for tea, and in the course of a short walk Mary came upon curious mounds of earth she took for some kind of animal's or bird's nest. But when she gingerly poked at them with her umbrella, she discovered that they were burial places. "Among the debris of an old one there [were] human bones, and out from one of the new ones [came] a stench and a hurrying, exceedingly busy line of ants, demonstrating what [was] going on." The beautiful, graceful crane and the stark white bones and decomposing flesh: these images symbolized the two extremes of the world Mary had come so far to find. Of course there was no turning back.

By the evening of the twenty-third they reached Lake Ncovi, "a lovely, strangely melancholy, lonely-looking lake," just as the golden sunlight of late afternoon was burnishing the still, mirrorlike water with its last gleams. On an island in the middle of Lake Ncovi was the Fang village of M'fetta where Pagan's friends were supposed to reside, and one and all sincerely hoped that Pagan did have friends there and that they would be at home because M'fetta had a decidedly bad reputation.

With some trepidation, then, they paddled across the lake to the island, just as darkness was falling. The villagers hastened down the forested hill from the town to the beach where Mary's party landed. "Pagan got out . . . alongside the canoe just as the inhabitants . . . came — a brown mass of naked humanity down the steep . . . path to attend to us." Pagan could not immediately pick out either of his friends among the welcoming party, and, as Mary put it, "things did not look restful nor these Fangs personally pleasant." Indeed, they were quite frightening to behold, these gun- and knife-armed M'fettan Fangs, with whom, as Mary describes the situation in *Travels in West Africa*, "it was touch-and-go for twenty of the longest minutes I have ever lived." Pagan called out the name of one of his friends, Kiva, in vain, and Mary nonchalantly strolled to the front of the party "saying to the line of angry faces 'M'boloani' in an unconcerned way, although I well knew it was etiquette for them to salute first."

At last Kiva appeared, and Pagan rushed to him and made a stylized, propitiating embrace; then Gray Shirt espied another Fang friend in the crowd and did the same. Mary "looked round to see if there was not any Fang from the Upper Ogooué whom I knew to go for." There wasn't, but now the ice had been broken. In her first confrontation with the "fearful Fang" Mary exhibited the respect and sensitivity she was always to show toward them, and her reward for this first meeting was, after initial tension and hostility, to be received warmly into their midst: after greetings and handshaking all round, "we all disappeared into a brown mass of humanity and a fog of noise" as they made their way up the hill to the village.

At last Mary had reached the Fang in their purest, uncontaminated, inland form, untouched by the coastal or European influences that had affected the Fang she had met in Libreville and on the Ogooué. Mary's knowledge of them and her decision to make them her "own" people derived largely from her four most admired predecessors in African exploration: Burton, Du Chaillu, Reade, and Brazza. Brazza knew the Fang best because he traveled extensively in their territory and dealt with them as a government agent, negotiating delicate treaties and establishing stations in their midst. Du Chaillu's and Reade's contact was more fleeting, and predictably they emphasized the Fangs' more sensational customs, especially their alleged cannibalism. Burton, while giving lip service to the established Fang notoriety for bloodthirstiness and savagery, also identified the source of the Fang appeal, not only for himself but also for Kingsley and for most intelligent travelers after her. He wrote a pioneering article on the Fang for the *Anthropological Review* in 1863, and in his best-selling *Two Trips to Gorilla Land,* published in 1876, Burton devoted more than thirty pages to them. The burden of what Burton has to say of the Fang is that unlike the Mpongwe and other coastal groups, the Fang remained largely uncorrupted by Western customs and mores.

At the core of Burton's and subsequent Europeans' vision of the Fang was the Romantic notion of the Noble Savage. The Fangs' origin was shrouded in mystery. They had only begun to migrate into Congo Français in the late eighteenth and early nineteenth centuries, perhaps from the grassy plateaus of northern Cameroon. Fang legends, however, held that they came from even farther away, from a land in the northeast of the continent inhabited by white men who rode horses and worked in iron. Thus they were connected by oral tradition with the civilizations of the upper Nile and Egypt.

But for Mary and for Burton the Fangs' nobility sprang not so much from their vague historical past as from their strength as warriors, for they swept through Congo Français, conquering or assimilating such peoples as the Galoa, Bakota, and Nkoni who stood in their way. They were skilled workers in iron, powerful traders of both rubber and ivory, and prosperous cultivators of cassava, plantains, and peanuts. They lacked an elaborate hierarchy of authority based on blood. Instead, "pre-eminent elders," or temporary clan chiefs and military leaders, were chosen to govern them on the basis of merit and talent. Their fetish focused on an ancestor cult that, like their witchcraft and secret societies, had successfully resisted missionary influence.

Such resistance was also integral to the Fangs' appeal to Europeans. They were "Noble Savages" not simply because of their noble heritage and noble conquests, but because, as Burton first pointed out, in the face of white domination the Fang had fought back and retained their own cultural integrity. Mary makes this clear in her discussion of Fang currency. Unlike most other groups, the Fang had minted their own money in the form of little iron imitation ax heads called *bikei,* but those Fang dwelling on the coast and in contact with the white missionaries, traders, and government officials had abandoned their own currency for that of the Europeans. As Mary explains it in *Travels in West Africa,* "you do not find bikei close down to Libreville, among the Fang who are there in a semi-civilized state, or more properly speaking in a state of disintegrating culture."

Mary discusses many aspects of Fang culture in *Travels in West Africa* and in *West African Studies.* She was particularly interested in their crafts — pottery, basket making, netting, weaving, and iron work — and she also describes their ivory and rubber collections at length. Furthermore, she paints a picture of sexual equality in Fang marriage that would have warmed the hearts of the most militant suffragettes back home. The Fang husband in fact is described by Mary as a paragon of masculine enlightenment: "He will turn a hand to anything that does not necessitate his putting down his gun outside his village gateway. He will help chop firewood or goat's chop, or he will carry the baby with pleasure, while his lady does these things; . . . and he will . . . tease out fibre to make game nets with, and plait baskets or make pottery with the ladies cheerily chatting the while."

Surprisingly, comparatively little of Mary's long chapters on fetish in *Travels in West Africa* and *West African Studies* deal specifically with the Fang. She does a fairly complete anthropological workup on them in her chapter "Bush Trade and Fang Customs" in *Travels in West Africa* just as she did on the Bubi earlier. But she fails to delve deeply into their complex spiritual beliefs. In fact, most of her writing on fetish is rather generalized, on "the West African mind forest," as she put it, as if this were one homogeneous territory. When she does single out particular groups, it is usually the Igbo or the Twi or the Fjort whom she knew a good deal about from her reading and from her friendships with such authorities as Mary Slessor and R. E. Dennett. Nassau, it is true, taught her much about the Fang, as well as about the Galoa and Benga, and certainly Mary's fieldwork among the Fang was far more extensive than was her fieldwork among any other African ethnic group. She knew the Fang intimately, she admired them almost without reservation and felt a profound kinship with them. All this Mary makes very explicit in *Travels in West Africa:*

> I have been considerably chaffed . . . about my partiality for this tribe, but as I like Africans in my way — not à la Sierra Leone [that is, Europeanized] — and these Africans have more of the qualities I like than any other tribe I have met, it is but natural that I should prefer them. They are brave and so you can respect them. . . . They are . . . a fine race . . . where one continually sees magnificent specimens of human beings, both male and female. Their colour is light bronze, many of the men have beards . . . the average height . . . is five feet six to five feet eight. . . . Their countenances are very bright and expressive, and if once you have been among them, you can never mistake a Fang. But it is in their mental characteristics that their difference from their lethargic, dying-out coast tribes is most marked. The Fang is full of fire, temper, intelligence and go.

For Mary the Fang came to represent the pure, uncontaminated African: physically handsome, intelligent, and brave. During her overland trek she lived among them day and night. She was in a region where no white person had been before (she loved to recount stories of the terror and wails of Fang children at the sight of her white face). Gradually, inexorably, she shed the skin of her English feminine identity. Even if she hadn't sought to become one of the Fang, the pressure toward assimilation would have been great. And of course she did little to resist. It was almost as if that route between the Ogooué and the Remboué were a darkened tunnel that Mary entered at Kangwe and emerged from at Agonjo, and what happened in the darkened space was like a dream somehow, unmoored as she was from everything familiar and stable in her old life.

It may be that Mary did not write extensively of the Fang — and especially of their law and fetish — because, as she said later, she always expected to return and study them with greater care and in greater depth and then publish a full-scale work on them. But it seems more likely that she held back because she could not speak of the Fang dispassionately as she had of the Bubi, with the necessary anthropological detachment. Occasionally in the huts of the Fang villages she stayed in Mary would find a jagged piece of mirror — a great treasure in such remote regions. She must have been startled by the reflection of her pale, narrow face, "full of fire, temper, intelligence and go," that stared back at her, reminding her that she was not, externally, akin to the people around her. And yet at bottom her failure to examine the Fang critically in writing her books, despite her repeated insistence that they were her "brothers," her people, must have come from her awareness that to do so would be an act of self-revelation, even self-exposure. And so praise is heaped on the noble Fang and the material manifestations of their culture described, but beyond this Mary will not take us, because the path would have led into some of the deeper reaches of her own heart and mind.

When she had climbed the first path at hand leading to M'fetta, however, Mary was not very taken with her first unadulterated Fang village. "The town was exceedingly filthy — the remains of the crocodile they had been eating the week before last and piles of fish offal, and remains of an elephant, hippo or manatee — I really can't say which, decomposition was too far advanced — united to form a most impressive stench." This initial impression was not enhanced when one of the women offered Mary "a mass of slimy gray abomination on a bit of plantain leaf — smashed snail to eat."

The first thing to be done, despite the lateness of the hour, was for Mary to augment her crew with several Fang, and so they made their way to the palaver house in the center of town. Such negotiations were always tortuous and of a leisurely duration. After a while Mary retreated to her hut for a cup of tea, but as she tried to relax a bit "the door hole was entirely filled with a mosaic of faces." Returning to the carrier deliberations, she found to her surprise that three of the richest men in M'fetta had volunteered their services: Pagan's friend, Kiva, a handsome young man named Fika, and a noted elephant hunter called Wiki. In addition, another unpaid traveler like Passenger attached himself to the party, "a Fang gentleman with the manners of a duke and the habits of a dustbin," whom Mary called the Duke. This brought her band to a total of ten men: the Galoa interpreter Ngouta; the four Adjoumba — Gray Shirt, Silent, Singlet, and Pagan; Passenger and the Duke; and now the three Fang. In return for their services Mary promised to pay them when they reached Hatton and Cookson's subfactory on the Remboué.

By this time it was past midnight. Mary returned to her hut, but the stifling heat, mosquitos, and lice all conspired to make sleep impossible. Shortly before 1:00 A.M. she stole out again into the silent, slumbering village, made her way down to the beach, and then borrowed a small Fang canoe and paddled out onto the dark lake. "Quantities of big fish sprung out of the water, their glistening silver-white scales flashing so that they looked like slashing swords. Some birds were making a long, low boom-booming sound away on the forest shore."

Spying out glowworms on the bank, Mary paddled to the shore to pursue them, only to find that she had dropped in on a hippo banquet — five ponderous beasts were tranquilly consuming vast quantities of the long saw grass growing at the water's edge. Not wishing to disturb their feast, Mary paddled back to the island without any glowworms and made for the opposite end to that which M'fetta occupied. This was deserted and quiet, and in the warm darkness Mary took off all her clothes, carefully folding her black skirt and white blouse, removing her boots and stays and chemise for the first time in days, and then letting down her long, pale hair. Entirely naked beneath the purple-black sky, she walked into the cool, clear water and slowly and luxuriously bathed: washing off all the day's accumulation of dirt and dust and sweat, letting her hair swirl free about her, floating flat on her back and staring at the stars' points of white light far above her. Only reluctantly did she regain the shore and don her clothes again: "Drying one's self on one's cumberbund is not pure joy but it can be done when you put your mind to it."

By 3:30 she was back in her hut, and after dozing for an hour or so on the hard wooden plank of a bed, she roused her men at 5:00 and had a cup of tea. By 5:30 they were off again. It was now Wednesday, July 24. They spent the day following the series of small streams and lakes past Lake Ncovi to their farthermost terminus. Here they banked the canoe and disembarked "into a fitting introduction to the sort of country we shall have to deal with before we see the Remboué — namely, up to our knees in black slime."

Bogs and swamps, however, were not a continuous feature of the first day's long, twenty-five-mile march. Instead, they trekked through the heavy gloom of dense rain forest, never once catching even a glimpse

of the sun. But all the usual residents of this landscape they did encounter — a small herd of elephants, a family of gorillas, and also an
impressive snake, "a beauty with a new red-brown and yellow-pat-
terned velvety skin, about three feet six inches long and thick as a
man's thigh" which they killed and ate for supper. Mary was also
personally visited by a tick of a terrific size whose head burrowed painfully in her flesh.

Their goal was to pass the night at the village of Efoua, where several of the M'fettan Fangs claimed to have friends. Toward evening,
shortly before reaching the outskirts of Efoua, Mary, who was in the
lead, noticed that the path petered out but then resumed at a short
distance ahead. Naturally she made for this point by the fastest route
possible, and "the next news was I was in a heap on a lot of spikes
some fifteen feet or so below ground level" at the bottom of a deep
game pit. What she had stepped on, in fact, was merely undergrowth
used to camouflage the hole of the trap. Her first impulse was to feel
vindicated in her choice of apparel; her second was to wonder how she
would get out. "It is at these times that you realize the blessing of a
good thick skirt. Had I paid heed to the advice of many people back
in England who ought to have known better . . . and adopted masculine garments, I should have been spiked to the bone and done for.
Whereas, save for a good many bruises here I was with the fullness of
my skirt tucked under me sitting on nine ebony spikes some twelve
inches long, in comparative comfort, howling lustily to be hauled out."

The Duke and Passenger approached and peered down the dark hole
at Mary, Passenger then inquiring, " 'You kill?' " " 'Not much,' "
Mary responded and then demanded that someone find her a bush rope
and haul her out. Here Wiki took charge of the situation and "went
and selected the one and only bush-rope suitable to haul an English
lady of my exact complexion, age, and size out of that particular pit.
They seemed rare round there from the time he took."

By dusk, however, they arrived at Efoua. Wiki's and Kiva's friends
were at home and arranged for the group's hospitable reception, and
one of the chiefs insisted that Mary stay in his own house. Then ensued
the standard trade palaver, for as usual the only way in which Mary
could account for her presence was by identifying herself as a trader for
Hatton and Cookson, familiarly known in these parts as Ugumu. She
bought twenty-five balls of rubber "to promote good feeling" and also
parted with her much admired red silk tie in exchange for some elephant hair necklaces given her by one of the chief's wives. The chief

himself pressed gravy spoons, meat, and plantain, on her, unsuccessfully tried to trade his clay cooking pots, and then promised her a very rare, special item he kept hidden away in his house. His hut was turned upside down in search of this treasure, as box after box was unpacked by the light of the bush torch; endless disputes ensued on the order of " 'I'm sure you had it last,' 'You must have moved it,' 'Never touched the thing,' " and so on. "At last it was found and [the chief] brought it across" the street to Mary. "It was a bundle of bark cloth tied round something most carefully with tie tie. This being removed, disclosed a layer of rag which was unwound from round a central article. Whatever can this be? thinks I; some rare and valuable object doubtless, let's hope connected with Fetish worship, and I anxiously watched its unpacking; in the end, however, it disclosed to my disgust and rage, an old shilling razor. The way the old chief held it out and the amount of dollars he asked for it, was enough to make anyone believe that I was in such urgent need of the thing, that I was at his mercy regarding price." Mary waved it off "with haughty scorn, and then feeling smitten by the expression of agonised bewilderment on his face, I dashed him a belt that delighted him, and went inside and had tea to soothe my outraged feelings." Value and interest of course lay in the eye of the beholder. Mary could pick up a razor at a chemist's shop on Kensington High Street any day of the week. It was the first time such an object had swum into the chief's view before, so naturally he guarded and treasured it, even though he had about as much use for it as Mary had for any of the juju articles she acquired.

As Mary prepared for bed, she once again had a large audience. "Every hole in the side walls" of the hut "had a human eye in it, and I heard new holes being bored in all directions; so I deeply fear the chief, my host, must have found his palace sadly draughty." Spectators didn't bother Mary; indeed, "the only grave question I had to face was whether I should take off my boots." They were soaked through, and her feet were very sore, but in the end she decided to "lef 'em" because she felt certain that if she took them off she wouldn't be able to get them back on in the morning.

So still fully dressed down to her wet boots, Mary curled up on some of the chief's boxes, using a tobacco sack as a pillow, and dozed until she was awakened by the violent smell in the house. She had noticed the stench when she first entered, but now, after an hour or so of the house's being shut up, it was quite unbearable and of "an unmistakable organic origin." Upon investigation, it appeared to emanate from some small bags hanging from the ceiling. These Mary fetched down, carefully untied, and then emptied out their contents into her hat: a human hand, three big toes, four eyes, two ears, and "other portions of the human frame. The hand was fresh, the others only so so and shrivelled."

The detritus of cannibalism it would seem. Certainly Mary subscribed to the popular view spread by Burton and Du Chaillu that the Fang were cannibals. In *Travels in West Africa* she explains that she kept the Fang in the minority in her party because it was rumored that they sometimes killed, neatly cut up, and smoked black traders who ventured into their territory, and Mary had no wish to "arrive at the Remboué in a smoked condition, even should my fragments be neat." But for the most part Mary downplays this sensational subject; indeed, she shortens the Fangs' name to *Fan* in all her writing on them because of the unfortunate suggestiveness of *Fang* (which, however, when pronounced correctly rhymes with *gong* or *wrong,* not *rang* or *sang.*)

Were the Fang cannibals? It is hard to say. Nearly all reports of African cannibalism are at second hand, by hearsay, and are thus suspect. Modern anthropologists argue endlessly with each other on this score, some saying that Fang sorcery forbade cannibalism, while others claim that certain rites required portions of the human body. To add to the confusion is the fact that, as is the case in a number of African languages, the Fang word for *kill* is the same as that for *eat.* In addition, the ancestor cult that lay at the heart of Fang fetish involved the careful preservation of ancestors' skulls, relics that Europeans would wrongly assume were acquired by violent acts of anthropophagy. The white man in Africa was often determined to see a cannibal behind every tree. And not infrequently Africans would encourage this "superstition" by telling Europeans of grisly acts of cannibalism committed by their enemies.

Though Mary believed that the Fang did practice anthropophagy and held that they did so for nutritional rather than sacrificial reasons — what contemporary anthropologists quaintly call "gustatory cannibalism" — her discussion of the subject is brief and demystifying. The European in Africa, she says, is in no danger of ending up in a Fang cooking pot, nor do the Fang fatten up slaves for consumption, as some other groups were reputed to do. The Fang, according to Mary, eats his fellow man from practical, commonsensical motives. "He has no slaves, no prisoners of war, no cemeteries, so you must draw your own conclusions. No my friend," she concludes, "I will not tell you any cannibal stories." As for the "mementos," as she calls them, that tumbled into her hat in Efoua, she carefully replaced them in their respective bags, hung these back up on the ceiling, and then opened the bark door of the hut for a breath of fresh air.

Thursday, July 25, the second day of their march, was "infinitely worse than the first" because they had to negotiate an uninterrupted series of steep hills, ravines, and swamps. The Fang took no special notice of Mary's agility and stamina, because unlike the "civilized" coastal Africans with long experience of Europeans, they didn't know that the white man in Africa is generally "incapable of personal exertion, requiring to be carried in a hammock or wheeled in a go-cart or a Bath-chair about the streets of their coast towns, depending for the defense of their settlement on a body of black soldiers."

Only toward the end of the afternoon did Mary begin to flag. They came upon a swiftly flowing river with a boulder-strewn bed. Some fifteen feet above the rushing water and the rocks was a bald, slippery tree trunk spanning the river's deep ravine. Everyone except Pagan and Mary opted to wade and swim across. Pagan then attempted the tree trunk bridge, but midway he slipped and only just barely caught onto the tree with his hands; he then crawled back to the bank and swam across too. This spectacle did not cheer Mary, because she knew she was too tired to fight the strong current of the river and so would have to cross by the bridge. "If only the wretched thing had had its bark on it would have been better, but it was bare, bald, and round, and a slip meant death on the rocks below." She took a deep breath and then "rushed it" successfully to the other side.

By nightfall they had reached Egaja, a notorious place even by Fang standards and also the first town they had entered in which they had no friend who could secure them a welcome. Lacking this sort of entrée, Mary adopted a clever new strategy. She decided to put her hosts on the defensive and instructed Pagan to tell the Egajan chief " 'that I hear this town . . . is thief town.'

" 'Better not, sir,' says Pagan.

" 'Go on,' said I, 'or I'll tell him myself.'

"So Pagan did. It was a sad blow to the chief.

" 'Thief town, this highly respected town of Egaja! A town whose moral conduct in all matters . . . was an example to all towns, called a thief town! Oh, what a wicked world!'

"I said it was, but I would reserve my opinion as to whether Egaja was a part of the wicked world or a star-like exception until I had experienced it myself."

In no time, Mary and the chief were close friends, and she gleaned a great deal of valuable fetish information from him. In return for such hospitality Mary held an open-air medical clinic, beginning with the chief's aged, shriveled-up mother. The poor woman had a dreadfully infected arm, a mass of abscesses and swollen ulcers, all crusted over with yellow pus, which Mary lanced, drained, and washed. No sooner was this unpalatable chore finished than the whole of afflicted Egaja turned up for treatment. "There was evidently a good stiff epidemic of yaws, . . . lots of cases of dum, . . . ulcers of course galore; a man with a bit of broken spear in an abscess in the thigh; one which I believe a professional would call a 'lovely case' of filaria, the entire white of one eye being full of the active little worms and a ridge of surplus population migrating across the bridge of the nose into the other eye, under the skin, looking like the bridge of a pair of spectacles." Mary of course by this time was well versed in all branches of tropical medicine. In fact she had a dual command of the subject, for she had on the one hand, her own formal training and experience, and on the other, she also knew a great deal about African medical practice and remedies. *Travels in West Africa* contains a lengthy appendix called "Disease in West Africa," and in *West African Studies* two chapters are devoted to African therapeutics.

When the impromptu clinic was over, it was well past eleven at night, and Mary gladly retired to rest in the chief's house, only to be abruptly roused at 1:45 A.M. "by the frantic yells of a woman. I judged there was one of my beauties of Fangs mixed up in it and there was, and after paying damages got back [to bed] again by 3:30 A.M. and off to sleep again instantly." "Woman palaver" was a recurrent problem during the march. Instead of collapsing with fatigue when they reached a new village, Mary's men would cast their eyes about in search of amorous adventures. Sometimes their advances were rewarded, sometimes spurned. And when they were unsuccessful, Mary had to deal with the scantily clad, indignant woman and often her enraged husband as well. On the surface it was a ripe scenario for farce, as Mary describes it, but who can say what effect such skirmishes had upon her or what currents of feeling they provoked. At any rate, by the time they reached the next village Mary had learned a few things from the nocturnal uproar at Egaja: "I chaperoned my men while among the

Mary Kingsley in deep mourning shortly after
her parents' deaths in 1892

George Kingsley before his marriage   Henry Kingsley

The house at 22 Southwood Lane, Highgate, with its bricked-in front windows, where Mary spent most of her childhood

When Charley entered Christ's College, the Kingsleys moved to 7 Mortimer Road, Cambridge.

Mary Kingsley in Calabar during the
1895 journey. Lady MacDonald is on
her right and Sir Claude MacDonald
on her left. Roger Casement is standing on the far right behind them.

Pictures of Fang used to illustrate *Travels
in West Africa*. The photographs were
probably taken by Mary Kingsley.

Studio photographs of "the intrepid explorer" taken about the time of publication of *Travels in West Africa* in 1897. The
inset bears Mary's signature and the inscription "The melancholy picture of one
who tried to be just to all parties."

Mary's brass armlets and carved ivory writing seal,
complete with her engraved signature

The nail-studded Muvungu who
kept sentry in Mary's entrance
hall and was the first presence
her visitors encountered

John Holt, around 1900

Mary Slessor wearing her engagement ring, around 1891

Mary Slessor's household at Calabar, with an unidentified guest

Matthew Nathan

The funeral procession through Simonstown, with Mary's coffin draped
with the Union Jack and borne by a gun carriage

The procession on Simonstown pier and the *Thrush* waiting
to carry her coffin out to sea

ladies of Esoon — a forward set of minxes — with the vigilance of a dragon; and decreed, like the Mikado of Japan, 'that whosoever leered or winked, unless connubially linked, should forthwith be beheaded,' have their pay chopped, I mean."

It seems that one of their party *did* have an acquaintance at Egaja. Kiva in fact owed one of the Egajan Fangs a coat for an ivory transaction that had taken place some time ago. Soon after the woman palaver Mary awoke again to the uproar of a Fang bankruptcy court, for Kiva was in no position to pay up and consequently had been tied up, "talking nineteen to the dozen; and so was everyone else; and a lady was working up white clay in a pot," presumably in preparation for Kiva's decease in lieu of settling his debt.

At this stage Mary intervened: "I dare say I ought to have rushed at [Kiva] and cut his bonds, and killed people in a general way with a revolver, and then flown with my band to the bush," but instead she shouted "Azuna," Fang for "listen to me," as loudly as she could and began intricate and lengthy negotiations for Kiva's release. "Fortunately for the reader," she writes in *Travels in West Africa,* "it is impossible for me to give in full detail the proceedings of the court. I do not think if the whole of Mr. Pitman's school of shorthand had been there to take them down the thing could possibly have been done in word-writing. If the late Richard Wagner, however, had been present he could have scored the performance for a full orchestra; and with all its weird grunts and roars, and pistol-like finger clicks, and its elongated words and thigh slaps, it would have been a masterpiece." In the end, Mary had to pay the Egajan Fang the equivalent cost of Kiva's coat from her own trade stock.

Clearly it seemed prudent to depart from Egaja as soon as possible. And so dawn found the group traversing the surrounding plantations and then entering into the familiar "gloom of the Great Forest again; that forest that seemed to me without end, wherein in a lazy, hazy-minded sort of way, I expected to wander through by day and drop in at night to a noisy . . . town for the rest of my days."

By nightfall they reached Esoon. The good news here was that they learned the Remboué was not far off now — perhaps only a long day's trek ahead. Proximity to the Remboué and "civilization" meant that "some . . . of the more highly cultured inhabitants" of Esoon spoke trade English. They also knew of Ugumu's (Hatton and Cookson's) factory on the river and even of the *Mové,* the paddle steamer that had taken Mary from Libreville to Lambaréné. In fact, all of Esoon was eager to learn if Mary was " 'a wife of them Mové man . . . or them other white man.' I civilly said them Mové men were my tribe and they ought to have known it by the look of me."

After an unprecedentedly quiet night in Esoon they set off for the Remboué early on Saturday, July 27, but the last stretch of the Remboué was not destined to be the dreamy forest wandering of the preceding days. Instead, they struck a series of tidal swamps. On the brink of the first they clung like monkeys to a network of aerial roots and took the bearings of "the lake of ink-black slime" that lay before them. There was nothing for it but to strike out across the swamp, Mary taking up the rear of her column and "deeply regretting that my ancestors had parted prematurely with prehensile tails for four limbs, particularly when two of them are done up in boots and are not sufficient to enable one to get through a mangrove swamp. . . . Added to [this] . . . were any quantity of mangrove flies, a broiling hot sun and an atmosphere three quarters solid stench from the putrifying ooze all round us." It took them an hour and a half to cross this first swamp, but emerging from this trial they were briefly rewarded with a path running through a beautiful flower- and fern-filled valley and a vista of pale, purple-blue mountains in the distance which reminded Mary of a Turner painting.

Eventually, however, this lovely landscape gave way to a new swamp, though unlike the first this one came equipped with an underwater bridge, another tree trunk, which Mary and her party attempted to use. "All of us," she reports in *Travels in West Africa,* "save one, need I say that one was myself, effected this with safety. As for me, when I was at the beginning of the submerged bridge and busily laying about in my mind for a definite opinion as to whether it was better to walk on a slippy [*sic*] tree trunk bridge you could see, or one you could not, I was hurled off by that inexorable fate that demands of me a personal acquaintance with fluvial and paludial ground deposits; whereupon I took a header, and am thereby able to inform the world that there is between fifteen and twenty feet of water each side of that log. I conscientiously went in on one side, and came up on the other."

The closer they got to the Remboué, the larger these tidal swamps and the more harrowing their crossing became. Finally, toward late afternoon, they found themselves on the rim of the largest and most forbidding swamp Mary had ever seen: "It stretched away in all directions, a great sheet of filthy water, out of which sprang gorgeous marsh plants, in islands, great banks of screw pine, and coppices of wine pine with their lovely fronds reflected back by the still, mirror-like water, so that the reflection was as vivid as the reality." Fortunately, a group of rubber carriers arrived as Mary's party was surveying this scene, and it was agreed that they would lead Mary's party through the swamp, but not until the rubber carriers had made an alarming series of preparations that included removing all their clothes and folding them into bundles that they stowed on top of their heads. The necessity for this soon became apparent, for shortly they were up to their chins in the slimy black water. It took them more than two hours to cross the swamp, and when they finally clambered out on the other side they were all "horribly infested with leeches, having a frill of them round our necks like astrachan collars." Mary herself was quite faint from the loss of blood, and, as she says, "of course the bleeding did not stop at once, and it attracted flies," so they were something of a spectacle when they straggled into N'dorko as night was falling.

But the hardships of the day, their faintness, fatigue, and hunger were all forgotten once they arrived in the village, for through the blood-smeared gateway at its farther end they glimpsed the goal of their week-long journey from Kangwe: the Remboué, flowing swiftly past on its way to the Libreville estuary. Mary made for its bank, surrounded by a noisy crowd, and then, having satisfied herself that it was indeed the Remboué — "a big river, but nothing to the Ogowé either in breadth or beauty" — and not a vision, she returned to the center of town in order to settle payment for her men.

First she encountered Hatton and Cookson's African agent, and as they were conversing, "a big, scraggy, very black man with an irregularly formed face the size of a tea tray and looking generally as if he had come out of a pantomime on the *Arabian Nights,* dashed through the crowd shouting 'I'm for Holty, I'm for Holty,' " in other words, "I am the agent for John Holt." Mary was perplexed by the smallness of both men's factories and worried too, because she had agreed to pay her crew as soon as they reached the Remboué, and now it turned out that there wasn't enough rum and no gunpowder at all in N'dorko. The situation was redeemed, however, when she learned that as usual she had not turned up precisely where she should have. The Hatton and Cookson man was not the major Remboué agent Mr. Sanga Glass as Mary had assumed, but rather was a subagent for him. Mr. Glass was an hour's paddle upstream at Agonjo, and he *did* have adequate supplies with which to pay Mary's party. A message was dispatched to Agonjo, and by 10:00 P.M. or so Mr. Glass duly arrived, "an exceedingly neat, well-educated M'pongwe gentleman in irreproachable English garments, and with irreproachable but slightly floreate English language." Mr. Glass, in turn, was quite astonished by Mary's appearance, "for no white man of any kind had been across from the Ogooué for years and none had ever come out at N'dorko."

Business soon suspended these expressions of mutual admiration and surprise. In *Travels in West Africa* Mary describes how "we started talking trade with my band in the middle of the street; making a patch of uproar in the moonlit silence." Finally, close to midnight each of Mary's Fang carriers had been paid off to his satisfaction, and Mary made a "touching farewell with the Fangs," parting company with them reluctantly "in peace, good feeling, and prosperity . . . for . . . they are real men."

The Galoa and Adjoumba members of Mary's party accompanied her and Mr. Glass to Agonjo in a fleet of canoes down the swift river illuminated by the moon and stars. It was past midnight when they finally arrived at this their proper destination, but even so Mr. Glass opened his large store and distributed the payment goods by the light of lanterns. Then Mary was welcomed by his wife into their neat home and given the largest room and the best bed, upon which she gratefully collapsed, too tired to remove her boots, even though there would be no need to force them on the next morning, for the great march from the Ogooué to the Remboué had been triumphantly completed.

Small wonder that after these exertions and adventures Mary chose to idle away a few pleasant days at Agonjo, thoroughly enjoying the hospitality of Mr. Glass and his wife. The only other member of the household was a handsome, clever young storekeeper, who was prone to sing "Partant pour la Syrie" with intense feeling and at full volume in the middle of the night.

Part of the reason Mary lingered in Agonjo — it was now early August — was that Mr. Glass was agonizing over how she should return to Libreville. He wouldn't hear of her traveling in an ordinary paddle canoe, and so deliberations over her mode of travel back to the estuary extended over a period of days, until into "the affair there entered a highly dramatic figure." This was one Obanjo, also known as Captain Johnson, an independent bush and river trader — a large, handsome, intelligent man, got up in a sombrero and a neat dungaree suit and endowed with a theatrical "Hallo-my-Hearty atmosphere coming off him from the top of his hat to the soles of his feet, like the scent off a flower." This "reckless, rollicking skipper" was Captain Johnson, but his eyes belonged to his other personality, Obanjo, and revealed "a man courageous in the African manner, full of energy and resource, keenly intelligent and self-reliant." He was an intriguing figure and a character worthy to play a significant role in the last act of Mary's Ogooué to Remboué saga.

But from Mr. Glass's point of view Obanjo/Captain Johnson's great drawing point was that he possessed a proper sailing canoe substantial enough to transport Mary to Libreville. This "noble vessel," as Mary calls it, was, however, not yet finished; its interior was still roughly hewn, and its sail was a "bed quilt that had evidently been in the family some years." It also contained a standard bamboo staging, which, however, was in an unfinished state and was thus rickety and insubstantial. Nevertheless, onto this "precarious perch" Mary installed herself and her gear. Partly to the worn bed quilt sail and partly to the amount of trading Obanjo indulged in Mary owed the "credit of having made a record trip down the Remboué, the slowest white man time on record." They took in fact the better part of four days to accomplish this last stage of the journey, and their first day's run was only about five miles.

They set off on the first morning, though, well before dawn, at 4:00 A.M. in the moonlight, and as Obanjo still seemed full of sleep, Mary offered to navigate, for she loved few things more than canoeing at night with the warm, soft, African darkness all about her. After a brief examination in practical seamanship, Obanjo gladly handed over the tiller. On subsequent nights he put her in charge as a matter of course, "and as I prefer night to day in Africa," Mary writes in *Travels in West Africa,* "I enjoyed it. Indeed, much as I have enjoyed life in Africa, I do not think I ever enjoyed it to the full as I did on those nights dropping down the Remboué. The great black, winding river with a pathway in its midst of frosted silver where the moon light struck it: on each side the ink-black mangrove walls, and above them the band of star and moonlit heavens that the walls of mangrove allowed one to see. Foreward rose the form of our sail, idealised from bedsheetdom to glory; and the little red glow of our cooking fire gave a single note of warm colour to the cold light of the moon." Now and then the mangrove walls would thin out, and she would catch glimpses of more vast swamps, gleaming like polished silver in the light of the moon. The only trouble with this nocturnal navigation was that Mary was subjected to a series of "horrid frights" when she steered onto tree shadows, mistaking them for mudbanks or trees themselves, they seemed so solid and real in the moonlight. As was so often the case in Africa, the boundary between illusion and reality was blurred or indistinct in the watches of the tropical night. And not a little of its magic derived from this subtle intermingling of illusion and fact.

On the second day they stopped at a village in which Obanjo had a wife and also a herd of goats, some of which he wanted to transport down to Libreville to sell. There ensued a mad chase for some of these goats on the beach before the village, a "spirited performance" uncannily similar to the skirmishes between the armies of Macbeth and Macduff that Mary had once seen on the London stage. While watching this activity, Mary was stunned to hear "a well-modulated, evidently educated voice say in most perfect English, 'Most diverting spectacle, madam, is it not?' " Mary turned around to her cultured interlocutor and beheld "what appeared . . . to be an English gentleman who had from some misfortune gone black all over and lost his trousers and been compelled to replace them with a highly ornamental tablecloth." This startling figure then introduced himself as Prince Makaga and profusely apologized for not having his case of calling cards on hand. Mary returned his civilities and contained her own astonishment at the figure the Prince cut until she and Obanjo and the captured goats had departed the village. Then Obanjo explained that Prince Makaga — a name that Mary recognized from reading Du Chaillu as designating the bravest and best hunter in a village — was a Mpongwe trader who had previously been an agent for one of the large European firms and had several times been to England and France.

The only other exciting event during the leisurely ride down the Remboué was the appearance of two runaway Fang boys who begged to be taken on board so that they could travel to the bright lights of Libreville and seek their fortune. Obanjo unwisely took the boys on, and in a short while they were being hotly pursued by the mother of one of the boys and a by large gun-bearing contingent of men from the boy's village. The appropriate boy was returned to his people, while the other remained on board and eventually reached the goal of his dreams.

By the third day they reached the point at which the Como River joins the Remboué, and that evening found them on the northern shore of the Gabon estuary at the village of Dongila. Here there was a large Roman Catholic mission, and when they arrived the first sight to meet Mary's eyes was a nun with a group of children on the shore catching shellfish and generally merry-making. Obanjo went ashore, and the nun extended an invitation to Mary through him for Mary to come spend the night at the mission. But Mary was soaked and dirty and "dead tired and . . . quite unfit for polite society"; she also learned from Obanjo that the kind sister knew no English, and Mary "shrank in my condition from attempting to evolve the French language out of my inner consciousness." So she declined the invitation and remained in the cramped canoe all night, or nearly all of it, for at "about midnight some change in the tide, or original sin in the canoe caused her to softly swing round and the next news was that I was in the water." Soaked through and highly disgusted, she hauled herself back on board and in the darkness got her portmanteau out of the hold and tidied up as best she could.

Before they left Dongila the next morning Obanjo tried to persuade Mary to go into the neighboring Spanish territory north of Congo Français and see "plenty country, plenty men, elephants, leopards, gorillas. Oh! plenty thing." But though Mary was tempted by this proposal, she felt it more prudent to linger for a bit in Libreville before striking out into the unknown again. Among other things, she knew that she had to reestablish credibility among her own kind before setting off on further adventures. Thus her prayer as they approached Glass was that Mr. Hudson would be away at Libreville on business, knowing as she did that many incidents and adventures had taken place in her career since she had last seen him that he would not approve of. "Vain hope! He was on the pier. He did not approve. He had heard of most of my goings on."

These had been fully reported by a German agent who had recently come from Lambaréné "in the legitimate way" — by steamer down the Ogooué rather than overland from Kangwe to Agonjo — and this agent had informed Mr. Hudson that Mary had departed from Kangwe and was bound for Remboué. In his anxiety for her safety Mr. Hudson had sent a surf boat up to Agonjo to fetch Mary — just the sort of vessel that Mr. Glass would have desired — but this they had somehow missed en route, perhaps because they were pausing at a village to trade or because they were moored to the shore and sleeping for the night. Anyway, the surf boat was only one more item to add to Mary's debt to Mr. Hudson, for it was only through his agency that she had been able to travel up the Ogooué and then through the beautiful region between the Ogooué and the Remboué. As Mary explains it in *Travels in West Africa*, "I tried to explain to him how much I had enjoyed myself and how I realised I owed it all to him; but he persisted in his opinion that my intentions and ambitions were suicidal."

It had been a quest, this journey into Congo Français by river and land, and all along the way Mary had been tested: at the Alemba rapids, at M'fetta, at Egaja. She had been tested by the environment, as she crossed terrain that seemed to her "to have been laid down as an obstacle race track for Mr. G. F. Watts's Titans, and to have fallen into shocking bad repair," by the peoples she encountered, by her own stringent demands on her physical and psychological resources. And she had succeeded magnificently by any standards, even her own.

Isolation from her own kind — "them Mové tribe," as she had called them at Esoon — had freed her to find her own destiny. But the goal of Mary's quest was not attained. She came out of swamps and forests never before beheld by Europeans. Having been received by the "irreproachably English" Mr. Glass, she was handed over to the redoubtable Obanjo/Captain Johnson. Perhaps not a little of Mary's fascination with this startling figure derived from his so successfully embodying both the African and European personalities. Obanjo was a transitional figure, an African guide back to white civilization on the coast. Although Mary turned down his invitation to go sky-larking and to see "plenty plenty thing" in even more remote territory than that which she had traveled through, her refusal was reluctant and only for the time being. "I am still thinking about taking that voyage," she says in *Travels in West Africa,* for she always meant to go back. Her farewells to the Ogooué and the Remboué, and to the Fang were provisional.

·⤳ 10 ⤴·

Corsico and Cameroons

A s soon as she returned to Glass Mary hastened to go round to Dr. Robert Nassau's to report on her travels and to indulge in one of their "frequent and intimate conversations" on fetish, as Nassau later described them. The two aficionados sat up late on Nassau's verandah, forming a secret society of two during these long hot Glass evenings. They discussed in exhaustive detail and with all the passion of initiates such matters as charms and incantations, witchcraft, funeral and sacrificial rites, the African underworld or afterlife, ancestor worship, reincarnation, and the various classes or varieties of spirits — spirits that permeated and determined every aspect of life in Africa. The forest and rivers and sky, the shadow you cast in the noonday sun, even your neighbor's canoe — everything indeed — was inhabited and animated by a spirit. To dwell in West Africa was to live in a realm full of their presence and power, a realm where the boundaries between the animate and the inanimate, the material and the ethereal, the living and the dead were all blurred and indeterminate. It was also a world in which for their own reasons Nassau and Mary felt at home and at ease, and from the beginning they recognized this in each other; it was the source of their closeness, their kinship.

The urbane, late middle-aged missionary and the angular, heterodox "odd woman" were both clearly fascinated to the point of obsession with West African cosmography and its underlying spiritual beliefs. In *Fetichism in West Africa* Nassau describes his relentless quest for fetish: "I began to search," he says, shortly after arriving in West Africa in the 1860s, "and thenceforward for thirty years, wherever I travelled, wherever I was guest to native chiefs, wherever I lived, I was always leading the conversation in hut or camp, back to a study of native thought." In *Travels in West Africa* Mary couches this quest in the terms of big game hunting, as a sport both dangerous and exhilarating. But she cautions that unless you possess a mind "pliant enough to follow the African idea step by step, however much care you may take, you will not bag your game." Even more telling, however, is Mary's comparison of her passion for fetish with a lingering and potentially lethal disease: "The fascination of the African point of view," she writes, "is as sure to linger in your mind as the malaria in your body. Never then will you be able to attain to the gay, happy cock-sureness regarding the Deity and the Universe of those people who stay at home." Doctor though he was, Nassau had no cure for this disease. Like Mary, he too was infected.

The source of the illness, for Mary at least, was the way in which fetish kept alive and vital and ever present fundamental spiritual and philosophical problems and beliefs. Fetish was not something one practiced one day out of seven or five a times a day while kneeling eastward. It affected the most mundane of daily chores and told one whence one came, where one was bound, and the meaning of existence in between these two points. And this all-encompassing power it possessed derived from the way in which it sprang from the empirical evidence of nature — it was, in fact, a species of pantheism.

Mary puts the case very clearly in her opening discussion of the subject in *West African Studies,* a work that contains her most systematic and mature views on fetish. She opens chapter 5 with the bald statement that "the final object of all human desire is a knowledge of the nature of God." This proclamation is less startling than it might seem if we construe her to mean that everyone wishes to fathom the meaning and purpose of his or her own destiny in particular and of human life in general. Mary then goes on to say that this desire can be satisfied in one of three ways: by divine revelation; by an apprehension of God apart from the material (and necessarily perishable) world; or, thirdly, by "the attempt to understand Him as manifest in natural phenomena." Mary confesses that her own sympathies lie with the third route to divine knowledge, and this route is also, she explains, the way of fetish. The follower of both pantheism and fetish holds that the natural world is *animated* by spiritual power and that when communing with Nature one makes contact with this Divinity. Hence the modern term for fetish: animism.

At first glance, Mary's long chapters on fetish in *Travels in West Africa* and *West African Studies* might look like rather disconnected, arcane monographs, oddly out of place in the rollicking travelogues that contain them. But if the travel episodes often read like a picaresque novel, the lengthy discussion of fetish comes close at times to being spiritual autobiography. It is in these chapters that Mary identifies the most important influences on her intellectual and psychological development: Aristotle, Spinoza, Goethe, Darwin, Burton, and Tylor. She also clearly discloses her own personal creed, a highly unorthodox one for the niece of Canon Charles Kingsley, combining as it did heterogeneous elements from Darwin's *Origin of Species,* Tylor's *Primitive Culture,* and Goethe's "Prometheus." It is to the latter, indeed, that she directs the student of fetish rather than to more obvious transcendentalists such as Wordsworth or Shelley. Mary's pantheism was of a distinctly Teutonic cast, as she confided to George Macmillan: "I think Fetish in German," and then alluding to her cockney accent, "and express it in (H) ammersmith." but Mary's real bible was not contained between the covers of any book. It was written instead in the great rivers and forests and mountains of West Africa. It is because she wants to make fetish more understandable and palatable to an uncomprehending reading public that she invokes her European jujus, Goethe and Spinoza. The natural world, she insists over and over again, is pregnant with meaning and power for the African, just as it was for some of Europe's greatest thinkers, and most of all, as it was for Mary herself.

But this was not perhaps, or not in the same way, as it was for Dr. Nassau, who subscribed to and preached the divine revelation in the New Testament and continued his missionary work against tremendous odds even as he pursued indefatigably his search for "native thought." What intellectual and spiritual acrobatics Nassau had to perform in order to align his quest for fetish with his quest for converts we do not know. But his deep knowledge of and sympathy for African belief was of inestimable value to Mary. Having sat up until all hours discussing fetish, Mary and Nassau found that the conversation naturally turned to Mary's other major pursuit, fish. And here too Nassau was eager to be of help. He suggested that Mary make an expedition to Corsico Island some twenty miles out to sea from Gabon, the island where he had first been stationed when he came out to Africa. In the middle of the island were several small freshwater lakes that might yield some interesting new fish. The Corsican women trapped these fish in specially woven baskets each August, and Nassau calculated that this annual event was now imminent. Furthermore, Nassau's successor at the Presbyterian mission at Corsico, an educated and ordained Benga named Ikenja Ibea, would be sure to welcome Mary. In fact, Nassau's all-around factotum, a young man named Eveke, was the Reverend Ibea's son, and Nassau insisted that Eveke accompany Mary and that they should go in Nassau's own boat, the *Lafayette*.

They made the crossing in one day under a broiling sun, Mary navigating for most of the way while Eveke and her small crew of Mpongwe slept. The Reverend Ibea was evangelizing on the mainland when they arrived, but Mary was warmly welcomed by Mrs. Ibea, who insisted Mary take possession of the largest room in the house and then offered her tea and avocados.

Since everyone knows "there is no time south of 40°" and Corsico hovers around the 1° latitude, Mary was not surprised to learn the next day that the women's great fishing trip was still a rather vague proposition, the problem having something to do with the special baskets not yet being ready. The next day the situation remained indefinite, though Eveke assured Mary that all would be set for the following day. "Internally blessing Eveke and the ladies," Mary decided to take an extended hike along the island's southern shore, hoping to collect some interesting shells. But shells on Corsico turned out to be as rare as fishing baskets; Mary didn't even find any common whelks.

What she did encounter, though, was a mob of "wholly malignant" wild and rowdy schoolchildren, who yelled and emitted howls, danced around her, spat, and shouted, "Frenchy no good, Frenchy no good." This unruly band was led by a male albino of about fourteen, "clad in the remains of an antique salt sack, which he wears unaltered inverted over him. Unfortunately," Mary observed, "holes have been roughly cut in the bottom and sides of it to let out his unnecessary head and arms." Just as she was about to deal with this figure, Mary noticed a sweet-looking nun sitting on the rocks doing needlework, apparently helpless to control her charges. The nun, Mary later learned, was part of the small Roman Catholic presence on the island — two Spanish priests and three nuns — but because the sister knew no English and Mary no Spanish, all they could do was smile and nod at each other. Mary then went on down the path bordering the shore and round a rocky point, only to be pursued in a matter of minutes by the howling pack of miscreant children. Shielded now from the view of their protectress, however, "things happened to those children that caused them to prefer the nun's company to mine." The albino's sack ended up in Mary's fist, and "not the albino alone has got out of repair this side of the rock, for neither that promising young lady who spat in my face nor the one who threw sand in my eyes are what they were this morning."

The sights of Corsico — a mere five miles long and three across — were fairly well exhausted in the two days Mary waited for the island women to mount their fishing expedition. On the morning of August 7 things at last seemed to be in a state of preparation. Mary set off with a contingent of women from the Ibeas' village for the fixed meeting point for fishing women from various parts of the island. And all along the way they shouted for others to join them, especially for one Engouta. "Notably and grievously we howl for En-gou-ta-a-a and Engouta comes not; so we throw ourselves down on the deliciously soft, fine, golden brown grass, in the sun, and wait for the tardy absent ones, smoking and laughing, and sleeping, and when any of these avocations palls on any of us we rise up and howl Engouta."

After more than two and a half hours of waiting, during which time most of her companions fell asleep on the grass, Mary was roused from observing some unusual beetles by what sounded like the crackling fusillade of guns. Raising her eyes from the beetles, she saw a cloud of blue smoke surmounting a wall of crimson fire, both rapidly moving toward them. As she tells it in *Travels in West Africa,* Mary hastened to spread the alarm among her dozing friends, "adding in the case of the more profound sleepers an enlightening kick and making a beeline to the bush in front of us. The others followed my example with . . . rapidity . . . but, in spite of some very creditable and spirited sprint performances, three members of the party got scorched and spent the balance of the afternoon sitting in mud-holes, comforting themselves with the balmy black slime." Shortly afterward the longed-for Engouta finally turned up and explained that the conflagration was the fault of "some fool man" who was overzealously burning down his manioc plantation before sowing the new season's's crop.

At last they were ready to move on to the freshwater lakes, a little chain of them in the middle of the island. The women's fishing methods were simple and were quickly put into action. One contingent of women waded into the water and formed a line facing the shore, and another group followed and stood opposite them with their special fishing baskets held just below the water. The first band of women then beat and splashed the water with their hands and with sticks and yelled and "skylarked generally," whereupon the terrified fish hastily swam toward the waiting baskets of the other women and were scooped up by the peck. Twelve to fourteen bushels of fish was an average haul. but when Mary eagerly inspected the catch she was dismayed to find only the common African mudfish, "a brute I cordially hate" precisely because of its ubiquity. The mudfish was what she found at the end of her own line nine times out of ten and what African fisherman were constantly trying to sell her. It was a bitter disappointment, for she had traveled out to Corsico specifically to collect some new specimens.

The moral Mary drew in *Travels in West Africa* from this venture was that it once more demonstrated the peculiar and perverse logic of the place: "But there! It's Africa all over; presenting one with familiar objects when one least requires them, like that razor in the heart of Gorilla-land; and unfamiliar, such as elephants and buffalos when you are out for a quiet stroll armed with a butterfly net, to say nothing of snakes in one's bed and scorpions in one's boots and sponge. One's view of life gets quite distorted; I don't believe I should be the least surprised to see a herd of hippo stroll on to the line out of one of the railway tunnels of Notting Hill Gate Station. West Africa is undoubtedly bad for one's mind."

By the time she returned from the disappointing fishing expedition with all her specimen bottles still empty, Reverend Ibea had come back from the mainland. Mary found him "a splendidly built, square-shouldered man, a pure Benga, of the finest type, full of energy and enthusiasm." Over tea they discussed the way the Fang had overrun, absorbed, and sometimes obliterated the older peoples in Congo Français, including the Benga in Gabon, Corsico, and on other neighboring islands. Fond as Mary was of the Fang, "Mr. Ibea and I got quite low about this." In fact Mary confesses that she felt it "more than Mr. Ibea, for I am not a Christian minister and am more of a savage than he is." As a man of God, Mr. Ibea ascribed his peoples' decline to indolence and to other moral failings. Though she must have held her tongue in company with her host, Mary looked to the white man more than to the "fearful Fang" or to paganism for the cause of the Benga's threatened state. In *Travels in West Africa* she bluntly says that "nothing strikes one so much, in studying the degeneration of these native tribes, as the direct effect that civilisation and reformation has in hastening it. The worst enemy to the existence of the African tribe is the one who comes to it and says: 'Now you must civilise, and come to school, and leave off all those awful goings-on of yours and settle down quietly!' " The Benga, alas, had settled down nearly to the point of extinction.

Shell-less, fishless, and with only a small stock of Benga fetish information, Mary decided not to linger on Corsico. She left on August 8, the day after the abortive fishing trip, with Eveke and her small crew and also a Corsican woman passenger loaded down with five bundles, one large tin box, a peck of limes, and a husband. The *Lafayette* was overcrowded as a result, with Mary herself seated in the middle of the boat "surrounded by a rim of alligator pears and bananas, as though I were some kind of joint garnished for table instead of a West Coast skipper." The Corsican woman complained incessantly and when not complaining occupied her mouth by eating intensely sour limes in a way that set Mary's teeth on edge. They failed to reach Cape Esterias, midway between Corsico and Libreville, by nightfall and had to spend the night on the anchored *Lafayette* a short distance from shore. All the other occupants, including a restless ram Reverend Ibea was sending to Libreville, slept under a makeshift tent. But Mary spent the night sitting up, dozing fitfully in the open air, and then waking to gaze at the clouds and mountains of mist furling and unfurling along the shoreline, alternately swaddling and exposing the dense forest-covered hills just beyond the ribbon of surf and sea. Finally the morning broke gray and cheerless and chilly, the sea looking angry and wicked. As the ghostly figures hunched beneath the white sail tent began to stretch and groan into wakefulness, Mary combed her tangled hair and meditated on her old problem: "Why did I come to Africa?"

By midafternoon they reached the cape, and here they spent the night, Mary in a European-style house in the process of construction, under the care of a beautiful young African woman named Agnes who was a subagent for John Holt. Agnes was a great linguist as well as a beauty and could speak pidgin English, proper French, and a smattering of Spanish. There was a small Catholic mission at Cape Esterias, and the next morning at 5:00 A.M. Agnes roused Mary to go to mass, a service Mary could follow for once because in this tiny settlement on the equator, the weather-worn white père conducted worship in Latin, the communicants "singing their Salve Maria responses in that musical, metallic twang that Latin seems to bring out so strongly in the African voice."

Just as they were about to board the *Lafayette* after church, Mary spied a ragged lunatic clambering among the rocks, crying out like a wild animal, and she recognized him as the source of the weird howls

and screams that had kept her up half the night. She learned that the
poor filthy man haunted the beach, screaming and moaning as he jumped
about among the rocks. Mary tried to approach him very slowly, holding out some biscuits to the gaunt creature, he glaring all the while,
but when she got within a few yards of him, he leapt up and tore off
into the forest.

The remaining short run to Libreville was enlivened by a near collision with a whale's enormous fluke — "a most charming spectacle
on the horizon," but not so picturesque within a few feet of one's tiller.
The crew informed Mary that it was the courting season for whales,
and she retorted that "I don't come again into Corsico Bay in canoes
or small craft while any of that wretched foolishness is going on." As
they approached the Libreville estuary they were unceremoniously
stopped by the estuary guardship whose officials demanded a bill of
health from the *Lafayette* and threatened quarantine if none was forthcoming. Mary explained that bills of health were unknown on Corsico,
"there being no Spanish official on the forsaken island to issue them."
After a considerable amount of palaver, the guardship doctor passed
the *Lafayette* but warned that they would not be allowed to do it again.
Mary solemnly promised that they wouldn't try, "nor will I," she says
in *Travels in West Africa,* "for it's not my present intention to revisit
an island that has only mudfish in its lakes and courting whales in its
encircling seas."

In Libreville, Mary spent several desultory (by her standards) weeks,
wandering the surrounding bush paths armed with her butterfly net
and cleft stick by day, and spending her evenings discoursing with
Nassau or Hudson and writing up her battered, bulging log. Finally
in mid-September the northbound *Niger* arrived, and Mary took passage on it for the town of Victoria in Cameroon. Out at sea, from the
deck of the *Niger,* she found herself confronted with her great temptation — the magnificent Mungo Mah Lobeh, or "Throne of Thunder,"
merely labeled Mount Cameroon on most West African maps. This
was the fourth or fifth time Mary had gazed from the sea on the awe-
some mountain, rising as it did more than thirteen thousand feet from
its surf-washed base to its towering, skyscraping summit. And each
time Mary had found its dramatically varying guises of beauty more
and more compelling: "Sometimes it is wreathed with indigo-black
tornado clouds, sometimes crested with snow, sometimes softly gorgeous with gold, green, and rose-colored vapours tinted by the setting
sun, sometimes completely swathed in dense cloud so that you cannot

see it at all; but when you once know it is there it is all the same, and you bow down and worship."

Of course, as Mary conceded, it was "none of my business to go up mountains. There's next to no fish on them in West Africa, and precious little good rank fetish." She could manufacture a motive, saying that she wanted to determine the extent and pattern of the Sierra del Cristal range of mountains from the top of Mungo. But the fact is that people climb mountains simply because they are there, beckoning, even imploring people to climb them — or so it seems to the mountaineer. And the most inviting mountains are those that few or none have been up before. On this issue Mary is, for once, quite precise. In *Travels in West Africa* she says that she was the twenty-eighth person to ascend Mungo, the third Englishman, and also the third person to climb it from the more arduous southeast face. (All the predecessors she enumerates of course were white; almost certainly a number of Africans had also reached the summit. It is a peculiar and misleading usage of travel and exploration books on Africa to talk of "discoveries" and "firsts" as if the continent were totally uninhabited, whereas Africans had usually "discovered" and often inhabited such "finds" for years if not generations before they were seen by European eyes.) What Mary does not mention, however, is that she was the first white *woman* to reach the top of Mount Cameroon, perhaps the very first woman, African or European, at all.

Gazing at Mungo from shipboard, Mary set her heart on climbing it, even though the *Niger*'s Captain Davies urged her "chuck it as it was not a picnic." Once she had landed in Victoria, Cameroon, she found that, unlike the French authorities in Gabon, the German colony's vice governor, Herr von Lucke, refrained from putting obstacles in her way, though he did grimly prophesy that Mary would either be drowned by the rain or would catch the worst cold of her life. Mary, for her part, was happy once again to be "under the dominion of Germany," in part because she could converse freely with her hosts in their language, and in part because they responded to her plans with a kind of fatalistic good will and cooperation. Herr von Lucke was himself an extremely conscientious though fundamentally melancholic young man. He dashed around "carrying on a series of experiments" to see if he could be in three, or even better, four places at once, and in the process he helped Mary to organize a small party of experienced guides and carriers for the ascent. Shortly after her return to England Mary learned that the poor man had committed suicide, ostensibly because he had been falsely accused of spreading calumny about the German emperor. But who could say for certain what drove men to take their lives on the Coast or describe the terrible depression and mental distortions that can prey upon the mind there?

On the morning of September 20, however, Herr von Lucke was still very much among the living, and he accompanied Mary and her men to the broad, new, government road leading inland from Victoria. For the first half mile or so this was a joy to follow, so smooth that "you could go over it in a . . . [wheel]chair. [But] the rest of it made you fit for one for the rest of your natural life," because it didn't have its top on yet and was a treacherous mass of broken rocks, lava, tree stumps, and tangled vines. Then, inevitably, it began to rain just as the unfinished road petered out into the thick, forest-covered foothills of the mountain. Soon their path was a torrent of mud-thickened water, and Mary was saturated to the skin, but the feeling was not wholly uncomfortable because of the high temperature, which produced a sort of hothouse effect. And even though the downpour prevented them from seeing more than two yards in any direction, the scene was weirdly beautiful. They seemed to be "in a ghost-land forest," for the great palms and redwoods loomed out of the enveloping mist when they approached and then dissolved back into the atmosphere as they passed by. All the rocks and boulders were smothered in moss of the most delicate shades of green, which made them look like soft emerald pillows strewn on the sides of the path, and here or there was one covered in bright gold-colored moss, as if a ray of sunshine had been trapped on the forest floor by the mist and was nestling among the rocks until it could escape and regain its home with the sun.

Early in the afternoon they reached the village of Buana at the base of the mountain, where the Basel Bible Mission was located; it was run by two Africans, one clad in a tidy white jacket and the other in an identical blue one. White Jacket and Blue Jacket, as Mary called them, offered her accommodation in their house and then lounged about and spat and chatted as she unpacked her gear. Soon all the chiefs in the neighborhood arrived and, shortly after, a veritable army of local sightseers. Soaked through and weary and cold now, Mary gently evicted her visitors, the chief, and the expectorating Bible teachers and then closed the shutters on the audience peering in from outside, telling them that "the circus was closed for repairs." She wrung as much water as she could from her saturated clothes, combed her hair and secured it with more hairpins, and then ventured out again and took a short stroll. But the scenery was "much like that you would enjoy if you were inside a blancmange," and she could scarcely see a few yards about her.

She did happen upon some highly interesting human scenery, though, in the person of an itinerant minstrel. She had not seen one of these performers since she had been in Sierra Leone and Accra in 1893. Each minstrel performed for a fee. He carried with him a "song net" very much like an ordinary fishing net, to which were attached various objects: python bones, pipes, feathers, pieces of hide, birds' and reptiles' heads, and so on. Each of these things was a title of sorts for a particular tale. One selected an object and asked, "How much that song?" The minstrel came back with an outrageous price, one haggled, reached an impasse, went on to another object, haggled some more, and in time — usually of an inordinate duration — came to an understanding. Then one sat down on one's heels and listened with rapt attention to the song, or rather, chant. As Mary says, "You usually have another. You sort of dissipate in novels in fact." Often the audience was augmented by passers-by who refused to pay. "Hence a row," Mary explained, "unless you are, like me, indifferent to other people having a little pleasure."

The minstrel Mary met that soggy afternoon in Buana was the most riveting and impressive she had ever encountered. She called him Homer on the spot

> because his works were a terrific two. Tied on to his small net were a human hand and a human jaw bone. They were his only songs. I heard them both regardless of expense. I did not understand them, because I did not know his language; but they were fascinating things, and the human hand one had a passage in it which caused the singer to crawl on his hands and knees, round and round, stealthily looking this side and that, giving the peculiar questing cough, and making the leopard mark on the earth with his doubled-up fist. Ah! that was something like a song! It would have roused a rock to enthusiasm; a civilised audience would have smothered its singer with bouquets. I — well, the headman with me had to interfere and counsel moderation in heads of tobacco.

Homer sang a cappella, without any orchestral accompaniment. But Mary was as enamored of African instrumental music as she was of vocal performances. She had a go, in fact, at nearly every instrument she came across and was assured by her African teachers that "with application I should succeed in becoming a rather decent performer on the harp and xylophone, and had the makings of a genius for the tom-tom." The tom-tom was her very favorite, and though she conceded that it was not suited to romantic serenading, "all else the tom-tom can do, and do well. It can talk as well as the human tongue. It can make you want to dance or fight for no private reason." In short, this "noble instrument" was the best for "getting at the inner soul of humanity."

After Homer's stirring performance, Mary returned to the mission house once again, shooed away eager callers, lit candles, and read Günther. Sleep on the wooden plank bed with an ad hoc pillow fashioned out of German and English Bibles wrapped round with a tattered pair of Blue Jacket's trousers proved elusive. Moreover, Mary's most loquacious carrier, Kefalla, was dogmatically holding forth in the next room. So she got out of bed again, oiled her revolver, and then sat up listening to the cacophony of Kefalla's pronouncements, mingled with the "coo-cooing" of the village women — apparently entreating utterances calling for their husbands, who were far out of earshot down in Ambas Bay, to come home. One man did return, however, in a bellicose state and began whacking his wives, whose screams only seemed to accelerate the cooing of the other women.

The next day, September 21, was spent much as was the day before: slogging through the mud in the rain. In the afternoon, shortly before reaching Buea, where there was a government station, Mary paused at a stream and attempted to "dispossess [herself] of the German territory" she had accumulated in the course of the day, swishing the mud out of her skirts and splashing the clear water over her hands and face, "but what is life without a towel?" That her exertions were not successful became apparent when she met the German officer in charge of the Buea station. As soon as Herr Liebert had cordially welcomed her to his house — an impressive structure that was, however, only partially finished — he suggested "an instant bath." Mary tactfully declined. "Men can be trying! How in the world is anyone going to take a bath in a house with no doors and only very sketchy wooden window-shutters?"

The next morning Mary reorganized her small party. Several men departed to return to Victoria. The headman, Bum, and the pontificating Kefalla remained, the latter having been renamed "the Professor" by Herr Liebert, though Mary thought "Windbag" was a more accurate sobriquet. To replace those who were leaving, Herr Liebert loaned Mary three men from the station. The first of these was a Liberian named Xenia, who Mary felt sure must have had a checkered past in the American colony: "I wonder whether he is a fugitive president or a defaulting bank manager. They have copies of all the high points of American culture there, I am told." In addition to Xenia, Mary acquired a local man named Sasu and another called Tomorrow who came "from some interior unknown district and who speaks no known language and whose business it is to help cut the way through the bush." By 8:00 A.M. they were off, despite Kefalla's remonstrances that it was Sunday: " 'You no sabe this be Sunday, Ma?' says he in a tone that tells me he considers this settles the matter. I 'sabe' unconcernedly."

The rain continued to pour down, making the steep path slick with mud. Mary wondered "now and again, as I assumed with an unnecessary violence a recumbent position, why I came to Africa; but patches of satin leaved begonias and clumps of lovely tree-ferns reconciled me to my lot." And when the rain let up every now and then and the mist lifted, they saw that they were traveling through a vast, fern- and moss-enshrouded forest "cathedral."

By evening they reached the timberline on the mountain, and here they decided to camp, though Mary felt that if she had "had a bull behind me or Mr. Fildes in front, I might have done another five or seven miles." At Buea Herr Liebert had pressed a military camp bed on her, and now there were "great times" trying to set the thing up on the steep, slanted hillside, Kefalla giving advice while viewing the proceedings in a manner that so annoyed Mary that she dispatched him to chop firewood. Nevertheless, they got the bed properly set up at last, then Mary had Xenia make her some tea, and she dined luxuriously on tinned fat pork and herring.

Before nightfall Mary climbed a short way up the mountain face to take compass bearings. When she got back to the camp, just as darkness was descending, she found that the men had been into the rum that she carried along for restorative purposes, for herself and the men, against exhaustion and the cold. Kefalla was laying down the law "with great detail and unction," and Mary's cook, normally a quiet, circumspect man, was "now weirdly cheerful" and singing incoherently. This aroused the ire of the others who wanted to slide into drunken slumber. After an hour, the cook's performance grew woollier and woollier and then died out altogether. Mary sat up late on her military camp bed and wrote in her journal by the light of an insect-haunted lantern.

The next morning, September 23, broke "gloriously fine," and all went well as they continued to scale the mountain until they reached a water hole, and, as one of Mary's men put it while gazing down the hole, "water no live" there. This provoked a crisis because, as Mary only now learned, they had exhausted the inadequate supply of water they had carried up with them from Buea. Mary quickly deduced from the behavior of the men that their dry state was evidently a trick and that they expected her to give up the climb and return with them to Victoria, where they would "get their pay and live happily ever after without having to face the horror of the upper regions of the mountain." In fact, they cited other Europeans' resignation in the very same waterless position as an example to Mary to abandon the climb. But Mary was not to be bullied or deceived into failure, quite the opposite, in fact. She sent a couple of men back to Buea with a note to Herr Liebert requesting a demijohn of water and then, to the others' dismay, recommenced her climb alone. By this time the sun was blazing, and it reflected back from the rocks in scorching rays, though simultaneously a biting, cold wind seemed to penetrate through to Mary's bones.

And yet, all her physical discomfort — thirst and sunburn and chill — was more than compensated for by the dazzling views and vistas on all sides. Far below the Atlantic looked like a plain of frosted silk and the mangrove swamps that hemmed it like a vast damson-colored carpet. Immediately below lay the town of Victoria, with Mungo's forested foothills encircling it like a diadem, and Ambas Bay beyond gemmed with its rocky islands. Meanwhile, above on the mountain a thunderstorm was brewing, sending forth a soft, billowy, cream-colored cloud. From below white mists began to rise from the mangrove swamps. A vibrant rainbow emerged, one arch of it buried behind the mountain peak while the other dissolved into the mauve sea of mist below. This mist continued to waft up toward Mary, turning from a pale rose color to lavender in the setting sun until it was at her feet, blotting out all the world below so that only the two summits remained: Mount Cameroon directly above her and the mountain island of Fernando Po some twenty miles out to sea.

In *Travels in West Africa* Mary writes how "it was like a vision, and it held me spellbound, as I stood shivering on the rocks with the white mist round my knees until into my wool-gathering mind came the memory of those anything but sublime men of mine; and I turned and scuttled off along the rocks like an agitated ant left alone in a dead universe."

The first man she met was Xenia, apparently lost and behaving oddly, behavior that reminded Mary that she had been told he was "slightly crazy." He had given Mary's black bag to one of the other men and was now carrying the lid of a saucepan and an empty lantern. As Mary observed, "this is not the sort of outfit the Royal Geographical Society *Hints to Travellers* would recommend for African exploration. . . . Nice situation this: a madman on a mountain in the mist."

"In a homicidal state of mind," she made tracks for the missing men, followed by the feckless Xenia. But they found only one of their empty soda water bottles — a wretched reminder of Mary's parched state. "I did not linger to raise a monument to them" she writes of the absent men, "but I said I wished they were in a condition to require one." At this point, however, at least the heavens were cooperative, for they discharged a good deal of rain, so that Mary could draw the long saw grass that grew so abundantly thereabouts through her lips and drink the beads of rain water from it. It was now evening and the only other liquid or any kind of nourishment she had had that day was a glass of sour claret early in the morning before setting off.

There were still no signs of the missing men, so Mary fired several shots in the direction in which they had made their camp, and instantly a chorus of voices was heard in response, leading Mary and Xenia back to the others. After giving them "a brief but lurid sketch" of her opinion of their behavior, Mary opened tins of food for supper and then sent more couriers down to Herr Liebert for additional food and water.

They spent the following day waiting for the supplies from Buea. Even if they hadn't been desperately short of food and water, Mary would have found it difficult to continue her climb because her face and lips — badly burnt from the previous day's exposure — were cracked and blistered, and in the night she had inadvertently whipped a large patch of skin off one cheek with the blanket.

The expected consignments of food and water arrived during the course of the day, including a sack of rice and beef for the men and a special box for Mary from Herr Liebert containing a generous supply of biscuits, candles, tinned meats, and a bottle of wine and another of beer. As they were happily dining on all these delicacies, another violent thunderstorm lurked and growled in the distance, sending out bursts of thunder and vibrant streaks of lightning. "One feels here," Mary observed, "as if one were constantly dropping, unasked and unregarded, among painful and violent discussions between the elemental powers of the universe."

The next day, the twenty-fifth, they were off at 7:00 A.M. climbing the steep, craggy mountain wall. By early afternoon they were all chilled through with the cold rain. So Mary called a halt, wrapped up each man in a blanket, built blazing fires, and then retired by herself behind some boulders to wrestle into her seaman's jersey — always a struggle but particularly so today, given her soaked cotton blouse. At first the pullover threatened to suffocate her and then got firmly jammed on her head, and she thought for a moment that she would have to call for help. But after a good battle, she successfully got her head and arms into the appropriate holes and rejoined the men. As for going any farther that day, it was clear that they wouldn't budge, and Mary's face also remained "a misery to me; as soon as it dries it sets into a mask and when I move it, its splits and bleeds." So rather than resuming the march, she wandered about some during the afternoon, taking compass bearings and collecting rocks. That night she sat up, partly because she wanted to keep watch over the men, who were sleeping in a huddle dangerously close to their fires. But in any event, Mary herself dozed off twice and toppled over and had to be rescued, wet blankets and all, from the fire by Xenia and Kefalla.

"The weather is undecided and so am I," Mary wrote in her log at dawn the next day. Cold and rainy, conditions were far from ideal for reaching the top of Mount Cameroon. But she didn't want to give up now, after six days of arduous climbing. She debated with herself whether it was right to risk her men in this last lap toward the summit. Her own fate, however, she breezily dismissed as "my own affair, and no one will be a ha'porth the worse if I am dead in an hour." In the end, she asked for volunteers, and only Bum, the headman, and Xenia agreed to go with her to the top.

And so they set off at 6:00 A.M. and plunged into the iron gray mist that poured down from the steep mountain face above. After an hour or so Xenia collapsed, and Mary wrapped him in a blanket, gave him a tin of meat and a flask of rum, and told him to take shelter in a depression beneath one of the rock ridges and await their return. Then she took compass bearings and proceeded with Bum. But soon Bum too gave up short of the peak — in his case for the third time, since he'd been up with previous parties — and Mary left him also with a blanket and provisions and then went "on alone into the wild, grey, shifting, whirling mist."

"After a desperate fight" against the elements she finally gained the summit, where she found something close to a hurricane raging and visibility of less than ten yards. Here she also found the empty champagne bottles of some of her predecessors piled near the cairn at the top, and among them she deposited her own memento — one of her printed calling cards — "as a civility to Mungo, a civility his Majesty will soon turn into pulp."

It was in truth a rather anticlimactic victory up there on the frigid, gale-swept peak of the Throne of Thunder, and in *Travels in West Africa* Mary confesses that "verily I am no mountaineer, for there is in me no exultation, but only a deep disgust because the weather has robbed me of my main object in coming here, namely to get a good view and an idea of the way the unexplored mountain range behind Calabar tends." She might just as well have been down at Buea or even Victoria for all she could see. Moreover, it was freezing cold. But in spite of her disappointment Mary must have felt some sense of accomplishment: old Mungo may have failed her, but it didn't vanquish her. Even more importantly, she didn't fail it.

Still, Mary didn't linger at the summit denouncing the foul weather or ruminating on her own triumph. Before her calling card began to disintegrate in the mist and rain, she started her descent and hastened down to pick up the waiting bundles of Bum and Xenia.

They got back to Buea in a day, though the relative speed of their return didn't mean it was smooth going. Mud-slickened paths are as tricky and hazardous going downhill as up. As usual Mary went in for "acrobatic performances," falling down on top of her lantern, taking flying slides of twenty feet or so until halted by a tree, and so forth. By the time they reached Herr Liebert's station, the only dry or clean particle of her was one cuff over which she had been carrying her shawl.

Herr Liebert of course again suggested an "instant bath," and perhaps this time Mary capitulated. At any rate, after tea and a change of clothes she joined Herr Liebert, who was engaged in making a much needed door for his rudimentary house, and they discoursed "on things in general and the mountain in particular" as the sun was setting and Mungo, perversely, shone clear and bright in the sun's dying rays above them.

Having no wish to stay with White Jacket and Blue Jacket again, Mary went through Buana and all the way to Victoria the next day, arriving back at her starting point on September 28, just eight days after they had set off for the top of Mungo. They reached Victoria just as night was falling and approached Government House by the private path through the botanical gardens, as Mary had no wish to be seen in

her bedraggled state. Fortunately, Herr von Lucke was out, so she had
time to wash and change before he returned. When he did reappear,
he had the satisfaction of learning that his grim prognostications for
Mary's adventure had come to pass: she had been nearly drowned to
death in the rains and had caught "an awful cold, the most awful cold
in the head of modern times."

And yet she refused to be sensible and go to bed early after the
exertions of the day's hike, which had only exacerbated her cold. Instead after dinner she went out alone onto the verandah and "sat . . .
overlooking Victoria and the sea, in the dim soft light of the stars,
with the fire-flies round me and the lights of Victoria away below, and
heard the soft rush of the Lukola River, and the sound of the sea-surf
on the rocks, and the tom-tomming and singing . . . all matching and
mingling together." And in the face of all this loveliness, she posed
her old question to herself: " 'Why did I come to Africa?' thought I.
Why! Who would not come to its twin brother hell itself for all the
beauty and the charm of it!"

Not content with scaling Mount Cameroon, Mary decided to follow
this feat with a canoe excursion to the Rio del Rey, which was farther
north on the other side of Mungo. It was not an easily reached or very
navigable waterway, and the route from the Rio del Rey to Calabar,
where Mary planned to travel next, was even more hazardous. For
once, Mary is perfectly honest about the hazards of her projected itinerary, perhaps in this case because her friends eventually succeeded in
persuading her to abandon it. She writes in *Travels in West Africa,*
"Had the desire to get myself killed, with which I am constantly being
taxed, been my real and only motive for going to West Africa, I should
have rigidly adhered to this fine variegated plan" of going on to the
Rio del Rey from Victoria. But Herr von Lucke, with dire tales of the
fearsome rapids, rocks, and tornadoes awaiting her along the river,
convinced Mary that she should chuck this particular, perilous picnic.
Instead he talked her into staying a few days longer in Victoria and
waiting for the Cameroon governor's yacht, the *Nachtigal,* to arrive
and take her on to Calabar.

In the meantime Herr von Lucke tried to console Mary with the
sights of Victoria. The day after she came down from the mountain,
he proposed a walk. Mary knew, however, that this would be no idle
stroll but instead "an affair of fourteen miles or so, taken at a good five
miles an hour," and she "being as stiff as a table-leg declined." Then
he offered a more modest invitation to go see the islands in Ambas

Bay, the cove round which Victoria was so picturesquely nestled. So they went out in a small skiff, and Mary found two of the bay's three islands, Ambas and Bobia, "perfect gems of beauty." Mondoleh she was less taken with; it reminded her of "one of those flower-stands full of ferns and plants — the sort that you come across in drawing rooms at home, with wire-work legs. I do not mean that Mondoleh has wire-work legs under water, but it looks as if it might have." Ambas was the outermost island in the bay, and it belonged to a German officer of the *Hyaena* who won it in a raffle for five hundred marks. Its only inhabitants were goats and pigs, and Mary says that the only really noticeable thing about it was that both the English and the Germans located it in the wrong place on their maps.

Bobia, though rocky and the least fertile of all three islands, contained both human and animal inhabitants, the human ones being fishermen for the most part and their families. The pigs of Bobia were legendary on the Coast, and Mary deeply regretted not having been able to bring one home, for she was sure it would have caused "a profound sensation" at the Royal Agricultural Show. "These interesting animals," she explains, "are black in colour, . . . two-thirds head, and after a very small and flat bit of body, end in an inordinately long tail. Their mental dispositions are lively, frolicsome and extremely nomadic and predatory." Mary was conversant on this subject of Bobia pigs because of one troublesome specimen owned by Herr von Lucke — a gift from a Bobia chief. This pig had a genius for slipping the rope that moored it to the vice governor's premises and then sauntering all over Victoria. Mary tells how "I used to meet it away in the Botanical Gardens, and in fact in so many unexpected places that I should not have been surprised to have met it anywhere."

Shortly after the Ambas Bay excursion, the *Nachtigal* arrived, but it was not en route to Calabar. Instead, the governor of Cameroon, Herr von Puttkamer, was on board, recuperating from a bad attack of fever, for it was thought that those stricken with tropical diseases had a better chance of recovery out at sea. Herr von Puttkamer was indeed on the mend, and he kindly asked Mary on board for breakfast, during which she acquired "a good deal of material for a work on the Natural History of Governors which I do not intend to publish." As they ate and chatted, the *Nachtigal* steamed about the bay, and since the sea was calm all was pleasant, until they received a sudden shock. They thought they had discovered a new rock but then found that they had in fact struck a sleeping whale.

The *Nachtigal* and the governor returned south to the Cameroon River, with promises, however, of the boat's returning soon en route to Calabar. Herr von Lucke continued to show Mary the sights of the area by taking her to Man of War Bay just south of Ambas Bay, and they also toured the large Woermann coffee, palm oil, and cacao plantation there.

Then another German ship, the *Hyaena,* called in at Victoria, and again Mary was asked on board for a meal — in this case a sumptuous dinner of roast beef and plum pudding, consumed at a temperature of 106 degrees while the equatorial sun poured down on the diners eating alfresco on the deck. Among those on board the *Hyaena* were two German officers who had preceded Mary up the southeast face of Mount Cameroon, and they compared their experiences of this unusual and dangerous approach at length.

Finally the *Nachtigal* returned to Victoria bound for Calabar, and Mary hastily packed all her gear, including her wardrobe, which, as she put it, had by now been reduced to a rather "rarefied state." The *Nachtigal* was commanded by Herr von Besser, and it steamed quickly and uneventfully to Calabar. Here Mary found, to her regret, that Sir Claude and Lady MacDonald had returned to England in preparation for another colonial posting to China.

But though she missed the MacDonalds, Mary did see her even dearer friend, Mary Slessor, when she went up to Okoyong to spend several days with her. And, as before, the two women sat up far into the night rocking the babies and talking — Mary Kingsley about all her adventures and experiences in Congo Français, Mary Slessor of her own exertions in the surrounding villages and about all the new additions to her family at the station. It must have been during this last visit that Mary learned so much from her friend about the Calabar Effik secret society, Egbo, which seemed to combine into one society Mary's two consuming interests, African law and fetish. In addition, she saw the initiated Okoyong girls emerge from the "fattening houses" where they had gorged on starchy fou fou and yams and palm oil in order to reach the large proportions deemed attractive for marriageable young women, dimensions, perhaps, that mimicked the state of pregnancy, which was their only goal and aim in life.

As soon as word reached Mary Slessor's village that the English ship, the *Bakana,* had arrived in Calabar, Mary hastened back to take passage. The *Bakana,* commanded by Captain Porter, was a sister ship to the *Batanga,* which had brought Mary out more than ten months earlier. Needless to say, she was now far more loaded down than she had been on the outgoing journey. Even though she had already sent several consignments of fish, reptile, and insect specimen back from Congo Français, she had bottles and bottles of new ones preserved in spirit, not to mention all the fetish items she had picked up along the way — carved figures, charms, amulets, baskets for catching vagrant souls, and so on — and then there were musical instruments and woven cloth and leatherwork of one kind and another. And on top of all this, Mary also had a large, live lizard for the London Zoo and a small monkey that perched on her shoulder.

It was mid-November when the *Bakana* departed from Calabar; it steamed almost directly westward along the five degree latitude until it reached the Grain Coast of Liberia, and then it rounded the western bulge of the continent and headed due north. It proved an uneventful, calm voyage until they reached Sierra Leone. Here "a gloom fell over the whole ship" when the purser, Mr. Crompton, suddenly died — a final, grim reminder for Mary of the precariousness and fragility of all things in Africa. This death, as Mary put it, "was one of those terribly sudden, hopeless cases of Coast fever, so common on the West Coast, where no man knows from day to day whether he or those round him will not, before a few hours are over, be in the grip of malarial fever, on his way to the grave." Mary ends *Travels in West Africa* with poor Crompton's death, and it casts a shadow back on everything that has gone before.

Several days later Mary wrote George Macmillan during their brief stopover in the Canary Islands. She had heard while in Sierra Leone that newspaper accounts of her travels had already begun to appear in England. In addition, she told Macmillan that the publisher Kegan Paul had been dispatching letters that had been haunting her like ghosts — offers, in fact, to publish her account of her adventures. These letters, she told Macmillan, had been appearing in "whacking blue envelopes marked 'most important' . . . off gigs, canoes, branch steamers, and surf boats." Kegan Paul, indeed, would seem to have pursued Mary up and down the Coast. And another publisher, which she does not name, she intimated, had also approached her. This same letter to Macmillan concluded with details of Mary's straitened financial position: "I am anxious to make money because I am now more than ever sure my brother won't and I have myself only £260 a year and that only for fifteen years more. If I keep on surviving in such a pointless way . . . there is nothing but the workhouse before me."

Altogether, this was a remarkably astute and persuasive letter, describing for Macmillan the interest that already existed at home in her travels — the fact that her reputation had actually beaten her back to England — informing him that other publishers were eager to snap up her account of her travels if Macmillan dallied, and finally, telling him, in so many words, that she needed to reach a profitable understanding with him. The only salient fact she omitted was that her underlying reason for wanting to write a financially successful book was that she would have the means to return to West Africa as soon as possible. Even before she had left the Coast, Mary was making shrewd calculations that she hoped would enable her to come back soon.

On the evening of November 30, 1895, in the chill, gray sleet of the English winter, the *Bakana* arrived at Liverpool, and Mary disembarked, her black waterproof bag clutched in one hand, the other holding the lead of the little monkey shivering on her shoulder. As she walked down the gangway, Mary saw by the flare of the gas lamps along the dock a young journalist, notepad in hand, come forward to meet her.

Part Four

We carry with us the wonders we seek without us; there
is all Africa and her prodigies in us.

Sir Thomas Browne

· ✧ 11 ✧ ·

"Travels in West Africa"

The eager reporter who greeted Mary on the Liverpool quay was a young Reuters correspondent named Charlton who had read the newspaper stories of Mary's travels that had preceded her home. And he was also a harbinger of the flood of ink that would be devoted to her in the weeks and months ahead. On the most fundamental level, Mary's voyage out had been an intensely private, personal journey, but its immediate, visible result was that she was catapulted into public prominence, even celebrity. Newspapermen pursued her to the extent that she wished, as she told George Macmillan, she could dispatch them all on "a yachting cruise down the coast." And the "haut politique," as Mary called the elite political, social, and intellectual circles of the day, soon began to shower her with invitations. She confided to her Cambridge friend Hatty Johnson that "I look back with envy on my Lady MacDonald, who had two personalities, one to deal with the outside public, with another underneath it." Of herself, Mary confessed, "I cannot be a bushman and a drawing roomer and so I get worried and bored."

To Mr. Charlton the next day at the Northwestern Hotel in Liverpool, however, Mary was excessively generous and cooperative. She offered to loan him her bulging journals, and when he protested that he had only an evening, not a week, to prepare his article, Mary obligingly gave him the first of many interviews to come. The fact was that Miss Kingsley was a journalistic scoop. On Monday, December 2, Mary took the train back to London, and, picking up the *Times* at Euston station, she found a lengthy story on her travels; to her con-

sternation she read in it that she had discovered portions of human
bodies tucked away in the larders of the mud huts she stayed at in
Gabon.

The article in the next day's *Daily Telegraph* was even worse. In the
florid, hyperbolic style Mary loved on occasion to parody, the *Telegraph*
identified Mary as the daughter of Charles Kingsley and then went on
to gush, "Always something new from Africa . . . and that which a
woman wills Heaven also wills." The *Telegraph* enrolled Mary in the
"great dynasty of modern African travellers which commenced with
Dr. Livingstone," and then compared the narrative of her travels —
"where cold missionary on the side-board would not sound like a
dreadful joke" — to the rousing and marvel-filled speech recited by
Othello to Desdemona, "Anthropophagi" and all. And since the *Telegraph* could not forbear moralizing as well as sensationalizing, its story
concluded with a tribute to the New Woman of which it considered
Mary such an outstanding type: "Yes! Anything seems possible in Africa, yet almost more wonderful than the hidden marvels of that Dark
Continent are the qualities of heart and mind which could carry a
lonely English lady through such experiences as Miss Kingsley has
'manfully' borne. It is a curious and a novel feature of the modern
emancipation of woman — this passion on the part of the sex to emulate the most daring achievements of masculine explorers."

This was going too far. Cannibal and gorilla stories Mary could put
up with, but celebration as a New Woman was more than she could
bear. Even before she had properly unpacked all her gear, she fired off
a "disclaimer" to the *Daily Telegraph* — her first appearance in print —
in which she set the record straight on three important points. First,
she was at pains to acknowledge all the help that she had received from
"the superior sex" on the Coast. She wondered, in fact, "that with the
amount of practical help to say nothing of good advice that I got from
all these gentlemen I was not, as it were, projected bang across the
continent," and in particular, she wanted to make clear how "dependent" she had been on the West African traders. Secondly, Mary wanted
to correct the story of her parentage, to say that she was the daughter
of George, rather than Charles, Kingsley. And finally, and most importantly, she flatly stated that "I do not relish being called a New
Woman. I am not one in any sense of the term. Every child I come
across tyrannises over me, and a great deal of time I ought to give to
science goes in cooking, etc. I do not think travelling now lays one
open to this reproach. Have you forgotten the Queen of Sheba?"

This was the first in what became Mary's periodic repudiations of feminism, which culminated in her public opposition to women's suffrage several years later. Like many other gifted Victorian women, including Charlotte Brontë, George Eliot, and Florence Nightingale, Mary was loath to identify herself with the contemporary women's movement. The fear of these women, most of whom were single and childless and hence anomalous in their society's eyes, was that to embrace the designation of New Woman would reduce them, in society's view, to unattractive, strident freaks. Despite all their accomplishments, and in Mary's case these were of a peculiarly "masculine" order, such women were plagued by a fundamental and debilitating failure of nerve. The lurking fear behind all their protests that they cooked more than they explored, darned more than they wrote, nursed more than they lectured, was the very primal one that they *were* unwomanly. As, in fact they were, if to dream of a life rich in incident and experience was "unfeminine" or manly. The "reproach" of New Woman Mary deflected by insisting upon the external female chores and obligations she fulfilled. Husbandless and childless, Mary invoked her cooking and her dependence on the "superior sex" in Africa as a defense against those who would call her a New Woman. But of course she protested too much and in time too long. And her protests were yet another manifestation of the split between public and private, fame and isolation — the abiding conflicts and inner divisions that were to characterize her life from now on.

Certainly emptiness and loneliness were her immediate portion when she unpacked all her bags at the top of 100 Addison Road. Charley was off in Singapore, and Mary's only companions were her army of cats, including one named Smiles and another Joseph Chamberlain, which a neighbor had cared for in her absence, and the three-foot-high, nail-studded idol, Muvungu, that she had brought back from the 1893 journey. It was dark, damp, and chill in the flat; bottles of specimens, insects pinned onto corkboards, heavy photographic plates, and dried grasses for Kew Gardens all cluttered up the parlor. Mary herself, as she wrote Günther, was "hopelessly cold and as torpid as the juju lizard" she had brought back for the Regent's Park Zoo. The first task at hand was to get this creature to his new home and some of the more cumbersome specimens into the Natural History Museum. Hence Mary's request to Günther that "if you have got a spare young man in your commodious basement, I think he had better come here and go through" her fish, shells, sponges, and assorted rocks, "for they are not particularly portable and I do not expect particularly interesting."

Then, as she had done after her first journey to Africa, Mary now stanched her feelings of homesickness for the Coast by writing. As early as December 10, scarcely a week after her return, she began submitting manuscript material on her second trip to Macmillan. She sustained that magical life by imaginatively reliving it at her small writing desk in the Addison Road library, a room now filled with bronze figures and bangles, ivory carvings, wooden masks, musical instruments, charms, and raffia baskets. A "cosy room," as one interviewer later described it, heated as far as possible to a tropical level, with folios and old travel books piled on shelves and on the floor, maps of Africa rolled up in the corners, and cats curled up before the fire.

And Mary retreated again to the past as well as to West Africa in her writing, for when she was not working on what was to become *Travels in West Africa,* she turned once again to the memoir of her father, which Charley, despite all his noises to the contrary, had made absolutely no headway on during the year Mary was away. By December 23, in fact she informed Macmillan that she was close to the end of the biographical preface for George Kingsley's *Notes on Sport and Travel.*

She had also made extraordinary progress on her *Travels* because along with her letter of the twenty-third she sent Macmillan selections of manuscript dealing with some of the Ogooué episodes of her trip. This chapter and indeed much of what was to go into the book was lifted directly from Mary's voluminous diaries, though as she later wrote Lady MacDonald, "the amount of expurgation my journals have required has been awful." In this particular section, for example, she told Lady MacDonald, "I . . . had to entirely eliminate a lovely scene in the Ogooué when I and the captain of a vessel had to take to the saloon table because a Bishop with a long red beard and voluminous white flannel petticoats was rolling about the floor in close but warful embrace with the Governor of the Ogooué, utterly deaf to the messages of peace the captain and I poured down on them." Such potentially libelous material Mary could excise on her own, but that she had difficulty reworking and condensing the more unwieldy, uncontroversial passages of her journal was shown by the fact that Macmillan suggested that Dr. Henry Guillemard edit the batches of manuscript Mary submitted. On the face of it, this seemed a reasonable plan, and Mary even agreed to pay Guillemard's editorial fee. Guillemard seemed a particularly good choice because quite apart from being an old family friend, he was also the geographical editor for the Cambridge University Press. But as things worked out in the coming months, Guillemard's contribution to the *Travels* became an irksome impediment, for he couldn't refrain from rewriting rather than reworking Mary's manuscript. And so along with all her other literal and metaphorical headaches in the months to come, Mary had to put up with this awkward and increasingly exasperating alliance with Guillemard.

Mary's writing schedule, however, was always liable to interruption. Her cousins Rose and Mary Kingsley called, of course, as did Violet Roy and Lucy Toulmin Smith. Dr. Günther's young man came to fetch the less portable specimens, and Mary herself went to the Natural History Museum with her choicest beetles, lizards, and fish. A sick friend in Cambridge summoned her to nurse. She visited her Bailey relations in Chancery Lane. And Sarah Kingsley and her ancient mother in South Wimbledon remained chronically ill and destitute and consequently were in need of Mary's attentions on both scores. In some ways it seemed as if Mary had never been away at all, as if the year in Africa had been some sort of protracted hallucination, so inexorably did her old life reassert its routines and responsibilities.

And yet dramatic developments also took place that showed that her London life would never again be the same. For example, a series of controversial articles appeared in the *Spectator* in December. The *Spectator* palaver, as Mary would have called it, began with an article entitled "The Negro Future," by Meredith Townsend, which appeared in early December and started off by saying, "Reading the accounts now appearing of Miss Kingsley's adventures in Cameroons, the question which all African narratives suggest comes again into the mind, What makes the African continent so bad?" Townsend then proceeded to ponder this weighty query and in the course of the article managed to articulate nearly every racist sentiment and prejudice of his day. For him the "total impression" of Mary's travels was "that of a people abnormally low, evil, cruel. . . . It is in Africa that the lowest depth of evil barbarism is reached." Moreover, "it has always been so." From the beginning of time, according to Townsend, the African has gone on in his stagnant, degraded way, subsisting on a murky, subhuman level: it remained a race that had "founded no empire, built no city, developed no art." About the chances of uplifting such a barbarous people Townsend was not sanguine, but he dimly perceived two possible grounds of hope. The first was that the African might not prove absolutely impervious to "the influence of a higher race": of Englishmen and Empire, for example. Instead of being a brute, perhaps the African was "a child to be turned into a man." The second ray of light Townsend made out for the Dark Continent was that of missionary effort — the "annealing quality" of Christianity that could save the degraded black man. But, on the other hand, Townsend cautioned that the African's destiny may be quite other than what we would wish. "We know nothing of the Divine purpose" and so cannot assume that the African has any significant role to play in it. "The destiny of the Negro," Townsend concluded, "may be for ever useless in our eyes, as were the worms in those of Darwin's gardener."

Townsend's article appeared on December 7, but it was not until Christmas Day that Mary sat down to compose a rejoinder, and when she did, this first extended appearance in print was a curiously vacillating though heartfelt production. Her long letter appeared in the December 28 issue and began by giving lip service agreement with Townsend's low view of African culture. Even though her flat was filled with African artifacts, Mary could still assert that Africans "have never produced an even fourteenth-rate sculpture, picture, machine, tool, piece of cloth, or pottery." But when it came to African society she was prepared to grant Townsend nothing, and she was particularly incensed that he should draw such pessimistic conclusions from the newspaper accounts of her travels. "In mental and moral affairs," she asserted, the African was not inferior and indeed possessed both a sense of honor and justice. "In rhetoric," she continued, "he excells and for good temper, and patience he compares favorably with any set of human beings." Then Mary proceeded to launch into a defense of the "barbarous" customs and rites Townsend deplored. The African is not cruel, she argued, nor are such things as his burial rituals and ceremonies. Indeed, in an analogy that must have raised the hackles of many a *Spectator* reader, Mary held that the importance given by Africans to "burial rites is quite Greek in its intensity. Given a duly educated native of the Niger delta, I am sure he would grasp the true inwardness of his Alcestis far and away better than any living European can." This, of course, was heretical. Even worse, however, was the salvo in the last paragraph of Mary's letter: "'I do not believe the African to be brutal or degraded or cruel. I know from wide experience . . . that he is . . . grateful and faithful and by no means the drunken idiot his so-called friends, the Protestant missionaries are anxious, as an excuse for their failure in dealing with him, to make him out."

The *Spectator* could scarcely publish what they called Mary's "cynical letter" without editorial comment. An unsigned article in the same issue called "Negro Capacity" reiterated Townsend's major points and glossed Mary's response with "the centre of her argument is that the Negro is very like other people, though in him the emotions which in other races lead to punitive proceedings, lead to torture, murder and . . . cannibalism — the latter a practice which our correspondent would apparently defend, or shall we say extenuate if she had dared."

The gauntlet had been flung down and the opening rounds of ammunition discharged; the lines of hostility had been clearly demarcated. From now on Mary would be embroiled off and on — mostly on — in numerous controversies, the combatant in various journalistic and political skirmishes. Sometimes she was on the offensive, sometimes on the defensive, and only very rarely did she inhabit the neutral zone of truce or cease-fire.

"Negro Capacity" in the *Spectator* was not the only response Mary had to her letter in defense of the African, his character, and society. On New Year's Eve she wrote Günther, "I was really afraid to open your letter this morning. Last night's post brought me three fearful blowings up from personal friends in regard to my letter in this week's *Spectator* and I feared you might have got an entirely new light on my character from it. Oh Dr. Günther, never, wander from the straight path of Evangelical orthodoxy. Be if you can possibly manage it . . . a Scotch Presbyterian. Nothing else gives you comforting, cocksure self-confidence, lots of nice people will agree with you then and you will not get called 'cynical' and 'unfair' and 'blind to *true* facts' then like I am now. I like 'true facts.' What are false facts?"

The dates of Mary's letters to the *Spectator* and to Günther, Christmas Day and New Year's Eve, are telling. For all her fame and notoriety and despite the demands of friends and relations, she was alone in the Addison Road flat at precisely those times of the year when others were in the midst of their families celebrating the holidays. On Christmas morning and on New Year's Day, Mary awoke to a cold, empty house. In the months and years ahead she often wrote letters on holidays or at 2:00 or 3:00 A.M. on weekend nights. And she never fails to date such letters and to add "midnight" or "2:45 A.M." at the end, after signing the letter with "yours very truly and dead tired" or "yours very truly and quite frozen." Only in this oblique way, though, did she reveal the extent of her isolation.

She was not, however, reluctant to talk about her illnesses, some of which were clearly psychosomatic. In early January she was down with fever and headache, which she claimed were lingering bouts of malaria. Then influenza struck, and when she finally got back to her writing desk, progress on *Travels in West Africa* was impeded by rheumatism in her hands, which made writing an agony. These were gray, bleak days and weeks, the early months of 1896. More interviews and articles appeared, but Mary ceased trying to correct or refute their distortions and inaccuracies. Despite migraine and flu she continued with her book, and writing it must have instilled in her some sense of vocation and fulfillment because she attended a special meeting for women authors at the Writers' Club in late January. But, as she wrote Hatty Johnson, in the midst of some of the most popular women writers of the day, she felt she came off as "an utter failure because I was frightened by a little woman about 4 feet 6 inches high who had been to South Africa. It wasn't that that terrified me but her shirt and fixings, real shirt, starched, studs, waistcoat and coat and hat on side of head, talked of how women should let them see they could *boss* it. I shrunk into a corner with a little lady who had really been to the Faroe Islands and who could have whipped up the other one, shirt and all, in fact the whole room full." This second woman, Mary continued, "told me lots of things and above all, she did not know who I was and asked me if I was related to Tinsley, the publisher. I said I thought I might be."

Also in January Mary traveled to Edinburgh to lecture before the Scottish Geographical Society. It was her first public performance, or "magic lantern entertainment," as she described her lectures with slides, and it was an enormous success. From the very beginning, Mary was a brilliant lecturer — a kind of combination music hall comedienne, university professor, and evangelical preacher. This first lecture, "Travels on the Western Coast of Equatorial Africa," was a racy account of her journey between the Ogooué and the Remboué in Gabon and was more or less extracted intact from the manuscript of *Travels in West Africa*. Most of the lectures Mary gave in 1896 were in fact lifted directly from her work in progress, in part to avoid diverting herself from her primary task of finishing the book, and even more important to create an audience for the book when it did appear. During the winter and spring of 1896 Mary spoke at Glasgow, Birkenhead, Liverpool, Vauxhall, and Dublin, among other places.

The lectures before geographical societies were smallish affairs and only open to members. But very quickly Mary's fame as a lecturer spread, greatly aided by vivid newspaper accounts of her talks, so that at the public events, she spoke to as many as seventeen hundred people on occasion, and even so crowds were turned away at the door. No one was going to mistake her for a relative of Tinsley in the future. By 1897 she had hired an agent from one of the large London literary and theatrical agencies on the Strand to handle her lecture dates and fees. Her fee hovered between five and ten guineas, about the going rate of the day, though Mary often spoke gratis for charities of one sort or another. In April, for example, she told Macmillan that she was speaking at the YMCA in aid of what she had been sententiously informed was "a home for dissolute girls under the auspices of the Elders of the Presbyterian Church." The good elders of course meant *destitute* young women, but Mary probably wouldn't have withdrawn her services even if they had been dissolute as well. But the paid lectures were important, as were the royalties from her books, for one reason only: they would enable her to return to the Coast. As she bluntly put it to her agent, she had calculated that every pound earned meant five miles in West Africa.

Given her inexperience and fundamental shyness, it might seem surprising that Mary proved such a popular and dynamic speaker, to the extent in fact that at the height of her fame men donned placards or sandwich boards and strutted up and down Oxford Street as human advertisements for her London lectures. The woman who always hesitated awkwardly on the thresholds of Kensington drawing rooms and who once flushed scarlet when her heavy African brass bracelet clattered to the floor at a smart dinner party could stand up before five hundred or a thousand people, tell jokes (usually at her own expense), then abruptly shift gears and talk fervently on English trade interests in West Africa or on the spiritual beliefs of the Fang, point out particular features of her magic lantern slides with a completely steady hand, and then gracefully acknowledge her delighted audience's applause at the end of her performance.

There was after all, a very real need in Mary to reach out and touch others — to connect, make contact. But the usual, informal kinds of intimacy were often inaccessible to or impossible for her, especially in these early years of her public life. Socially, indeed, Mary saw herself as a misfit. As she described her plight to Lady MacDonald, that most confident of hostesses and social creatures, Mary watched the "game" of English society as a perpetual outsider: "I was yesterday at two At Homes and a dinner," she wrote her friend later that spring, "at every one of which I saw people who had abused their hosts up hill and down dale or who their hosts had abused ditto. Yet there they were all together smiling and calling each other by their Christian names and so on — it all seems to me silly and sinful and it's uncommon dull."

Instead of "reaching" people through the normal routes of at-homes and over tea, Mary spoke out from a podium and in the pages of her books. The lectures of course were perhaps the more psychologically rewarding, for writing is an inherently solitary business, and the response one gets — in the form of reviews and letters — is delayed and received long after the immediacy of the utterance has passed.

But Mary's lectures gave her a structured means of moving and being moved by others. Moreover, they afforded a situation that was not only formalized and so largely immune to social insecurity and awkwardness, but was also largely under Mary's own control. Not infrequently she would open her talks with humorously self-deprecating remarks, as if to say, "Yes, I may seem a bit odd and angular and uneasy, but let's have a laugh about it and then get on to the real thing — travel or fish or fetish — at hand." And so ultimately Mary's lecturing did far more than create an audience for her forthcoming books or bring in cash for the constantly planned-for and then deferred trip to the Coast. More basically, it brought contact to the solitary reaches within: the lectures carried her, however briefly, in from the cold.

The newspaper stories and her growing reputation as a lecturer naturally led to a dramatic enlargement of Mary's literary and social world. Lionization ensued and with it invitations to countless teas and dinners, precisely the sort of affairs where she found herself an "utter failure," and this sense of failure in turn led to further redemptive lecturing. Hence a vicious circle was started, with all its attendant headaches and insomnia and despair over proper clothes and inadequate hairpins. Whether she liked it or no, Mary was in demand and even shed reflected glory on those who knew her. Guillemard reported from Cambridge that "I am quite a distinguished person here because I am a friend of Miss Kingsley. I enliven the dinner talk with anecdotes about you: how you invariably travel disguised as an Arab sheik; and generally have a well-hung leg in your portmanteau."

In late February Mary herself wrote Günther — a man with a generally acknowledged "difficult" personality and even less social savoir faire than his protégée — that "I was at a big dinner party given in my honour last night and got an awful dose of the wrong sort of incense so I am feeling very dingy-minded and extra humble. I felt highly inclined to ask them why they did not ask the lady who dives through the roof at the aquarium and the female lion tamers — the side of me they pretend to admire is no higher than this sort of thing. 'Oh Miss Kingsley, how many men did you kill?' I who never lost a porter and who have set up o' nights 5 mortal weeks at a time nursing a fever epidemic to say nothing of individual cases."

Perhaps it was this lecturing and attendant lionization that prompted Mary to sit for a professional photographer that spring. She was becoming aware — however self-consciously and unpleasantly — of her "image." No doubt, too, George Macmillan was hoping for a photograph for the frontispiece for *Travels in West Africa,* though in any event he was to be disappointed. In the early illustrated articles on Mary that were published in magazines like the *Illustrated London News,* the picture of Mary that was used was one that had been taken in Cambridge in 1892, shortly after her parents' deaths. It is a three-quarters profile, and Mary sits in a straight-backed, wooden rocking chair, stiff and gaunt, encased in deep mourning, her head done up in a veil-enshrouded pill box hat, her hands demurely folded in her lap. She is not yet even thirty in the picture but could pass for forty with the grim frown lines around her mouth and the look of weary abstraction in her eyes. The photograph, as Amy Strachey, wife of the *Spectator* editor, later said of Mary, looked less like an explorer than anyone could imagine. Instead, Mary here resembles someone, as another friend put it, on the order of a duke's housekeeper.

But the new photographs, one a face portrait and the other a full-length picture, were also in their decor and artificial studio setting highly uncharacteristic and misleading. However, they were at least more flattering than those of the gaunt figure in the rocking chair. Here Mary looks much younger; there is a hint of a smile on her lips and high spirits in her eyes. A very distinctive yet approachable woman is captured in these pictures and a handsome one too. She seems handsome and striking rather than beautiful or pretty, because there is a strength of character in Mary's looks that is very different from the softness and vulnerability of conventional feminine beauty. And there is also a very real but repressed sensuality, in her face particularly. She looks here in fact uncannily like her father in the only surviving photograph of him as a young man.

And yet everything in Mary's clothes and in the studio background conspires, or attempts to conspire, to deny the essence of the woman posed before the photographer's camera. She stands woodenly before what is an obviously painted scene of willows and manicured shrubs, one hand limply holding white gloves, the other an umbrella leaning

against a stone parapet that looks inappropriately solid and real before
the painted backdrop. The spray of artificial flowers at Mary's feet are
more in keeping with the photograph's general aura of unreality. Mary
is still dressed in mourning in an antiquated looking, stiff dress of
black watered taffeta, complete with outmoded muttonchop sleeves,
elaborate ascot, and pinched-in waist, the latter attesting to the presence of constraining stays underneath. Her fair hair is parted in the
middle and pulled severely back from her face. But what is perhaps
most astonishing in these photographs is the utter frivolity and incon-
gruity of the little hat perched on Mary's head: it is an insubstantial
production composed mostly of artificial flowers and a bizarre set of
what are probably small feathers but which look like insect antennae
in the middle, just above her forehead.

These photographs seem to speak volumes, albeit cryptically and
ambiguously. Is this woman who walked through stinking swamps in
a serge skirt and cotton blouse laughing at her predicament in this
artificial setting and uncomfortable, unflattering attire? Perhaps the
photographer tossed the bouquet of fake flowers at her feet and put the
gloves and umbrella into her hands. But we can't hold him responsible
for the armorlike dress, which must have weighed heavily on her slight
frame, and the ridiculous headgear. The only authentic pieces of
adornment here are the ring and bracelet on Mary's left hand and wrist.
One thinks of Henry Morton Stanley's studio portraits, with stuffed
lions and Stanley himself done up in tropical khaki and sun helmet.
Mary, by contrast, is doing her utmost in her pictures to seem like the
last person one would accuse of having traveled in West Africa. And
far from looking like the *Daily Telegraph's* New Woman, she is the
Victorian lady par excellence, down to the last artificial flower bud.

This was a role, a persona, that Mary was reluctant to give up, and
she tried to hold on to it when a journalist named Miss Sarah Tooley
interviewed her in March for the popular monthly magazine the *Young
Woman,* whose motto was "the sweetest lives are those to duty wed."
Miss Tooley was charmed by Mary, who was dressed for the occasion
in a dark silk dinner dress, and Miss Tooley also admired the cosy
Addison Road flat, except for the forbidding Muvungu and a large
carved mask hanging on the wall: an "exceptionally hideous carved
mask which Miss Kingsley thought might be of use at a fancy dress
ball — let hostesses beware!"

For much of their pleasant chat Mary and Miss Tooley collaborated to perpetuate Mary's image as a perfectly ordinary Victorian woman who happened to have traveled in West Africa. Her childhood was unexceptional, Mary said, because, for example, her "father had a perfect horror of highly educated women," so that Mary was not allowed to study any academic subjects until she proved herself able "to starch and iron a shirt." Such "practical domestic training," Mary insisted, had "proved of great service" to her both in Africa and at home, especially in the long, bleak years when she was nursing her mother. On the subject of these "very onerous filial duties" Miss Tooley was eloquent and acute to the extent of refuting her magazine's motto. Nothing was "sweet" about Mary's domestic servitude in the years directly before she went to Africa. "Indeed," Miss Tooley wrote, "the . . . strain of those long years of sick nursing, although they were lightened by tender love was in reality greater than anything Miss Kingsley has undergone in West Africa."

And here, over the teacups and cakes, the submerged feminism of the interview breaks through the surface of the Victorian ladylike decorum that the two women were at pains to establish. Mary was amazed "that her travelling exploits are spoken of as something extraordinary for a woman to have accomplished, while no one would have marvelled if she had continued the heavy strain of her home duties to the end of her days. It is a curious inconsistency that little account is taken of a woman if she sacrifices herself on the domestic hearth, while should she follow in the track of men — frequently a much easier course — and undertake public or scientific work, everybody cries 'How marvellous!' "

After these revealing remarks the interview proceeded on fairly predictable lines, with the usual complement of cannibal and gorilla stories, though interestingly, Miss Tooley asked Mary for the first time about African women: "I suppose, Miss Kingsley, that the African woman is a very degraded specimen of humanity?"

Mary measured her response as she poured out more tea. "Not altogether; her position has been greatly exaggerated by travellers and as most of them were men they had small opportunity for judging. As a woman I could mix freely with them and study their domestic life, and I used to have long talks . . . and gleaned a lot of information. I believe, on the whole, that the African married woman is happier than the majority of English wives," a view Mary ascribed to the "unsentimental" African attitude toward marriage.

Mary went on to give more vivid details and to tell anecdotes from her travels, many of which were foremost in her mind because she was then using them in writing *Travels in West Africa*. But before Miss Tooley rose to go, yet again the contrast between Victorian conventionality and West African adventure manifested itself in Mary's stuffy sitting room.

Sarah Tooley asked Mary pointblank, "Do you think . . . that a woman can undertake travel involving so much physical endurance and exposure with impunity?"

And Mary shot back, "Certainly. Why not? It seems to me such nonsense to make a fuss about everything which a woman happens to do. As a matter of fact, I believe that a woman has more deep-down endurance than a man." And then to prove her point, Mary compared the hardships of her travels, not with any conventional masculine activities, but instead with the mundane routines of someone like Lady MacDonald or Lady Goldie, or even her cousins Rose and Mary Kingsley. "Take a society woman in London," she said to Miss Tooley, who undoubtedly knew the species through and through. This society woman "spends her days in a busy round of social duties and pleasures and dances all through the night — that is physical work if you like. I would much sooner wade through a swamp up to my neck in mud or climb the Peak of the Cameroons, than go through such a treadmill life as that; it would simply kill me." It is the word *treadmill* that gives away Mary and Miss Tooley's departure from the magazine's maxim that "the sweetest lives are those to duty wed."

The *Young Woman* interview didn't actually appear until June, and in the meantime Mary published a handful of articles herself, all culled from the manuscript of *Travels in West Africa*. As she put it to Macmillan, she was deliberately keeping herself before the public eye until the book came out. In March "The Development of Dodos," a frontal attack on missionaries in Africa, appeared in the *National Review*. Mary also published two travel pieces on her climb up Mount Cameroon and an article on fetish entitled "Black Ghosts" in the June issue of *Cornhill*. The talk before the Scottish Geographical Society also came out in print, as did another talk Mary gave in March before the Liverpool Geographical Society.

The Liverpool talk was important on a number of scores. Interestingly, because of the society's bylaws, which included the prohibition of women members, Mary's lecture was actually read by a member of the society, James Irvine, rather than by Mary herself. She sat next to

Mr. Irvine on the platform, however, and undoubtedly was amused to hear her racy prose issue from his mouth: the passage, for example, describing the immense hippo that stared at Mary and her crew, "yawned a yawn a yard wide, and grunted the news of our arrival to his companions, who also rose up, and strolled through the grass with the flowing grace of Pantechnicon vans."

Among the audience who heard Irvine read Mary's lecture was the prosperous and politically astute Liverpool merchant John Holt, head of the trading concern with which Mary was so familiar as "Holty" on the Coast. Holt must have been particularly interested in Mary's concluding remarks in the lecture, for after the lively account of her "picnics" climbing Mount Cameroon, Mary ended with her first articulation of her own brand of economic imperialism. She had been convinced since her first trip in 1893 that England's role in West Africa should be that of "the greatest manufacturing country of the world" and that what it should seek on the Coast was not colonies of Kiplingesque, expansionist Empire, but markets for English goods. Colonies, especially colonies in the White Man's Grave of West Africa, drained the mother country, while markets employed and enriched the laboring classes safe and sound back at home. Of course Mary's underlying motive, as always, was the preservation of indigenous African culture, which she felt the traders would secure while the Colonial Office would smash the whole show up. But this fundamental point is not stressed in the Liverpool lecture. Instead, Mr. Irvine wound up with an impassioned peroration to the West Coast trader — "those heroes of commerce, whose battles have been fought out on lonely beaches, far away from home or friends. . . . Of such," Mary concluded, "is the kingdom of England."

John Holt saw that he had a potential ally in the mute "lecturer" seated on the podium, and Mary herself must have been gratified by Holt's interest and appreciation of her talk. Holt was nearly twenty years Mary's senior. In fact, he had gone out as a struggling trader to Fernando Po in 1862, the year Mary was born. When his English employer died Holt worked for the man's African widow as manager of the concern until he had saved enough to buy the business from her. Through diligence, luck, and a deep understanding and respect for Africans and African ways, Holt prospered. Soon he had stations on the mainland in Gabon and Cameroon. His brother came out to join him, and they employed additional Englishmen and African traders as well, as the business thrived on the largely untapped sources of rubber, palm oil, and ivory on the Coast. By the mid 1870s, Holt himself returned to England and set up the Liverpool headquarters of his growing business. John Holt and Company soon vied with Hatton and Cookson and with Goldie's Royal Niger Company as the major mercantile power in West Africa. Mary and Holt met at the Liverpool lecture in March of 1896, but it was only after *Travels in West Africa* was published the next year and after Mary emerged as a political force as well as a celebrity that the two became close and Mary, as one historian put it, "the intellectual spokesman" for British commercial interests in West Africa.

Also at Liverpool Mary met another English trader named Forshaw, the only white man who had ever been initiated into the Calabar Effik secret society, Egbo. As an authority on the subject, he agreed to go through the fetish chapters of *Travels in West Africa*, "a great stroke of good fortune," as Mary wrote Macmillan. When Forshaw's final, positive verdict came in, Mary was elated and forwarded his letter to her publisher. As she told Macmillan, she desired scientific validation far more than popular acclaim. "Everything I write now," she told him in a letter, "is written with one eye on Günther and one on the coast." The Coast in the person of Forshaw had stamped a seal of approval on Mary's labors. And so too did Günther. Mary fired off another letter of "mere vanity" to Macmillan when she received Günther's report. It exceeded, in fact, her wildest dreams, for among the sixty-five species of fish and eighteen of reptiles that Mary had brought back were some valuable discoveries and very little that was dross. Three entirely new species of fish were named after her: *Ctenopoma kingsleye, Mormyrus kingsleyae,* and *Alestes kingsleyae.* In addition, she had returned with sixteen modifications of known forms, another fish of which the Natural History Museum had only one other specimen, acquired forty years earlier, and a new snake and a lizard that the museum had been waiting ten years for.

Despite Forshaw's and Günther's approval, however, Henry Guillemard continued to function as scientific arbiter and editor of Mary's book; in fact the term *editor* is inadequate to describe Guillemard's self-appointed role in the composition of the book. The increasingly unsatisfactory arrangement was that Mary turned in her handwritten manuscript to Macmillan, who then had it transcribed by a typist. The typescript then was submitted to Guillemard, who proceeded to rewrite rather than merely check or correct it. Then this incongruously hybrid product of the typist's and Guillemard's labors was returned to

Mary, who could scarcely recognize it as originating from her own hand.

The opportunities for muddle seemed endless. Mary wrote Lady MacDonald that the typist "strange to say . . . finds some difficulty in reading my handwriting . . . and produces some strange effects in the work. Yesterday I was knocked endways by reading in the proof 'a careful young man does not buy a ballet-girl for a wife.' Now I know I had never uttered this great truth. Besides, the most reckless young Central African blade could not buy a ballet-girl with india rubber. On referring to the original text I find I had written 'baby.' " She complained to Macmillan that the typist was making "a farrago of nonsense" of the manuscript and urged that he (for it was a male typist) be "loosened from the machine to do original work of his own."

Eventually a new typist was called into service who learned to decipher Mary's barely legible scrawl. But the palaver with Guillemard was not so easily resolved. For a time Mary tolerated his "mania" for Latinized words and his needless injections of "perhaps," "however," and "dear reader" throughout the text. But by the end of the summer a crisis had been reached, as Guillemard's pretentious and obfuscating editing distorted Mary's work beyond all recognition. Besides Guillemard's verbosity and penchant for multisyllabic words — *appalling* for *awful, dwelling* for *house,* and *terminus* for *end,* for example — he was grotesquely, even ludicrously, changing the meaning of Mary's text. At last, on August 20, after eight months of uneasy collaboration with "the good Doctor," Mary put her foot down. In a candid and heated letter to Macmillan she wrote: "I am going down the Coast again and I have no character to lose as a literary person but I have got a very good character to lose as a practical sea man and an honest observor of facts on the West Coast and I cannot put my name to this sort of . . . panorama affair, and if my log is published as I have written it I feel I can face any man." If published as "corrected" by Guillemard, however, Mary felt she could never face the people whose judgment she valued most. How, for example, could she face Captain Murray after Guillemard had amended her text to say that Captain Heldt had "housed" Mary. As Mary told Macmillan, "to house means to lower a mast to half its length and then secure it by lashing its heel to the mast below. As I dare say you know, I assure you Captain Heldt *never* lashed my heels nor lowered me to half my length." Another instance among countless Guillemard emendations: Mary had said a boat crosses Forcados bar drawing eighteen feet of water; Guillemard blithely altered this to mean that Forcados bar was only eighteen feet deep. Mary's reaction to Macmillan was: "I fear you will think these things of no importance but they are important to me. I have taken vessels of 2000 tons across the bay and up the Forcados creeks as a pilot three times. I should never get the chance of taking another if I published such rot, and I would rather take a 2000 ton vessel up a creek than write any book."

Mary wrote Guillemard on the same day she sent her letter to Macmillan, and though this communication was far more temperate than the Macmillan letter, it was no less firm. She was calling a halt to the whole arrangement. "Your corrections," she wrote Guillemard, "stand on stilts out of the swamps and give a very quaint but patchy aspect to the affair so that I do not know my way about it at all. I never meant you to take this delicate labour over the thing but only to arrange it and tell me point blank if I was lying about scientific subjects. I would rather have the rest of the stuff published as it stands. I have no literary character to lose at present and no ambition to gain one."

It was also apparently Guillemard who proposed to Macmillan that the rapidly expanding manuscript of *Travels in West Africa* be split into two books: a travelogue, containing the travel chapters and also the earlier "Bights of Benin" account Mary had produced after her 1893 journey; and a more scientific volume containing the fish and fetish portions of the book. Macmillan was greatly enamored of this plan and told Mary in May that they could bring out the travel book almost immediately, "in June if possible for light summer reading and then the larger book in October for the long winter evenings." The rollicking travelogue, he predicted, would "whet public appetite for the larger book which is to follow."

But on this score Mary was as adamant as she was on the subject of Guillemard's editing. "It is a ridiculous situation to find oneself in — that of *not* wishing Macmillan & Co. to bring out a book instantly," she wrote her publisher. "It's unique in literary history I expect." Nevertheless, she firmly vetoed the two book plan. However fragmented *Travels in West Africa* might seem to Macmillan and Guillemard, for Mary it was an organic and indissoluble whole: buffoonery, "picnics," danger, naturalistic investigation, fishing, fetish, philosophical reflection — they were all inextricable parts of her experience on the Coast, and to parcel them out into separate books would be to shatter or dismember the beauty and magic of the life she had found there.

And so "Guillemardese," as Mary called it, and the two-book proposal were unconditionally rejected, but this did not mean that all was smooth sailing after these issues had been decided. Macmillan wanted to include a map in the book, but Mary refused to use the only ones available because they were grossly inaccurate. She complained that the printer was ruining her photographs and not using the ones she considered particularly valuable. Then there was a skirmish over the typeface of the appendix. Mary wanted to make sure that it was the same size used for the rest of the book: "The type usually used for appendices is so repulsive no one ever reads them and this trade and labour appendix is the moral to the whole tale." It contained her harshest attack on missionaries, a spirited defense of the liquor traffic, and her analysis of the African vis-a-vis other races. Furthermore, she was determined that Guillemard should not dip his spoon into this particular stew. She warned Macmillan to "take no heed of the Dr.'s observations on the trade appendix; he knows nothing about it." In fact she told Macmillan that she didn't want any more of the appendix typescript shown to Guillemard at all. And finally there was the matter of the title. Macmillan rejected out of hand Mary's flippant "Log of a Light-hearted Lunatic." For a while the book was called *West Africa,* then *West African Travels and Observations,* but it was only on the eve of publication that *Travels in West Africa* was settled on. And chapter titles could cause trouble too. In December, when she was already correcting proof, Mary wrote Macmillan that she had changed the title of the last chapter on her climb up Mount Cameroon from "The Final Ascent," "as it might give the idea that I went up like a rocket from the top and am still going and what is more that my ascent is final and no one could do it again."

In the meantime Charley, who had come back to England in June, had volunteered to do the index, a rare and uncharacteristically generous gesture. For the most part, though, Charley did not make life any easier for Mary as she fought off Guillemard, wheedled George Macmillan, and pushed herself to the breaking point to finish the book.

Charley's return had been dramatic but true to form. He cabled Mary from Plymouth to "meet me at Albert Dock with money," so she had to drop everything and rush down to Plymouth to "unship" him. They had not seen each other since Mary's departure for West Africa some eighteen months earlier, but they were scarcely back in London before "Master Charles" began to tell on Mary's nerves. At the height of the Guillemard affair she turned to Charley for advice, with what results she reported to Macmillan. "I . . . asked Charley for advice about Guillemard and he sententiously observes that I had better only write and say to you that I do not approve of Dr. Guillemard's corrections. On being pressed as to how this statement will injure the publication of the work he says he does not know." Charley's only further "profound observation" was that "unless you can write in the grand style you had better write naturally." Mary might as well have gone to Muvungu for advice. In a significant aside in this letter Mary mentions that Charley has read none of the book in manuscript "because I never bother him with these things."

Only when he offered to do the index for the book did Charley evince any interest in his sister's work and finally read it in proof. And very likely, his contribution of the index was undertaken in part to atone for the fact that his promised memoir of their father for *Notes on Sport and Travel* was still not forthcoming. In early August Mary wrote Macmillan that she hoped "Master Charles will let you have the *Memoir* forthwith," but that she was dubious of this eventuality was made clear when she continued, "but who would not have a family like mine! Whenever we Kingsleys go and commit a crime we do *not* repent. Oh no! We go and persuade ourselves we have done *quite* the right thing." Charley's "crime," of course, was that he had made no progress on the memoir whatsoever in the past two years despite all his assurances to the contrary. Finally, in late August at just about the time the Guillemard crisis was coming to a head, Mary had a showdown with Charley over *Notes on Sport and Travel,* with the result, as she wrote Macmillan, that once again she would take over the biographical essay on top of finishing *Travels in West Africa.* "It was more suitable that he should do it," she said, and his failure to come through with it made her "very unhappy about him because this disinclination of his to grind at anything but abstract metaphysics cannot lead to Fortune and he is not like me indifferent to creature comforts."

Thus life in the Addison Road flat in the summer and autumn of 1896 was anything but serene. Charley lounged about, buried in his abstruse philosophical tomes but liable now and then to "attacks of activity" on Mary's index. Mary meanwhile was constantly working at a frenetic pace on her book, the memoir, and more articles. And when she was not at her writing desk, she was at some friend's or relative's sickbed. The only thing that pleasantly interrupted this hectic and wearying round was Mary's meeting in September with her great fetish juju, the eminent Oxford anthropologist E. B. Tylor. Earlier that year in May Mary had met the more famous "Golden Bough," as she called Sir James Frazer, at Cambridge where she had gone for an editorial conference with Guillemard. But as Mary makes clear in her letters and even in her published work, she was not dazzled by Frazer's monumental study. Tylor's *Primitive Culture,* in contrast, she called her bible.

It was at the Macmillans' at Danby that Mary found herself "really face to face with the greatest of ethnologists," as she described Tylor in a letter, and soon they were exchanging frequent letters, and Mary became a welcome weekend guest at the Tylors' home in Oxford. The Tylors' friendship meant a great deal to her because for the first time she was able to talk openly and at length about what so engrossed and fascinated her. As she confided to Mrs. Tylor after one visit, "I cannot tell you how much I enjoyed myself because I should have to make it clear to you firstly how very lonely I am in my interest in Fetish. No one of my own people understand anything about it and utterly fail to see why I should care so much about what seems to them a mass of utter rubbish so that I always feel rather in disgrace with them." And it was to the Tylors too that Mary confessed, as she had to no one else, her deep sense of affinity and kinship with Africans. "I seem to have a mind so akin to that of the Savage," she wrote E. B. Tylor in one letter, "that I can enter into his thoughts and follow them." Indeed, it was to this almost mystical bond that Mary ascribed the gifts Tylor soon came to admire deeply in her, such as her ability to collect and analyze ethnographical information.

For as was the case with most early ethnographers, Tylor, apart from an early expedition to Mexico, had little experience in the field. But his theoretical understanding of animism and his knowledge of everything that had been written on the subject — from travelers' accounts to articles in learned journals — were both immense. Hence he and Mary were invaluable to each other. For her, Tylor was an endless font of ethnographical wisdom. Soon after they met in fact she asked him to read the fetish chapters of *Travels in West Africa* in proof. At the same time, Mary furnished Tylor with countless photographs of fetish houses, shrines, and charms, and also told him as much as she could about totemism, his particular area of interest at the time, on the Coast. And if Victorian propriety prevented Mary from telling Tylor about certain practices — perhaps those concerning female circumcision or beliefs connected with menstruation — she told *Mrs.* Tylor about "a lot of queer things," which Mrs. Tylor in due course passed on to her learned husband.

It was a good thing that the Tylors entered Mary's life and summoned her to Oxford for weekend visits precisely at this juncture, for she was feeling harassed and tired and often ill as well. As long as Charley was rattling around the flat, there was a latent tension in the air that broke out now and again into exasperation and even fleeting hostility. Clearly the sight of his sister writing day and night, besieged by newspapermen, and enjoying an ever increasing circle of friends in high places could not have enhanced Charley's own self-esteem. He would announce that he was going back to Burma or Ceylon but would then dawdle and run up to Cambridge or Wales for a week or two, returning to his old inert existence in Kensington with no further mention of traveling. The upshot of this erratic behavior was that Mary could make no plans of her own, for it goes without saying that as long as Charley remained in England, so perforce did she in order to keep house for him. Meanwhile the drudgery of the final stages of *Travels in West Africa* drained her, and she became wretchedly depressed: she was full of doubts over the book, less and less able to tolerate the situation with Charley, and a prey to migraines, insomnia, and exhaustion.

And the usual social and familial demands persisted. At the end of October Mary wrote Macmillan, "I am dead tired. I have two particular friends of mine up now and they are deadly enemies of each other — so have to be kept apart, done twice over as it were." A bit later she confided that she had been ill and in bed for more than a week and "fit for nothing but a cheap funeral." Several days after she was still "wretchedly low and weak."

To Lady MacDonald and Hatty Johnson Mary was even more candid. To the first she wrote "I am low in mind, principally from being low in my health with everlasting colds and headaches but also from having sort of lost the power of enjoying life in England." With Hatty she was even blunter: looking ahead she prophesied continued "wretched health," and if Charley didn't bestir himself and Mary consequently had to stay put, she said, "I am going to absolutely loathe being in England."

Winter was closing in, with its icy sleet and knife-sharp winds. On November 5, Guy Fawkes Day, Mary gave Macmillan the last portion of the manuscript of *Travels in West Africa:* "Lo the Appendix." For much of that month and the next she was consumed with the wearisome, mechanical labor of correcting proof. Macmillan set the publication date for the beginning of the year, and Mary ticked the days off her calendar with increasing apprehension. No authorial pride buoyed her days. She had deep misgivings about the book; fearing alternately that it would be thought too flippant or too ponderous. She even went so far as to ask her cousin Mary Kingsley, the daughter of Charles Kingsley, who wrote best-selling novels under the name of Lucas Malet, to read the manuscript. But Lucas Malet's generally favorable opinion did little to assuage Mary's anxieties.

Christmas passed with no celebration for Mary or for Charley. On December 26, Boxing Day, Mary had her Uncle William Bailey and the Brownlows, old family friends, over for supper.

It had been more than a year now since Mary had returned from the Coast — a year of extraordinary productivity, a year in which she had emerged from social obscurity to controversial fame. But it had also been a year of illness, anxiety, and depression. Mary *had* lost the power to enjoy life in England, and the prospect of similar years unrolling ahead was loathesome to her. The only cure, then, for her malaise and unhappiness was to return to West Africa. That she was confident that she would soon do this is indicated in a letter she wrote Macmillan at the end of December. She was "perfectly satisfied" with Macmillan's "liberal terms" in regard to the book, but she had only just realized that her contract stipulated that royalties would be paid annually in January. *Travels in West Africa* was scheduled to be published in January 1897, which meant that Mary wouldn't receive any royalties until January of 1898, and, as she said, "I hope to be on the Coast before then and . . . I should like to have part of the profits for my outfit."

Macmillan obligingly amended the payment schedule so that Mary would receive her first royalty check well before the following year. But as events would prove, his adjustment was unnecessary. New Year's Day and the beginning of 1897 arrived, but far from feeling any sense of renewal Mary felt played out and at loose ends. After all the frenetic activity of her life since she had returned from West Africa, these days directly before her book was published were passed in a kind of chilly hush. Mary's lot now was the usual one of unnatural silence and abrupt cessation of work that always precedes publication. She awaited the appearance of *Travels in West Africa* with all the conflicting feelings of intense expectation, doubt, and hope that any new writer feels welling up within.

Growing Influence

The book *Travels in West Africa* was published on January 21, 1897, and by the end of the month it was clear that Macmillan had a best seller on its hands. Who would have thought that "Only Me" as Mary used to identify herself on the Coast, could have pulled it off? Certainly not her West Coast trader friends who wrote to Liverpool about it. A first book by a thirty-five-year-old woman with no formal education, a book moreover running to an excess of six hundred densely packed pages, more than a hundred of which were devoted to an arcane disquisition on fish and fetish, would not seem to possess the essential ingredients of a blockbuster. But the booksellers on Charing Cross Road had trouble keeping enough copies of *Travels in West Africa* in stock, and the society lady patrons of Mudie's Lending Library had to wait their turn patiently to read it on an ever lengthening waiting list. To Macmillan Mary professed herself amazed at the book's reception. All year she had been writing with the sinking feelings of "a prize fighter who knew he had got money on him." But it turned out that Macmillan knew the G.P., as Mary liked to call the General Public, better than she did: "I thought they really cared for nothing but art and geographical facts, though I . . . had a sneaking feeling there must be some people who care for things as they are — with all the go and glory and beauty in them as well as the mechanism and the microbes."

But the popular and commercial success of *Travels in West Africa* — it had gone into a fifth edition by June and made more than three thousand pounds for Macmillan in the first twelve months after it appeared — did not make Mary any less anxious about its reception among the "big jujus" who were in a position to judge the authenticity and value of the book, and she was scarcely less apprehensive about the reviews to be published in the daily and monthly press. Hence she was delighted once again to receive positive verdicts from Tylor, Goldie, and Günther. She had sent Günther an advance copy, she said, "in fear and trembling," knowing that he would read it with care and "not just say, 'Oh how very strange and charming' " like the "ordinary superficial person." It was the "ordinary superficial person" indeed who wrote most of the glowing reviews of *Travels in West Africa* and who, in the course of extolling its strangeness and charm, further reinforced the "explorer in petticoats" image of Mary that had haunted her ever since she returned from the Coast. The *Illustrated London News* opened its review, for example, with "In a romping style which disdains the trammels of a too accurate syntax, the intrepid lady carries us across the deadly mangrove swamps of the Dark Continent to its tangled forests. We are tortured by leeches and terrified by gorillas, but never by Mrs. Grundy who may read with profit of Miss Kingsley's remarks on polygamy . . . and barbaric morals generally. Heedless of perils by day and night, we eagerly press on to gather information about native manners and customs mostly as to the absence of the one and to the disagreeable features of the other." The *Morning Post, Daily Telegraph, New York Times, Bookman,* and *Nation* all followed suit, giving favorable notices that marveled at Mary's rollicking adventures, praised her racy style, quoted stories of some of her choicer "picnics," and either ignored or gave only the most cursory attention to the wealth of ethnographic and scientific information that was at the heart of the book.

Several reviews, however, were more searching in their analysis. One reviewer, Bruce Walker, qualified as another big juju because he had traded for some fifteen years in Gabon, explored the middle Ogooué, and married a Gabonese woman; he devoted more than nine columns in the February 6 *Athenaeum* to a meticulous appraisal of *Travels in West Africa,* correcting various minor errors but by and large praising the accuracy and profundity of Mary's portrayal of a land and people with which Walker was intimately familiar. Mary was immensely gratified by Walker's intelligent praise, but one point in his review rankled, and she replied publicly in a letter to the *Athenaeum* that was published on February 27. Walker had rather gallantly opened his review with high praise for Mary's womanly courage, but had unfortunately contrasted it with the less eventful, sedentary lives led by traders' and officials' wives on the Coast.

In her rejoinder Mary echoed her response to the *Daily Telegraph*'s praise of her as a New Woman a year earlier: "As my visiting West Africa has brought down on the ladies there . . . the disparaging remarks of your reviewer," Mary wrote, "I must combat his statements and assure you that the wives of the officials and missionaries and traders who are resident there, not for their own pleasure or instruction, but from the noble motive of duty to their husbands do not lead either an easier or a safer life than I do in the bush." She followed this up with a rather lengthy and unconvincing argument that it is actually more unhealthy to remain in one place in West Africa than "to wander far and wide in the forest, however uncomfortable the surrounding conditions may be." Not to mention, she went on, the additional taxing responsibilities wives have of young children, tropical domestic crises, and often "the moral and physical strain" of a large mission school of African girls. And finally Mary wound up by naming the names of the unsung heroines she had met on the Coast — Madame Jacot, Madame Forget, and Mary Slessor — and went even further to praise "the equally creditable behaviour under difficulties of hundreds of women who have never left England in their lives." It was "Only Me," the *Young Woman* version of Miss Kingsley, who responded to Walker's *Athenaeum* review, insisting once again that there was nothing in the course of her travels that called upon her to exhibit any heroic, or, even more important, any unwomanly characteristics.

The *Athenaeum* review was the only one Mary responded to in print, but like most first authors, she was morbidly thin-skinned about the handful of unfavorable notices she got. She wrote Macmillan in February that she was in "a terrific rage" over "the horror" perpetrated on *Travels in West Africa* in the *New York Tribune* and a little later remarked that she wouldn't be seen dead in the same street with the *Nature* reviewer. But the review Mary dreaded most was the one she expected to see in the *Times,* whose opinion would carry more weight with the specialist and with the popular reader than would any other paper's notice. Throughout January and February Mary opened the *Times* at breakfast every morning with trepidation. She calculated that the review would almost certainly be done by the *Times* expert on African colonial affairs, Flora Shaw. And from her careful study of the *Times*'s colonial policy on Africa, Mary well knew that she and Miss Shaw — perhaps the two leading popular authorities of the day on that continent — were not, in Kingsley's parlance, of the same tribe. Mary found Shaw's jingoistic, Kiplingesque brand of imperialism repugnant, and no doubt Flora Shaw was equally dismayed by Mary's championship of trade interests in West Africa. Though the two women both moved in the "haut politique" their paths had never crossed, and indeed they were not destined to meet until 1899. But they knew "who they ate foo foo with," as Mary put it, and in any event, the *Times* failed to publish any review of *Travels in West Africa* at all, not even the briefest or most dismissive of notices. This of course was an even worse affront than a hostile review. Mary never forgave the *Times* for snubbing her book and in the future rarely let pass any opportunity for ridiculing, exposing, or damning it.

Perhaps the two most perceptive reviews were found neither in the big metropolitan papers nor in the erudite scientific journals that Mary scrutinized so carefully, but rather in the pages of Mary's old admirer the *Young Woman* and also in the monthly magazine the *Spectator*. Apparently forgetting for the moment that "the sweetest lives are those to duty wed," the *Young Woman* bravely and accurately praised *Travels in West Africa* as "a book of defiance, . . . the liveliest, cheeriest, most resolute defiance all round — friends and relatives, laws of health, notions of what is proper and becoming, danger to life and limb, and the rest. Whether there are any notions left of what is proper and becoming for women may be doubted." But these bold assertions are words of unorthodox praise rather than criticism. Notions of what is proper and becoming for women "are not things to mind about if you have a good object in view. Nurses are absolved from them, doctors, and missionaries' wives. So too is Isabella Bishop" who explored the Rocky Mountains in Colorado. In this tradition, the *Young Woman* asserted, "Miss Kingsley has proved her own right to freedom." Of all the reviews, only the *Young Woman* grasped the fundamental truth that Mary's travels were a journey of liberation.

The *Spectator* perceived the other important thread in the variegated, richly woven fabric of the book: "The only general impression . . . that one gets from Miss Kingsley's eminently cheerful pages is curiously enough the impression of death in its myriad forms hovering over the whole West Coast." The reviewer, St. Loe Strachey, seized upon the essential, informing principle of contrast in *Travels in West Africa* and indeed in Mary's personality: that the light and beauty and comedy of life on the Coast were intensified by the precariousness and vulnerability of all things in that world. West Africa took the color out of all other kinds of living because life itself there could be such an ephemeral and hence infinitely precious commodity. Strachey's re-

view struck a chord in Mary, who felt herself perpetually misunderstood by others — by admirers and foes alike. So touched in fact was
she by Strachey's appreciation that she wrote him privately to thank
him for the review, and thus began a sustaining friendship that lasted
until the end of her life. Oxford-trained and also a barrister, Strachey
was editor of the *Cornhill Magazine* at the time he wrote the review of
Travels in West Africa for the *Spectator*. Two years later he moved on to
edit the *Spectator* itself. Handsome, dynamic, and astute, Strachey was
at the center of the London literary, social, and political elite of the
1890s. Perhaps more than anyone else he drew Mary into the inner
circle of its haut politique, but he and his wife also became Mary's
close personal friends, as was not unexpected, given Strachey's acute
understanding of her book.

Strachey and his set did not constitute the only enlargement of Mary's
social world as a result of the favorable reception of *Travels in West
Africa*. In March Mary met the Anglo-Indian administrator, philosopher, man of letters, and all-around *éminence grise* Sir Alfred Lyall at a
dinner party at Henry Morton Stanley's. She had pored over Lyall's
masterly *Asiatic Studies*, a comparative study of religions, during her
Cambridge days, and she now embarked on a rarefied correspondence
with him that focused on the finer points of diverse religious systems;
in her letters Mary always rather obsequiously signed herself "Yours
very respectfully, M. H. Kingsley." In July Lyall published what was
probably the most erudite review of *Travels in West Africa*, a long essay
in which Mary kept very learned company with F. B. Jevons, author
of *An Introduction to the History of Religion*, and Max Müller, who wrote
Contributions to the Science of Mythology.

Meanwhile the number of Mary's acquaintances also multiplied as a
result of her renewed schedule of lecturing, lecturing that of course
enhanced the sales of her book. In February Mary spoke at Newcastle,
South Shields, and Durham, and in March in "Yorkshire at Large,"
Richmond, and Liverpool, not to mention such London venues as the
Folklore Society, where she spoke on "The Fetish View of the Human
Soul," and the Highgate Literary and Scientific Institution, where she
alliteratively discoursed on "Trials of a Tropical Traveller." And at one
of these affairs early in 1897, Mary met Alice Stopford Green and
thence began what was probably the most important relationship in
the coming, crowded years.

Mary had had other important women friends in her life. Lucy Toulmin Smith, who went back to her Highgate days, was a kind of com-

bination mother figure and intellectual mentor, but there was and remained a certain degree of emotional reserve between them. With Hatty Johnson and Violet Roy, friends dating from the hard, lonely Cambridge years, Mary was more intimate. Indeed, Mary withheld little of her trials with Charley and her Kingsley relatives from Hatty and Violet, and they in turn came to her when they were troubled and in need. But neither Hatty nor Violet had the intellectual gifts or the personal courage of Mary, and both in fact came close to idolizing their friend because of these traits. And then of course there was the gallery of wives in Mary's life: Lady MacDonald and Lady Goldie, Mrs. Macmillan, Mrs. Holt, Mrs. Tylor, and Mrs. Kemp — women Mary was always sending her love to at the end of letters written to their husbands. But even with the wives with whom Mary felt a true bond, such as Mathilda Goldie, there was an unbreachable emotional distance: the nineteenth-century social chasm that yawned between the socially secure matron and the anomalous spinster.

But Alice Stopford Green combined the status and freedom of both species of women. Some fifteen years Mary's senior, she had been the wife of the eminent historian John Richard Green, author of such books as *A Short History of England, The Making of England,* and *The Conquest of England.* But Green had died after a long illness in 1883, and in the years since his death Alice Green had gone on to produce valuable works of her own after successfully seeing several posthumous volumes of her husband's through the press. Among these solo works of hers were a biography of Henry II and one of the earliest works of English urban history, *Town Life in the Fifteenth Century.* At the same time Alice Green became a social presence, like St. Loe Strachey, among the intellectual elite of the day, and her Kensington Square house was the center of a brilliant, heterogeneous salon that regularly drew such figures as Florence Nightingale, Beatrice and Sidney Webb, Winston Churchill, Roger Casement, the Humphrey Wards, and Henry James. And at the center of this coterie, the handsome, tall, red-haired Alice Green presided with the social grace and ease of a Lady MacDonald, combined with the startling mixture of dead seriousness and mordant wit of her new friend Mary Kingsley.

Mary was attracted far more by Alice Green's intellectual gifts, sympathy, and generosity than by her social standing and savoir faire. But beyond attraction there was a deeper kind of identification that drew the two women together into a special closeness. Partly this derived from important similarities in their upbringing. Like Mary, Alice

Stopford Green had learned German in order to assist her clergyman
father in his research on biblical studies. Again, like Mary's, Alice
Green's adolescence had been an unremittingly lonely one. At the age
of sixteen she was struck with semiblindness; for a year she did not stir
from her darkened bedroom, and for seven more years she scarcely left
the house and was unable to read for more than a short period each day
until an operation restored her sight at the age of twenty-four. Six
years later she married Green, a man ten years older than she, who had
already had one foot in the grave. The marriage by all accounts was
"fantastically happy," but it was also rather unusual. No children diminished the intensity of the intellectual and medical ties that bound
the couple into complete symbiosis. Green submitted his wife to a
rigorous course of historical study and also ordered her to abandon the
novel that she had been working on before their marriage. Soon Alice
was sufficiently well trained to act as her husband's research assistant
and amanuensis, and, as his condition deteriorated, she also performed
the duties of a sick nurse. In her relation to her brilliant, invalid husband, then, Alice Green combined the roles Mary had so dutifully
played in relation to her parents. And when J. R. Green expired some
six years after their marriage, his thirty-six-year-old widow did precisely what Mary Kingsley had done upon the deaths of her father and
mother. Her servitude and her apprenticeship having abruptly termi-
nated, Alice Green resolved — tentatively at first, but in time more
and more decisively — to strike out on and to achieve something of
her own.

There was very little in her life that Mary held back from Alice
Green: her chronic exasperation with Charley; her bouts of depression;
all the irritating demands of her tedious Kingsley relations; the various
quotidian headaches of her hectic life throughout 1897. On Marxh 22,
for example, she wrote Alice of the "dreadful, tiring day" she'd had.
First of all, Violet Roy had been visiting and was worried sick over her
husband and the obscure brain disease that caused him to black out
suddenly. After Violet left, the "soulful Maxses" called, swiftly followed by "two gay young medical women one of whom is going to
ride to Fez on a bicycle . . . and came to ask *me* how to do it." A bit
later she returned from lecturing and socializing in Ashridge "a wreck."
Propriety had dictated that she refrain from smoking, apparently a new
practice in which she indulged with Alice Green, and she confessed,
"I *cannot* converse coherently on the Godhead and galoshes within a
space of ten minutes to half an hour. As for being coherent for hours

like you right on end without cigarettes, it passes me to do dem ting for sure," lapsing in the end into pidgin.

After a lecture tour in the North that autumn she regaled Alice with a highly characteristic account of her adventures. "Lordy! the times I have had this past week," she wrote.

> Awful adventures at Leicester — champion of the liquor traffic had to sleep at a temperance hotel because of horse races. Sheffield also weird. I realized at Leeds I did not know where I was to lecture at Sheffield so telegraphed to ask. They answered Literary-Philosophical, so I thought it was there. Well when I went there ten minutes before the time — it wasn't. Building deserted; frantic rush into chemist's shop to ask where the philosophical was holding its meeting. Gay young chemist says, "Oh, I can't tell you. I know they've got a big pot down for the Fil." Briefly mentioning I was the big pot, I left him and toiled into a stationer's. Young woman at stationer's knew and would take me there — saved!!! Off we went full speed, landed at Hall placarded "Escaped Nun and Father Slattery" — hissed by crowd for escaped nun — fled back to philosophical Society outside which were two gentlemen evidently devoid of philosophy and they told me they were the secretaries who had lost their lecturer and had 1400 people getting savage round the corner in an old music hall.

Mary could also give way to her "innate coarseness," as she put it, with Alice Green, which was altogether an enormous relief, for the London haut politique seemed oppressively strait-laced and thin-lipped after the unorthodox society of the Coast.

The standard taboos of the day did not mar or inhibit Mary's friendship with Alice. She felt free to speak of whatever she wished to Alice Green, and some of her most candid feelings on love and sexuality are expressed only in her letters to her closest friend. Just as she had been called in as "a pause in affairs" or as a "smokescreen" for friends embroiled in elaborate courtship maneuvers during her younger days, Mary now found herself the confidante of various friends and acquaintances in the throes of what in the parlance of the day were known as "irregular relations." And only to Alice Green could Mary divulge the details of some of these adulterous affairs with a mixture of irreverent humor, impatience, and pity. On one occasion, the wife of a Cambridge don, one Mrs. A., summoned Mary up to Cambridge where she found a scientist, Mr. B., in a semicomatose state on Mrs. A.'s parlor sofa, Mrs. A. having dosed him with a sedative to subdue his ranting proclamations of undying passion. The exact location of Mr.

A. seemed uncertain, which, of course, did nothing to calm the situation. After she reported these goings-on to Alice, shortly upon returning to London Mary received a frantic letter from Mrs. A., enclosing another positively vitriolic one penned by Mrs. B., from whose eyes the proverbial scales had suddenly fallen. What, Mrs. A. implored Mary, should she do? Mary wrote back that Mrs. B. seemed "a common sense, narrow-mindedly proper person," and that the best course was to give Mr. B. no more medicine, no matter how desperate his psychological state might appear, and make no reply whatsoever to Mrs. B.'s abusive letter. Altogether, sensible and sympathetic counsel, but Mary knew full well how hard it would be for the participants to follow it. Writing of this episode to Alice, Mary said, "You are the only person I know who seems to have the same make of mind that I have on . . . sex relationships, only you have had more expansive experience, that is to say, you know personally what love is, I don't." Once again she denies direct knowledge of passion, and yet why did Mrs. A. and others turn to Miss Mary Kingsley in extremity? Surely they did not merely because of her lack of cant and social hypocrisy. Mary and Alice Green knew the often uncontrollable currents of feeling and passion that lead people to such passes despite the high stakes involved. For as Mary said to Alice of this particular messy entanglement, it "is a very dangerous state of affairs — if it goes on, it must go smash."

Mary could speak with complete freedom and intimacy to Alice Green, and she could shed her dismaying assortment of public and private personas as well. So close was she to Alice that she half humorously, half seriously asked her to identify which of these versions of her self was the authentic one: "I wish you would say which form of me you approve of — or I should say tolerate most, and I'll cultivate it and cast the others off. I can't go on with about a dozen different souls inside. I shall leave one on an omnibus some day; besides they take it out of me cruel and give me headaches." "Only Me" needed Alice to recognize, respond to, even love the "Real Me" that Mary had buried within. And this need was all the greater now that she was back in England and was being pulled in different directions by the variety of roles she was called upon to play: author, lecturer, political partisan, sister, relative, nurse, and general doer of odd jobs for others. Life on the Coast had bestowed wholeness and authenticity. Life in England wrought fragmentation.

This feeling of fragmentation was particularly real during the flurry surrounding the publication of *Travels in West Africa*. Then once the book was out Mary was again assailed by homesickness. As she wrote Macmillan in March, "This London life takes all the go out of me. I have not written a poem for months which is an awful bad symptom." And a bit later: "If I were rich I would buy a barrel organ that is going on outside . . . and keep it by me to play on when I am low in my mind." At about the same time Mary wrote Tylor that she was "going out" to West Africa in a month or so. The exact date was contingent, as always, on the departure of Charley, who said that he intended to go to Malaysia, but, as Mary observed, "all that palaver live for mouth." Charley seems, however, to have roused himself and made some definite plans, because Mary abruptly announced to Macmillan on April 2 that "I should sail by the boat that leaves Liverpool on the 12th of this month."

But at the last moment she had to cancel her longed-for departure for the simple reason that Charley, who had been suffering from "a perpetual cough and dingy mental state" all winter, suddenly took a dramatic turn for the worse. As Mary wrote Hatty Johnson, he "would not see a doctor, the sort of performance men call 'not making any fuss' which means worrying their devoted female relations to thread papers." Mary nursed him for several weeks at home, and then the two, at just about the time Mary should have set sail again for West Africa, took a convalescent trip to Colwyn Bay in northern Wales, which "set Charley partially up again and he was therefore extremely bored by it and insisted on going on to Llanberies and he went up Snowden and things in general."

Even after the recuperative holiday in Wales, however, Charley remained sufficiently unwell to prevent Mary from booking passage again. The prison house doors seemed to be clanging shut once more, and Mary lived now with a haunting déjà vu sensation — life seemed to be reverting to the pattern of her pre-African years when her ailing, dependent mother was still alive. She confessed to Hatty, "I feel the fear coming down on me like a black cloud that there is something wrong with his lungs, and I feel so powerless in the matter. It is just as if the old days were coming back and I do not feel able to work or think on outside things as I could were it not for this."

That Mary had dedicated *Travels in West Africa* to Charley did not disguise the continuing friction that existed between them. Charley did not bask gracefully in the reflected glory of Mary's fame after *Travels in West Africa* was published. Nor could he have been pleased when she booked passage once again for the Coast. And so he got ill, and the trip was canceled, and Mary turned again to the only remedy for her homesickness: writing about Africa.

By the end of April she was already sending Macmillan manuscript and promising "to be as serious as I can and to not be diffuse." Guillemard, she firmly stipulated, was not to be in on this book. Instead, both Lucy Toulmin Smith and Alice Green would read the batches of manuscript Mary produced, mending split infinitives, lassoing stray prepositions, severing her "interminable Teutonic sentences." In addition, John Holt would read the political and trade sections and Tylor the chapters on fetish. Mary was especially gratified when the latter said she was "a lamp post in a fog," because, as she told Macmillan, "I always thought I was the fog myself."

The number of editors called into service with *West African Studies* reflected its heterogeneous elements. If *Travels in West Africa* was a "vast word swamp," *West African Studies* was, as Mary put it, a "patchwork affair." Into its portmanteau Mary stuffed willy-nilly the travelogue of "The Bights of Benin," various passages excised in manuscript from *Travels in West Africa,* most of the lectures on trade and fetish she delivered in 1897 and 1898, a reworking of the Corsico fishing episode, which had already appeared in her first book, two historical chapters on the European discovery of and early trade in West Africa, two more chapters on African property, a three-chapter frontal attack on the Crown Colony system of government, and finally her own elaborate scheme for trade rule in West Africa.

This last she was at first reluctant to formulate. As she wrote Holt, she felt it would be "cheeky" of her to dictate the best mode of West African administration. She was, she demured, "a brickmaker, not an architect." But as a "drag chain" the Crown Colony system became more and more of a threat to African institutions, Mary screwed her courage to the sticking point and came out with her own "alternative plan." It clearly reflected her own peculiar brand of economic imperialism and her fundamental belief that traders caused the least harm to African society because their profits depended upon the well-being of their markets. Like Goldie's plan for the Royal Niger Company, Mary's tortuously devised trade rule scheme was in fact one of the earliest expressions of the idea of indirect rule in West Africa — the notion that colonial powers should use existing African governing structures, such as chieftaincies and African legal courts, rather than impose alien direct rule, which would be carried out solely by representatives of the

British Colonial Office. But the most novel element of Mary's plan was not its articulation of the concept of indirect rule, but rather her conviction that the source of indirect rule's power should be a council of men representing the industrial and commercial centers of England rather than the Colonial or Foreign Office in London. Her plan, however, came to naught and survives now only as an obscure footnote to West African colonial history. But for her it was the center of the book and the most carefully as well as painfully thought out and articulated part of it.

At first the writing of *West African Studies* served the underlying purpose of transporting Mary back to the Coast, especially as she revised the Corsico fishing chapter and the "The Bights of Benin" account of her 1893 voyage out. The fetish chapters were also absorbing as Mary deciphered the notes from her battered bush journals, reread her favorite ethnographer jujus, and wove the whole into a coherent account of African thought and its connection with Western philosophy. She wrote Macmillan, for example, of how "grubbing in the rag bag of my mind I found the tail end of a passage from a big philosopher that was the glue I wanted to stick the facts together with . . . through Kant and Hegel . . . and Spinoza."

Soon, however, the unwieldiness of *West African Studies* became oppressive; Mary was especially plagued by doubts about the chapters on the Crown Colony system and the "alternative plan": Would her arguments and ideas make sense to anyone? Beyond this point, the book refused to cohere, and Mary could not integrate its disparate components. By October she was writing Macmillan, "I cannot get outside the seething mass of things in this new book; though it will seem flippant enough to spare when it is done, it is heavy work for me. I am holding on to the main idea around which it is written by the scruff of its neck, but selection of the facts that will bring that idea clearly out to the minds of people who do not know it, is hard work. If I were a Sir Henry Maine or if I did not know so much, it would be easier." There was also a disconcerting stylistic unevenness in the manuscript. As Mary put it to one friend, "it is as usual very flippant or very heavy. The flippancy is bad, the other rocky . . . being technical." She veered from the broad burlesque, even farce, of the Sierra Leone and Corsico chapters, to learned discussion of schools of fetish, to lively historical narratives, to heated propaganda in the Crown Colony and trade rule chapters. There was something to please everyone in *West African Studies,* but few people she knew would be pleased with the whole thing.

The numerous editors did little to unify the book's medley of ingredients, for Mary parceled out different chapters to different readers. Only
Lucy Toulmin Smith and possibly Alice Green read the whole work in
progress, and Lucy Toulmin Smith seems to have functioned primarily
as a copy editor — correcting grammar, halting run-on sentences, and
so forth. George Macmillan perhaps had a few qualms, but on the
other hand he knew that he would have little trouble selling anything
issuing from Mary's pen.

Meanwhile of course Mary continued to be plagued by various social
and familial demands. The Kingsleys, in particular, remained a chronic
drain on her emotional and financial resources, to say nothing of the
hours and days of her time they consumed. She had scarcely begun the
opening chapters of *West African Studies* when her cousin Mary Kingsley Harrison (the novelist Lucas Malet) summoned Mary to Brighton
because her husband, the Rev. William Harrison, was dying. This was
the "full-blown vicar" with the foaming heels whom Mary had taken
charge of when his spectacles broke so many years before. And now he
was at death's door and his wife prostrate with pleurisy as well as grief.
So Mary, as she wrote Hatty Johnson, had to go down to nurse them,
and at Brighton she found herself "surrounded with a mephitic mental
atmosphere of weird emotionalism with little or no real feeling under
it. The smell of eau de cologne and other scents; to say nothing of a
beast of a bottle of lavender salts that was always getting upset and
destroying things, ladies' maids, stuff first class carriages, ditto
broughams. Then the funeral at Clovelly and throughout it all rows
raging . . . and Mary and Rose telegraphing and writing ill-advised,
row-making letters in all directions and needing to be suppressed."
Mary could have endured all this histrionic behavior, she told Hatty,
if anyone "had been genuinely heartbroken . . . but save for Mary none
of them seemed really sad. All the rest was nothing but selfishness they
gave grand names to."

Of Charles Kingsley's daughters, who lived together in London after
Harrison's death, Mary said bluntly to Alice Green, "I never pretend
to understand them. . . . Mary is the easiest but there is a touch of
something that seems to me almost morbid in her. Rose is I fancy
entirely artificial and so totally unknowable to me." Mary took to making her obligatory calls on them when she thought they would be out
so that she could merely leave her card and depart with an easy mind.
But more often than not she would find Rose at home, "flourishing
but very deaf."

Henry Kingsley's widow, Sarah, and her aged mother decidedly were not flourishing down in South Wimbledon. They were, as always, both destitute and dying, and Sarah in consequence made an urgent, emergency appeal to Mary. Mary's response, as she described it to Macmillan, was to "send a doctor . . . to see her, go over myself. Then if she *is* in this sad physical state something must be done, by me of course: pay her debts." Mary was *not* going "to pother on" as Sarah's other Kingsley relations had for years: dispensing sympathy but no cash. Mary told Macmillan that she planned to make Sarah a fixed weekly allowance "if she is as . . . she says, but I must find out first. Like my father, who cut himself away from them, I have such a des-tation of the humbug and equivocation that the Charles and Henry Kingsleys have . . . that I am not patient in this matter. But I cannot have her dying like a dog in a ditch."

Mary in fact had had about all she could take from this illustrious side of her family. It was her mother's family, the déclassé Baileys, she felt were her real kin. Her uncle William Bailey, a law stationer in Chancery Lane, and his daughter, Annie Bailey, were frequent visitors, and it was Annie, rather than Rose Kingsley or Mary Harrison, who came to 100 Addison Road to look after things when Mary or Char-ley was ill. Needless to say, the Baileys' and Kingsleys' paths did not cross in Mary's parlor, or anywhere else for that matter. And it goes without saying, too, that Mary excepted the Baileys from the scathing remarks she made about her family in a letter to Hatty Johnson in May. "You have one thing to be thankful for," she wrote Hatty, "and that is that you have not got my relations. I have always envied you your Aunt Fanny on general grounds, but really now it's more than that and I feel inclined to advertise in the Exchange and Mart: 'Fine set of relatives,pedigree strain, will exchange for fire-irons or anything useful.' It's the Charles Kingsleys I am referring to, but I would throw in the Chanters [in-laws of the Kingsleys] and Aunt Sarah with plea-sure."

One person whose incursions on her time and energies Mary did not resent this spring, however, was Dennis Kemp, the Wesleyan mission-ary Mary had made friends with and stayed with in the Gold Coast in 1895. Kemp was on leave in Tunbridge Wells during the spring and summer of 1897, and soon after Mary returned to England he wrote to her, including in his letter some mild remonstrances for her treatment of missionaries in *Travels in West Africa*. Mary replied, as was her style, with both humor and seriousness. She had seen Kemp's photograph in

a recent issue of the *Methodist Recorder* "looking simply dangerous, roused,
I presume, from reading . . . my remarks on missions; and I only hope
the Missionary Society will not print a flyleaf with your protrait and
that of Mr. Todd [another Wesleyan missionary] and underneath thus,
'Portrait of the Wesleyan missionary who had read Miss K. and portrait of the one who did not, for Mr. Todd's unruffled expression is a
contrast to your own." But joking aside, Mary couldn't unsay what
she said about missionary activity in West Africa, nor could she "ignore the truth . . . of their destroying the honesty and morality of the
native." At this impasse, the two decided to meet again, and Kemp
took to calling regularly at 100 Addison Road, often staying right
through tea to dinner and well into the evening, talking endlessly
about the Coast.

They agreed to cease disagreeing — or rather to place a moratorium
on discussing missions in West Africa. Mary encouraged Kemp in his
work on a book on his African experiences, and once it was completed,
she submitted it for him to George Macmillan, who published it as
Nine Years at the Gold Coast in 1898. There was a further exchange of
photographs, Kemp giving Mary a more cheerful one than that which
had appeared in the *Methodist Recorder* and inscribing it with "the photo
of the missionary after he was kicked downstairs." Mary, in turn, gave
Kemp her portrait photo (the one in which she is wearing the antennae
hat), with the inscription "the melancholy picture of one who tried to
be just to all parties."

The inscription — startling in its contrast to the jocular undercur-
rent that had so far characterized their relationship — was perhaps a
covert plea for intimacy. Although she was aware of his Methodist
tenets, Mary perceived a well of human sympathy beyond narrow par-
ochialism in Kemp, and slowly she began to unburden herself to him
as she had with no other person, not even Alice Green. When Kemp
gratefully acknowledged receipt of the photograph and asked her about
the cryptic inscription, she replied, "I am really a very melancholy
person inside. But I don't show that part of myself. I feel I have no
right to any one's sympathy, and I have so much more than I deserve
of what is worth having in this life." Moreover, she confessed to Kemp
as she had to no other person, with the exception of Mary Slessor, that

> far under the melancholy there is an utter faith in God, which I fear I
> could not make you believe I have. Nevertheless, it is there and it has
> survived my being educated among agnostics, and the dreadful gloom
> of all my life until I went to Africa. . . . I do not mean that my faith

is of any use to anyone except the owner, or that it is comfortable or restful; for I have always a feeling of responsibility. All through the fifteen years during which I nursed my mother and watched over my brother's delicate health I never "felt it was all for the best," and I know I failed, for my mother's sufferings were terrible, and my brother's health is now far from what I should wish. So you see I have too gloomy a religion to want to convert other people to it.

Kemp unlatched Mary's spiritual and psychological floodgates and out rushed all the unarticulated doubts, fears, beliefs, regrets,and dreams that had been locked within for years. As Mary put it in another letter:

It is a sad situation for you as a Wesleyan to be Father Confessor to what is honestly and truly a tortured soul. As for my not showing the best part of me — well, the best part is all this doubt and self-distrust, and melancholy and heartache. . . . Why should I show it to people I don't care for, and I don't know? I put on armour (corruscating wit) . . . when I go out to battle. If I did not, well, I should be like Goldie, hurt and embittered and, in my case, not in his, unfit for combat.

Why was Kemp singled out by Mary to be her "father confessor"? The immediate pretext was that she had agreed to give several lectures for the benefit of the Wesleyans. But she explained to Kemp that if she was going to lecture on his behalf, she ought to make clear to him her own spiritual state. It could be highly unpleasant if he found her out as a rank heretic after the fact, and so she wanted him to be forewarned. This perhaps was more of a rationalization, however, than a motive. It would seem that Mary's need, the desire that Kemp awakened in her, to alleviate her profound isolation, was the real origin of their close friendship, which commenced in the spring of 1897.

Kemp was also a link with the Coast — that world that kept receding from her grasp. He was a man of God, accustomed to listening to the sorrows and doubts of others, a man possessed of empathy, insight, and intelligence. And moreover he was entirely removed from the haut politique surrounding Mary now. He seemed to call her back to the far more authentic life she had known in West Africa, and at the same time, he called her back to herself: the essential self that Alice Green also recognized.

Throughout the summer and autumn of 1897 Mary continued to do a great deal of lecturing, usually delivering chapters or lengthy sections of *West African Studies* that she was currently working on. In May she spoke at Glasgow, Hull, and Liverpool and in June at both Cambridge and Oxford, the talk at the latter being on "African Religion and Law." It must have given her a wry kind of pleasure to speak *h*-lessly at these two ivy-smothered bastions of British upper-class learning. She had a very different sort of audience for two charity lectures, one for the building fund of the Working Men's College at Westminister Hall, the other for the Boys' Institute in the slums of North London. As she described it to Alice Green, the audience at the Boys' Institute was composed of "the street sweepings of the back of Oxford Street, . . . dirty, anaemic creatures," who were transfixed by Mary's slides of Africans, whom they found "awful low. It was a real pleasure to them I am sure to see something they felt superior to." Shortly after, in Tunbridge Wells, an upcoming lecture of Mary's was billed as being given by an entomologist, and, Mary was told, "it will be so interesting to the farmers." "I said ethnologist," she wrote Alice, "and now I suppose I must discourse on wire worms and turnip fly."

October and November were her busiest months. By then she had made sufficient progress on *West African Studies* to have a good supply of talks on hand that had been culled from the manuscript. On November 11 she gave a paper entitled "West Africa from an Ethnologist's Point of View" to the Liverpool Geographical Society, this time reading the paper herself rather than using a male interpreter as she had the year before. The Liverpool Geographical Society was now hosting the author of *Travels in West Africa,* and to accord her due respect, they overruled their own bylaws. The next day she spoke at Hull, and when her lecture was written up in the local paper Mary was described as being of "a quaint but modest appearance." The balance of the month was taken up by talks at Leicester, Sheffield, Highbury, Manchester, Whitechapel, and at Liverpool again. At Highbury, Mary wrote Macmillan, she had an audience of seventeen hundred, and she "addressed them from a red velvet pulpit surrounded by ministers and elders."

By and large all this lecturing was helpful for the book, despite its taking Mary away from her writing desk so frequently. In the course of a talk she could see at which points the audience was most attentive and at which their attention began to wander. And in the question and answer sessions following her presentations, she discovered what issues or arguments were overly technical or "rocky" for her listeners, and these she honed or reworked in the book. In this way she got immediate feedback on this book from potential readers as well as from her various editors. Clearly she needed to be reassured on numerous fronts that her struggles over it were not in vain. And the lectures, too, constituted a kind of promotion tour for *West African Studies:* they created an audience and buyers for the book and not merely among those who actually attended the lectures but also among those who read the newspaper accounts of the talks.

A hiatus occurred in all the writing and reading activity in early October, however, when Violet Roy's husband, Professor of Pathology at Cambridge, died suddenly during an epileptic fit at the age of forty-three, leaving Violet, as Mary put it, "with nothing but debts." Of course, Mary had to go up to Cambridge to orchestrate the funeral arrangements (a task that she had become adept at by this point) and to try to console Violet and make some sort of financial plans for her. Violet's precarious economic situation remained a constant source of worry over the next several years. Soon she became something of a personal secretary to Mary — reading proof, handling correspondence, arranging lecture dates with Mary's agent — and Mary almost certainly gave her some sort of remuneration for these services. In fact, she probably handed over these duties to Violet so that Violet wouldn't feel like a charity case.

In addition to writing *West African Studies,* lecturing, and looking after friends in need, Mary had two other projects brewing in the second half of 1897: an abridged version of *Travels in West Africa* and an introduction to a book by her old trader friend, R. E. Dennett, *The Folklore of the Fjort.* The first was a fairly straightforward affair, involving lifting out most of the fetish material from *Travels in West Africa* and leaving the travelogue intact. In the end, then, George Macmillan had his way with the two-book plan Mary had vetoed the year before, for the abridged *Travels in West Africa* was the popular "light reading" he had urged her to produce. The preface to the folklore book she took considerable pains over, and it contains her fullest defense of the West African trader, arguing for his sympathy and respect for African culture.

Perhaps it was Mary's tireless efforts on all these fronts that provoked Charley finally to make an attempt at some sort of professional future for himself. His biographical memoir of his father for *Notes on Sport and Travel* remained of course in abeyance; Malaysia now seemed to be off the horizon; his desultory studies in Buddhism and Chinese literature had begun to pall. It had been eight years now since Charley had finished his LL.M. at Cambridge. Since then he had done nothing with his legal studies. Indeed, he had really done nothing profitable at

all. In early November, however, he was admitted to the Inner Temple
in London, the first step for one who wished to be called to the bar and
to practice as a barrister. Mary must have been heartened by Charley's
enrollment at the Inner Temple, but like everything else in his life,
Charley's plan to practice law came to naught. He was never called to
the bar, and after this single abortive burst of ambition, he never again
attempted to earn his own livelihood. Charley's seemingly congenital
parasitism did nothing of course to ease the tense relationship between
sister and brother in the cramped Addison Road flat. They seemed to
have tacitly agreed in fact to occupy it simultaneously as seldom as
possible. Charley was forever dashing down to Devon or back to Cambridge to stay with friends, while Mary of course spent a considerable
amount of time on the road lecturing.

In December, however, both she and Charley were at home, for
Mary invited Major (later Lord) Frederick Lugard to visit them on
Addison Road. Lugard, who had made his name leading military and
commercial expeditions in India and in East and Central Africa, would
in the next decade go on to become the chief architect of indirect rule
in West Africa, the first high commissioner of northern Nigeria, the
primary force behind the amalgamation of northern and southern Nigeria, and the first governor general of this vast, new, unified colony.
In time, too, he married Mary's great adversary at the *Times*, Flora
Shaw. But in the closing months of 1897 Lugard had only reached
midstream in his career. He was in London to organize a West African
frontier force to protect Goldie's Royal Niger Company, for it was
becoming increasingly clear that trade interests in West Africa could
not be entirely self-sufficient: they needed military protection both
against recalcitrant African chiefs who would not acquiesce and surrender up their lands to the company and against the French, who were
encroaching on this territory, especially in the regions to the north of
Goldie's dominions.

No doubt Mary's and Lugard's paths would have crossed sooner or
later in someone's drawing room without any precipitating event or
occasion. But as it turned out, Lugard himself initiated a head-on
collision with Mary by writing a highly provocative article on the liquor traffic in West Africa for the November issue of the popular and
widely circulated *Nineteenth Century*. Lugard's long, detailed attack on
the liquor trade revolved around two central arguments: that it de-
moralized Africans, and that it was actually harmful to other trade
interests in West Africa. But the most remarkable feature of the article

was that Lugard singled out Mary Kingsley no fewer than eight times as a kind of personification of the proliquor party he was at pains to denounce. At times his piece even approaches an ad hominem attack. One by one Lugard enumerated and tried to demolish Mary's carefully thought-out reasons for maintaining the liquor trade: that there is more drunkenness in England than Africa; that African alcoholic drinks are more potent and dangerous than trade gin or rum; that the climate in Africa requires some kind of stimulant; that to withhold liquor from the African is to treat him like a child; and finally, that liquor is a highly efficient trade good because it is easily portable and does not perish. Lugard then went on to wrap up his article by calling for a complete prohibition of the liquor trade in the long run and over the short term increasing duties and taxes on the liquor, for to halt the trade suddenly and totally would seriously injure England's economic interests in West Africa.

Mary was stunned by Lugard's attack on her and almost immediately began drafting a heated response to it, though events were to prevent her from finishing and publishing it until April. In the meantime, Goldie, no doubt with undisguised glee, decided to stage what would certainly be a highly volatile meeting of his two friends by asking them both to dine on December 9. Mary accepted the invitation with considerable trepidation; as she put it in a letter to Holt on the sixth, "I've got to dine at Goldie's to meet *Lugard* on Thursday. I'd rather be on the road to Oyo way when the flying fishes play and the dawn comes up in thunder from behind Corsico Bay. . . . Perhaps you will understand now . . . why I enjoy a swamp." On the afternoon of the ninth she wrote Holt again and promised, "I will write after seeing Lugard tonight."

But her report of this momentous meeting was not in fact made until the eleventh because, as she told Holt, she was "too livid" immediately after the dinner party to write a balanced account of the evening. There were no grand fireworks, but Lugard irritated her; she found him naive and uninformed, and thus she was all the more chagrined by his attack on her over the liquor trade. "Of course," she wrote Holt, "we did not say a word about the liquor question to each other, though Goldie did his best to make us. But in a crowded dinner party one cannot quietly talk over facts calmly and facts regarding West African· liquor Lugard evidently has not got." Her opinion of him was that "he is plainly a dreamy partisan of the missionary party — a very fine explorer and soldier, I have no doubt — but a man who acts under orders, and does not think. Order him to go anywhere and he will go; tell him such and such a thing is good or bad and if he recognizes the person who tells him so is a proper, pious person he throws all the weight of his authority in backing up what he thinks is the proper pious thing. No man who thought for himself would have written that article. He is a strangely simple-minded creature," Mary concluded, "without an atom of an idea of the elementary laws of evidence."

To Lugard himself, however, Mary donned her humble "Only Me" guise to the extent at times of self-abasement. A week after meeting Lugard at Goldie's, she finally broached the subject of the liquor controversy and his article in a letter to him beginning, "I am totally unfit for the higher forms of cultured intelligence — [but] my dear Sir you have attacked me, so it's no use asking a person of my limited thinking power to think that you have not, but I hastily beg to say I do not mind being attacked."

Despite this rather coy opening, however, Mary went on to enumerate and defend her assertions that the liquor traffic was a harmless and economically beneficial form of trade, the very same arguments that Lugard had so laboriously attempted to refute in his article. The two were clearly at an impasse and, given Mary's assessment of Lugard's mind and character, a rather hopeless one at that. And yet she went to some lengths to ingratiate herself with him, beginning with an invitation to visit Addison Road. "I live while in England with a brother whose health is delicate and whose mind is wrapped up in metaphysics and who hates society — as much as I do," she wrote Lugard. "The consequences are we live in a congested den-like flat together and rarely see people at home, but I should like to see you before I go out again. When that will be I do not know to a month or so for I am only Master Charles's satellite."

But in her next letter to Lugard at the end of December she makes no reference to sailing for West Africa as she did in her first invitation. Instead Mary and Charley are all "too delighted" at the prospect of the call Lugard promised to make. "We will show Polynesian and Malaysian things and old maps of Africa etc., in fact, we will do our unconventional best."

That Mary and Lugard remained on friendly terms, at least until he returned to Nigeria the following spring, is indicated in one of her letters to another friend in which Mary explained that her social schedule was uncertain because "I am at the mercy of Major Lugard for he and I are at war with each other and we have now and then, behind

the scenes, to arrange details of the next fight." But once she published
her rejoinder to him in an article entitled "Liquor Traffic in West
Africa" in the April issue of the *Fortnightly Review* Mary had crossed
the Rubicon as far as cordial relations with Lugard were concerned.
The article ran to more than twenty pages, and with an adept blend of
humor, closely reasoned argumentation, and technical knowledge, Mary
one by one toppled Lugard's arguments and reasserted her own position that trade liquor is not poisonous, does not degrade or injure the
African, and is positively necessary to English trade. And in the course
of her argument Mary also exposed the underlying paternalistic racism
of Lugard's article, especially his proposed gradual phasing out of the
liquor traffic, first by increased taxation and then by total prohibition.
This plan, Mary said, was both "unsound and pernicious." Even worse,
it was dishonest to "humbug" the African by saying that England was
not withdrawing liquor, only making it more expensive, and then in
the course of time turning around and banning it.

Lugard's *Nineteenth Century* article was the main object of her animus
in the *Fortnightly Review* article, but Mary also released some long pent-
up salvos against the *Times,* which she considered — especially in the
person of Lugard's future wife, Flora Shaw — to be the most powerful
organ of the antiliquor party in England. The *Times* embodied "the
superior form of the English mind," which, when confronted with the
issue of the liquor trade, gave "rise to a feeling of great personal moral
superiority, combined with a conviction of the iniquity and absence of
high moral ideals in other nations and persons, persons of non-superior
type like myself." Mary, of course, had borne the *Times* a personal
grudge ever since its refusal to notice *Travels in West Africa* the year
before. Hence her wholly ironic insistence in the *Fortnightly Review*
article that she had nothing but "the greatest admiration for the *Times,*
and moreover I owe it many debts of gratitude for I always made it a
point, when on my extremely occasional visits to an English Government House, on the West Coast of Africa — the only sort of place in
that country where you can get that newspaper — of securing articles
and storing them because when well wetted and beaten into a pulp and
mixed with gum and then boiled gently in a pipkin, there is simply
nothing equal to the *Times* for stopping cracks or holes in one's canoe,
which is, as Mr. Pepys would say, an excellent thing in a newspaper."
The *Times*'s utility in West African affairs, however, halted here, for
like Lugard and Shaw, it was invariably either mis- or uninformed.
Mary had "never met the apparition of the *Times* in its human form

walking about the West African bush; and it does not say in its leading articles where it gets its information from."

Shortly before the *Fortnightly Review* article appeared, Mary only slightly exaggerated in a letter to a friend the furore she anticipated that it would arouse: "It is fire and brimstone for me when it comes out, and all Liverpool can do is to put up a memorial window to me." As for the design of the stained glass window, she feared Liverpool "in its devotion to me might select a West African ju ju hung round with square-faced gin bottles." Certainly the article was one of the boldest and most controversial Mary had written, but its impact was muted somewhat by the four-month period between Lugard's attack and Mary's response and also by new, overshadowing events in Africa, such as the Sierra Leone Hut Tax War and the Fashoda crisis in the Sudan.

The closing weeks and days of 1897 were busy ones for Mary. She lectured twice at Bournemouth in mid-December, and the balance of the month was taken up with nursing a woman, an old family friend, who died shortly before Christmas. Charley's chronic cough was exacerbated by the cold weather, with the result that he now rarely went out. Mary made what progress she could on *West African Studies* in the sporadic moments she could secure in the midst of all these demands. Winter was closing in. The days became shorter and shorter, and colder and darker. Christmas came and went once more with no celebration. For Mary these bleak winter months were the hardest part of the year to endure, and they were made an even greater trial by her vivid recollections of December, January, and February on the Coast — when the dry season reigns and the sun, a huge bronze globe, hangs low in a cloudless, electric blue sky.

On January 1, 1898, the British government imposed a property tax of five shillings on all houses in the Protectorate of Sierra Leone in order to raise revenue to administer the colony in Freetown and the protectorate hinterland. The Sierra Leone house or hut tax was the brainchild of the protectorate's energetic governor, Sir Frederick Cardew, who cherished dreams of transforming his small colonial backwater into a larger gem in Victoria's crown of Empire. Cardew envisioned new drains for Freetown, a larger police force for the colony, and most of all, he yearned for that quintessentially Victorian symbol of progress — a railroad. No one outside the Colonial Office was consulted about the feasibility of the tax, which was almost without precedent in the African colonies: not the English traders and missionaries in Sierra Leone, not political and anthropological experts on the country, and not, above all, the peoples of the protectorate — the Mende, Temne, Limba, and Kono inhabitants who would somehow have to wring five shillings per annum out of an average annual income of no more than one pound. Cardew wrote Whitehall that he needed the tax. The urbane colonial secretary, Joseph Chamberlain — the architect of British imperialism in Lord Salisbury's Tory government — rubber-stamped the plan, and almost immediately chaos ensued.

The peoples of the protectorate refused to pay the tax, and when the frontier police tried to collect it by force the householders revolted. By March reports were appearing almost daily in the British newspapers of violent skirmishes in remote villages, involving looting, burning, and, even worse, the wholesale slaughter of anyone who seemed to be connected with the British government. Traders, missionaries, and educated Africans were murdered in cold blood, often when they were helpless in their beds in the middle of the night. With his monocle securely screwed into one eye and a hothouse orchid attached to his lapel, Chamberlain sat at his mahogany desk at Whitehall and wondered what had gone wrong. He began dispatching telegrams to Cardew asking him to "reconsider" the tax. He consulted his advisors, Colonial and Foreign Office officials with experience on the Coast, and in the midst of his baffled chagrin over the tax, he read a letter to the *Spectator* from Mary Kingsley that set out in no uncertain terms the folly of the tax and the reason why the attempted implementation of it had so disastrously failed.

The explanation was absurdly simple: the tax violated African law, which stipulated that what one paid for regularly quite logically belonged to the person who collected the money. Or as Mary put it in the *Spectator:* "One of the root principles of African law is that the thing that you pay anyone a regular fee for is a thing that is not your own — it is a thing belonging to the person to whom you pay the fee — therefore if you have to pay the Government a regular and recurring payment for your hut, it is not your hut, it is the property of the Government; and the fact that the Government has neither taken that hut from you in war, bought it of you, or had it given as a gift by you, the owner, vexes you 'too much' and makes you, if you are any sort of man, get a gun." Privately Mary told Chamberlain that the tax amounted to little more than "confiscation tempered by bribery." For after her letter appeared in the *Spectator,* Chamberlain turned to Mary for counsel. With Liverpool and Manchester trade interests solidly be-

hind her, she urged immediate and total repeal of the tax on two
grounds: "It is not morally right and . . . it is not practically worth
it" because of the strategic difficulties of relying upon hostile chiefs in
remote villages to help collect the tax.

Chamberlain listened attentively, even encouragingly, to Mary's advice. As she wrote Holt, "Chamberlain is manifesting a desire to be
taught. He is horribly frightened of being known to communicate
with me à la Saul and the Witch of Endor. . . . I am secretly inserting
into him on a dozen sides . . . the horror of the thing he has done
with this hut tax and he turns to me, asking me if I can give 'any
suggestions as to an alternative method of collecting revenue.' " Mary's
alternative plan was to raise revenue through increased customs dues
and fines and also by means of government monopolies on tobacco and
timber. Again, Chamberlain listened but withheld action.

He did not act in fact until after the hut tax came up in the House
of Commons in May. The Irish M.P. Michael Davitt delivered an impassioned speech against the tax in the course of which he denounced
Cardew as a lunatic and repeatedly cited Mary's call for the abolition
of the tax as the only way of ending the chaos reigning in Sierra Leone.
Chamberlain now was beginning to get hot under the collar, but still
he wavered. Finally, he decided to send a commission of inquiry out
to the colony, and at the head of this commission he appointed a Scottish lawyer named Sir David Chalmers who had served nearly ten years
in West Africa as a colonial judge.

For Mary the hut tax controversy that broke out in early 1898 was
important living history, and she incorporated what she felt were its
all too glaring lessons into the political chapters of *West African Studies,*
which she was then working on. In mid-January, however, she took a
respite from her writing and from her myriad domestic demands and
went on a lecture tour to Ireland, speaking at both Belfast and Londonderry. As usual, she had a certain quota of odd experiences. She
found the audience at the Field Club "savage," and the Northern Hotel
at Londonderry was "full of . . . commercial gentlemen kissing cook
maids on stairs and that sort of thing." "I don't want to say anything
actionable," Mary wrote her agent, "but the Hotel at Grand Canarie
or at Bomea, Congo Free State are kings to it."

Unfortunately, the immediate result of the lecturing in Ireland was
a virulent and nearly fatal case of influenza. By the time Mary returned
to London on January 17 she was in a state of collapse. Dennis Kemp
called and was told by Charley of the gravity of Mary's condition,

which did not seem to be responding to the "severe doses of strychnine" administered by the doctor. There was ample cause to be alarmed; the attack was bad and had come on when Mary was in an overworked and mentally and physically exhausted state. Kemp immediately went to George Macmillan and told him that Mary was dying, whereupon Macmillan cabled Alice Green — then on holiday in Paris — who, as soon as she received the telegram, took the next boat train back to London to nurse her close friend. Eventually Mary Kingsley Harrison and Rose Kingsley learned that Mary was seriously ill and were positively "rampagious," as Mary put it, when they flew to her bedside and found Alice Green already installed there. Mary herself was incensed at both Kemp and Macmillan for raising such an alarm and summoning Alice Green home. Slowly she began to mend, though there was the constant risk of relapse. On the thirty-first she reported to a friend that "I cannot say I am altogether well, as I am shaky on my legs and generally just conscious that I am supremely weak and wretched. But I made my first venture out today and was brought home ignominiously in a cab. Still, ten days ago if I had gone out at all the chances were that I should have gone in a hearse and not come home."

As she recovered Mary worked on the political chapters of *West African Studies* — nerve-wracking writing for her — and dispatched batches of manuscript to Holt and Alice Green. For the farther along she got the more unsure and unhappy she felt about what she was producing. Once she recovered, the usual social round resumed, along with, and as a constant distraction to, her writing. Bruce Walter, the *Athenaeum* reviewer, came round on March 3 with a colorful figure named Count Charles de Cardi, a Liverpool merchant of Corsican descent who had spent some thirty-four years in trade in West Africa. On the thirteenth Mary wrote Holt that she had been "lunching with Goldie and spending the balance of my day with Stanley so I am tired and gloomy and more convinced than ever of my errors." Three days later she met privately with Chamberlain to discuss the hut tax and found the Colonial Secretary "mighty civil and all that sort of thing," although "he said one or two things that grated on me severely," such as his boast that he sat "like a spider in his web" and let everyone who had anything to say come to him and tell him. Mary was determined not to be one of Chamberlain's ensnared flies, though she again lectured to him on the folly of the hut tax and also discussed such matters as sanitation, drainage, and nursing in West Africa.

On April 26 Mathilda Goldie died suddenly at the age of fifty-one. The blow nearly broke her husband, who was rendered "intensely and intentionally wretched" by the loss. In his grief Goldie turned to Mary, who was scarcely less desolate. Mathilda Goldie was one of the few people Mary confessed to loving. For weeks she could barely work or think of anything other than this loss and Goldie's irremediable pain. Goldie sealed up his drawing room and turned away callers. Mary could do nothing other than formulate a strange, cryptic dedication for *West African Studies:* "To my brother Mr. C. G. Kingsley and to my friend who is dead."

In late May Mary went to hear E. B. Tylor speak on totemism at the Anthropological Society, and in a long letter registering her admiration for his lecture, she also asked him if he would recommend or sponsor her as a new member in "the Anthropological," as she called it. She assured Tylor that she wouldn't disgrace him, adding that "I am for a West Coaster fairly respectable and will not steal the other members' umbrellas or hats." In due course Mary was nominated and accepted as a member, and shortly thereafter she also joined the British Empire League and the Folklore Society.

Nevertheless, she remained, in theory at least, opposed to women's participation in learned societies. When a movement was afoot to admit women into the august Royal Geographical Society Mary denounced the "shrieking females and androgyns" who wanted to append F.R.G.S. (Fellow of the Royal Geographical Society) to their names. To one Mrs. Farquharson, whose petition in favor of female membership in the Royal Geographical Society Mary refused to sign, she was more temperate. "If we women distinguish ourselves in Science in sufficiently large numbers at a sufficiently high level," she wrote Mrs. Farquharson, "the great scientific societies like the Royal and the Linnaean will admit women on their own initiative or we shall form scientific societies of our own of equal eminence. The great thing for us in this generation to do is to show a good output in high class original work." Mary preferred to operate, as she wrote Holt, behind the scenes, affirming that "every bit of solid, good work I have done has been through a man." She clearly thought that "the presence of petticoats" would necessarily bring about a lowering of standards in learned societies. Women didn't have the time or flair for such matters, Mary further told Holt, or only women such as herself or Flora Shaw did, clearly implying that such as they would not enrich any erudite gatherings. Even when Mary proposed the creation of an African society

along the lines of the Royal Asiatic Society, she vetoed the idea of
extending membership to women, which meant that she "dared not
show a hand in it for ladies *must not* be admitted." Eventually, she
shelved the plan, for she feared that any African Society would inevitably become a tool of political partisanship.

But Mary never relinquished her position against allowing women
into scientific societies. Once again, she refused to ally herself with
even the faintest stirrings of feminism in English society. And once
again her motives were mixed. She had worked hard to become "one
of the men" in the intellectual circles she moved in, and she no doubt
enjoyed her anomalous position in them. More important, she clearly
felt that if she associated herself with any feminist agitation she would
damage her own credibility. The stakes were too high; indeed, they
involved nothing less than the integrity of African culture and the
economic welfare of Britain. To participate in the causes of the contemporary women's movement would, she felt, undermine her influence and authority in West African affairs.

In late May Mary was summoned to Great Berkampstead to nurse
the ailing widow of her father's former patient-employer, Lord Pembroke. When Lady Pembroke was sufficiently recovered Mary moved
on to Liverpool for a visit to the Holts before returning to London for
three political dinners and a lecture before the women's press dinner in
late June.

On July 8 she gave one of her most lively lectures at Cheltenham
Ladies' College, the lecture that included the anecdote about the hippopotamus ("like a furniture van in hysterics") on the rampage through
the village, the advice that spinsters in West Africa, when queried
about the location of their husbands, should not futilely try to explain
that they don't have one but should instead say "you are searching for
him and then . . . locate him away in the direction in which you wish
to travel; this elicits help and sympathy." This, too, was the lecture
that Mary ended by describing the "painful charm" of West Africa
that haunts those in exile in England, so that "everything that is round
you grows poor and thin in the face of that vision, and you want to go
back to the Coast that is calling you, saying, as the African says to the
departing soul of his dying friend, 'Come back, this is your home.' "

Mary's appearance and mode of delivery at the Cheltenham lecture
were calculated to enhance the strangely appealing mixture of the lu-
dicrous and the profound, the zany and the poetic that animated her
talk. She was dressed, as always, in black, in a stiff, full-length silk

dress, with an enormous cameo brooch at her throat, both in a style at least thirty years out of date. "But then," as one in the audience recalled more than seventy years later, Mary's "hairbreadth escapes and thrilling adventures made one forget completely her appearance which of course was a bit of stagecraft designed to heighten her achievements." Some of the adventures were rather "hot stuff" for Victorian schoolgirls, and the headmistress, Miss Blake, fidgeted nervously now and then on the platform behind Mary. Miss Blake must also have been taken aback by Mary's opening gambit. In her perfectly clear, vibrant voice she launched into her talk with, "I expect I remind you of your maiden aunt" — a pause for effect — "long since deceased."

In August work on *West African Studies* was suspended once again when Mary and Charley moved from the dark, cramped flat at the top of 100 Addison Road to a small house at 32 Saint Mary Abbott's Terrace, about a mile to the south and just off Kensington High Street. They were both no doubt tired of their congested "den-like" quarters on Addison Road, and perhaps the imminent publication of *West African Studies* — along with her lecture earnings — gave Mary enough financial confidence to merit taking on the expense of a house. The process of moving "3½ tons of books and the makings of a museum" was left of course almost exclusively to her, as was in addition the transfer of a "blood drum, blood dish, [and] blood bowl packed into wheeled vans regardless of expense." A special cab had to be hired to carry the nail-studded Muvungu, who, in the new house as in the old flat, held a central position in the front hall and was the first object visually and olfactorily to greet the visitor to 32 Saint Mary Abbott's Terrace. "The funny little house," as one friend described it, was a considerable improvement over the Addison Road flat, even taking into account its two malfunctioning chimneys, which Mary christened "Chimborazo and Valparaiso because they alternately vomited dense clouds of smoke into her rooms."

It was at just about the time when Mary was moving into Saint Mary Abbott's Terrace that she met the journalist Stephen Gwynn, with whom she swiftly became close friends. Gwynn was a young, ebullient Irishman, a prolific journalist who also produced a steady stream of verse, novels, and biographies. When Mary met him he was writing a good deal on Africa in the daily press and soon would be among the group of contemporary journalists who wrote on and exposed the atrocities perpetrated in King Leopold's Congo Free State.

Initially Mary's friendship with Gwynn was occasioned by a shared absorption in West African political affairs. Then Gwynn gave her his first novel to read — it was a love story, which prompted Mary to confess that she had never been in love and to recount the foaming heels episode with her cousin Mary's suitor. This broke the ice, and soon Gwynn became one of Mary's inner circle of confidants along with Alice Green and Dennis Kemp. Forty years later, after a colorful career as an Irish nationalist, novelist, literary critic, and general all-around man of letters, Gwynn was to become Mary Kinglsey's first biographer.

Once the domestic situation was more or less under control at 32 Saint Mary Abbott's Terrace, Mary got down to the last chapters of *West African Studies*, hoping, however to delay publication until Sir David Chalmers's report on the Sierra Leone hut tax was completed. Without it, Mary's discussion of the tax remained inconclusive, and yet in the end the report was so delayed that she had to go ahead and allow *West African Studies* to appear in January 1899. As always, the last stages of writing were the most painful, and Mary's doubts grew proportionally. She felt incapable of making her position clear, of doing justice to her arguments. She was also far more apprehensive about the impending response to *West African Studies* than she had been over *Travels in West Africa*. She was not apprehensive about the literary judgment on the book, but rather about the political uproar she feared her discussion of the Crown Colony system and the hut tax would precipitate. In early December she wrote Gwynn, "My book will be out Macmillan says early in January and as I feel certain every friend I have will cut me on its appearance, I am anxious to see as much of them as possible before the catastrophe."

What distractions Mary had during this period were scarcely welcome or cheerful. Charley, who had spent much of the summer in Cambridge, now transferred his headquarters back to London, with the result that more than ever Mary found herself "tied by my apron strings to domestic affairs." She did manage to run up to Cardiff in mid-November for a lecture, but for the most part her outings took her no farther than the outskirts of London. On November 13, for example, she called on Henry Morton Stanley and found him "very ill" and quarrelsome. But she went to Stanley to be bullied, she wrote Holt, and even confessed, "I'd black his boots if it gave him pleasure, likewise yours and Goldie's." But "I go *no* further," she added, "*no* I won't black Joe's," thus excluding the colonial secretary, Chamberlain, from her servile ministrations.

In December Charley announced he was going to China, and Mary told Holt that "the moment he does, I am off to West Africa." *West African Studies* was in its last throes, and Mary yearned to escape as soon as she had deposited it in the printer's hands. But Charley's projected Chinese expedition amounted to nothing more than had his previous travel plans. Instead of going to China, he went to Devon for Christmas, and this time Mary stayed up alone until 3:00 A.M. on Christmas Eve doing the *West African Studies* index herself.

This Christmas was even worse than the previous two. As Mary wrote Mrs. Holt, "I have had an extra bad time lately." Mary herself came down with flu shortly before Christmas, and then one of her mother's oldest friends fell ill, and Mary had to nurse her until the woman died on the twenty-sixth, Boxing Day. Then the eighteen-year-old son of another friend died of influenza; his mother consequently went mad, and Mary had to remain with her until other friends filled the breach and saw to the poor woman's care over the long run.

Sickness, death, madness — none of them were strangers of course in Mary's life, but in their combined, simultaneous strength, on top of all the labor of the last stages of *West African Studies*, they were enough to threaten even her tough, resilient spirit. Once again it was the dead of winter, and once again Mary was on the brink of publication, with all its attendant anxiety and fatigue. Once again West Africa inexorably receded from her grasp because of Charley's immobility. Despite all her productivity, despite her growing political power and ever widening circle of friends and associates, Mary felt trapped in England. A fine web of social, political, and domestic demands and obligations had ensnared her. Africa called to her no less insistently — in fact even more so — but she could not find her way home.

·❧ 13 ❧·

Valediction

On January 31, 1899, *West African Studies* was published — almost exactly two years after *Travels in West Africa*. The early weeks of the new year before the book came out were fraught with anxiety for Mary. This time around of course she didn't fear the reaction of her great jujus — Günther, Tylor, and Holt — since they had already read and approved much of the book in manuscript. But Mary was apprehensive about the reception she might find among the G.P. (general public). She was afraid that it would find the book alternately too flippant and too heavy and that Macmillan as a consequence would lose money on her account. But all Mary's grim prognostications for *West African Studies* were, as usual, completely unfounded. Just how eager the G.P. was for the new book was demonstrated by the fact that it sold twelve hundred copies the first week it was out. And the book reviewers were scarcely less enthusiastic. The *Saturday Review, Spectator, Athenaeum,* and *Literature* all showered encomiums on *West African Studies*, several reviewers insisting furthermore that it was "more solid and satisfactory and matured" than *Travels in West Africa*. Of course there were the occasional carping reviews, some of which rankled, but more often amused, Mary. The *Glasgow Herald,* for example, condemned her style as "unladylike," and the *Echo* reviewer was critical of the book's "colossal" size; "the sheer labour of cutting the pages," he complained, had reduced him "to a state bordering upon muscular atrophy." Mary's favorite negative review, however, appeared in a small provincial paper that singled out a quotation from Coleridge's *Rime of the Ancient Mariner* that she had used and sternly advised her to stick to prose and not attempt such feeble verse again.

Perhaps the most substantial, and to Mary the most gratifying, review of *West African Studies* was that which appeared in the *Daily Chronicle* on the day *West African Studies* was published. The unsigned review was by a young, unknown journalist named Edmund Morel who nevertheless pronounced judgment on the book with the ring of authority: "The general verdict on this book will be that it is the most weighty and valuable contribution on the internal politics of western Africa that has yet seen light. Like her first effort, *Travels in West Africa*, . . . Miss Kingsley's *West African Studies* will take its place among the standard works of West African knowledge to be preferred by coming generations as monuments of painstaking research, immense powers of observation and remarkable ability." In short, according to Morel, *West African Studies* was already and would remain a classic.

Mary contacted the *Daily Chronicle* in order to learn the identity of her appreciative reviewer and was not the least bit taken aback to discover Morel to be a twenty-six-year-old struggling reporter who had left school at the age of fifteen, worked as a clerk for the Elder Dempster steamship line in Liverpool, and now was attempting to establish himself as a Fleet Street newspaperman in London. Almost immediately Mary became something of a mentor to Morel. They discovered that their views on the hut tax, missionaries, the liquor traffic, and other issues were in perfect accord. Mary recognized Morel's talents and gave him vital encouragement. She began reading his articles in draft, advising him where to submit them, and even on occasion acting as his literary agent and sending pieces on to editors like Strachey and others with her strong recommendation. Her efforts on Morel's behalf were unstinting, for in addition to helping him place his work, she also introduced him to her circle of politically powerful friends. Though she would never have admitted it, she was in fact herself a great juju to Morel.

Mary had heard rumors that the *Times* would ignore *West African Studies* as it had *Travels in West Africa*, and even before *West African Studies* came out, she reported to Holt that "the *Times* means to wreak its most awful curse on me — not notice the book at all." The person who had placed this curse on Mary's work was of course the *Times* colonial editor Flora Shaw. Small wonder, then, that when Mary was invited to a small dinner party in mid-February at which Flora Shaw would also be present, she felt some trepidation at the prospect of meeting her long-standing adversary. Or, as she wrote Holt, she foresaw "lovely work" for this momentous occasion, "for there is much gossip up here to the effect that she hates me and uses all her power at times to smash me."

Just why Flora Shaw was one of the very few people capable of intimidating Mary is unclear. There were in fact so many similarities and parallels between the two women's lives that one could just as well imagine a sustaining intimacy to have grown up between them. Shaw was exactly ten years older than Mary and like her had essentially been a domestic captive well into young womanhood because of the invalidism of her demanding mother. When Mrs. Shaw died, Flora at the age of eighteen had had to shoulder all the family domestic responsibilities and somehow also manage to continue her own self-education, for, like Mary, she never received any formal lessons at home or went to school. When she reached her late twenties, by which time her thirteen younger brothers and sisters had all grown up, Flora began to travel — to Gibraltar, Morocco, Egypt, and to other exotic places from which she sent back articles that were published in the *Pall Mall Gazette,* the *Manchester Guardian,* and the *Times.* And when she eventually returned to England from her travels, Flora was drawn into the leading political and literary circles of the day and soon became the intimate friend of men such as John Ruskin, George Meredith, Cecil Rhodes, Sir George Goldie, and finally, her future husband, Frederick Lugard. It was her friendships with the last three men of course that brought Shaw into Mary Kingsley's orbit. But Shaw's relations with these three great "Empire Builders" of the 1890s were both more complicated and intense than were Mary Kinglsey's. While Mary felt something close to contempt for Rhodes and his followers, Flora idolized the man who had carved out and named a whole country for himself in southern Africa, and she indefatigably championed Rhodes's own vehement brand of imperialism. With Goldie she was uncontrollably and in the end tragically in love. Some sort of liaison — probably a consummated one, given Goldie's romantic history and Flora's adoration — existed between them from as early as 1891 or 1892, but Goldie of course was married. Then when Lady Goldie died suddenly in 1898, Flora allowed her own extravagant desire to overrule Goldie's obviously grief-stricken state as well as the prevailing social conventions and proprieties, and she proposed to the man she had loved so unhappily for more than seven years. Goldie refused her, and Flora suffered what amounted to a nervous breakdown from which she seems never to have fully recovered. She married Lugard some five years later, when she was fifty-one, almost with an air of resignation. Shortly before they wed she wrote him, "You once said you would win my love. I, too, hope to win yours. We cannot force it. Let us not try on either side, but let us be content to marry as friends."

When Mary and Flora finally met face to face on the evening of February 16 at a select London dinner party, the resemblance between the two women was almost uncanny: both were tall and slender, and both were dressed in stiff black dinner dresses with mutton chop sleeves, for, like Mary, Flora always dressed as if in mourning. But such external similarity couldn't disguise a fundamental antipathy, especially on Shaw's part. Mary wrote Holt how she found Shaw "civil but in a smouldering rage with me. . . . She is a fine, handsome, bright, upstanding young woman, as clever as they make them, capable of any immense amount of work, as hard as nails and talking like a *Times* leader all the time. She refers to the *Times* as 'we' and does not speak of herself as a separate personality and leads you to think the *Times* is not a separate personality either. She is imbued with the modern form of public imperialism. It is her religion. A person who comes along and says imperial control can be wrong is therefore naturally regarded as an enemy and hated as such." Mary Kingsley of course was just such a person.

Also at the party was the celebrated Isabella Bird Bishop, who had traveled and written about her journeys in the Rocky Mountains, Tibet, Japan, China, and Persia. In the account of the evening she made to George Macmillan, Mary related the tense little colloquy that took place among the three women. Mary was baffled, she said, as to why Shaw "should have her knife in me. . . . She only spoke a few words to me, but while talking with Mrs. Bishop"; Shaw obviously alluded to *Travels in West Africa* and *West African Studies* when she observed that " 'books that were amusing were not always accurate,' " a sentiment that, Mary added, "Mrs. B. profoundly agreed with." As Mary was leaving, however, Flora addressed her directly and said, " 'I fear you will find West Africa much changed when you go there again, Miss Kingsley,' " to which, Mary reported, "I merely laughed and said I didn't think so," keeping in mind that Shaw had never been south of the Sahara. There was no way, after all, for Mary to know that Shaw was not talking like a *Times* leader and behaving like imperialism personified simply because she was a kind of intellectual and political automaton. Rather, Shaw was feeling crushed at this time by Goldie's rejection of her, and at least part of her frigid behavior to Mary and to others during this period must be ascribed to her emotional anguish.

Soon enough Mary would experience a similar kind of anguish herself. She had embarked in fact on her own sad romantic course the very evening before she met Flora Shaw when she dined at the opulent home of the Jewish banker Sir Samuel Montagu on February 15. Even though she was a confirmed if unwilling "drawing roomer" by this point, Mary was enormously impressed by the silver, china, and general luxury that prevailed at the Montagus'. But the decisive event of the evening occurred when she was taken in to dinner by a handsome Jewish army officer named Matthew Nathan who since 1895 had been serving as secretary of the Colonial Defense Committee. "I dote on the military and have a weakness for the nation Israel," Mary wrote Gwynn of her first meeting with Nathan. Her attraction to Jews, she said, sprang from "their dreamy minds, their hard common sense and their love for beautiful material objects — it is just the same thing that makes me love African society." From the very beginning, then, Mary associated her feelings for Nathan with her love for Africa. Nathan on his part made only a laconic, prosaic notation of his meeting with Mary when he recorded, as was his inveterate habit, all the previous day's events in his diary. At the bottom of the page for February 16 he jotted: "Dined at the Montagus' and took in Miss Kingsley — writer on West Africa — a cheerful person who advocates no direct taxation in Sierra Leone but government monopolies on salt and tobacco."

Matthew Nathan was, in the parlance of the day, something of a catch, though his Jewishness would cancel out his appeal in many young women's eyes. For Mary, though, it was an asset, not merely because she perceived an affinity between Jews and Africans, but also because as a Jew, Nathan was something of an outsider, just as Mary saw herself on the fringes of the social world she inhabited — a perpetual "looker-on of life," as she put it.

Nathan was exactly Mary's age (thirty-six) in 1899 and at a crucial stage in his career. Most of his energies were devoted to penetrating the inner circles of the professional, intellectual, and social elite in London, and he quickly realized that the "cheerful" Miss Kingsley could greatly aid him in this task. His course so far had been steady if undramatic: he had been educated at the Royal Military Academy at Woolwich, commissioned as a Royal Engineer, and he had gone on to serve in Sierra Leone, the Sudan, India, and Burma. When he met Mary, he had been on the Colonial Defense Committee for more than three years and, like one of Mary's favorite fictional characters, Mr.

Micawber, was "waiting for something to turn up." In the meantime, he pursued a tranquil and utterly conventional London existence: working diligently at the War Office, dropping in at his club every day, indefatigably making the round of social calls, and dining out at select dinner parties or at home with his doting, widowed mother, with whom he lived. Not infrequently he presided over his own dinner gatherings, and he would note in his diary the menu, who escorted whom in, and would even draw a diagram of the dinner table, marking the location of the guests seated between himself and his mother, who were positioned at either end of the table.

Four days after the Montagu dinner Nathan called on Mary "to talk West Africa," a tête-à-tête that only confirmed Mary's attraction to him. Nathan was a handsome man and possessed of a muted but compelling charm. He had the gift of appearing to be intensely interested in and in sympathy with whomever he wished to ally himself. Hence Mary swiftly became convinced that Nathan cared as deeply about West African affairs as she did. Nathan departed at dusk without his gloves, and when Mary discovered them two days later, she wrote him a note that she dispatched with his gloves, regretfully, since the gloves, she told him, were "just the things I want to give me an air of dignity and power." In a calculated afterthought she added that she was "hoping to have the pleasure of seeing you again soon."

Since "dignity and power" were commodities that Mary possessed in greater quantities than Nathan, she did have the pleasure of seeing him again soon in early March. But in the meantime something had turned up for Nathan: at the end of February Chamberlain informed him that Governor Cardew was being recalled from Sierra Leone in connection with the inquiry into the hut tax war. Nathan was tapped by Chamberlain to go out and serve as acting governor in Cardew's absence, and despite all the evidence that Chalmers had amassed, Chamberlain told Nathan to continue implementation of the tax at least until the Colonial Office had heard Cardew's side of the story.

On Sunday, March 5, Mary went to call on Sir Alfred Lyall with Isabella Bishop, and when she returned home she found Nathan and Count de Cardi awaiting her in her sitting room. Nathan was restless, the conversation disjointed and stilted. Finally he asked pointblank if he could have a few words with Mary out in the hall. Of course she complied, and as she wrote Gwynn, "I took him into the hall when after throwing down poisoned arrows and so on he poured into my ears a strange tale as to how he was going to take over Sierra Leone and

Cardew [would] come home and finally he went with my blessing and I returned to the imprisoned de Cardi who I found in a flustered state, hoping he did not intrude, etc."

If Nathan saw Mary as a vehicle to higher things and sought her "blessing" before embarking on them, she on her part increasingly saw Nathan as holding some of her deepest political and moral convictions. She had already equated Nathan's Jewishness with her love of African culture. Now she saw him as the instrument of preserving that culture. Nathan would go out and quell the unrest wrought by the hut tax war; he would restore peace to the colony and protect British trade interests there. In short, when Mary fell in love with Nathan she fell in love not merely with an individual man but with the world, values, and beliefs that she thought he embodied. She felt an intense kind of identification with him, which is perhaps the most dangerous sort of love. And because Nathan was something of a social and political chameleon and could assume the protective coloration of the views Mary projected onto him, he began to allay her deep-seated feelings of isolation.

It took very little on Nathan's part to open the floodgates of Mary's need. Shortly after his Sunday evening announcement, Mary wrote him a long letter outlining her political views, including her abhorrence of the hut tax, the destructive effects of which she felt confident that she could convince Nathan. It was a strange letter and opened with an expression of fear that he would not understand her. She then went on to fulminate against the hut tax, affirm her own prestige among the Liverpool traders, invoke her Kingsley relatives, declare her agnosticism, and, most important as far as Nathan was concerned, assert her power and authority at the Colonial Office. "I have a very lively hatred for those arm chair fools who sit up here and play the cat and banjo with Africa and call it civilising the African and spreading Christianity," she continued. "But I have nothing but respect for you. I would no more do a thing to hamper or worry you than I would mean of flying. I am capable of making the Colonial Office's flesh creep whenever I get half a chance so if there is ever anything that the C.O. does that you do not want . . . you let me know and I'll cry hands off."

The very next day, March 9, Matthew Nathan replied to this first substantial letter he had received from Mary. Although Mary eventually destroyed the handful of letters he wrote to her during the course of 1899 and early 1900, Nathan's March 9 reply survives in fragmentary pencil draft form in a small pocket notebook of his, sandwiched

between a list of things he had to do that day and a record of expenses
connected with his imminent departure for Sierra Leone. Nathan opened
with the emphatic statement that "I do want to understand you and I
shall." "That I do not yet do so at all completely with regard to West
Africa," he continued, "is due to the fact that when I saw you first my
interest in that part of the world had not received the stimulus which
has since come to it and if you will forgive my saying so, it was your
personality rather than your work which engaged my attention at the
dinner where we met." The letter then went on to more mundane,
practical concerns that Mary's eyes must have rapidly skimmed over
before returning to its opening: "I do want to understand you and I
shall. . . . It was your personality rather than your work which engaged my attention." Benign enough, if gallant, statements to any
woman who was accustomed to receiving compliments from men. But
as Mary had asserted so many times to her close friends, no man had
ever declared that he *would* understand her, that he was more drawn to
herself than to the issues and causes she championed. She had endured
thirty-six years of emotional fasting, and now she construed the few
crumbs that Nathan had tossed her as a veritable feast.

Mary received Nathan's letter on March 10. The very next day he
sailed for Sierra Leone. It was a tedious voyage, but Nathan whiled
away the evenings by playing five rubbers of whist after dinner and
also by reading the copy of *West African Studies* that Mary had given
him shortly before his departure. He wrote home to his mother than
he found the book "amusing," though "too humourous which after a
time has the effect on one of a number of *Punch* as well as of depreciat-
ing her more serious statements, but she certainly gives a good impression of West Africa beginning with the life on an Elder Dempster
boat."

While Nathan was being mildly amused by *West African Studies* on
shipboard, on May 12, the day after he left, Mary sat down at her
writing desk in the small library at Saint Mary Abbott's Terrace and
let forth the deluge of her reply to Nathan's March 9 letter. For twenty-
four pages her sprawling, angular script kept it up, becoming less and
less legible the more intimate and revealing she became. She was pen-
ning an apologia, a confession. Nathan had insisted that he *would* understand her, and now she did everything in her power, exploited all
her uncanny eloquence, summoned every buried desire, need, and fear
in order to help him to do just that.

*

The letter was headed with the caveat "Of no importance, Private," a habitual warning Mary perversely affixed to many of her most important communications. Then after the salutation, "Dear Major Nathan," she launched into the heart of the matter.

I shall keep that letter of yours until the day I leave for the coast again and then I shall burn it. No one but myself shall see it. . . . it would . . . give people the idea you were a diplomat or had a strange taste in ladies if it was my "personality" that made you throw away five minutes time on me. . . . All I can hope from you . . . is that you will not dislike me and keep judgments in suspense until I go hence and am no more seen. . . . You know perfectly well that if I were King of Babylon and you were a Christian slave as Mr. Kipling wildly says, I should not have the power to willingly and wittingly mislay your matchbox ever. I should be just as much afraid of you as I am now — I don't suppose you know why I am and it is difficult to explain. The fact is I am no more a human being than a gale of wind is. I have never had a human individual life. I have always been the doer of odd jobs and lived in the joys, sorrows, and worries of other people. It never occurs to me that I have any right to do anything more than now and then sit and warm myself at the fires of real human beings. I am grateful to them for letting me do this. I am fond of them, but I don't expect them to be fond of me and it's just as well I don't for there is not one of them who has ever cared for me apart from my services. Yes, that is why I offered to help you. . . . I am no better than the human beings I deal with in this matter of feeling — when they are happy and comfortable and smug, I lose all interest in them as well as they in me. It is quite mutual save that I have more reason to be grateful to them than they to me for it is through them I know this most amusing human world. But it is the non-human world I belong to myself. My people are mangrove swamps, rivers, and the sea and so on. We understand each other. They never give me the dazzles with their goings on like human beings do by theirs repeatedly.

My life has been a comic one. Dead tired and feeling no one had need of me anymore when my Mother and Father died within six weeks of each other in '92 and my brother went off to the East, I went down to West Africa to die. West Africa amused me and was kind to me and was scientifically interesting and did not want to kill me just then — I am in no hurry. I don't care one way or the other for a year or so. Well then my brother came back and I came home to look after him domestically as long as he wants me to do so. I must do it — it is duty, the religion I was brought up in. When he does not want me I go back to West Africa for the third time, perfectly content to stay there if it chooses: it is not the restful kind of place I thought it. It is just as fond of giving me odd jobs as up here has been, but taken as a whole I like the sort of Englishman that gives me odd jobs to do in West Africa better than I like the people in London drawing rooms. They seem better worth bothering after. . . .

There are men up here I like but am not afraid of, the Rt. Hon. Joe [Chamberlain], Antrobus, and dozens more including A. S. Jones. Then there are a better group of men I am afraid of in a scientific way. They depend on me and trust me . . . Tylor, Günther . . . Sir Alfred Lyall . . . but apart from this trust in me I do not care. And there is you and Sir George Goldie who don't trust me but who whether you do or no, I must be able to face clean handed. It would be so much easier to be cheaply cruel and cowardly, so much easier to lie by silence and save peoples' feelings, things it hurts me to hurt. But if I do it once I could not look you in the face again and I must be able to — it is the only thing worth having living or dead. I have never done one thing in my life I cannot face you with, I never shall. If you did not exist I should not be dishonourable. I should be just hard. There is no mortal reason why you should care one way or the other what I am. Sir George Goldie has to tolerate me because his wife loved me and he loved and loves her. You have no such link so I explain to you — but not to him — I am of no account to you, and I know it. I don't revel in it or should not write to you thus.

And finally Mary concluded her letter with, "Some day forgive me boring you with this, and remember as kindly as you can that melancholy thing that will always serve and fear you."

It is at the same time both the most ingenuous and calculating of letters. By insisting on the fundamental, unassailable isolation and alienation and the reckless despair that drove her to Africa, Mary presents herself as something of a romantic heroine. But she lacks the pride and defiance of the true romantic; instead, she confesses again and again her fear and need. There was no earthly reason why Mary should have feared Matthew Nathan; as she herself asserted in other letters, her own political power and influence were greater than his. Mary's fear of him sprang instead from the unexpressed declaration that permeates nearly every carefully chosen word in the letter: she had fallen in love with Nathan, and the power wielded by a loved one is far more terrifying than any other kind of power. To her grief, Mary discovered that to love was to be disarmed, reduced almost to a victim. Hence her highly uncharacteristic, cringing posture here. Her portion now was the helpless anxiety of all who love intensely and hopelessly — waiting in a state of tense expectation for the knock on the door, the postman's call, while a pale unreality bathes everything else in daily life. Her stated and reiterated fear of Nathan was also a kind of provocation; by insisting that she was afraid of him and that she knew he didn't "care one way or the other what I am. . . . I am of no account to you," Mary was also challenging him to refute these statements and declare once again that he *would* understand her.

The whole letter, written immediately after Nathan's departure, no doubt late at night when daytime emotional caution subsides, had an air of urgency. It was a gamble, this act of self-revelation and supplication, for it would be impossible for Nathan to respond to it temperately or noncommittally. He would either have to answer it in kind or not at all. The letter swiftly followed him out to the Coast. He reached Sierra Leone on March 24 and was sworn in as acting governor on the twenty-eighth. Mary's letter arrived two days later on the thirtieth. Nathan noted in his diary, "letter from Miss Kingsley" and then added in parentheses "her open soul." It is impossible to know whether he hesitated or debated in his own mind what he should do about the letter. All that is certain is that he did not answer it and indeed did not write Mary at all until the following August after she had sent him a letter of introduction for Maj. Ronald Ross, the medical doctor who went out to Sierra Leone in July and conducted research there that led to his discovery that malaria was not airborne but rather was transmitted by anopheline mosquitos.

For days, weeks, perhaps months, Mary must have waited for Nathan's reply as if her life hung in the balance. And then, as the silence stretched into April and May and she calculated and recalculated how long it would have taken her letter to reach Nathan and how long his reply would have taken to return to her, despair and regret must have supplanted anxiety and hope in her heart. What might she have given to retrieve or revoke the letter? It languished instead in some drawer or wastebasket in Government House in Freetown, and Nathan's refusal to answer it could have only one interpretation: that she was correct in her accusations that he did not care for her, that she was of no account to him. By June she must have realized that she had lost the gamble, that she had misunderstood Nathan's interest and gone too far. But writing the "gale of wind" letter was not an aberration for Mary; it was in fact of a piece with the rest of her actions since her parents had died. In pursuit of intensity, beauty, meaning, experience, even of duty, she did not flinch from taking risks. This letter to Matthew Nathan was one of the riskiest things she had attempted and one of the few that had unambiguously failed. Silently, unobtrusively, and completely alone, Mary endured the crisis of Nathan's rejection during the spring and summer of 1899. And when she had fully comprehended her loss — if one can speak of loss in connection with something that has never really been possessed — Mary was all the more ready and willing to take additional risks and to return to West Africa again since the one person in the London political world who might have reconciled her to it — Nathan — had made it clear there could be no real intimacy between them.

Once again Mary began the various preparations for returning to West Africa. In the course of answering Nathan's delayed and perfunctory August letter, she told him that she hoped to go out by the end of the year because Charley was making noises about going to China in December. She informed Tylor that she wanted to go to the middle Congo region this time. But then Charley as usual brought all Mary's plans to a halt. First he announced that he wanted to accompany her on her third journey, a prospect that dismayed her. As she wrote to a friend, "Unfortunately, my brother has taken it into his head to come with me this time which complicates matters for he is only fit to travel in savage countries where people can get about comfortably." Eventually Mary persuaded Charley that he was not cut out for the Coast, with the result that he remained an impediment to her for she had to stay in England with him. By the end of the year her plans once again had all come to naught, and she wrote Sir James Frazer's wife in December, "When I shall go out to West Africa I am not sure because of my brother. He is . . . a duty to me so I cannot leave him for my own pleasure, but I am . . . wearying to be away for life up here tires without interesting me."

She dealt with the tedium of London life and her homesickness for the Coast as she had previously: by engaging in a strenuous regimen of writing and lecturing. Much of the spring and summer was devoted to two projects: a short history of West Africa for the *Story of Empire* series published by Horace Marshall, and the long-deferred collection of George Kingsley's writings, *Notes on Sport and Travel*. Mary finally wrested the memoir of their father out of Charley's incompetent hands and finished it herself by the end of August. *The Story of West Africa* was also done with Kingsleyesque alacrity. "The little book," as Mary called it, involved "knocking off" West African history from Herod-

otus to the present "on a cabbage leaf," and the most congenial part of
it for Mary was rereading all her favorite travel and exploration books
from the days of Prince Henry the Navigator and the Portuguese explorations right through to the great nineteenth-century English explorers. Though two concluding chapters focused on Goldie's Royal
Niger Company and on Chamberlain and the Crown Colony system,
The Story of West Africa was essentially a historical survey of the European exploration of West Africa, synthesizing diverse sources into a
short (by Mary's standards, for it was only 165 pages) and highly readable account. It contained no mention of missionaries or the liquor
traffic, and Mary's discussion of the slave trade was severely edited and
defused in the galley proof stage. The result was one of Mary's most
entertaining but also least original and controversial books. When it
and *Notes on Sport and Travel* were published together in January 1900
they scarcely caused a ripple. Both were minor efforts compared with
Travels in West Africa and *West African Studies*, and by this time, too,
public interest in the continent was riveted on the escalating war in
South Africa.

During the spring Mary met the man Nathan had been sent out to
replace, Sir Frederick Cardew. Cardew was one of those cheerful, ob-
tuse colonial officers who blithely and unwittingly caused so much
damage in the countries they administered. He was back in London to
explain the hut tax war and to defend continued implementation of
the tax, and he and Mary — the most vocal opponent of the tax —
were destined to meet. On May 19 their paths crossed at an afternoon
at home, and they arranged to meet three days later to discuss the
situation in Sierra Leone in detail. Mary wrote Holt a full account of
what took place during her three-hour interview with Cardew and concluded that "I have learnt nothing beyond what I knew before, namely:
a) that he is an honest man, b) he believes in the hut tax as a civiliser,
c) he does not regard the African as anything but a savage." Subsequent meetings were equally fruitless, and all Mary's careful explanations of African law so much wasted breath. And yet she recognized in
Cardew a decent if completely misguided human being. "I believe in
Cardew's honesty," she wrote Holt, "just as I believe he could live in
an African colony for a century and know no more about it than a
policeman in the British Museum knows about cuneiform inscriptions
which he sees before his eyes every day for years."

Cardew had been recalled in expectation of the negative verdict on
the hut tax that the Chalmers report was expected to pronounce. Pub-

lication of the Chalmers report, in fact, had been seriously delayed so that Cardew could mount his defense. For Chamberlain at the Colonial Office was in a very awkward position; like Cardew, he considered it economically imperative to retain the tax, but at the same time he was responsible for appointing Sir David Chalmers to conduct an inquiry into the hut tax war and could scarcely ignore Chalmers's findings. In any event, Chamberlain did what nine out of ten men in his position probably would have done: he stalled. Chalmers's draft of the report was submitted to the Colonial Office in January 1899, but it was not published until the end of July. In the interim, a sequence of events occurred that muted its indictment of the tax. Cardew promulgated his own protax views; Chalmers himself became seriously ill and finally died scarcely a week after the report was published; and the events in South Africa made the hut tax war in tiny Sierra Leone shrink by comparison to something approaching insignificance. The end result of all this was that Cardew was vindicated and the tax retained.

Mary followed all these events with a kind of fatalistic dismay. And in a similar fashion she wearily submitted to the inevitable social round of her London life. However much she felt herself a supernumerary in the haut politique, friends and acquaintances did all they could to keep her center stage at their country weekends, homes, and dinner parties. In August St. Loe Strachey invited Mary to their house near Dorking to see Lord Cromer, who had specially requested to meet the celebrated Miss Kingsley. But some sort of domestic crisis was reigning at Saint Mary Abbott's Terrace, and Mary regretfully wrote that she would not be able to manage coming. Mrs. Strachey was thus highly surprised when she looked out the window on the Saturday morning Cromer was expected to see "the baker's cart trundling up the drive with a strange figure seated beside the baker." It was Mary, "sitting very stiff in her little black bonnet, and conveying somehow the impression of the figure-head of a ship." "A most interesting afternoon followed." Cromer afterward told Mrs. Strachey he had never met a woman who impressed him as much as Mary had, and Mary herself wrote Mrs. Strachey the next day, profusely thanking her for the "honor and pleasure" of meeting Cromer, "the big Ju-Ju of administration."

Far less congenial was Mary's attendance at a reception for Sarah Bernhardt. It was precisely the sort of occasion amidst precisely the sort of people that was calculated to bring Mary the maximum amount of social discomfort. Another guest observed that Mary looked as if she had just walked out of one of the books of the popular novelist, Charlotte Yonge, the maiden aunt, say, in the best-selling *Dynevor Terrace*. The Bernhardt fans milled about in the reception room of the Grafton Galleries while "the Diva was having a little supper with some fellow artistes in an inner salon. It was an exhilarating occasion, everyone seemed in the highest spirits except Miss Kingsley. Holding aloof from the animated groups around, grave as a judge, for an hour or more she paced up and down, her antiquated coiffure and dress rendering her all the more conspicuous." Finally the divine Sarah issued from her inner sanctum and "flashed by, electrifying the assemblage." But while the actress's thronged admirers pressed forward to meet her, Mary "retreated, gazing at Sarah Bernhardt from behind a hedge of eagerly craned heads."

If Mary was an awkward failure as a "drawing roomer," she still drew her own admiring crowds as a lecturer. She lectured throughout 1899, but her schedule became especially crowded after August, by which time she had finished both *The Story of West Africa* and *Notes on Sport and Travel*. In September she lectured at Torquay, Bradford, and Leicester, in October at Middlesbrough and at Bradford and Leicester again. But it was November that proved to be the real nightmare. She wrote Holt on the nineteenth how she had spoken on Friday the tenth at York for an organization "devoted to Roman remains and £3000 in debt." Then "Saturday evening I made Newcastle in spite of bad weather; Sunday I lectured to 2000 people in a theatre — drafty — on W.A. Monday ditto . . . Tuesday to Edinburgh and lectured to a high-toned Scotch audience on W.A. successfully. Wednesday partially recovered. Thursday Glasgow: awful goings-on, bonfire with magic lantern; Friday Dundee, 1800 people, great enthusiasm. Saturday reached Edinburgh again for repairs. Tomorrow, Monday, Aberdeen; Tuesday Glasgow again; Wednesday Horwich . . . Friday Birmingham, Saturday home . . . then Halifax and Birmingham again. But I will not dwell on the painful subject further," she told Holt, adding "what there will be left of me at the end of the month will be a mere memory, 10,000 colds, and an indifferent photograph which after all is more than I deserve."

One event Mary did not include in the lecture itinerary that she described to Holt was a debate she participated in at Trinity College, Cambridge, in early November. The Magpie and Stump Society left the motion up to Mary, and she proposed: "That it is better for us to understand alien races than for alien races to understand us." She spoke for sixty-nine minutes before the audience of more than two hundred undergraduates and according to the minutes of the meeting led "the house down the flowery paths of anecdote," before carrying them away with "the most cogent and convincing arguments." The two other speakers' brief contributions seemed both perfunctory and unconvincing after Mary's impassioned speech, and she carried the house by a large majority. Then before they adjourned at 11:30 P.M., the group unanimously elected Mary an honorary member of the society. Thus she finally entered the citadel of male learning that had been denied her all those years in Cambridge when she had only been able to glimpse it through the activities of her father and brother.

On occasion Mary presided over similar gatherings herself. When de Cardi gave a talk at the Anthropological Institute entitled "Ju Ju Law in the Niger Delta," which included a detailed account of female circumcision, Mary led the discussion after the lecture. She wrote E. D. Morel how she had also braved a tedious and interminable meeting of the British Empire League. Both she and Flora Shaw had recently been elected to its council, and so they shared the podium "side by side all the afternoon in sweet silence, listening to indistinct utterances from the speakers."

In the midst of all this frenetic lecturing Nathan returned to England from Sierra Leone at the end of October. Since her "gale of wind" letter back in March, Mary had only written to him twice: in July to introduce Major Ross and then again in August after Nathan had responded to the Ross letter. They both seemed to have agreed tacitly to pretend that Mary had never bared her "open soul." Mary's July and August letters are direct but impersonal. She speaks of her meetings with Cardew, the Chalmers report, ethnological matters, and the Liverpool traders, but says nothing of her own activities, much less her frame of mind. Still, her old idolizing of Nathan creeps in at the end. In July she wrote, "I often hear of you and nothing but praise," from indirect reports, in other words, for she had not heard *from* Nathan at all. She closed the August letter with even warmer words: "Believe me, Major Nathan, the *wonderful* way you have soothed down that restive colony, and made all men connected with it love you, I esteem as a great achievement, but who am I! Only yours very truly, M. H. Kingsley."

Nathan arrived back in London on October 29, but he did not call on Mary until November 9, and she was out. The next day she went to York to lecture and wrote him from there of her deep disappointment at having missed him. She implored him to come again as soon as she returned home, but Nathan didn't bother to call again until early January. For two months, then, Mary was on pins and needles: she was keenly aware that Nathan was close at hand, that she might run into him at any tea or dinner, that each time she opened her door to a caller she might find him on the threshold. She had also heard reports that he might be sent to South Africa — an alarming prospect — and she knew that he would be perfectly capable of departing without seeing her at all.

In the autumn of 1899 the long-smoldering crisis in South Africa came to a head. Chamberlain wanted a federated South Africa that would assimilate the independent Afrikaner republics, especially the Transvaal, which Britain had lost to the Afrikaners, who were led by Paul Kruger, in the first Boer War of 1880–81. Since then gold had been discovered in Witwatersrand, and Cecil Rhodes had obtained a royal charter for his British South Africa Company, become a millionaire, and established Rhodesia. Diamonds were still pouring out of Kimberley. As a result of all these developments, the influx of British settlers in South Africa increased dramatically. They and Chamberlain and Rhodes wanted more than the large piece of the pie they already possessed — Cape Colony, Natal, and Rhodesia. They also wanted the Transvaal back, and they wanted it soon.

In 1896 one of Rhodes's associates, Dr. L. S. Jameson, tried to annex the Transvaal by force. The idea was that the numerous non-Afrikaner inhabitants of the republic, most of them British, would spontaneously rise against their rulers if a conquering force were to arrive. Jameson organized a party of four hundred Rhodesian police to come to the rescue of the "Uitlanders," as these non-Afrikaner settlers were called. Across the border and into the Transvaal rode the four hundred to storm Johannesburg. But the Jameson Raid failed miserably. The Uitlanders did not rise up against the Afrikaners; instead they made peace with Kruger. Jameson and his men, deprived of the reinforcements they expected from Johannesburg, were swiftly and easily defeated by the Boer forces.

The spectacular failure of the Jameson Raid did not, however, extinguish British aspirations for the Transvaal. But now both Chamberlain and the new High Commissioner for South Africa, Sir Alfred Milner, were in favor of a strategy of gradual annexation, which they hoped could be initiated by extending the franchise to the Uitlanders in the Transvaal. Although the new non-Boer settlers constituted a sizeable portion of the population in the republic, they did not possess the vote and so were politically powerless. In order to debate this issue of the franchise for the Uitlanders, Milner and Kruger agreed to meet in the late spring of 1899, but they found it impossible to arrive at any sort of agreement. Milner broke off negotiations and cabled Chamberlain that he thought Kruger posed a real threat to the British colony of Natal. In September the British cabinet sent ten thousand men to defend Natal, and Kruger followed suit by mobilizing his own forces. Then on October 9 Kruger issued an ultimatum demanding that the British immediately withdraw their troops from the area of Natal bordering the Transvaal. When Milner and the Colonial Office failed to recall the troops or even to acknowledge the ultimatum, war broke out on October 11, as Kruger ordered his men to invade Natal. Thus commenced one of the "longest (two and three quarters years), the costliest (over £200 million), the bloodiest (at least 22,000 British, 25,000 Boer, and 12,000 African lives), and the most humiliating war for Britain between 1815 and 1914."

Despite the rumor, Nathan did not go to South Africa in a military, Colonial Office, or any other capacity. Instead he installed himself at his old desk in the War Office and resumed his duties as secretary of the Colonial Defence Committee. He was destined to observe the war from afar; for he sat at the receiving end of the telegraph line from which issued bulletins about the escalating situation at the Cape. Mary's response to the war was complex. She deplored the way it diverted attention and funds from the still pressing problems in West Africa, and it was definitely not her kind of "imperial show." But of course it had all the potential to be a heart-breaking affair, and she was in no frame of mind to watch passively in London as the war unrolled. Accordingly, in December she volunteered to go to the Cape — or wherever else she was needed — to nurse. For some time now she had been actively involved in the Colonial Nursing Association, writing and speaking on its behalf and lobbying for the establishment of of a regular corps of female and male nurses to serve on hospital ships and in coastal stations in all the colonies, but most especially in West Africa where "King Death" reigned supreme. Well did she know from her own experience the truth of the old adage, "Beware, beware the Bights of Benin; for every ten who go in, nine remain."

It was not surprising, then, that as a champion of the C.N.A. and with her own years of nursing experience Mary should apply to the War Office to be sent to South Africa to serve as an army nurse. But she also contacted various journalists and newspaper editors to sound out the possibility of covering the war as a correspondent. And she called on Dr. Günther too at the Natural History Museum to see whether he was in need of some freshwater fish from, say, the Orange River, right in the middle of the war zone. Finally, to close friends Mary confided an even more far-reaching scheme: after nursing, reporting, and fishing in South Africa, she planned to return finally to West Africa. But it was northern Nigeria and Lake Chad, far inland from the Coast, that she set her heart on this time. Remote terrain, devoid of missionaries and traders, for the most part, this region had ancient walled cities like Kano and Sokoto and a rich Islamic culture reaching back as far as any European civilization.

South Africa, then, was to be a kind of diversionary route back to the West African world Mary had been longing for and abortively planning to return to for nearly four years now. It also offered a duty that could transcend the perennial impediment of Charley. Duty to Empire, especially the peculiarly female duty of nursing the sick and the wounded, overruled even domestic duty to hearth and home and to an irksome, dependent brother. But liberation from the drawing rooms of the haut politique and from the drafty lecture halls of learned societies was not to be so easily achieved. Mary's initial application to the War Office was turned down: she was told that she "was not wanted and [the war] would all be over in no time."

Mary was not so sanguine about the speedy conclusion of the war and so patiently bided her time. When Matthew Nathan belatedly turned up at Saint Mary Abbott's Terrace on January 10, 1900, he brought all the latest news of South Africa, but according to his diary, he spent nearly all of his visit talking to Mary's friend Mrs. Im Thurn. Mary had not seen Nathan for nearly a year now, and she had been waiting more than two months for him to call, but then when he finally did come there was no real opportunity to talk in anything other than standard teatime formulas. Such were the givens of Victorian social life. Unless one hemmed and hawed and requested a few words out in the hall as Nathan had on the brink of his departure for Sierra Leone, there was virtually no privacy, no possibility of intimacy. So they chatted over the teacups and cakes, and then Nathan went away again while the other guests remained, leaving Mary in a pall of frustration and regret.

Several days later she sent Nathan a copy of *Notes on Sport and Travel,* which he duly acknowledged. Mary then responded to his note by asking him to tea, and Nathan obligingly stopped by on Friday, January 26, on his way home from the office. This time it was a tête-à-tête, but they talked impersonally — if intensely — of political issues, especially the hut tax, which Nathan persisted in supporting to Mary's dismay. The next day Mary wrote him a long addendum to their conversation, reiterating her attack on the tax: "I know I am beaten on that West African thing. I am always beaten, but for all that I never submit. . . . I won't lift a finger to help Cardew and the Bishop of Sierra Leone and the Crown Colony system at large out of the mess it is in." She then went on to assert that she wielded power among educated Africans, whose confidence she said she alone possessed, among whites. The veering patterns of Mary's behavior toward Nathan — oscillating between the extremes of servility and intellectual and political arrogance — was thus reestablished. But because Nathan had made it clear that he would not respond to her fawning "open soul," Mary was cornered into her combative, political spokeswoman role as she tried to resume regular communication with him.

The letters she wrote Nathan in January, February, and early March concern such matters as the Colonial Nursing Association, educational reform in Sierra Leone, and the increasingly grave developments in South Africa, as well as the perennial theme of the hut tax. Only occasionally does she strike a personal note, observing, for example, in early February that she "was sorry to see you looking not well yesterday." For they were meeting at fairly regular intervals in these months, though rarely alone. Indeed, Mary was often careful to couch her invitations in terms that would indicate to Nathan that others would also be present. She would humorously reassure him that "you will not have unmitigated me, but it will be tempered by Lady Macgregor," or that "if you come on Saturday you can help me shout down Leslie Stephen's trumpet and wrestle generally with a group of depressed metaphysicians." Still, despite the company of deaf Leslie Stephen and depressed metaphysicians, the frequency of Mary's letters and invitations to Nathan show that she was still trying to sound his depths and also that she was still unable to realize that he had none to fathom. Nathan was consolidating his gains with Mary; he knew very well, without her telling him, that she possessed power and influence. He came round after the office or on Sunday afternoons and argued the hut tax or discussed hospital ships in West Africa and then disappeared to his club or home to dinner with his mother while Mary closed out the day in her sitting room, which seemed palpably steeped in frustration and longing.

These opening weeks and months of the new century were, by Mary's standards, especially lonely and unproductive. She saw little of Alice Green; a lull occurred in her correspondence with Holt; and Gwynn was also an infrequent visitor. For the first time in five years she had no book underway, and so her contact with George Macmillan languished too. Her lecturing was also in abeyance: she spoke only once in January, on colonial nursing, and twice in February, on West Africa from an ethnographical point of view at the Imperial Institute and on the issue of the vote for women at the Fawcett Society, which was founded in honor of the famous Victorian suffragette, Millicent Fawcett. It was in this lecture that Mary's antifeminism reached its fullest expression, though, sadly, the transcript of the lecture is now lost. Her flippant report of it to Nathan — geared almost certainly to his own hostility to women's rights — survives, however. She wrote him how "I have been opposing women having the parliamentary vote this afternoon and have had a grand time of it and have been called an idealist and had poetry slung at me in chunks. Argument was impossible so I offered to fight the secretary in the back yard but she would not so you can all write me down impracticable."

This antisuffrage lecture no doubt ran along the same lines as Mary's statements opposing the admission of women into learned societies: women could do more good and achieve greater things by sticking to their own separate sphere, by playing a complementary though not necessarily inferior role to men. "Shrieking androgyns," on the other hand, were apt to accomplish nothing at all or, by virtue of their strident demands, provoke a backlash that would actually hinder progress for women. Such were the views that Mary must have propounded before her female audience at the Fawcett Society, yet most of these women surely grasped how all Mary's endeavors — her travels, books, political activities — wholly contradicted every word she uttered. Except for the constraints created by her family — by her mother in the pre-African years and by Charley ever since — no separate sphere had ever confined Mary. She had made contributions, become famous, wielded power in an almost exclusively male world; her "sphere" was the sphere of Macmillan, Holt, Tylor, Günther, Gwynn, Chamberlain, and Nathan.

Many of these men in fact were in the audience when Mary delivered

her Imperial Institute lecture on February 12. It was a brilliant, moving, and funny talk, offering no new information or views, but rather
synthesizing and skillfully weaving together all Mary's cherished themes:
economic imperialism, indirect rule, West African medicine, fetish,
secret societies, and so on — a kind of coda to everything she had been
writing and lecturing on for the past five years. Some of the comic
moments were brought about inadvertently. At one point Mary broke
out into a eulogy of a former colonial administrator in the Far East. At
the end of the lecture an elderly gentleman approached Mary on the
platform and identified himself as the object of her praise. " 'Hullo!'
said Mary, 'I thought you were dead.' 'No,' he replied, 'but I thought
I was forgotten.' " The other farcical episode in the lecture Mary confided to a friend in a letter the next day. She had been more mobile
than usual on the lecture platform, not standing statuesquely behind
the podium, as was her wont. She dryly observed, "I dare say you
noticed that I was jumping about like a cat on hot bricks last night."
Something had gone awry with the heating apparatus under the stage,
with the result that she had had to stand for more than an hour on a
surface so hot that the soles of her boots were burnt through.

What made the lecture deeply moving, however, was that it was a
kind of valediction. By this time, mid-February 1900, Mary had been
told by the War Office that she could expect to be sent to South Africa
early in March, and her awareness of her impending departure permeated the talk, a departure for a war front from which she openly
confessed she might not return. She began the lecture with an apology
for speaking on West Africa "when it is South Africa you are all so
deeply interested in" and then went on to confess, "I often feel as I am
sure the lady who told the tales in the *Arabian Nights* often felt, namely
that I shall get killed before I am half through with my information,
and moreover, I have more real cause for fear . . for the information I
have had to give about West Africa is far less charming than her tales
were and my grammar and composition infinitely inferior to hers. But
up to tonight you have been very kind and tolerant to me about my
West African discourses and I humbly beg to thank you all most sincerely on this, the last night I shall, in all human probability, have
the honour of speaking to London."

The lecture concluded on the same elegiac note and echoed back not
merely to Mary's opening words but to the whole course of her life
since she had returned from the Coast in 1895. "I thank you for your
toleration of me," she closed. "I know I owe it to the name I bear; I

know I owe all that is good in me to the blood of my ancestors; my Imperialism is their Imperialism, rather out of fashion in late years . . . but if I were to depart from that and preach certain doctrines in modern imperialism, it's a warm reception I should get from my family and the old merchant adventurers when I arrive at where they are held now to dwell — Fiddler's Green. Goodbye and fare you well, for I am homeward bound."

Home — West Africa — was the longed-for destination. But South Africa was Mary's immediate terminus, and most of her departure preparations in February were geared to her arrival at Cape Town. She negotiated with both the *Evening News* and the *Morning Post* to report on the war. She had several khaki drill nursing uniforms made up and bought a felt broad-brimmed hat to complete the outfit. For the first time in years she would shed her black silk dresses and woolen skirts like a mourning chrysalis. Then there was fish-collecting gear to be got from Dr. Günther and countless other matters to be looked after. As she wrote Nathan, "I am as busy as the devil in a high wind, and very feeble from having had another attack of influenza this past week."

Yet all these predeparture maneuvers were unmitigated chores because Mary lacked the keen excitement and eager anticipation she had felt on the eve of her West African travels. She wrote Nathan how she had been trying "to get an idea of South African politics before going out and have done it to the extent of realising what an awful mess they are and horribly sad. I wonder why I am not allowed to have a cheerful single port of call in this world — I suppose I am saving up for Fiddler's Green."

On Sunday, March 4, Mary wrote Holt, "I have only got things definitely settled within the last 24 hours. I sail Saturday from Southampton on the Union Liner Moor so I shall not see Liverpool again for a dreary long time." On Thursday the eighth, she wrote Nathan the same news. She had last seen him on February 28 at the Montagus' — almost exactly a year after they first met at the properous banker's home — and now she asked him please to call on the next evening: "It goes without saying I shall be glad if you can come."

By Friday afternoon all of Mary's elaborate preparations were complete, and she dined early with Charley at home. Alice Green had managed to persuade Mary to allow her to go to Southampton the next day, and all Mary's other farewells — to Holt, Morel, Gwynn, Macmillan, and others — had been made. So she was on her own Friday evening, waiting for Nathan. No more letters to write, nothing left to pack, and it was impossible to read. The evening stretched ahead like a prison sentence; time — measured out by the clock's pendulum — slowed to a halting gait. Mary sat in her overheated sitting room alone this last night in England, while across town Nathan dined with his mother, worked on an encyclopedia article he had been commissioned to write, and then retired to bed early.

It is impossible to know how late Mary sat up before the fire waiting, or whether she even went to bed at all. But clearly this final vigil closed certain doors within her. It must have seemed that she was leaving nothing behind — no one, no work, no legacy of any sort. She had been stranded in England for more than four years, and now the ties that had moored her unwillingly were severed. Early on the morning of March 10 she took the train to Southampton with Alice Green to embark on her last voyage "homeward bound."

Part Five

Exultation is the going
Of an inland soul to sea,
Past the houses — past the headlands —
Into deep Eternity —

Bred as we, among the mountains,
Can the sailor understand
The divine intoxication
Of the first league out from land?

Emily Dickinson

·ᔑ 14 ᔐ·

The Final Bound

Mary's farewell to Alice Green on the crowded, congested Southampton dock was a heart-wrenching one. The *Moor* was a twenty-eight-hundred-ton mail ship of the Union Line now called into service as a troop carrier. As the two women embraced on the quay, troops in dull khaki milled about them, cases of ammunition were wrestled into the ship's hold, guns and artillery carried on board, not to mention copious supplies of food and other provisions to sustain the ship's teeming population on the nearly three-week voyage to the Cape. Mary and Alice stood "harrowing each other's feelings," as Mary later put it, in a turbulent sea of soldiers, sailors, and deck hands — saying goodbye in the chill gray air of a March morning with the unspoken urgency of those who know they may never meet again. Then Mary went up the gangplank, and as the *Moor* weighed anchor, she waved from the deck to the solitary figure of Alice left behind on the pier.

This passage to South Africa bore no resemblance to Mary's previous voyages out. The *Moor* was no *Lagos,* nor was its harassed and overworked Captain Tysen at all like the genial Captain Murray. Instead of an eccentric collection of coarse traders, prim missionaries, neophyte shipping agents, and weatherbeaten seamen, the *Moor* carried more than 650 soldiers, two brass bands, and other assorted military personnel destined for the war front. The decks, cabins, and saloons — all conceivable nooks and crannies — were occupied. Toilet facilities were minimal, water scarce, and ventilation, because of the abundance of supplies, very poor. Hygiene and sanitation under such circumstances deteriorated drastically, and the daily diet of tinned pork and fish was inadequate to counteract the unhealthiness of the abysmal living conditions. The result was that after only several days at sea the war already began to take its toll as men succumbed to dysentery and other ailments. Then, as they moved farther south, the heat brought about further suffering for the soldiers, who were garbed in thick gray flannel shirts and khaki woolen trousers. And the heat also nourished the *Moor*'s resident microbes and bacteria, which increased the number of sick on board. Mary perforce commenced her nursing duties as a consequence of all these miserable conditions. She began innoculating the men against enteric fever, in the long run a wise move, but in the short run the vaccine itself made them ill, and if they weren't suffering from the enteric serum or from other ailments, they could be counted upon to be acutely seasick. "Flat ironing the ocean would not avail" to prevent it, Mary wrote Strachey. In addition, several men contracted pneumonia, and one poor fellow died and had to be buried at sea. Inadvertently, Mary found herself on what amounted to one of the hospital ships she had been trying to convince the Colonial Office to establish, except that the *Moor* of course lacked sufficient medical supplies and personnel to cope with all its suffering passengers.

There was also perpetual uproar on board from sources other than the vocally ill. Those men who managed to remain reasonably well or at least vertical whiled away their time by discharging upwards of six thousand rounds of ammunition at the waves, since they were unable to devise a floating target. Such shooting practice gave them an opportunity to learn how to handle their guns, but the real reason was that the bullets were dumdums, the most lethal kind of bullet, which explodes on impact, and dumdums were illegal in South Africa and could not be unloaded at Cape Town. Of the bungling and waste of shipping out thousands of rounds of ammunition that could be used only against blameless dolphins, seagulls, or offending waves, Mary cryptically observed to Strachey, "thereby hangs a tale *not for publication*." Finally, as a kind of background accompaniment to the groans of the sick and to the firing practice, the military bands practiced daily out on the decks, and in the evenings a gramophone took over musical duty.

Of all these lively and noisy goings-on Mary gave a full report to Matthew Nathan in a letter written in the Bay of Biscay on March 14, four days after she sailed from Southampton. It was a friendly, amusing, but carefully neutral letter, and it made no mention of Nathan's failure to appear on the eve of her departure. When Nathan received

Mary's letter on March 23, predictably he did not reply. And thus their relationship, fraught with so much need and anxiety and pain on Mary's part and met with urbane indifference or embarrassment on Nathan's, dwindled to its undramatic end. Mary had destroyed Nathan's few letters, including the one in which he declared that he would understand her, perhaps on her last night before sailing when Nathan did not come to say "goodbye and fare you well." This last Bay of Biscay letter was an empty gesture — like throwing a life line to someone who is in no danger of drowning.

Mary also wrote to Alice Green from the Bay of Biscay and to St. Loe Strachey on March 22, the latter letter locating her somewhere in the "South Atlantic Ocean." More surprisingly, however, given the hubbub and lack of privacy on the *Moor,* Mary wrote two highly interesting pieces on shipboard, perhaps late at night in her cramped cabin, perhaps in some empty corner of the poop deck above the crowd of soldiers. The first was an article entitled "An Early African Voyage" and is a swashbuckling account of the voyage of one Captain Phillips on the *Hannibal* to Africa and to the West Indies in 1693 and 1694. Captain Phillips had more than his full share of catastrophes and diversions: sea battles and shipwrecks, pirates, madmen, hostile African rulers, tropical storms, plague epidemics, and so forth. Quite possibly Mary had worked up Captain Phillips's gripping picaresque tale for *The Story of West Africa* and then had to omit it for reasons of space. In any event, it must have been a great relief for her to be able to retreat from life on the *Moor* to Captain Phillips and the *Hannibal.* This was the world in which Mary had dwelt in her childhood reading long ago in Highgate: a world where captains brandished gleaming swords and pirates had hooks for hands and patches over their eyes. Africa then had been a continent of dream and desire, not a political arena, not a geographical pie to be randomly carved up, not the battleground of fetid trenches and guerrilla commando units the *Moor* was inexorably moving toward.

Mary's second work written on the *Moor* was a long letter to the African editor of the *New Africa*. If Captain Phillips's story was a nostalgic celebration of the Africa of Mary's imagination, the *New Africa* letter was one of her most definitive statements on African culture and government. One has the sense reading it that she is setting the record straight and that she is speaking here not to uncomprehending colonial officials but to Africans themselves. As a testament the letter synthesizes all of Mary's long-held convictions: that the African's future should *not* lie in the direction of progressive westernization, and that Africans must protect their institutions and laws from colonial interference and from those "stay-at-home statesmen [who] think that Africans are awful savages or silly children." Mary's fear here is that Africans rely too heavily upon Christianity as their weapon against cultural and legal colonization by the English and the French. "I know," she says, "that there is a general opinion among the leading men of both races that Christianity will give the one possible solution to the whole problem. I fail to believe this. I fail to believe Christianity will bring peace between the two races, for the simple reason that though it may be possible to convert Africans *en masse* into practical Christians, it is quite impossible to convert Europeans *en masse*. . . . I have had to stand up alone these two years," Mary continues, "and fight for African freedom and institutions while Africans equally and better educated in English culture have been talking about religious matters, etc. to a pack of people *who do not care* about Christianity at all."

In place of Christianity, Mary comes out and calls for the power of African nationalism to thwart colonial oppression. You must, she asserts, "come forward and demonstrate that African nationalism is a good thing . . . [for] unless you preserve your institutions, above all your land law, you cannot, no race can, preserve your liberty." She is calling, in short, for racial and cultural integrity and pride. The Colonial Office and the missionaries had contaminated both and in so doing divided and ruled Africans. Only a self-conscious and even militant African nationalism could avert further harm, in Mary's view, and this nationalism should come from Africans themselves.

On March 28 the *Moor* finally reached Cape Town. The place, ironically, almost seemed a vision of paradise. Here the deep blue of the Atlantic and the vibrant turquoise of the Indian Ocean merge at the southernmost tip of the continent. Cape Town lies nestled beneath the massive, brooding shadow of Table Mountain and with its straight, paved, bustling streets, well-built, gabled houses, and solid, brick buildings seems oblivious to the geographical splendor of the mountain looming up behind it. To Mary, Cape Town must have looked as if it had been plucked from the shores of some placid Netherlands lake. But the mountain and the confluence of the two mighty oceans encroached on this particle of domesticated Europe dropped down in their midst. It wasn't West Africa, it wasn't "the Coast," but the grandeur of Table Mountain conjured visions of Mount Cameroon and the pounding surf and the endless ribbon of ocean and bleached sand that bordered the whole west side of the continent. If the Cape wasn't home, it felt at first like a way station or bivouac on the way there.

Almost immediately upon arrival Mary reported to General Wilson, the principal medical officer at Cape Colony, to receive her assignment. It was not a congenial one, and Wilson in fact expected her to refuse it. The most pressing medical need was not among the British troops but rather among the large number of sick and wounded Boer prisoners of war who had been herded down to the Cape. The healthy ones were being held in internment camps, the sick on ill-equipped hospital ships in Simonstown Bay. But a new, makeshift hospital had just been opened in the old Palace Barracks in Simonstown, and it was in desperate need of staff. Would Mary go? Without hesitation she said she would. Sickness and death obliterated the distinction between countryman and foe; both the British and the Boers were victims of Imperialism gone amuck, the "heart-breaking smash" of this war.

And so Mary went to Simonstown, on the other side of the the peninsula from the Cape of Good Hope and found a kind of miniature Cape Town: it was neat and tidy, with well-laid-out, tree-lined streets running parallel to the graceful arc of Simonstown Bay. The Palace Barracks, or Palace Hospital, as it was now called, lay at the northern end of the town. It had been built at the end of the eighteenth century as a private house and was now in a sorry state of disrepair. Wards were set up in the largest rooms on the first and second floors. Here narrow iron beds with rough, sacking cloth sheets were lined up. The walls were streaked with dirt and peeling paint. Recumbent patients who were not unconscious or delirious could imagine designs or pictures in the sprawling cracks in the ceiling.

When Mary began duty at the "Palace" there was only one doctor, Gerard Carré, and two nurses, Nurse Rowlandson and Nurse Jackson, to care for upwards of two hundred patients, though by the end of April the staff was augmented by two more doctors, three more nurses, and a number of male orderlies. Most of the patients were victims of the February battle at Paardeberg, in which the Boer Gen. Piet Cronje had finally surrendered at the end of the month, but not before an appalling number of lives had been lost on both sides. Paardeberg had been trench warfare at its ghastliest. As Mary wrote Alice Green, most of her patients were "Cronje's men who . . . had been living underground with dead men and horses and drinking the decoction thereof." The result of these conditions was a virulent epidemic of typhoid or

enteric fever among the surviving captured Boers, with here and there
a case of measles thrown in for good measure. In addition, the Palace
housed failed escapees from the prisoner-of-war camps; these were men
wounded in the act of flight who were then brought to the Palace, to
suffer, more often than not, an agonizing death as the price for their
bid for freedom. As Mary wrote to Strachey, "I never struck such a
rocky bit of the Valley of the Shadow of Death in all my days as the
Palace Hospital."

The only relief Mary had from this grim world of suffering and
death was on her visits to the home of Rudyard Kipling and his American wife Carrie at nearby Wynberg. Kipling, the unofficial poet lau-
reate of the British Empire, was on the scene to observe this greatest
of imperial battles. Mary had known Kipling slightly in London and
admired some of his work, though she intensely disliked his jingoistic
"White Man's Burden." Indeed, she publicly refuted it in the pages of
West Africa and claimed that "it is the black man's burden that wants
singing . . . for the poor [African] has to put up with a lot of windy-
headed fads and foolishnesses no good to him or to the white man, and
a jest for the Gods." Kipling, on his side, admired Mary without
reservation. "Being human," he said, "she must have feared some things,
but one never arrived at what they were." Mary's life now at the Palace
Hospital only confirmed Kipling's awe for her bravery. She got into
the habit of coming round to the Kiplings' for tea or an early supper,
just as the sun was setting. And "sitting on the stoep, her hands quite
still in her lap, and looking across the Cape flats to the coloured ranges
beyond, she would tell of single-handed night vigils over fever-striken
men whose speech she hardly understood."

But the Kiplings left South Africa for England in the middle of
April, and then when Mary was off duty she remained alone in her
small room in the officers' quarters attached to the hospital. But even
when she was off the wards, she couldn't leave them behind. She could
not get out from under this rocky bit of the Valley of the Shadow of
Death any more than she had been able to escape her mother's darkened sickroom so many years before. The commissioned newspaper
articles remained unwritten, the fish-collecting gear unopened. Instead, Mary sat up late into the night trying to explain to those she
felt could understand the heart-breaking spectacle she was participating in at the Palace in Simonstown. She wrote St. Loe Strachey, "with
my usual luck I have dropped in for a repulsive job," and then went
on,

It is no use attempting to describe the thing: the rows of narrow iron bedsteads with sack-cloth sheets and mud-coloured blankets mixed among the aforesaid. More or less on the bed [is] a big bearded man, or a boy of sixteen or seventeen, delirious, in a typical typhoid way moaning and muttering, and now and then talking to his people at home or fighting a fight over again, in kitchen Dutch and in English. One boy, who for twenty-four hours kept on calling "Miss Johannes, please come down, down here," I shall not forget in a hurry, nor a giant of a man in mortal agony ten hours, and three sizes too big for the bed even if he had been quiet — and for the matter of that many more.

Well, the hospital is on two floors, divided into wards on each. Suppose you are tackling the giant, putting some of him in bed, and feeding him, you hear "Miss Johannes" going on, an under chorus of groans and racking coughs, then a "flump" which means some man whose life depends on his being quite quiet in bed is out on the floor, and you leave the giant, or whoever you have in hand, and go for the flumper, for if you don't he'll kill another man by getting in on top of him. Meanwhile, there is an unutterable stench and things Herodotus would not name in all directions. Moreover, the Boers are family men, and when you rouse one to feed or physic him he asks after his family and then after his trousers because of the money in them. If there is a member of his family in the hospital, as in very many cases there are, that man is dead or dying. As for his trousers, they are in a heap in the back yard, so you lie both ways. I do, and say "It's all right" in both cases which I know it isn't, or that "I will find out" which I know I can't, and the patient returns to his oblivion and I to another patient.

The other two nurses are equally endangering their bodies and souls with other patients on the other floors. Here there is another feature in the affair which is unpleasing. When a man is dying definitely, you don't like the two next to turn to see the performance, so you trot off and find two little screens. Well, the other two know what those screens mean perfectly well, only they think they are there for them, so they start off on dying too. We have had four or five a night dying under these conditions since I was here on Sunday. Then there are the never-to-be-forgotten bugs and lice. They swarm. The Palace supplies the bugs free of charge, the patients the lice; they get on well together and make common cause on humanity, of course including you.

Well, I will dwell no more on this thing. I am back on night duty tonight, and things are mending. We had yesterday a new doctor sent in all to ourselves, and he is doing marvels, for we had no deaths last night and only two in the afternoon, and we also had three more nurses, two hospital ones and a good lady who is district nurse, and who keeps on assuring the doctors, myself, and the other nurses that she is especially experienced in midwifery. Now until that woman came I should have said that there was no resource of civilisation that could not be found useful and thoroughly wanted by the Palace. Now I see I was hasty, and a midwife is a thing not required. She is a good soul, however, and very kindly and useful, and failing the performance of her practice, she does her best. And under the influence of the food we have poured into them and the new doctor's physic, the patients are quieting down somewhat, for how long we do not know.

To keep things cheerful, last night when we were at dinner we heard guns, which means prisoners were escaping from the camp. About 2:30 this morning there were brought in two men, a black shot through the kidneys fatally and accidentally in the skirmish, and a bayoneted Boer, one who had tried to get away. We got them into bed and expect they will die tonight when we are on duty again, and as we rather expect three more deaths tonight too, I shall be glad when it is tomorrow.

Mary's letter to Strachey remained unfinished and unsent, and so too did another, written to Flora Shaw of all people. The latter was a more somber, briefer version of the Strachey letter; it was almost certainly addressed to Shaw in her capacity as the *Times*'s colonial editor and intended for publication in the paper. She neglected most of her other habitual correspondents — John Holt, George Macmillan, George Goldie, Hatty Johnson, and Violet Roy — in part, perhaps, because of her grueling nursing schedule and the paralyzing exhaustion that overcame her during her few off-duty hours. But Mary's uncharacteristic silence must have also stemmed from her overwhelming conviction that there was no way she could make those back in England comprehend the unrelieved nightmare she was living out at the Palace. Disease, suffering, pain, and death were no strangers to her; she had lived with, struggled against, and been periodically, even repeatedly, defeated by them in England as well as in West Africa. One can face and accept King Death when he strikes unaided by human volition: in old age or through incurable diseases, in deadly climates, as a result of accidents. But what Mary was having to witness and attempt to combat at the Palace was the deliberate, wanton destruction of human life by human beings. She saw farm boys brought in pierced by bayonets, Boers with their intestines spilling out of ghastly wounds, bones protruding from limbs destined to gangrene, bodies maimed, crushed, mutilated. Kipling was right in saying that Mary was fearless, but even the brave can be broken — not by fear or loss, but by an irremediable despair that infects the heart, poisons hope, annihilates meaning, and finally destroys the will to live. And when one travels to those barren reaches within there is no returning.

It was from this inner wasteland that Mary wrote her last letter to Alice Green from Simonstown. After describing the epidemic of enteric fever in general terms, she told Alice how "today I have had over 100 patients under my own charge. Killing work." But even in extremity Mary couldn't refrain from striking a macabre, humorous note. The patients, if sufficiently strong, tended to "flit about" the wards in their night shirts when delirious, and capturing them was tricky work. "In malarial fever wanderers," Mary explained, "I had always the seat of the patient's pyjamas to get a grip on, but they wear no pyjamas here. Nothing but a flying shirt tail, but I am getting handy with that and am regularly called in to field wanderers in the other wards."

"One man," she continued in a different vein, "who has given me a twister of a time of it, and whom I felt sure I would lose, came through his crisis today all right and the first thing he said was, 'You are always here.' 'Count on it,' said I, 'stay in bed.' 'You must be so tired,' he said. I agreed with him."

And so she was — always there and always tired — but as Mary frankly confessed to Alice at the end of the letter:

> I am down in the ruck of life again. Whether I shall come up out of this . . . I don't know. It is a personally risky game I am playing here and it is doubtful. . . . All this work here, the stench, the washing, the enemas, the bedpans, the blood, is my world. Not London society, politics, that gateway into which I so strangely wandered — into which I don't care a hairpin if I never wander again. Take care of yourself. You can do so much more than I in . . . the "haut politique" and remember it is this haut politique that makes me have to catch large powerful family men by the tails of their night shirts at midnight, stand over them when they are sinking, tie up their jaws when they are dead. Five and six jaws a night have I had of late to tie up. *Damn* the haut politique.

The world of the Palace — the stench, the washings, the enemas, bedpans, and blood — was of course a dangerously infectious one. Mary began to smoke again, even while on duty, and to drink wine in the evenings. She explained to Dr. Carré and to Nurse Rae, the two people she was closest to at the Palace, that she hoped the cigarettes and wine would help ward off infections. Undoubtedly, too, she resorted to them as stimulants and sedatives, for the physical and psychological strain of attempting to convert the Palace "from a mortuary to a sanitorium," as Carré put it, was slowly but inexorably grinding Mary down. By the middle of May she was almost constantly feverish and found it next to impossible to take any food, but she insisted to the other nurses that it was merely "a touch of the West Coast fever" she had had and recovered from so many times before.

But Mary had been nursing typhoid patients for nearly two months and could not hide from herself, as she did for a time from others, the true significance of her symptoms. First came headache, fever, dizziness, and aching joints — symptoms similar to but more intense than those of malaria. Then the real horror of enteric fever set in as the typhoid bacilli invaded and proliferated: bleeding from the nose, slowed pulse despite a very high fever, a sore, thickly coated tongue, and worst of all, acute stomach pain, diarrhea, dehydration, and delirium. Mary needed no map for her prognosis. She lay on her bed in her small room in a fog of pain, weakness, and delirium. Sometimes oblivion would blot out the pain and transport her back to the Coast, to the moon-silvered Ogooué and the forests possessed of the hush and beauty of a cathedral. These were the redemptive reveries, and in them she dwelt again with "my people . . . mangrove swamps, rivers, and the sea and so on." But other memories must also have obtruded and featured figures like Nathan, Charley, George Kingsley, and finally her mother, Mary Bailey Kingsley, supine on a bed, muffled in depression, dying by slow degrees.

Nurse Rae's room was adjacent to Mary's, and on the morning of June 1 Mary managed to stumble from her bed and ask Nurse Rae to summon Dr. Carré. Her stomach pain was unbearable, and when Carré came he confirmed Mary's suspicion that the virulent enteric bacteria must have perforated her intestine. Her only hope now was surgery, and she consented when Carré said it must be performed immediately.

The operation was successful and the perforation sewed up. Mary regained consciousness early the next day, June 2. But she was very weak and aware of the severity of her condition. All her life she had been waging battles, but over this one, within her own body, she had the least control. In the end it was her heart that mutinied. By the evening of the second she knew she was dying, and she asked to speak to Dr. Carré in private. Back in Highgate Cemetery there was a narrow, dank, brick-lined vault designed to hold four coffins stacked one on top of the other. The vault was already half filled, and thousands of miles away in Simonstown Mary saw its yawning darkness opening to receive her. The thought was unendurable; she could never rest in that cold, subterranean prison. She made Carré promise her that she would be buried at sea, off the Cape of Good Hope, at the bottom of the heart-shaped continent that had governed her life and that now would claim her as one of its own.

At first Carré demurred, insisting that she was rallying, that the operation had saved her. But when he saw that Mary was in earnest, he conceded the gravity of her condition and the onset of heart failure, and he promised to carry out her last wishes. Mary then made one final request of him and Nurse Rae and the others. It was a simple but for them an exceedingly painful one to fulfill. She asked them all to leave her, to let her die alone, to close with life on her own terms and in her own way. She explained that she did not want them to see her in her weakness, but even more important, she knew that she must make this last, fearful journey in a life marked by dangerous travels, alone.

Reluctantly they did as she asked, only leaving the door of her room ajar. When Mary was "beyond knowledge," as Nurse Rae put it, and unconscious, they went back to her. The coma did not last long. Mary Kingsley had never shrunk from, never lingered over, any task, any duty, any "odd job," and now she did not protract the process of her dying. Dr. Carré and Nurse Rae remained with her throughout the night. Early on the morning of Sunday, June 3, her breathing began to falter, and soon after her heart peacefully and painlessly ceased to beat.

Dr. Carré began seeing to the funeral arrangements almost immediately. The body was moved from the hospital to the main army barracks, and Carré gained permission from the authorities not only for the burial at sea but also for a combined naval and military ceremony. Mary no doubt would have objected strenuously, but to those who had known and worked with her at the Cape she was a war heroine and had to be laid to rest with full military honors. Carré also signed the death certificate, giving Mary's age erroneously as thirty-five rather than thirty-seven. He repeated this error on the inscribed plate attached to her heavy teak coffin with brass fittings. The plate was engraved thus:

Mary H. Kingsley
Aged 35
Died at Simon's Town
Whilst Nursing Boer Prisoners of War
June 3, 1900

The day after Mary's death, Monday, June 4, the funeral party set out from the army barracks at 2:00 P.M. First came a detachment of gunners dressed in bright blue tunics and white helmets and under the command of Capt. J. R. Lightowlers. The band of the Fourth West Yorkshire Regiment followed playing the Dead March. Immediately behind the band was the gun carriage bearing the coffin covered by the Union Jack, the corners of which were held by the pallbearers, two of whom were the Palace Hospital doctors, Dr. Carré and Dr. Greenwood Hall. And finally, following in the wake of the gun carriage, was a throng of mourners, including Nurse Rae and others from the hospital, numerous colonial and military personnel, representatives of the Boer community, whose people Mary had served at the Palace, and the Rev. Phillip Legg, rector of Simonstown and acting military chaplain. All along the way, from the barracks to the town jetty, crowds gathered to watch the imposing procession moving slowly toward the sea to the solemn strains of the Dead March.

At the pier the cortege was met by a firing party of the Royal Marine Light Infantry commanded by Lt. H. S. Lecky, and the coffin was borne by the pallbearers onto the torpedo boat, the H.M.S. *Thrush.* Dr. Carré, the Reverend Legg, Nurses Rae and Rogers, Captain Lightowlers, and a number of the Fourth West Yorkshire Regiment also boarded the *Thrush,* which then weighed anchor and, turning its back on Simonstown Bay, steamed out past Cape Point to the high seas. At about 4:00 P.M. the *Thrush* stilled its engines some three or so miles out from land, and the Reverend Legg commenced the funeral ceremony. These last rites, addressed to a God Mary Kingsley had never believed in, were soon completed. The pallbearers removed and folded up the Union Jack. The Reverend Legg pronounced a final benediction, and then the coffin was carefully lowered over the deck rail into the ocean.

But to the amazement and consternation of all the mourners, it refused to be committed to the deep. No one had thought to weight the coffin properly, and now, instead of sinking out of sight, it floated off, bouncing to and fro, on the brilliant aquamarine waters. Lecky and Carré and Legg were aghast. And yet this last freakish episode of her life surely would have amused Mary Kingsley herself, especially occurring as it did after all the funereal solemnity of the procession and the lofty words spoken on the *Thrush.* The unsinkable coffin was her last joke in the teeth of death. Still, the living could not allow her remains to float blithely out to sea like a cryptic message contained in a glass bottle. Lecky leapt into action and ordered one of the *Thrush*'s lifeboats to be readied, and he and several of his men set off in it.

The lifeboat crew — on its mission to sink the dead — pursued the bobbing, wayward coffin. After several attempts, they managed to haul it in with a cable they threw out and hooked on to the coffin's brass fittings. From a distance, on the deck of the *Thrush,* the Reverend Legg, Nurse Rae, and Dr. Carré squinted into the late afternoon sun at the little lifeboat and the runaway coffin. Lecky and his men finally succeeded in attaching one of the *Thrush*'s spare anchors to the coffin; they then cast the anchor over the side of the boat. Instantly, the heavy iron hook sank into the depths, bearing its unwilling burden with it down to the bottom of that silent, watery world of coral and pearls and waving plants and starfish and the gentle manatee, a realm with no boundaries, where death was but "a sea change into something rich and strange." The group in the lifeboat watched the coffin sink, casting circles of ripples that grew wider and wider until they dissolved altogether into the smooth, glassy surface of an undisturbed and unyielding sea.

Notes
Selected Bibliography
Index

Notes

The notes refer to three types of sources: archival material, contemporary magazines and newspaper stories, and published books. Full references for the latter may be found in the Bibliography. Frequently cited texts are abbreviated as follows:

TWA   *Travels in West Africa*
WAS   *West African Studies*
NST   *Notes on Sport and Travel*
Gwynn   Stephen Gwynn, *Mary Kingsley*
MAP   *Mainly About People*

The major archival collections I have used are in the possession of the following private individuals or libraries: Mr. Peter Charles Kingsley Bailey; the Bodleian Library, Oxford; the British Library, London; the British Museum (Natural History); the Cambridge University Library; the Highgate Literary and Scientific Institution; Mr. D. J. Holt; the Library of the House of Lords; the London School of Economics; Mrs. Dorothy Middleton; the National Library of Ireland; the Rhodes House Library, Oxford; the Royal Commonwealth Society; the Royal Geographical Society; the South African Library; and the University of Birmingham Library.

1 The Kingsley Family

page

5   "The old English family": *NST*, pp. 1–2.
9   "Dreadful bad business this": Ibid., p. 4.
     "Charles was the greatest": Ibid., p. 3.
12 "tales of corroborees": Ibid., p. 38.

13   "knot of nigger philanthropists": William Scheurerle, *The Neglected Brother: A Study of Henry Kingsley*, p. 95.

"out of sticks and stones": Susan Chitty, *The Beast and the Monk: A Life of Charles Kingsley*, p. 242.

14   "Infinite were the points of collison between him and me": *NST*, p. 198.

"Histories of the globe": Ibid., p. 12.

15   "a ragged, resolute, ruffian-looking young vagabond": Ibid., p. 16.

16   "Settle down": Charles Kingsley, *Two Years Ago*, p. 231.

17   "The sunlight": *NST*, pp. 28–29.

2 Mary's Childhood: Inner and Outer Worlds

20   "the only thing": *NST*, p. 204.

"the hot baking sand": *NST*, p. 379.

21   "Before I can remember": *MAP*, May 20, 1899.

"A GALLANT RESCUE": Ibid.

"the minister of the chapel": Ibid.

22   "all sorts of dangerous wild-fowl": *NST*, p. 36.

23   "The whole of my childhood": *MAP*, May 20, 1899.

"I do not know": Mary Kingsley to George Macmillan, n.d.; British Library.

24   "being seized": *MAP*, May 20, 1899.

"mother's chief officer": *NST*, p. 197.

26   "a letter eloquently setting forth": Ibid., p. 203.

27   "volcanic temper": Ibid., p. 195.

"a performance": Ibid., p. 196.

"with just a twinkle": Ibid., p. 198.

"took an early opportunity": Ibid., p. 199.

32   "choice spots": *TWA*, p. 354.

"was the greatest of all": *TWA*, p. 353.

3 Changes

35   "at this time I developed": *MAP*, May 20, 1899.

"went home. I saw it was silly": Ibid.

36   "What I should": Ibid.

"connected with odd jobs": Ibid.

37   "incredible wrongs": *NST*, p. 139.

38   "one cannot be surprised": Ibid., pp. 127–128.

"A fearful period of anxiety": Ibid., p. 203.

38   "Oh! That I had the pen": Ibid., pp. 134–35.

39   "After his wanderings": Ibid., p. 190.

41   "she was": Henry Guillemard to Stephen Gwynn, November 21, 1932;
      National Library of Ireland.

42   "The society of cultivated men and women": *Athenaeum,* June 23, 1900.

43   "I heard boys": Mary Kingsley to Stephen Gwynn, November 20, 1898;
      National Library of Ireland.

45   "years of work": *MAP,* May 20, 1899.

4 *The First Voyage Out*

51   "too civilised": Henry Guillemard to Stephen Gwynn, November 21,
      1932; National Library of Ireland.

52   "Liverpool boats": *WAS,* p. 10.
      "it displayed itself": *TWA,* p. 13.
      "formed from fantastic-shaped": Ibid.

53   "a lovely lustrous blue": Ibid., p. 14.
      "I have been having": Mary Kingsley to Hatty Johnson, June 9, 1892;
      South African Library.
      "occupied by four gentlemen": Ibid.

54   "but he is dead now": *TWA,* p. 9.
      Batty claimed responsibility: James Henly Batty to Stephen Gwynn,
      October 7, 1932; National Library of Ireland.
      "who most energetically assert": *TWA,* p. 11.

55   "my brother came back": MK to Matthew Nathan, March 12, 1899;
      Bodleian Library.

57   "to creature comforts": MK to George Macmillan, November 21, 1895;
      British Library.
      "It was in 1893": *TWA,* p. 1.

58   "My motive": *WAS,* p. xxii.
      "dead tired": MK to Matthew Nathan, March 12, 1899; Bodleian Li-
      brary.

59   "the vast cavity in [her] mind": *TWA,* p. 1.
      "The dangers": Ibid., p. 2

60   "deadliest spot on earth": Ibid., p. 3.
      "abstain from exposing yourself": Ibid., p. 4.
      "to labour": Ibid.
      "two devices": Ibid., p. 684.

61   "always have your revolver": Ibid., p. 330.
      "Help! ": Ibid., p. 5.
      "you have no right": Ibid., p. 19.

62   "As for encasing": Ibid., p. 502.

62 She had read a book by a German ethnographer: *WAS*, pp. xxii–xxiii.
63 "in the guise": Gwynn, p. 101.

5 *The Second Voyage Out*

64 "but most unnecessarily": Mary Kingsley to Hatty Johnson, August 16, 1893; South African Library.
65 "poor chap": *WAS*, p. 6.
    " 'Brought any dress clothes' ": Ibid., pp. 6–7.
    "poor D.": Ibid., p. 8.
    "so far": MK to Hatty Johnson, August 16, 1893; South African Library.
66 "they had known": *WAS*, p. 11.
    "Can I live": Ibid., p. 15.
67 "surrounded by a wild, strange sky": Ibid., p. 16.
    "a sandy promontory": *TWA*, p. 14.
68 "It was with a thrill": *WAS*, p. 31.
    "On my first voyage": *TWA*, pp. 5–6.
    "he had looked": MK to Violet Roy, August 17, 1893; Royal Geographical Society.
    "acute delapidation": *WAS*, p. 15.
69 "has got more noise": Ibid., p. 33.
    "One wants the pen": *TWA*, pp. 21–22.
70 "a brown cloud": *WAS*, p. 33.
    "I should say": Ibid., p. 9.
    "bearing a name": *TWA*, p. 24.
71 "Why none": *WAS*, p. 34.
    "eternal sameness": Ibid., p. 38.
    "Night and day": Ibid., pp. 38–39.
72 "and getting behind a pile": MK to Violet Roy, August 26, 1893; Royal Geographical Society.
    "Woe to the man": *WAS*, p. 53.
73 "You remember": Ibid., p. 54.
    "who seems eternally engaged": Ibid., p. 57.
    "deeply trying creature": Ibid., p. 91.
74 "crawling about": MK to Violet Roy, August 26, 1983; Royal Geographical Society.
75 "a revolting animalism": MK to Violet Roy, August 17, 1893; Royal Geographical Society.
77 " 'Good Heavens!' ": *TWA*, p. 97.
    "barely necessary": Ibid., pp. 97–98.
78 "there being no gas": *WAS*, pp. 242–43.

78 "in an alarmed state": *Cornhill Magazine*, March 1897, p. 357.
    "I began": *Young Woman*, June 1896, p. 292.
79 "we either talked": *Cornhill Magazine*, March 1897, p. 357.
    "a dreamer": Gwynn, p. 49.
80 "an alarming place": *WAS*, p. 103.
    "you must make allowances": *TWA*, pp. xxii–xxiii.
81 "go two or three times": *WAS*, p. 9.
    "came the owner": Ibid., pp. 24–25.
82 "five unpleasant looking objects": *TWA*, p. 467.
83 "with a wild, palpitating": MK to Violet Roy, n.d.; Royal Geograph-
    ical Society.
84 Account of Congo Free State Railway episode: MK to Violet Roy, n.d.;
    Royal Geographical Society.
85 "method of progression": MK to Violet Roy, October 30, 1893; Royal
    Geographical Society.
    "On first entering": *TWA*, p. 101.
86 "life slid away": *WAS*, p. 83.
    "a three-foot long": Ibid., p. 83.
87 "there was no policeman": Ibid., pp. 454–55.
    "S.S. Rochelle was . . . surprised": MK to Violet Roy, October 30,
    1893; Royal Geographical Society.
88 "I went to the rescue": MK to Violet Roy, n.d.; Royal Geographical
    Society.

6 Exile in England

89 "takes all the colour": *TWA*, p. 102.
    "I am never quite happy": Gwynn, p. 97.
    "The charm of Africa": "A Lecture on West Africa," *Cheltenham Ladies'
    College Magazine*, Autumn 1898, p. 280.
91 "if you would be likely": Mary Kingsley to George Macmillan, August
    23, 1894; British Library.
    "undammable logorrhea": Henry Guillemard to Stephen Gwynn, No-
    vember 21, 1932; National Library of Ireland.
92 "you pulled": *MAP*, June 16, 1900.
    "I really cannot draw the trail": MK to George Macmillan, December
    18, 1894; British Library.
93 the still uncompleted manuscript: George Macmillan to MK, May 13,
    1896; British Library.
    "the best stuff": MK to George Macmillan, n.d.; British Library.
    "burn all your notions": *TWA*, p. 435.
    "read [it] until you know": Ibid.

94   "his books are . . . models": *WAS*, p. 190.
     "to go measuring peoples' ": *TWA*, p. 435.
97   "unalterably compromised": John Flint, *Sir George Goldie and the Making of Nigeria*, p. 6.
101 "courage in going": *TWA*, p. 12.
102 "to join her": Ibid.
103 "instinctively . . . because of the patience": *WAS*, p. 391.
     "who study the African": Ibid., p. 379.
104 "very hard": MK to George Macmillan, n.d.; British Library.
     "I am at present": MK to Hatty Johnson, August 2, 1894; South African Library.
     "I am getting rather nervous": MK to Albert Günther, December 10, 1894; British Museum (Natural History).
     "nearly broke the carpenter's heart": *TWA*, p. 13.

7 The Third Voyage Out

109 "all sorts": *TWA*, p. 12.
110 "valuable beings": *WAS*, p. 17.
     "The sailor officer": Ibid.
     "is a hard-working individual": Ibid.
     "a bad First": Ibid., p. 20.
111 "like danger signals": Ibid., p. 37.
112 "ill unto death": Mary Kingsley to John Holt, n.d.; Rhodes House Library.
113 "appearance of permanent substantialness": *TWA*, p. 26.
114 "a mass of rubbishy": Ibid., pp. 29–30.
     "the governmental cumberbunds": Ibid., p. 31.
115 "Hence the place": Ibid., p. 33.
     "you only saw": Ibid., p. 34.
     " 'You should have been here' ": Ibid.
116 "so as to get used": Ibid., p. 32.
117 "and noticed a most peculiar noise": Ibid., p. 86.
118 "the one set": Ibid., p. 217.
     "entirely celestial phenomenon": Ibid., p. 48.
119 "the very dullest town": Ibid., pp. 50–51.
     "the end of it": Ibid., p. 51–52.
120 "all pigs without rings": Ibid., p. 61.
     "and Spain at large": Ibid., p. 45.
121 "the most unfortunate set": Ibid., p. 51.
123 "white men are fish": Ibid., p. 71.

125 "the position of A.D.C.": Gwynn, pp. 268–70.
     "great sport": Ibid.
126 "seemed to remind him": Rudyard Kipling, *Mary Kingsley*, p. 4.
127 "I have made it a rule": MK to Hatty Johnson, n.d.; South African
     Library.
     "any of us": Ibid.
     "to its merely normal state": MK to Albert Günther, April 15, 1895;
     British Museum (Natural History).
     "most of my time": *TWA*, p. 74.
128 "my companions rowed": MK to Albert Günther, April 15, 1895;
     British Museum (Natural History).
     "a crocodile drifting down": *TWA*, pp. 88–90.
130 "right through the south end": Gwynn, p. 109.
131 "By the time": *TWA*, p. 474.
132 "her knowledge": Ibid., p. 74.
133 "To give you an account": Gwynn, pp. 278–79.
134 "I dare not betray": Ibid., p. 279.
     "My mind has a different feeling": MK to Robert Nassau, August 8,
     1899; National Library of Ireland.
135 "respected [the Africans'] religious beliefs": Mary Slessor to John Holt,
     August 17, 1900; Rhodes House Library.
     "it is the non-human world": MK to Matthew Nathan, March 12,
     1899; Bodleian Library.
     "The majesty": *TWA*, p. 178.
136 "a thing you ought": Ibid., p. 275.
     "I assure you": Ibid., p. 76.
137 "rats ran freely": Ibid., p. 79.
     "the little Eko": Ibid., p. 80.
     "a gigantic, lithe, powerful Dane": Ibid.
138 "Still the Benguella": Ibid., p. 82.
     "The next morning": Ibid.
     "one of that class of men": Ibid., p. 84.

8 Traveling the Ogooué River

142 "giving me a feeling": *TWA*, p. 107.
143 "a perfect gem": Ibid., p. 110.
     "lost all sense": Ibid., p. 112.
144 "remembering the awful state": Ibid., p. 115.
     "while so employed": Mary Kingsley to Albert Günther, May 22, 1895;
     British Museum (Natural History).

146 "with an amazing knowledge": *TWA*, p. 216.
147 "I may confide": *Cheltenham Ladies' College Magazine*, Autumn 1898, p. 270.
     "a fine little vessel": *TWA*, p. 122.
     "Most lighthouses": Ibid., p. 124.
148 "The day closed": Ibid., p. 127.
     "made up of malaria microbes": Ibid., p. 137.
     "very rickety stilts" *Cheltenham Ladies' College Magazine*, Autumn 1898, pp. 272–73.
     "a Cleopatra": *TWA*, p. 129.
     "a great glorious strange world": *Cheltenham Ladies' College Magazine*, Autumn 1898, p. 272.
     "Doubtless it is wrong": *TWA*, p. 129.
149 "I behave exquisitely": Ibid., p. 132.
     "Edmond the Sententious": Ibid., p. 133.
     "Through Fula": Ibid., p. 134.
150 "it is one": Ibid.
     "usual uproar": Ibid., p. 143.
     "is grand": Ibid., pp. 155–56.
     "no Fang village": Ibid., p. 159.
151 "sensational meetings": Ibid., p. 161.
     "there are only two things": Ibid., p. 200.
152 "My own clothes": *Cheltenham Ladies' College Magazine*, Autumn 1898, pp. 278–79.
     "be-gemmed with fire-flies": Ibid., p. 280.
153 "then down came disappointment": *TWA*, p. 165.
     "neither the Royal Geographical Society's list': Ibid., p. 167.
     "seeing we were becoming amusing": Ibid., p. 171.
154 "knock-about farce": Ibid., p. 191.
     " 'That's a thunderstorm' ": Ibid., p. 186.
     "the lily of the spirit": MK to Albert Günther, July 6, 1895; British Museum (Natural History).
155 "that fine hymn": *TWA*, p. 190.
     leopard episode: MK to Albert Günther, June 28, 1895; British Museum (Natural History).
156 "they squattered across": *TWA*, p. 267.
     "Always take measurements": Ibid., pp. 244–45.
     "have produced results": Ibid., p. 659.
     "I know no more": *WAS*, p. 106.
157 "The teaching even of sewing": *TWA*, p. 207.
     "I have no hesitation": Ibid., pp. 663–64.
158 "Now polygamy": *TWA*, p. 212.
     "the more wives": Ibid.

158   " 'A blow must be struck' ": Ibid.
159   "It was a moral mess": Ibid., p. 213.
      "I own that if": *WAS*, p. 320.
161   "a basket constructed": *TWA*, p. 346.

9 *The Journey to the Remboué*

162   "of course [I] had to go": *TWA*, p. 233.
163   "done die": Ibid., p. 235.
      " 'How are we going' ": Ibid., p. 238.
164   "Among the debris": Ibid., p. 241.
      "Pagan got out": Ibid., pp. 247–49.
      "looked round": Ibid., p. 248.
165   "we all disappeared": Ibid., p. 249.
166   "you do not find bikei": Ibid., p. 321.
      "He will turn": Ibid.
167   "I have been considerably chaffed": Ibid., pp. 328–29.
168   "The town was exceedingly filthy": Ibid., p. 249.
      "a mass of slimy gray abomination": Ibid., p. 251.
      "the door hole": Ibid., p. 252.
      "a Fang gentleman": Ibid., p. 264.
169   "Quantities of big fish": Ibid., p. 253.
      "Drying one's self": Ibid., p. 254.
      "into a fitting introduction": Ibid., p. 256.
170   "a beauty": Ibid.
      "the next news": Ibid., p. 270.
      " 'You kill?' ": Ibid.
171   " 'I'm sure' ": Ibid., p. 272.
      "Every hole": Ibid., p. 273.
172   "other portions": Ibid.
      "arrive at the Remboué": Ibid., p. 252.
      "He has no slaves": Ibid., p. 332.
173   "infinitely worse": Ibid., p. 271.
      "incapable of personal exertion": Ibid., p. 276.
      "If only the wretched thing": Ibid., p. 280.
      " 'that I hear this town' ": Ibid., p. 282.
174   "There was evidently": Ibid., pp. 283–84.
      "by the frantic yells": Ibid., p. 284.
      "I chaperoned": Ibid.
175   "I dare say I": Ibid., p. 286.
      "gloom of the Great Forest": Ibid., p. 289.
      "some . . . of the more highly": Ibid., p. 296.

176 "the lake of ink-black slime": Ibid., p. 299.
"All of us": Ibid., p. 301.
"It stretched away": Ibid., p. 302.
177 "horribly infested": Ibid., p. 303.
"a big river": Ibid., p. 304.
"a big, scraggy, very black man": Ibid., p. 304.
"an exceedingly neat": Ibid., p. 305.
178 "we started talking trade": Ibid.
"touching farewell": Ibid., p. 307.
"Partant pour la Syrie": Ibid., p. 308.
"the affair": Ibid., p. 335.
179 "a man courageous": Ibid.
"credit of having made": Ibid., p. 336.
"and as I prefer": Ibid., p. 338.
180 "a well-modulated": Ibid., pp. 340–41.
181 "dead tired": Ibid., p. 351.
"about midnight": Ibid.
"plenty country": Ibid., p. 348.
"Vain hope!": Ibid., p. 351.
"I tried to explain": Ibid., p. 352.
182 "to have been laid down": Ibid., p. 307.
"I am still thinking": Ibid., p. 349.

10 *Corsico and Cameroons*

183 "frequent and intimate conversations": Robert Hamill Nassau, *Fetichism in West Africa*, p. ix.
"I began to search": Ibid., p. vi.
184 "pliant enough": *TWA*, p. 434.
"The fascination": Ibid., p. 441.
"the final object": *WAS*, p. 95.
185 "I think Fetish in German": Mary Kingsley to George Macmillan, March 1, 1899; British Library.
186 "Frenchy no good": *TWA*, p. 390.
"things happened": Ibid.
187 "not the albino alone": Ibid., p. 391.
"Notably and grievously": Ibid., p. 396.
"adding in the case": Ibid., p. 397.
188 "But there!": Ibid., p. 399.
"a splendidly built": Ibid.
"Mr. Ibea and I": Ibid., p. 402.

188   "more than Mr. Ibea": Ibid., p. 403.
      "nothing strikes one": Ibid.
189   "surrounded by a rim": Ibid., p. 413.
      "Why did I come": Ibid., p. 419.
      "singing their Salve Maria": Ibid., p. 423.
190   "I don't come again": Ibid., p. 425.
      "there being no Spanish official": Ibid., p. 426.
      "for it's not my present intention": Ibid., p. 427.
      "Sometimes it is wreathed": Ibid., p. 550.
191   "none of my business": Ibid., p. 549.
192   "you could go": Ibid., p. 553.
193   "much like that": Ibid., p. 558.
      "How much that song?": *WAS*, 126.
      "because his works": Ibid., p. 127.
      "with application": Ibid., p. 56.
194   "all else the tom-tom": Ibid., p. 55.
      "Men can be trying!": *TWA*, p. 563.
195   "I wonder whether": Ibid., p. 606.
      "from some interior unknown district": Ibid., p. 568.
      " 'You no sabe' ": Ibid., p. 567.
      "now and again": Ibid., p. 570.
      "had a bull behind me": Ibid., p. 571.
      "with great detail": Ibid., p. 572.
196   "get their pay": Ibid., p. 574.
      "it was like a vision": Ibid., p. 578.
197   "this is not the sort": Ibid.
      "In a homicidal state": Ibid., p. 579.
      "a brief but lurid sketch": Ibid., pp. 579–80.
      "One feels here": Ibid., p. 584.
198   "a misery to me": Ibid., p. 591.
      "The weather is undecided": Ibid., pp. 592–93.
      "on alone": Ibid., p. 593.
      "After a desperate fight": Ibid., p. 594.
199   "verily I am no mountaineer": Ibid.
200   "an awful cold": Ibid., p. 608.
      "sat . . . overlooking Victoria": Ibid.
      "Had the desire": Ibid., p. 609.
      "an affair of fourteen miles": Ibid., p. 610.
201   "perfect gems": Ibid., pp. 610–11.
      "These interesting animals": Ibid., p. 613.
      "I used to meet it": Ibid.
      "a good deal of material": Ibid., p. 621.

203   "a gloom fell": Ibid., p. 627.
      "whacking blue envelopes": MK to George Macmillan, November 21, 1896; British Library.

11 *Travels in West Africa*

207   "a yachting cruise": Mary Kingsley to George Macmillan, December 10, 1895; British Library.
      "I look back": MK to Hatty Johnson, January 28, 1896; South African Library.
208   "Always something new": *Daily Telegraph*, December 3, 1895.
      "that with the amount": *Daily Telegraph*, December 5, 1895.
209   "hopelessly cold": MK to Albert Günther, n.d.; British Museum (Natural History).
210   "the amount of expurgation": Gwynn, p. 131.
211   "Reading the accounts": *Spectator*, December 7, 1895.
212   "have never produced": *Spectator*, December 28, 1895.
213   "I was really afraid": MK to Albert Günther, December 31, 1895; British Museum (Natural History).
214   "an utter failure": MK to Hatty Johnson, January 25, 1896; South African Library.
215   "I was yesterday": Gwynn, p. 130.
216   "I am quite a distinguished person": Henry Guillemard to MK, December 20, 1895; British Library.
      "I was at a big dinner party": MK to Albert Günther, February 26, 1896; British Museum (Natural History).
218   "exceptionally hideous carved mask": *Young Woman*, June 1896, p. 290.
219   "the . . . strain of those long years": Ibid., pp. 290–91.
      "that her travelling exploits": Ibid.
      " 'I suppose, Miss Kingsley' ": Ibid., p. 293.
220   "Do you think . . . that a woman": Ibid., p. 294.
221   "those heroes of commerce": *Liverpool Geographical Society*, March 1896, p. 52.
222   Günther's report on MK's fish: MK to George Macmillan, February 18, 1896; British Library.
223   "strange to say": Gwynn, p. 133.
223   "a farrago of nonsense": MK to George Macmillan, April 25, 1896; British Library.
      "I am going down the Coast": MK to George Macmillan, August 20, 1896; British Library.

224 "Your corrections": MK to Henry Guillemard, August 20, 1896; British Library.

"in June if possible": George Macmillan to MK, May 13, 1896; British Library.

"It is a ridiculous situation": MK to George Macmillan, May 18, 1896; British Library.

225 "take no heed": MK to George Macmillan, November 7, 1896; British Library.

"as it might give the idea": MK to George Macmillan, December 16, 1896; British Library.

226 "I . . . asked Charley": MK to George Macmillan, August 20, 1896; British Library.

"Master Charles will let you": MK to George Macmillan, August 10, 1896; British Library.

"It was more suitable": MK to George Macmillan; August 14, 1896; British Library.

227 "I cannot tell you": MK to Mrs. E. B. Tylor, December 7, 1896; D. J. Holt.

"I seem to have a mind so akin": MK to E. B. Tylor, October 1, 1896; D. J. Holt.

228 "a lot of queer things": MK to Mrs. E. B. Tylor, December 7, 1896; D. J. Holt.

"I am dead tired": MK to George Macmillan, October 30, 1896; British Library.

"I am low in mind": Gwynn, p. 130.

"I am going to absolutely loathe": MK to Hatty Johnson, January 28, 1897; South African Library.

12 Growing Influence

230 "a prize fighter': Mary Kingsley to George Macmillan, n.d.; British Library.

231 "in fear and trembling": MK to Albert Günther, January 20, 1897; British Museum (Natural History).

"In a romping style": *Illustrated London News*, February 6, 1897.

232 "As my visiting West Africa": *Athenaeum*, February 27, 1897.

233 "a book of defiance": *Young Woman*, November 1897.

"The only general impression': *Spectator*, March 6, 1897.

236 "dreadful, tiring day": MK to Alice Green, March 22, 1897; National Library of Ireland.

"I *cannot* converse coherently": MK to Alice Green, September 27, 1897; National Library of Ireland.

237   "Lordy! the times I have had": MK to Alice Green, November 22, 1897; National Library of Ireland.

238   "You are the only person": MK to Alice Green, January 31, 1898; National Library of Ireland.
"I wish you would say": MK to Alice Green, April 30, 1898; National Library of Ireland.

239   "This London life": MK to George Macmillan, March 24, 1897; British Library.
"If I were rich": MK to George Macmillan, May 8, 1897; British Library.
"all that palaver": MK to E. B. Tylor, February 21, 1897; D. J. Holt.
"I should sail": MK to George Macmillan, April 2, 1897; British Library.
"would not see": MK to Hatty Johnson, May 1, 1897; South African Library.
"I feel the fear": Ibid.

240   "to be as serious": MK to George Macmillan, April 24, 1897; British Library.
"a lamp post in a fog": MK to George Macmillan, May 1, 1897; British Library.
"a brickmaker": MK to John Holt, October 21, 1898; Rhodes House Library.
"alternative plan": *WAS*, p. 281.

241   "grubbing in the rag bag": MK to George Macmillan, n.d.; British Library.
"I cannot get outside": MK to George Macmillan, October 4, 1897; British Library.
"it is as usual": MK to Saxon Mills, September 17, 1898; Rhodes House Library.

242   "surrounded with a mephitic mental atmosphere": MK to Hatty Johnson, January 5, 1897; South African Library.
"I never pretend": MK to Alice Green, September 22, 1897; National Library of Ireland.
"flourishing but very deaf": MK to Alice Green, September 22, 1897; National Library of Ireland.

243   "send a doctor": MK to George Macmillan, January 23, 1898; British Library.
"You have one thing": MK to Hatty Johnson, May 1, 1897; South African Library.

244   "looking simply dangerous": *London Quarterly Review*, July 1900, p. 138.
"ignore the truth": Ibid., p. 139.
"the photo of the missionary": Ibid., p. 141.

244 "I am really": Ibid., p. 142.

245 "it is a sad situation": *Work and Workers,* February 1901, p. 69.

246 "the street sweepings": MK to Alice Green, September 22, 1897; National Library of Ireland.

"it will be so interesting:" MK to Alice Green, September 27, 1897; National Library of Ireland.

"addressed them": MK to George Macmillan, November 20, 1897; British Library.

249 "I've got to dine": MK to John Holt, December 6, 1897; Rhodes House Library.

"I will write": MK to John Holt, December 9, 1897; Rhodes House Library.

"Of course, we did not say a word": MK to John Holt, December 12, 1897; Rhodes House Library.

250 "I am totally unfit": MK to Frederick Lugard, December 19, 1897; Rhodes House Library.

"We will show Polynesian": MK to Frederick Lugard, December 31, 1897; Rhodes House Library.

"I am at the mercy": Edward Clodd, *Memories,* p. 79.

251 "the superior form": *Fortnightly Review,* April 1898. p. 537.

"the greatest admiration": Ibid., p. 538.

252 "It is fire": Edward Clodd, *Memories,* p. 81.

253 "One of the root principles": *Spectator,* March 19, 1898.

"confiscation tempered by bribery": MK to Joseph Chamberlain, April 4, 1898; University of Birmingham Library.

254 "It is not morally right": Ibid.

"Chamberlain is manifesting": MK to John Holt, March 19, 1898; Rhodes House Library.

"full of . . . commercial gentlemen": MK to Mr. Christy, January 25, 1898; Rhodes House Library.

255 "I cannot say": Edward Clodd, *Memories,* p. 78.

"lunching with Goldie": MK to John Holt, March 13, 1898; Rhodes House Library.

"mighty civil": MK to John Holt, March 19, 1898; Rhodes House Library.

"I am for a West Coaster": MK to E. B. Tylor, May 25, 1898; D. J. Holt.

"shrieking females": MK to John Holt, n.d.; Rhodes House Library.

256 "If we women": MK to Mrs. Farquharson, November 26, 1899; Royal Geographical Society.

"every bit of solid, good work": MK to John Holt, April 26, 1899; Rhodes House Library.

257 "dared not show a hand": Edward Clodd, *Memories,* p. 78.

257 "everything that is round you": *Cheltenham Ladies' College Magazine,* Autumn 1898, p. 280.

258 "hairbreadth escapes": E. Muriel Joy to Dorothy Middleton, June 22, 1966; Dorothy Middleton.

"I expect I remind you": Ibid.

"3½ tons of books": MK to E. B. Tylor, September 9, 1898; D. J. Holt.

"The funny little house": Amy Strachey, *St. Loe Strachey,* p. 97.

259 "My book will be out": MK to Stephen Gwynn, December 2, 1898; National Library of Ireland.

"tied by my apron strings": MK to John Holt, November 22, 1898; Rhodes House Library.

"I'd black his boots": MK to John Holt, November 14, 1898; Rhodes House Library.

260 "the moment he does": MK to John Holt, December 13, 1898; Rhodes House Library

"I have had an extra bad time": MK to Mrs. John Holt, January 1, 1899; Rhodes House Library.

13 Valediction

261 "more solid": *Athenaeum,* February 11, 1899.

"the sheer labour of cutting": *Echo,* January 31, 1899.

262 "The general verdict": *Daily Chronicle,* January 31, 1899.

"the *Times* means to wreak": Mary Kingsley to John Holt, n.d.; Rhodes House Library.

263 "for there is much gossip": MK to John Holt, February 14, 1899; Rhodes House Library.

264 "civil but in a smouldering rage": MK to John Holt, February 20, 1899; Rhodes House Library.

"should have her knife": MK to George Macmillan, February 19, 1899; British Library.

265 "I dote on the military": MK to Stephen Gwynn, February 16, 1899; National Library of Ireland.

"Dined at the Montagus' ": Matthew Nathan diary, February 16, 1899; Bodleian Library.

266 "just the things": MK to Matthew Nathan, February 2, 1899; Bodleian Library.

"I took him into the hall": MK to Stephen Gwynn, n.d.; National Library of Ireland.

267 "I have a very lively hatred": MK to Matthew Nathan, March 8, 1899; Bodleian Library.

268 "I do want to understand you": Matthew Nathan Papers, Bodleian Library.

"too humourous": Matthew Nathan Papers, Bodleian Library.

269 "Of no importance": MK to Matthew Nathan, May 12, 1899; Bodleian Library.

"letter from Miss Kingsley": Matthew Nathan diary, March 30, 1899; Bodleian Library.

272 "Unfortunately, my brother": MK to Miss Mahaffy, n.d.; Highgate Literary and Scientific Institution.

"When I shall go out": MK to Mrs. James Frazer, December 23, 1899; Cambridge University Library.

273 "I have learnt nothing": MK to John Holt, May 21, 1899; Rhodes House Library.

"I believe in Cardew's honesty": MK to John Holt, August 17, 1899; Rhodes House Library.

274 "the baker's cart": Amy Strachey, *St. Loe Strachey*, p. 101.

275 "the Diva was having a little supper": *MAP*, June 23, 1900.

"devoted to Roman remains": MK to John Holt, November 19, 1899; Rhodes House Library.

276 "side by side": MK to E. D. Morel, June 22, 1899; London School of Economics.

"I often hear": MK to Matthew Nathan, July 11, 1899; Bodleian Library.

"Believe me": MK to Matthew Nathan, August 28, 1899; Bodleian Library.

278 "longest (two and three quarters years)": Thomas Pakenham, *The Boer War*, p. xv.

279 "was not wanted": MK to John Holt, February 14, 1900; Rhodes House Library.

280 "I know I am beaten": MK to Matthew Nathan, January 27, 1900; Bodleian Library.

"was sorry to see you": MK to Matthew Nathan, February 9, 1900; Bodleian Library.

"you will not have unmitigated me": MK to Matthew Nathan, February 6, 1900; Bodleian Library.

"if you come": MK to Matthew Nathan, February 24, 1900; Bodleian Library.

281 "I have been opposing women having": MK to Matthew Nathan, February 27, 1900; Bodleian Library.

282 " 'I thought you were dead' ": *St. James Gazette*, June 7, 1900.

"I dare say you noticed": Ibid.

"when it is South Africa": *WAS*, pp. 430–31.

"I thank you for your toleration": Ibid., pp. 456–57.

283 "I am as busy as the devil": MK to Matthew Nathan, March 8, 1900; Bodleian Library.
"to get an idea": MK to Matthew Nathan, March 23, 1900; Bodleian Library.
"I have only got things": MK to John Holt, March 4, 1900; Rhodes House Library.
"It goes without saying": MK to Matthew Nathan, March 8, 1900; Bodleian Library.

14 The Final Bound

287 "harrowing each other's feelings": Mary Kingsley to Alice Green, March 14, 1900; National Library of Ireland.
288 "Flat ironing the ocean": MK to St. Loe Strachey, March 22, 1900; House of Lords.
"thereby hangs a tale": Ibid.
290 "stay-at-home statesmen": Gwynn, p. 283.
"I know that there is a general opinion": Ibid., p. 284.
"come forward": Ibid.
291 "Cronje's men": MK to Alice Green, April 11, 1900; National Library of Ireland.
292 "I never struck": MK to St. Loe Strachey, May 1900; House of Lords.
"it is the black man's burden": *West Africa,* July 1900, p. 52.
"Being human": Rudyard Kipling, *Mary Kingsley,* p. 2.
"sitting on the stoep": Ibid., p. 4.
"with my usual luck": MK to St. Loe Strachey, May 1900; House of Lords.
295 "today I have had over 100 patients": MK to Alice Green, April 11, 1900; National Library of Ireland.
296 "a touch of the West Coast fever": Gwynn, p. 275.
297 The details of Mary Kingsley's last illness, death, funeral, and burial at sea come from a number of sources, including Gwynn's biography; letters from Dr. Gerard Carré to Charles Kingsley dated June 6 and September 5, 1900, now in the possession of Mr. Peter Charles Kingsley Bailey; and the following newspaper and magazine accounts: *Daily Graphic,* June 26, 1900; *Cape Times,* June 27, 1900; *West Africa,* July 1900; and *MAP,* August 8, 1900. I am especially grateful to Mrs. Charity Hodge and to Mr. John Whale for the bizarre details of the burial at sea, which were related to Mrs. Hodge by her father, Capt. H. S. Lecky.

Selected Bibliography

This is a selected list of published work by, on, and related to Mary Kingsley; it is "selected" because one could wander endlessly in the "word swamp" of books dealing with African studies. The list of primary sources by Mary Kingsley is, however, essentially complete, though I have omitted some minor appearances in print, such as unimportant letters to newspapers, and magazine and newspaper interviews and summaries of Kingsley's lectures. Unpublished manuscript material, upon which the book is largely based, may be found in the notes.

Primary Sources: Publications by Mary Kingsley

BOOKS

Travels in West Africa, Congo Français, Corsico and Cameroons. London: Macmillan, 1897.

West African Studies. London: Macmillan, 1899.

The Story of West Africa. The Story of the Empire Series. London: Horace Marshall, 1900.

Notes on Sport and Travel. By George Henry Kingsley, with a memoir by his daughter Mary H. Kingsley. London: Macmillan, 1900.

ARTICLES

"The Negro Future." *Spectator,* December 1895.

"The Ascent of Cameroons Peak and Travels in French Congo." *Liverpool Geograpical Society,* March 1896.

"The Development of Dodos." *National Review,* March 1896.

"Travels on the Western Coast of Equatorial Africa." *Scottish Geographical Magazine*, March 1896.
"Fishing in West Africa." *National Review*, May 1896.
"The Throne of Thunder." *National Review*, May 1896.
"Black Ghosts." *Cornhill Magazine*, June 1896.
"Two African Days' Entertainment." *Cornhill Magazine*, March 1897.
"The Fetish View of the Human Soul." *Folklore*, June 1897.
"Native Populations of Africa." *Spectator*, June 1897.
"African Religion and Law." *National Review*, September 1897.
"A Parrot's Tale." *Cornhill Magazine*, September 1897.
Introduction to *Notes on Folklore of the Fjort*. By R.E. Dennett. London: The Folklore Society, 1898.
"The Hut Tax in Africa." *Spectator*, March 1898.
"The Position of Britain in the World." *Spectator*, March 1898.
"The Liquor Traffic in West African." *Fortnightly Review*, April 1898.
"The Law and Nature of Property Among the Peoples of the True Negro Stock." *Proceedings of the British Association*, September 1898.
"A Lecture on West Africa." *Cheltenham Ladies' College Magazine*, Autumn 1898.
Life in West Africa. In the *British Empire Series*, vol. 2, 1899.
"Administration of Our West African Colonies." *Monthly Record, Manchester Chamber of Commerce*, March 1899.
"The Forms of Apparitions in West Africa." *Journal of the Psychical Research Society*, July 1899.
"The Transfer of the Niger Territories." *British Empire Review*, August 1899.
"The Colonial Nursing Association." *British Empire Review*, October 1899.
"The Future of Negros." *Spectator*, November 1899.
"West Africa From an Ethnographical Point of view." *Imperial Institute Journal*, April 1900.
"Efficiency and Empire." *Spectator*, June 1900.
"Nursing in West Africa." *Chamber's Journal*, June 1900.

Secondary Sources

Arens, W. *The Man-Eating Myth: Anthropology and Anthropohagy*. New York: Oxford University Press, 1980.
Bell, E. Moberly. *Flora Shaw*. London: Constable, 1947.
Blyden, Edward Wilmot. *The African Society and Miss Kingsley*. London: West Africa, 1901.
Briggs, Elizabeth Charlotte. *The Staff Work of the Anglo-Boer War*. London: Grant Richards, 1901.

Brodie, Fawn. *The Devil Drives: A Life of Sir Richard Burton.* New York: Norton, 1966.

Buchan, James. *The Expendable Mary Slessor.* Edinburgh: Saint Andrew Press, 1980.

Campbell, Olwen. *Mary Kingsley: A Victorian in the Jungle.* London: Methuen, 1957.

Carrington, Charles. *Rudyard Kipling: His Life and Work.* 1955. Reprint. Hammondsworth, Middlesex: Penguin, 1970.

Chitty, Susan, *The Beast and the Monk: A Life of Charles Kingsley.* New York: Mason/Charter, 1975.

Clair, Colin. *Mary Kingsley: African Explorer.* Watford, Hertfordshire: Bruce and Gawthorn, 1963.

Cline, Catherine Ann. *E. D. Morel.* Belfast: Blackstaff Press, 1980.

Clodd, Edward. *Memories.* London: Chapman and Hall, 1916.

Fernandez, James. *Bwiti: An Ethnography of the Religious Imagination in Africa.* Princeton: Princeton University Press, 1982.

Flint, John. *Sir George Goldie and the Making of Nigeria.* London: Oxford University Press, 1960.

———. "Mary Kingsley: A Reassessment." *Journal of African History* 4, no. 1 (1963): 95–104.

Freshfield, Douglas W., and Wharton, W. J. L. *Hints to Travellers, Scientific and General.* London: Royal Geographical Society, 1893.

Fyfe, Christopher. *A History of Sierra Leone.* London: Oxford University Press, 1962.

Gardiner, David. *Historical Dictionary of Gabon.* Metuchen, N.J.: Scarecrow Press, 1981.

Gertzel, Cherry. "John Holt: A British Merchant in West Africa in the Era of Imperialism" Ph.D. diss., Nuffield College, Oxford, 1959.

Gwynn, Stephen. *The Life of Mary Kingsley.* London: Macmillan, 1933.

Hall, Richard. *Stanley: An Adventurer Explored.* London: Collins, 1974.

Haydon, Anthony. *Sir Matthew Nathan.* Saint Lucia, Queensland: Queensland University Press, 1976.

Hayford, Mark C. *Mary H. Kingsley from an African Standpoint.* London: Bear and Taylor, 1901.

Howard, Cecil. *Mary Kingsley.* London: Hutchinson, 1957.

Jay, Richard. *Joseph Chamberlain: A Political Study.* Oxford: Clarendon Press, 1981.

Johnston, Harry H. *The Story of My Life.* Indianapolis: Bobbs-Merrill, 1923.

Judd, Denis. *Radical Joe: A Life of Joseph Chamberlain.* London: Hamish Hamilton, 1977.

Kemp, Dennis. *Nine Years at the Gold Coast.* London: Macmillan, 1898.

Kingsley, Charles. *Two Years Ago.* London: Macmillan, 1857.

Kingsley, Francis. *Charles Kingsley: His Letters and Memories of His Life Edited by His Wife.* London: Henry S. King, 1879.

Kingsley, George, and the Earl of Pembroke. *South Sea Bubbles.* London: Macmillan, 1872.

Kingsley, Henry. *The Recollections of Geoffrey Hamlyn.* London: Macmillan, 1859.

—————. *Ravenshoe.* London: Macmillan, 1862.

Kipling, Rudyard. *Mary Kingsley.* Garden City, N.Y.: Doubleday, 1932.

—————. *Something of Myself.* 1937. Reprint. Hammondsworth, Middlesex: Penguin, 1977.

Livingstone, W. P. *Mary Slessor of Calabar.* London: Hodder and Stoughton, 1915.

Lynch, Hollis R. *Edward Wilmot Blyden.* London: Oxford University Press, 1967.

McDowell, R. B. *Alice Stopford Green.* Dublin: Allen Figgis, 1967.

Middleton, Dorothy. *Victorian Lady Travellers.* 1965. Reprint. Chicago: Academy Chicago, 1982.

Morel, E. D. *Affairs of West Africa.* 1902. Reprint. London: Frank Cass, 1968.

Morgan, Charles. *The House of Macmillan.* London: Macmillan, 1943.

Oliver, Caroline. *Western Women in Colonial Africa.* London: Greenwood Press, 1982.

Nassau, Robert Hamill. *Fetichism in West Africa.* London: Duckworth, 1904.

Pakenham, Thomas. *The Boer War.* London: MacDonald, 1982.

Perham, Margery. *Lugard: The Years of Adventure, 1858–1898.* London: Collins, 1956.

—————. *Lugard: The Years of Authority, 1898–1945.* London: Collins, 1960.

Porter, Bernard. *Critics of Empire.* London: Macmillan, 1968.

Robinson, Ronald, John Gallagher, and Alice Denny. *Africa and the Victorians.* London: Macmillan, 1961.

Scheurerle, William H. *The Neglected Brother: A Study of Henry Kingsley.* Tallahassee: Florida State University Press, 1971.

Stevenson, Catherine Barnes. *Victorian Women Travel Writers in Africa.* Boston: Twayne, 1982.

Strachey, Amy. *St. Loe Strachey: His Life and His Paper.* London: Gollancz, 1930.

Trollope, Joanna. *Britannia's Daughters: Women of the British Empire.* London: Hutchinson, 1983.

Wallace, Kathleen. *This is Your Home: A Portrait of Mary Kingsley.* London: Heinemann, 1956.

Warwick, Peter, ed. *The South African War.* Harlow, Essex: Longman, 1980.

Weinstein, Brian. *Gabon: Nation Building on the Ogooué.* Cambridge: MIT Press, 1966.

Index

225, 243–44, 262, 290; Mary's dealings
with, 76, 85, 104, 111, 114, 130–34;
Mary Slessor, 130–34; in Congo Français,
141–42, 145–50 *passim,* 166, 180–89
passim; in Cameroon, 192, 194; and hut
tax, 252, 253. *See also* Religion
Missionary Record, 132
Montagu, Sir Samuel, 265, 266, 283
Moor (British troopship, 1900), 283, 287–
89, 290
Morel, Edmund, 262, 276, 283
Morrison, Charles, 133
Mount Cameroon: Mary climbs, 191–99,
200, 202, 220, 221, 225
Mové (river steamer, 1895), 147, 148, 175
Mpongwe people, 140, 141, 144, 165, 178,
180, 186
Müller, Max, 234
Murray, Capt. John (of *Lagos,* British trading
vessel), 64–69 *passim,* 77, 83, 84, 104,
110, 111, 223, 287
"Muvungu" (idol), 3, 90, 209, 218, 226,
258

Nachtigal (Cameroon governor's yacht,
1895), 200, 201–2
Napoleon III, 97
Nassau, Dr. Robert Hamill, 112, 134, 145–
46, 150, 167, 185–86, 190; quoted,
183–84
Nathan, Maj. Matthew, 265–72, 273, 276–
84 *passim,* 288–89
Nation, 231
National African Company, *see* Royal Niger
Company
National Review (periodical), 221
Natural History Museum (Kensington), 96,
154, 209, 211, 222, 279
Nature (periodical), 232
New Africa (periodical), 289
Newman, John Henry, 10
New York newspapers: *Herald,* 30; *Times,*
231; *Tribune,* 232
Niger (British trading vessel, 1895), 190,
191
Niger Coast Protectorate, 88, 99–100, 123
Nigeria, 77, 92, 248, 279
Nightingale, Florence, 209, 235
Nile debate, 29–30
Nineteenth Century (periodical), 248, 251
Nine Years at the Gold Coast (Kemp), 244
Nkoni people, 165

"Noble Savages," 165–66
Nonconformism, *see* Religion
Notes on Sport and Travel (G. Kingsley), 5,
95, 210, 226, 247, 272, 273, 275, 279

Obanjo ("Captain Johnson"), 178–81, 182
Origin of Species, The (Darwin), 93, 185
Orungu people, 140
Oxford University, 11, 42, 246

Paget, Sir George, 42
Pall Mall Gazette, 263
Park, Mungo, 29, 32
Pembroke, Lord, 4, 5, 25–26, 37, 39
Pembroke, Lady, 257
Petherick, Katherine, 32
Phillips, Captain (of *Hannibal,* Mary's story
about), 289
Polygamy: Mary's stand on, 75, 76, 146,
157, 158–59, 160, 231
Port Douglas (British ship, wrecked 1892),
66
Porter, Captain (of *Bakana,* British trading
vessel), 202
"Porto" people, 122
Portuguese explorations and territory, 77–
81, 140
Primitive Culture (Tylor), 93, 185, 227
Ptolemy, 28, 29, 30
Pursuit of Knowledge under Difficulties (Craik),
35
Puttkamer, Herr von (Cameroon governor),
201

Quinee, Mme. (explorer), 153

Rae, Nurse (in Mary's final illness), 295,
296, 297, 298, 299
Ranulph, earl of Chester, 6
Reade, W. Winwood, 140, 165
Recollections of Geoffrey Hamlyn, The (H. Kingsley), 11
Regent's Park Zoo, 203, 209
Religion: Christianity, 10, 159, 162,
(Mary's view of) 133–36, 156–57, 159,
188, 213, 245, 267, 290; family views of,
10, 21, 35, 66, 244; agnosticism, 21,
134–35, 244, 267; Nonconformism, 21,
35, 112; duty as form of, 58, 269; Mary's
study of, 79, 94, 134 (*see also* Fetish); Roman Catholic, 112, 121, 141, 147, 180,

ABOUT THE AUTHOR

Katherine Frank was educated at the University of Illinois and the University of Iowa, from which she holds a Ph.D. in English literature. For the past six years she has lived and taught in West Africa, at the University of Sierra Leone and currently at Bayero University in Kano, Nigeria. She is now writing a biography of Emily Brontë.